WILLIAM POWELL FRITH

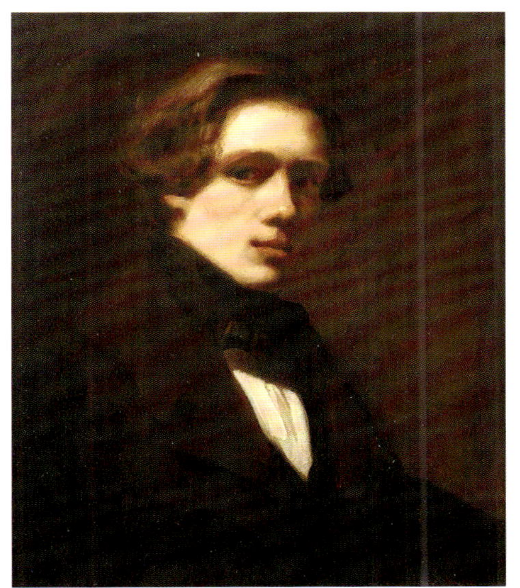

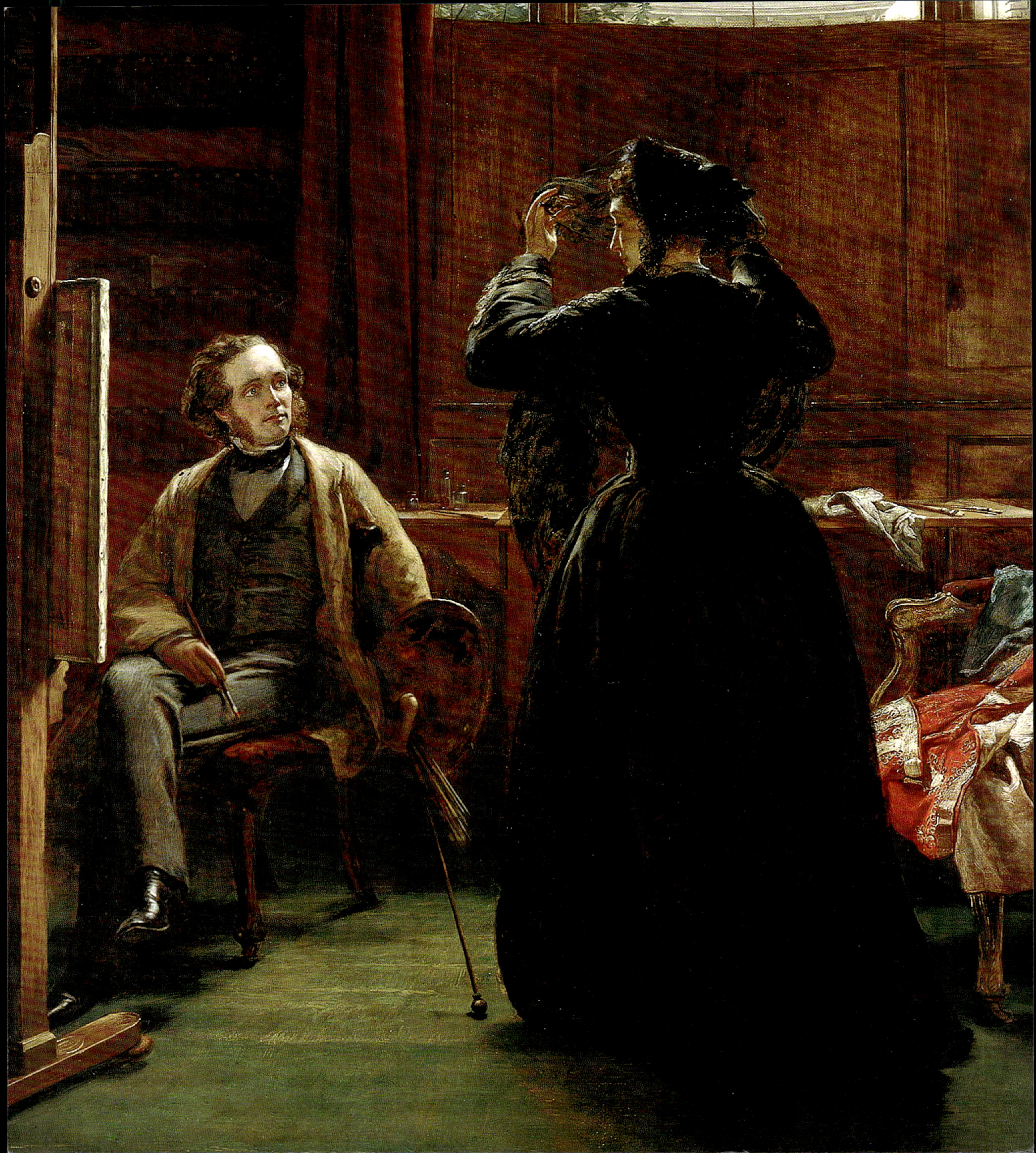

WILLIAM POWELL FRITH

PAINTING THE VICTORIAN AGE

EDITED BY
MARK BILLS AND VIVIEN KNIGHT

YALE UNIVERSITY PRESS
New Haven and London

in association with
Guildhall Art Gallery, City of London
The Mercer Art Gallery, Harrogate Museums and Arts

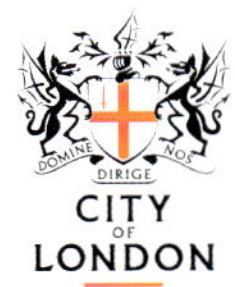

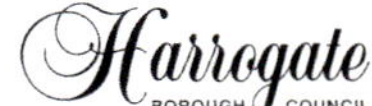

First published by Yale University Press in association with
Guildhall Art Gallery City of London and the Mercer Art Gallery Harrogate Museums and Arts
on the occasion of the exhibition *William Powell Frith: Painting the Victorian Age*

Designed by Sally Salvesen
Typeset in Monophoto Baskerville
Printed in Italy

LIBRARY OF CONGRESS CATALOGING-IN-PUBLICATION DATA
William Powell Frith : Painting the Victorian age / edited by Mark Bills and Vivien Knight.
p. cm.
Includes bibliographical references and index.
ISBN 0-300-12190-3 (alk. paper)
1. Frith, William Powell, 1819-1909--Criticism and interpretation. 2. Genre painting, Victorian--Great Britain. I. Bills, Mark. II. Knight, Vivien.
ND497.F8W55 2007
759.2--dc22
2006015523

HALF TITLE PAGE: *Self Portrait with a Model*, 1838. National Portrait Gallery, London
This picture was presented to the National Portrait Gallery in 1926 by Frith's daughters Louisa and Fanny. It may be the one he described as influenced by John Opie, stolen from his studio and discovered forty years later from an old furniture shop in Great Titchfield Street, where he had gone to buy studio props. The proprietor claimed the artist had died of drink, but as Frith had one of his sons with him he did not argue and just bought it for the asking price of £20.

FRONTISPIECE: Detail from *The Artist in his Studio*, 1867. National Portrait Gallery, London

Contents

Introduction and Acknowledgements

No book on Victorian art is complete without at least one illustration of William Powell Frith's three great social panoramas – *Life at the Seaside (Ramsgate Sands)*, *Derby Day* or *The Railway Station*. Frith was virtually a household name in his lifetime, and even today many people will have grown up with a print of *The Railway Station* on their parents' or grandparents' walls. An innovator in the field of modern-life painting that flourished in the 1850s and 1860s, his pictures were admired by Queen Victoria herself no less than by the crowds of ordinary Londoners who jostled to see them at the annual Royal Academy exhibitions.

But there is so much more to this iconic painter. Frith's output was prolific and his position within English painting pivotal. Yet the range of his influence has often been underestimated, and it is surprising how little has been written about him. Accompanying the first major exhibition on Frith since 1951, this book aims to provide a long-needed investigation of the artist and to place him within the context of his age. Alongside insightful art-historical arguments on the implications of his approach to depicting the Victorian crowd, its wide-ranging essays also examine the day to day realities of forging a career alongside a crowded family life, the influence on him of William Hogarth and his friend Charles Dickens, his own influence on contemporary art and illustration, and even his painting method and framing practice. Individually they present reflections on important aspects of Frith's art; together they paint a rounded portrait of a quintessential yet exceptional Victorian artist.

As editors, our first debt of gratitude is to the authors of the essays in this book: Caroline Arscott, Mary Cowling, Victoria Doran, Edwina Ehrman, Jane Sellars, David Trotter, Alex Werner and Sally Woodcock. Our second deepest debt is to Sally Salvesen and Catherine Bowe at Yale University Press. We are enormously grateful to Christopher Wood for his selfless and generous help over a long period, and to Professor Brian Allen and the Paul Mellon Centre for Studies in British Art, which provided the grant to fund the book's illustrations. The Friends of The Mercer Art Gallery have been exceptionally generous, and we are most grateful also to the Friends of Guildhall Art Gallery and to Mr Hilary Bachelier Carasco.

Finally, we are glad to thank Matthew Bailey (National Portrait Gallery), Martin Beisly and Peter Brown (Christie's), Sarah Fahmy (Tate), John Fisher and Seamus McKenna (Guildhall Library), Mark Frost (Dover Museum), Charlotte Grant (Christie's Images), Museum of London, Peter Nahum and Christine Hourdé (Peter Nahum at the Leicester Galleries), Terry Parker, Brian Perry, (The Beaverbrook Art Gallery, Ontario), Roxanne Peters (Victoria and Albert Museum), the Watts Gallery, and Danny Wettreich (the European Art Gallery, Dallas, Texas), as well as the many other museums and private owners who generously gave us access to their paintings and allowed them to be reproduced.

Mark Bills and Vivien Knight
May 2006

Chronology

1819 9 January, born Aldfield near Ripon.

1826 Frith's father takes over the Dragon Hotel in Harrogate. Attends boarding school at Thorp Arch, Yorkshire.

1832 Cliff House Academy, St Margaret's-at-Cliffe, Dover for 2 years.

1835 4 March, becomes a pupil at Sass's school at 6 Charlotte Street, Bloomsbury, London.

1836 First visit to Brighton and Hastings, August.

1837 Admitted as a probationer at the RA in January and admitted as full student in December. Death of his father in April.

1838 Exhibits *A Page with a Letter* at the British Institution (BI) and *Sketch of a Boy Reading* at the Society of British Artists.

1839 Living at 11 Osnaburgh Street, Regents Park with his mother, brother Charles and sister Maria Jane. Exhibits *Two Lovers* at the Liverpool Exhibition, *Scene from the 'Lay of the Last Minstrel'* at the Society of British Artists, and *A Study from Nature* at the BI. Spends four months painting portraits in Lincolnshire.

1840 Exhibits *Othello and Desdemona* at the BI, *Shylock Watching Antonio, Rebecca and Ivanhoe in the Turret at Front de Boeuf's Castle, A Study for the 'Last Minstrel'*, and *Madge Wildfire and Jeannie Deans* at the Society of British Artists, and *Malvolio before the Countess Olivia* at the RA. Second tour of Lincolnshire painting portraits. Visits Paris with his brother Charles and makes copies in the Louvre.

1841 Exhibits *Imogen Sleeping – Iachimo comes from the trunk* (a scene from *Cymbeline*) at the BI, *A Day Dream* and *The Mort or Death Blast* (with A.D. Cooper) at the Society of British Artists, and *The Parting Interview between Leicester and his Countess Amy, after one of his Stolen Visits to Cumnor* (a scene from *Kenilworth*) and *A Portrait* at the RA.

1842 Exhibits *Scene from Sterne's Sentimental Journey* at the BI, *Dolly Varden* at the Society of British Artists and *A Scene from the Vicar of Wakefield* at the RA.

1843 Exhibits *The Duel Scene from 'Twelfth Night'* and *Dolly Varden* at the BI and *Scene from the 'Merry Wives of Windsor'* at the RA. August: trip with Augustus Egg to Belgium, the Rhine, Strasbourg and Paris; learns Dadd has murdered his father. September: *Scene from Sterne's 'Sentimental Journey'* and *A Scene from the 'Vicar of Wakefield'* exhibited in Birmingham. First contact with patron John Gibbons.

1844 *Scene from the 'Merry Wives of Windsor'* exhibited at the BI and *One of the Interviews that took place between John Knox and Mary Queen of Scots respecting her Marriage with Darnley* and *The Squire describing some Passages in his Town Life – a Scene from the Vicar of Wakefield* at the RA.

1845 Exhibits *A Scene from the 'Sentimental Journey'* at the BI and *A Portrait* and *The Village Pastor* at the RA, securing his election as an Associate of the Royal Academy (ARA) on 3 November. In June marries Isabelle Baker; lodges in Charlotte Street.

1846 Exhibits *Norah Creina* and *A Sleeping Girl* at the BI and *The Return from Labour*, (from Gray's 'Elegy in a Country Churchyard'), and *Madame Jourdain discovers her Husband at the Dinner which he gave to the Belle Marquise and the Count Dorante* [from Molière's *Bourgeois Gentilhomme*] at the RA. Birth of daughter Isabelle.

1847 Exhibits *An English Merry-Making a Hundred Years Ago* and *A Scene from the 'Spectator'* at the RA. Birth of Jane Ellen (Cissie). Moves to 13 Park Village West, Regent's Park.

1848 *An Old Woman Accused of Witchcraft*, *A Stage Coach Adventure* and *Scene from the 'Bourgeois Gentilhomme'* exhibited at RA. June – July holiday in Scarborough and visit to York. November: moves into 12 Park Village West.

1849 April: birth of Willie. Exhibits *Coming of Age in the Olden Time* at the RA. August: holiday in Hastings.

1850 Exhibits *Portrait of a Lady*, *Sancho Panza tells a Tale to the Duke and Duchess* (a scene from Don Quixote), and '*Mr Honeywood introduces the Bailiffs to Miss Richland as his Friends*', (a scene from Goldsmith's *The Good-Natured Man*) at the RA. Birth of May Louise (Louey). Visits Belgium and Holland with Egg and Stone.

1851 His portrait painted by Augustus Egg. *A Gleaner* (background painted by Creswick) and *Hogarth brought before the Governor of Calais* exhibited at the RA. Summer holiday at Ramsgate. Death of his Uncle Scaife, his brother Charles and his mother. Birth of Charles George Frith.

1852 Exhibits *Wicked Eyes* at the BI. Exhibits two female portraits, *When we devote our Youth to God, 'Tis pleasing in His Eyes* (also known as 'Bedtime' or 'Evening Prayers') and *Pope makes Love to Lady Mary Wortley Montagu* at the RA. Summer holiday at Ramsgate. Moves to 10 Pembridge Villas, Bayswater.

1853 Elected RA. 10 February, filling the vacancy left by the death of J.M.W. Turner. Birth of Alice Frith.

1854 At Hampton in April and visits Kempton Park racecourse. *Portrait of Mrs E.M. Ward*, *Life at the Seaside (Ramsgate Sands)*, *Anne Page*, *The Love-Token: a scene from the 'Bride of Lammermoor'*, *The Poison Cup: a scene from 'Kenilworth'*, exhibited at the RA. Birth of a baby who dies the same year. Trip to Boulougne. Summer holiday in Dover.

1855 Exhibits *Feeding the Calves* (background by Richard Ansdell), *Lovers*, *At the Opera*, and *Maria Tricks Malvolio* at the RA and is awarded gold medal in the Universal Exhibition, Paris. Birth of Fanny Frith and of Mary Powell Alford.

1856 Exhibits *A Dream of the Future* (with landscape background by Thomas Creswick and dog by Ansdell), *Garden Flowers*, and *Many Happy Returns of the Day* exhibited at the RA.

1857 Exhibits *The Pliant Hour* (a scene from *Othello*) at the BI and *A London Flower Girl* and *Kate Nickelby at Madame Mantalini's* at the RA. *A Stage Coach Adventure* exhibited at the Manchester Art Treasures Exhibition (lent by Mrs Gibbons). Birth of Walter Frith. Summer holiday at Weymouth.

1858 Exhibits *Derby Day* at the RA. Birth of Alfred Elmore Frith and Agnes Catherine Alford. Summer holiday at Weymouth.

1859 Exhibits *Charles Dickens in his Study* at the RA. Elected member of the Athenaeum Club.

1860 Exhibits *Claude Duval* at the RA. Birth of Philip Frith.

1862 Exhibits a portrait of Thomas Creswick at the RA and *The Railway Station* at Louis Victor Flatow's gallery, 7 Haymarket. Birth of William Powell Alford. Summer holiday at Hastings and a week's shooting at Wareham, Dorset.

1863 Queen Victoria commissions Frith to paint the Marriage of the Prince of Wales and Princess Alexandra of Denmark in St George's Chapel, Windsor on 10 March. Exhibits *Juliet* at the RA. Gives evidence to the Parliamentary Commission appointed to enquire into the position of the RA relative to the Fine Arts.

1864 Death of Thomas Frith. Marriage of eldest daughter Isabelle to Captain Charles Oppenheim.

1865 Exhibits *Marriage of the Prince of Wales*, *Mrs Charles Oppenheim*, and *Miss Braddon* at the RA. Summer holiday at Scarborough. Birth of Ronald Alford and of first grandchild.

1866 Exhibits *Mrs J.F. Mounsey* and *Widow Wadman laying Seige to Uncle Toby* at the RA. *Life at the Seaside* exhibited at the Exposition générale des beaux-arts, Brussels and the Order of Leopold conferred on Frith. Birth of Evelyn Shirley Frith and of Reginald Alford.

1867 April: death from diphtheria of Evelyn Shirley Frith and stay at Tunbridge Wells. Exhibits *King Charles II's Last Sunday* at the RA. Summer holiday at Ramsgate.

1868 Exhibits *Before Dinner at Boswell's Lodgings, Sterne and the French Innkeeper's Daughter, Sterne's Maria, Scene from 'She Stoops to Conquer', Mr Sothern of the Theatre Royal, Haymarket, in the character of the Marquis de Tourville* at the RA. Birth of Guy Alford.

1869 Exhibits *Hope and Fear, Nell Gwyn, A Man in Armour, Altisidora Pretending Love for Don Quixote, feigns a Swoon at the Sight of him,* and *Malvolio, married to the Countess in Imagination, soliloquises* at the RA. Visit to Homburg with Henry O'Neil and Basil Hodges. Marriage of Jane Ellen (Cissie) Frith to James Panton.

1870 Exhibits *Sir Roger de Coverley and the Perverse Widow, The Pulse, the Husband, Paris* (a scene from Sterne's 'Sentimental Journey'), *Mrs Rousby as Princess Elizabeth in 'Twixt Axe and Crown', Two Doves, Amy Robsart and Janet, Gabrielle d'Estrées* and *At Homburg, 1869* at the RA. Birth of Bertram Septimus Alford.

1871 Exhibits *The Salon d'Or, Homburg,* and *I know a Maiden fair to see, Beware!* at the RA. Summer holiday at Boulogne.

1872 Exhibits *At my window, Boulogne, Lord Foppington describes his Daily Life* (from *The Relapse*, by Vanbrugh), *The Miniature, The Love Letter, An Incident in the Life of Lady Mary Wortley Montagu* and *Henry the Eighth and Anne Boleyn deer-shooting in Windsor Forest* at the RA.

1873 Exhibits *English Archers, Nineteenth Century, A Boulogne Flower Girl, A London Flower Girl, Breakfast Time* and *A Winning Hazard* at the RA. Elected Member of Academy of Fine Arts, Stockholm.

1874 Exhibits *Pamela* (from Richardson's *Pamela*, or *Virtue Rewarded*), *Wandering Thoughts, Blessing the Little Children, Sleep* and *Prayer* at the RA.

1875 Exhibits *Sophia Western at the Inn Fire* (a scene from Fielding's *Tom Jones*), *La Belle Gabrielle, Tom Jones shows Sophia her Image in the Glass as a Pledge of his Future Constancy, St Valentine's Day, Black and Blue Eyes, Polly Peachum, Flowers* and *New Earrings* at the RA. Tour of Italy with Isabelle and unmarried daughters. Elected Member of the Académie royale des beaux-arts at Antwerp, in place of Landseer.

1876 Exhibits *Scene from Molière's 'L'Amour Médecin', The Lover's Seat, Scene from 'The Vicar of Wakefield', Below the Doge's Palace, Venice, 1460* at the RA and *The Marriage of the Prince and Princess of Wales* at the International Exhibition, Philadelphia (British Section).

1878 Exhibits the five canvases forming *The Road to Ruin* and *Mrs Hetherington* at the RA. Appears as a witness for the defence in the Ruskin–Whistler libel trial, alongside Burne-Jones and Tom Taylor. Visits Paris Exposition universelle with Millais, where *Charles II's Last Sunday* is exhibited.

1879 Summer holiday at Tenby.

1880 28 January: death of Isabelle Frith. April: *The Race for Wealth* exhibited at Marsden's Gallery, King Street. Exhibits *Tenby Fishwoman* and *Prawn Seller, Tenby* at the RA. Visits Belgium and Holland with his unmarried daughters.

1881 30 January: Marries Mary Alford. Their son William Powell Alford is one of the witnesses. Exhibits *For Better, for Worse* at the RA.

1882 Exhibits *Miss Emile Levy* at the RA. Summer holiday in Switzerland.

1883 Exhibits *The Private View of the Royal Academy, 1881, Mrs William Lee of Downside, Honeymooning in Switzerland, Kate Kearney 'Beware of her smile etc.'*, and *A Guitar Player* at the RA.

1884 Exhibits *Beatrice hears that Benedick loves her, Dr Johnson and Mrs Siddons, Cruel Necessity* and *A London Flower Girl* at the RA.

1885 Exhibits *Mrs Alfred Pope, John Knox at Holyrood* and *The Old, Old Story* at the RA.

1886 Exhibits *The Sick Doll*, *The Troth Plight*, *Dr Johnson's tardy Gallantry*, and *Match Sellers* at the RA. Works included in the Adelaide Jubilee Exhibition, British Fine Art Section.

1887 Exhibits *Violets* and *Sir Roger de Coverley and the Beautiful Widow* at the RA; Eleven paintings lent by private owners to the Manchester Royal Jubilee Exhibition. Publishes *My Autobiography and Reminiscences*.

1888 Exhibits *Poverty and Wealth* and *Christmas Morning: Santa Claus's Gifts* at RA. Sells 7 Pembridge Villas and moves to Ashenhurst, 7 Sydenham Rise in South London. Publishes his *Further Reminiscences*.

1889 Exhibits *The Hon. Mrs Robert Foster*, *The New Frock* and *Walter Frith aged 5* at the RA.

1890 Retires from Royal Academy 26 March, but exhibits *Mrs Gerald Crecy Parnell* at RA this year.

1891 Exhibits *The Sweetest Beggar that e'er asked for Alms* at the RA. Publishes *John Leech, His Life and Work*.

1892 Exhibits *A New Model* at the RA.

1893 Exhibits *L'Adieu de Marie Stewart* at the RA.

1894 Exhibits *Five o'clock Tea, 1893* at the RA.

1895 Death of Mary (Alford) Frith. Exhibits *Mrs Gresham and her Daughter* at the RA.

1896 Exhibits *Juliet and the Nurse* at the RA. Moves to 114 Clifton Hill, St John's Wood, London.

1897 Exhibits *Juliet on the Balcony* at the RA.

1898 Exhibits *Olivia Unveiling* (a scene from *Twelfth Night*) at the RA.

1899 Exhibits *Charles II and Lady Castlemaine* at the RA.

1900 Exhibits *She gives a Side Glance and looks down* at the RA.

1901 Exhibits *The Intercepted Letter* at the RA.

1902 Exhibits *In the Conservatory: a Critical Moment* at the RA.

1908 9 January, his birthday: awarded the CVO at Buckingham Palace.

1909 Dies 2 November. Funeral at St Augustine's Church, Kilburn. Cremation at Golders Green Crematorium and interment at Kensal Rise Cemetery, North London.

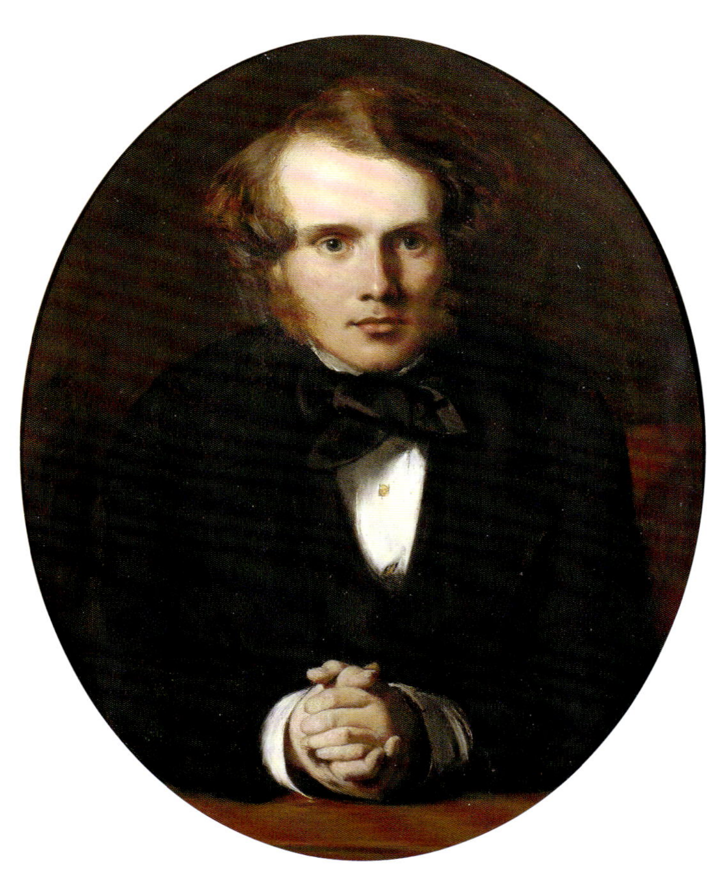

Chapter 1

The Private Life of William Powell Frith

VIVIEN KNIGHT

In terms of prices and popular appeal, William Powell Frith (1819–1909) was the most successful painter of his generation. At the peak of his career, in 1875, his picture *Before Dinner at Boswell's Lodgings* (1868) achieved the highest auction price to that date for a work by a living painter, and on no fewer than six occasions the Royal Academy had to protect his pictures from the crowds with an iron rail.[1] He was a pioneer in the field of modern-life painting, and *Life at the Seaside (Ramsgate Sands)* (1854; Fig. 14), *Derby Day* (1858; Fig. 61), and *The Railway Station* (1862; Fig. 63) remain unsurpassed as icons of the Victorian age. Yet such subjects – expensive and time-consuming to produce – formed a comparatively small part of Frith's output. The needs of his private and family life determined the shape and development of his work and circumscribed his ambition. This chapter examines the domestic background to Frith's public career.

Frith was born at Aldfield near Ripon on 9 January 1819. His family lived at Studley Royal, where his father Thomas (1777–1837) was House Steward;[2] his mother Jane Powell (1779–1851; Fig. 2) came from a family of gentleman farmers in the Shropshire village of Fitz.[3] There were three other children – George (1816–31), Charles (1822–51) and Maria Jane (b.1825). In 1826 the Friths moved to Harrogate when Thomas became tenant of the Dragon Hotel where he prospered.[4] William attended boarding school at Thorp Arch[5] and then spent two years at the Cliff House Academy at St-Margaret's-at-Cliffe near Dover (Fig. 3), which he enjoyed because his father (an amateur artist and collector of old prints and pictures) had instructed that he should copy prints in preference to academic study. When he returned home aged fifteen, his portfolio of copies from 'Dutch prints' were 'the wonder of High Harrogate' (Fig. 7).

Frith would have preferred to become an auctioneer, but he was reluctantly persuaded to consider an artistic career. In March 1835 he and his father took the York coach to London to show his copies to Thomas Phillips RA, staying at Scaife's Hotel at 7 Lower Brook Street, which was run by Jane Frith's sister Maria and her husband Francis Scaife. Phillips being away, the next day the Scaifes' artist neighbour John Partridge agreed to look at Frith's portfolio (Fig. 4). While the boy was struggling with a classical bust Partridge lent him to copy (the first time he had been asked to draw from a three-dimensional object rather than a print), his father visited Henry Sass and arranged for Frith to enter his school as an indoor pupil, living and eating with Sass's own family.

Sass was an undistinguished artist but his school at 6 Charlotte Street was good at preparing students for the Royal Academy Schools.[6] The students copied antique figures (Fig. 5) and outlines from Michelangelo, Guercino, the Carracci and Poussin, but Frith also set himself to draw 'from chairs, tables, stools, etc., because if a man can't draw a chair, how can he draw a head, when one is so much more difficult than the other?'[7] He retained the habit of drawing even common objects from actual models for the rest of his life, whereas the study of perspective and anatomy he

1. *Self Portrait.* Private Collection. Frith gave this picture, apparently based on a portrait of him by his friend Augustus Egg, to his daughter Isabelle in 1908.

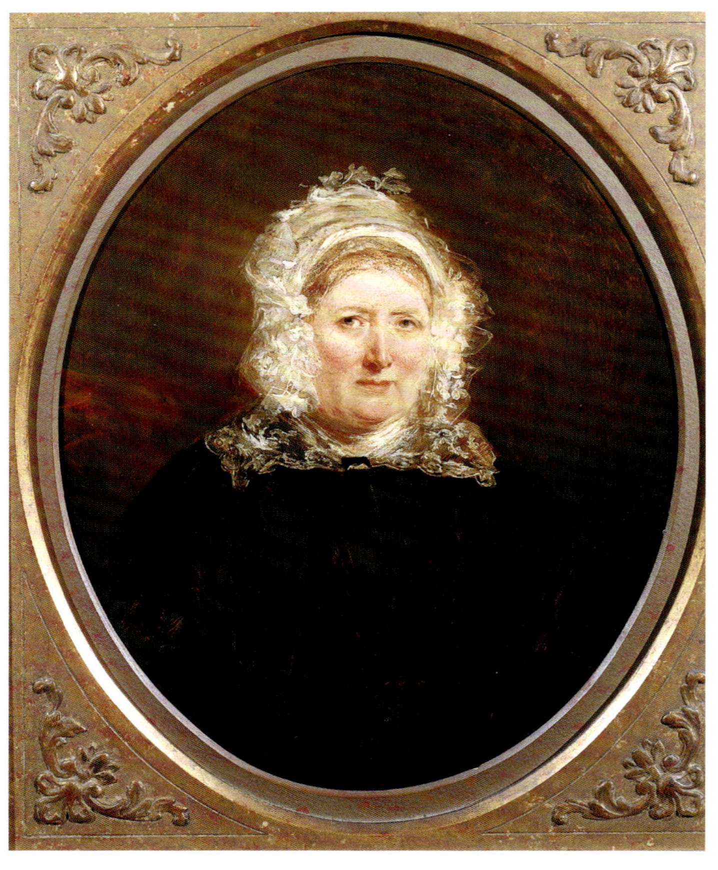

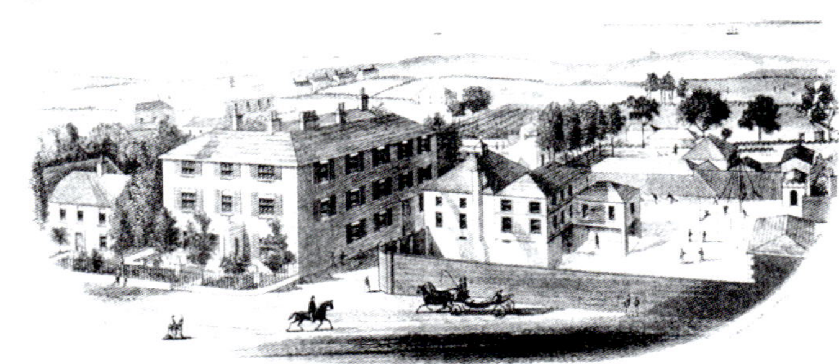

2. *Jane Frith, the Artist's Mother.* Private Collection. Frith painted the original of this portrait in 1840, and late in life made several copies to give to his children. He gave this one to his daughter Louisa on 2 August 1896.

3. Cliff House Academy, St Margaret's, Dover, from the school's letterhead. Dover Museum. Frith was a boarder at the school 1832–4.

4. John Partridge (1790–1872), *The Artist and his Family.* Museum of London. A neighbour of Frith's uncle and aunt Scaife in Brook Street, Partridge's success and wealth perhaps reassured them that an artistic career could be rewarding.

5. *Venus de Milo.* The Mercer Art Gallery, Harrogate Museums and Arts. The *Venus de Milo* was one of the antique casts at Sass's art school. Frith wrote he was drawing a 'broken Venus' in a letter to his mother of 1 March 1836, and of sending a drawing of the Venus home in December.

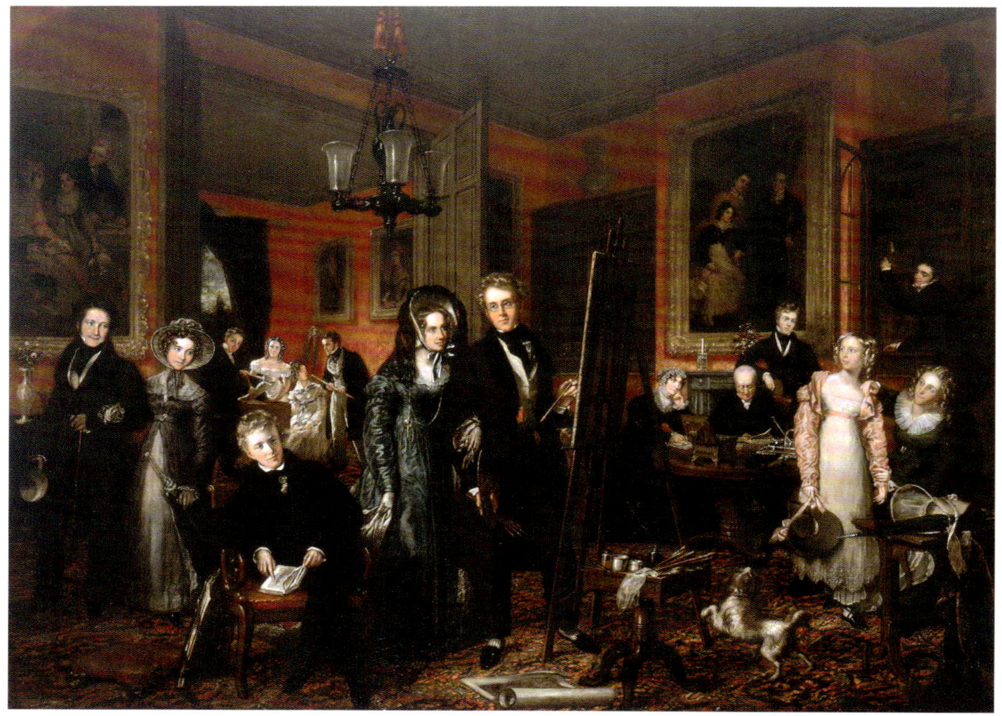

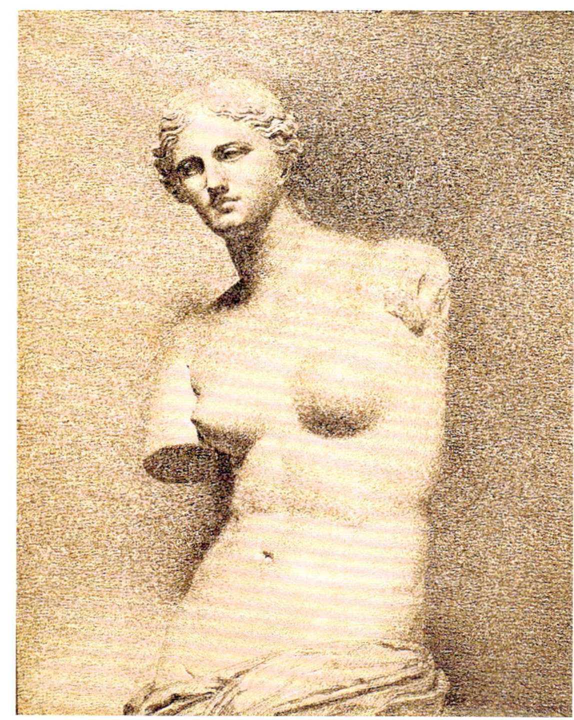

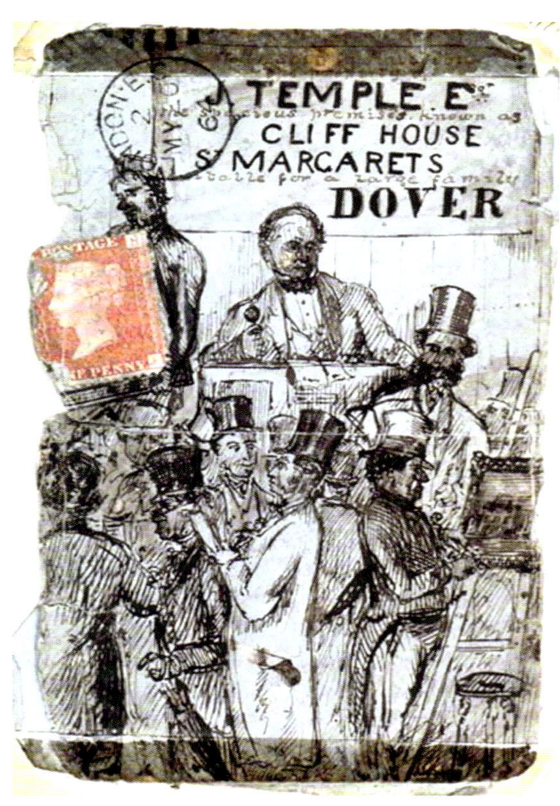

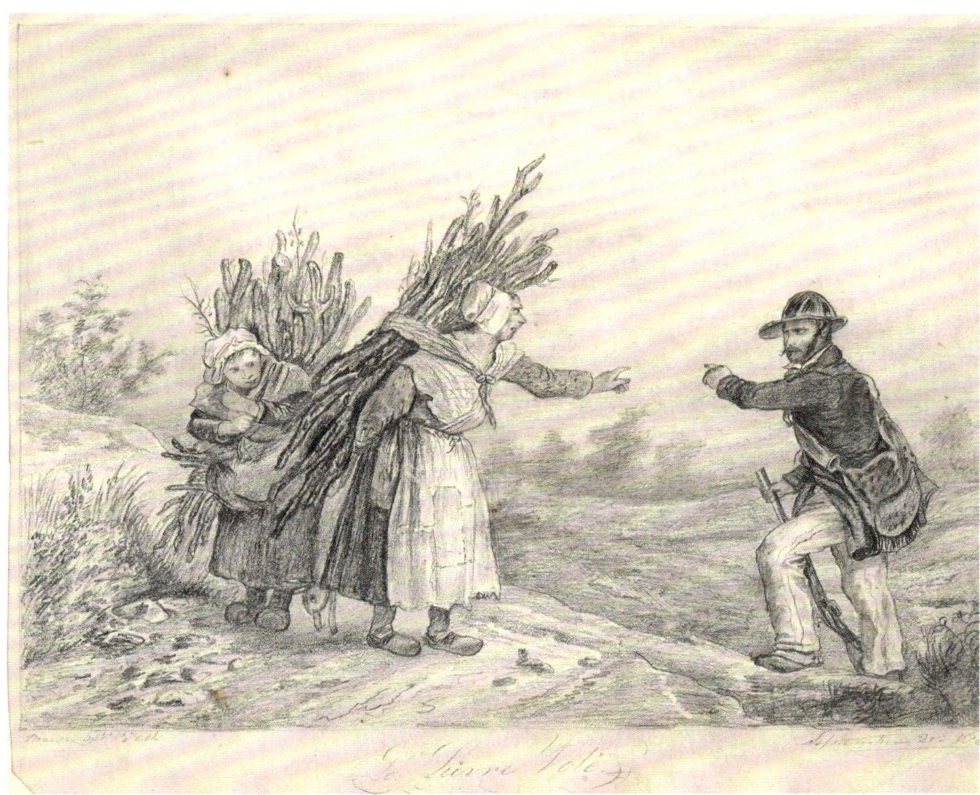

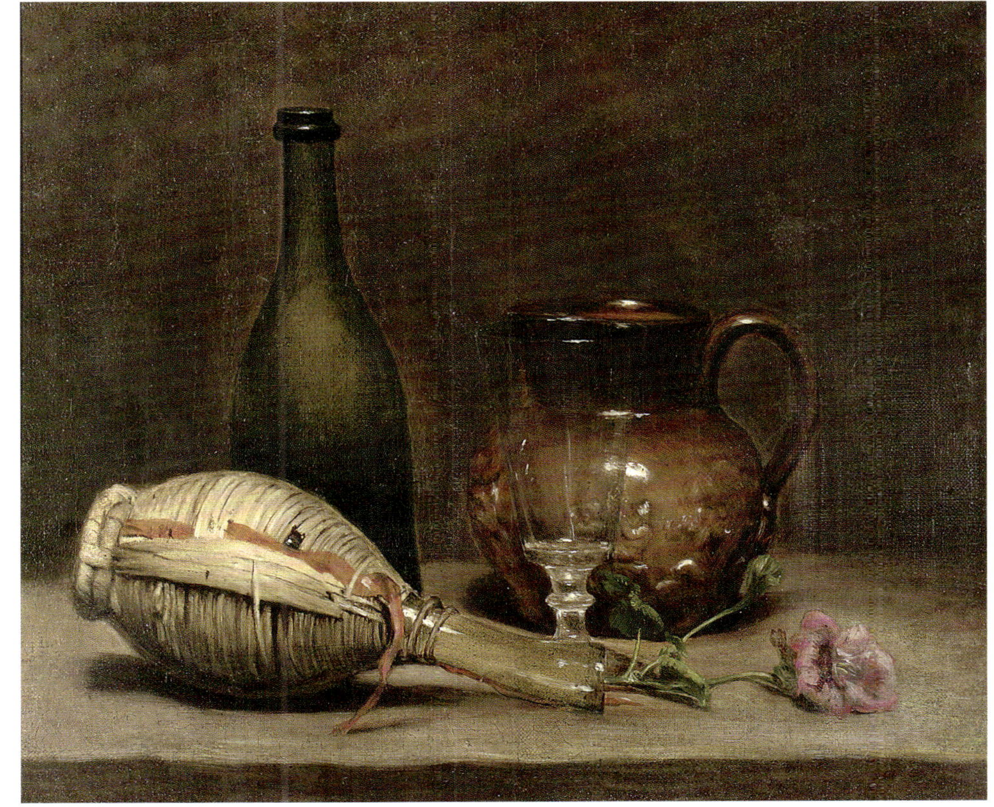

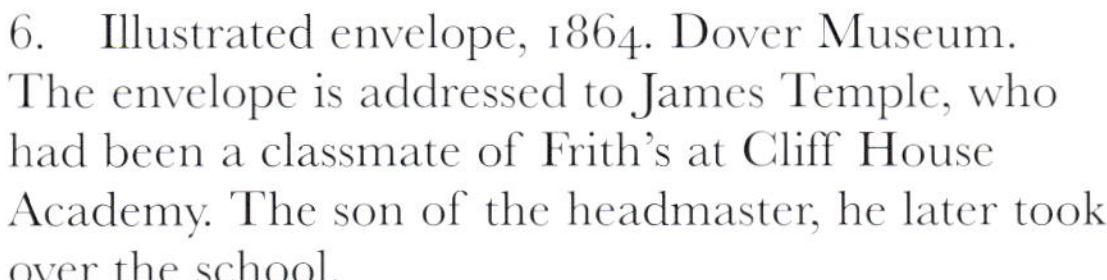

6. Illustrated envelope, 1864. Dover Museum. The envelope is addressed to James Temple, who had been a classmate of Frith's at Cliff House Academy. The son of the headmaster, he later took over the school.

7. *Le Lièvre volé*, 1832. The British Museum. Frith's early training consisted of copying prints. He made this copy when he was thirteen years old.

8. *My First Attempt from Nature*, *c.* 1837. Private Collection.

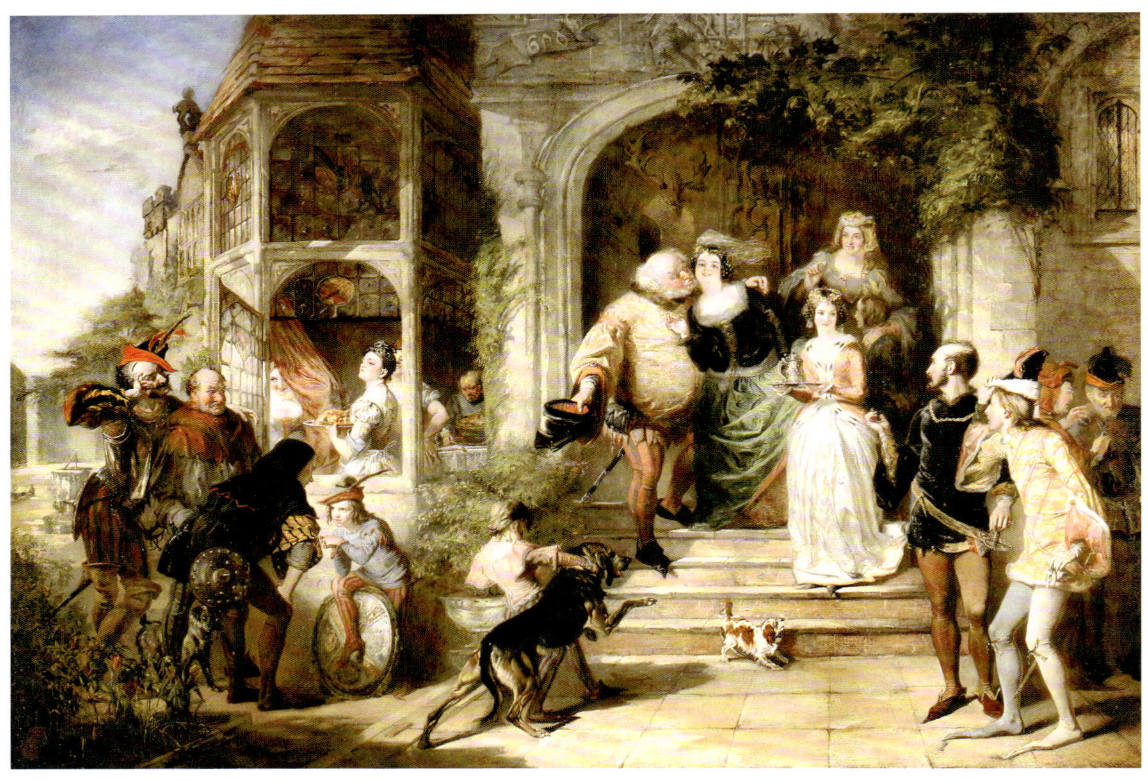

9. *The Merry Wives of Windsor*, 1843. European Art Gallery, Dallas, Texas.

found difficult and uninteresting and abandoned as soon as possible.

Frith's letters home to his mother[8] reveal an active and alert teenager, avid to see exhibitions and to meet artists, impressed by social occasions, keen on new clothes and conscious of his appearance, anxious to reassure his family he is working hard, living within his means and behaving correctly, always hoping for more pocket money and presents of cake, Yorkshire ham and grouse for himself and Mr and Mrs Sass. In December 1836 Sass let him 'try for the Academy' with a drawing of the Laocoön (one of the antique casts that lined Sass's hall) and on 3 January 1837 he was admitted as a probationer, becoming a full student the following 5 December. In the meantime he stayed on at Sass's, learning to paint by making monochrome copies from antique figures and copies of the Old Masters. When he rebelled Sass threatened to write to his father, but a compromise was reached whereby Frith made one more copy and was then allowed to arrange and paint his first still life (Fig. 8).

In April 1837 Thomas Frith died of influenza while staying at Scaife's Hotel. His widow found a tenant for the Dragon and brought Charles and Jane to London, staying with the Scaifes while she looked for a house. By 1839 the family were installed at 11 Osnaburgh Street, Regent's Park. Using the small back parlour as his painting-room, Frith painted himself ('hour after hour spent staring into a mirror, with results unrecognisable by my friends as likenesses of myself') and his aunt and uncle, and scoured the streets for other models ('Italian organ-boys . . ., chair-menders, knife-grinders'), selling the portraits at Jones's auction-rooms in Great Portland Street.[9] A portrait commission from a man whose daughter was a governess in Lincolnshire led to another from her employer and thence to a four-month tour of Lincolnshire in 1839, painting the wives and daughters of gentleman farmers. Frith found it good practice and made a second Lincolnshire tour – painting a slightly wealthier clientele – in 1840, the year in which he made his first trip to France with his brother Charles and copied in the Louvre and which also saw his first appearance at the Royal Academy Exhibition with *Malvolio before the Countess Olivia*. Frith painted Malvolio's legs from his own in front of the mirror in the back parlour at Osnaburgh Street[10] but large pictures would have been difficult in this limited space, and by 1842 he was also renting a separate studio in Charlotte Street.[11]

Shakespeare was only one of the sources trawled by Frith at this time (Fig. 9).[12] Many early (and later) subjects were drawn from Scott, Cervantes, Molière, Goldsmith and Sterne, carried out with the high degree of 'finish' that appealed to contemporary middle-class taste. This kind of subject and treatment was common to the group of his friends and former fellow-students, Richard Dadd, Augustus Egg, John Phillip, Henry O'Neil, Alfred Elmore and E. M. Ward, who made up the informal sketching club known as 'the Clique' (not to be confused with the later St John's Wood Clique). Frith was also influenced in this direction by his patron, Birmingham industrialist John Gibbons, whose first commission in 1843 was a subject from Sterne's *Sentimental Journey* (Fig. 131): Gibbons demanded literary subjects over historical ones, female figures over male, Goldsmith in preference to Shakespeare as coming 'nearer home to one's everyday sympathies' and illustrative detail over broad effects.[13]

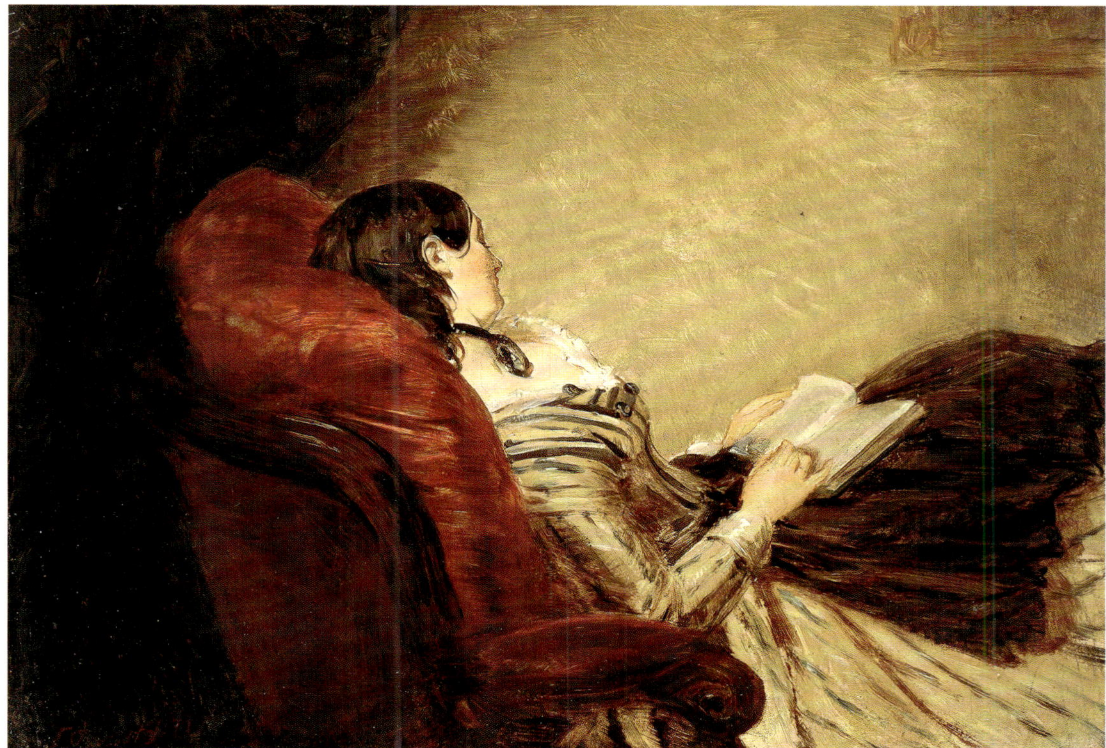

10. *Isabelle Asleep*, 1867. With Christopher Wood, London.

Frith's best friends at this time were Richard Dadd and Augustus Egg.[14] In 1842 Dadd accompanied a patron to the Middle East, returning ten months later in the early stages of insanity. Egg and Frith were in Paris in 1843 when they learned from a newspaper that Dadd had murdered his father and escaped to France where he was captured after a second murder attempt. A search of Dadd's studio revealed portraits of Frith, Egg and their other friends, all with their throats cut.[15] The experience doubtless fuelled the interest in insanity and its characteristics which recurs throughout Frith's *My Autobiography*. Later, Frith – who seems to have done a lot to relieve artists in distress and their families, both informally and through support for the Artists' Benevolent Fund – employed one of Dadd's sisters as a governess to his children.[16]

On his last visit to Frith's studio, Dadd had seen one of Frith's several versions of *Dolly Varden*, a character in Dickens's *Barnaby Rudge* (1841; Fig. 31). Frith had been an admirer of Dickens since reading the collection of early pieces published in 1836 as *Sketches by Boz*. What attracted him to *Barnaby Rudge* was Dolly's picturesque eighteenth-century costume, which he modelled on the wedding dress he had just inherited from his maternal grandmother. After Dickens saw the 'Dolly' painted for Frank Stone, in November 1842 he commissioned another version together with a companion picture of Kate Nickleby.[17] It was the beginning of a close friendship which lasted until Dickens's death in 1870, despite Frith's wife Isabelle – the close friend and confidante of Catherine Dickens – banning him from her house after the break up of the Dickens marriage, just around the time Frith was beginning the portrait of Dickens commissioned by his friend John Forster (Fig. 32).[18]

Isabelle Baker (1822–80; Fig. 10) married Frith in York on 26 June 1845. They left for their honeymoon in the Derbyshire Dales on a train that stopped at the bottom of her parents' garden,[19] an arrangement possible because Belle's father George Baker was Secretary to the York

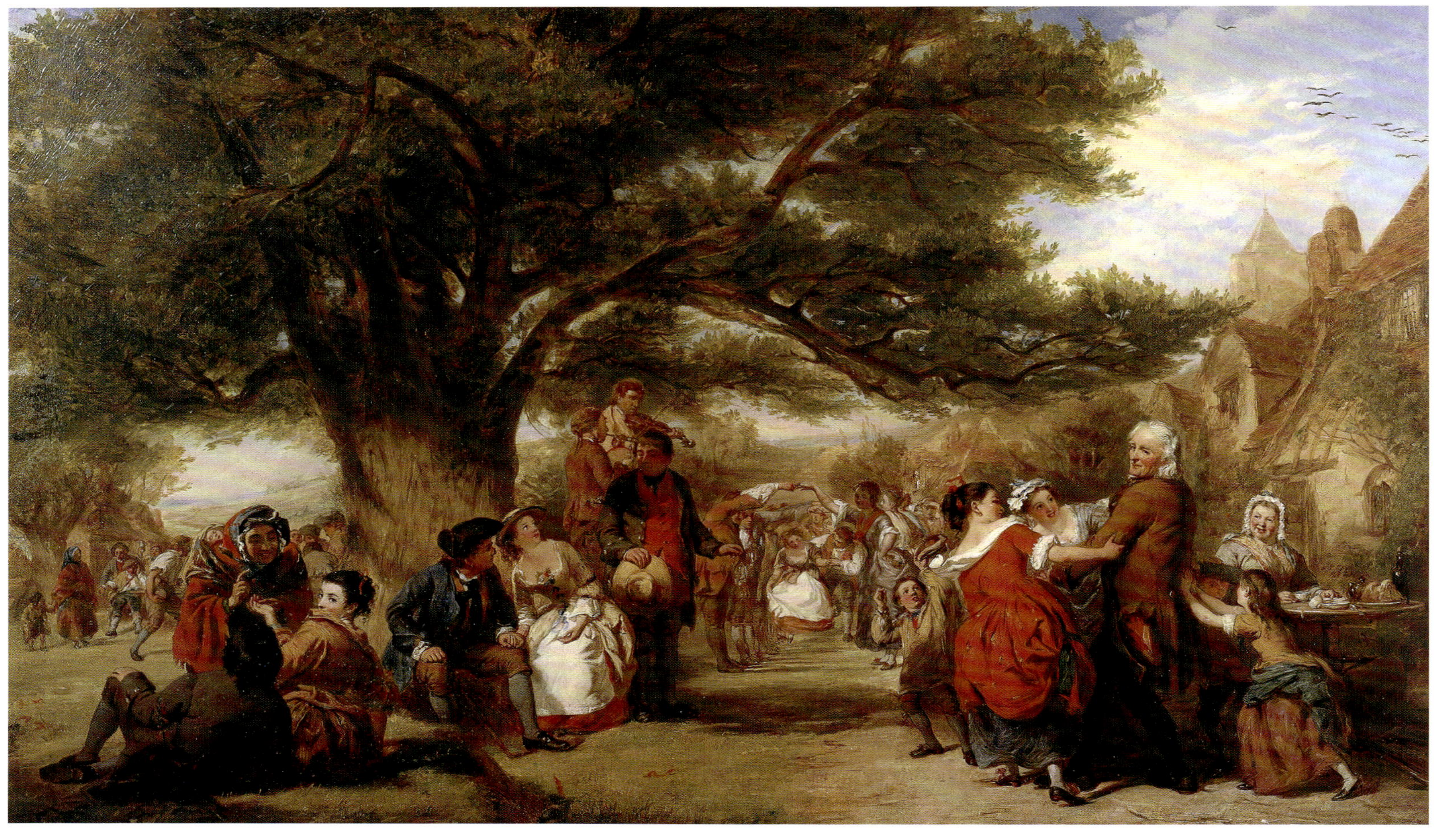

11. *An English Merry-Making a Hundred Years Ago.* Private Collection. Also known as *An Old English Merry-Making*, this is a smaller version of Frith's 1847 picture, either a preliminary study or, more probably, a later replica.

and North Midland Railway, whose Chairman was the infamous 'railway king' George Hudson.[20] Perhaps it was Baker who introduced Frith to a friend of Hudson's, Mr G. T. Andrews of York, who in 1847 bought Frith's painting *A Scene from the Spectator*. Andrews made a fortune in the 'railway mania' that reached its peak in that year and he persuaded Frith to buy shares in one of Hudson's lines, but when the bubble burst Frith saw the shares he had bought at £8 10s quoted in *The Times* at half a crown each. Frith was forced to ask his friend and patron Thomas Miller for help, and perhaps he still remembered this time when painting the *Race for Wealth* (1878), in which he aimed 'to illustrate also the common passion for speculation, and the destruction that so often attends the indulgence of it'.[21]

On his marriage Frith's mother settled £150 a year on him, and he and Isabelle moved into lodgings in Charlotte Street[22] where their first child, Isabelle, was born in 1846. The number of pictures Frith produced in the two years he lived in Charlotte Street testifies to his industrious working habits.[23] The largest at 44 × 73 inches was *An English Merry-Making a Hundred Years Ago* (Fig. 11). Frith painted its numerous figures from both professional models and people he knew or sought out: Isabelle's washerwoman Mrs King at the tea-table on the right, the grandfather an old man from the Paddington Workhouse, and the fortune-telling gypsy on the left, a real one encountered selling matches in the street outside the Regents Park house into which the Friths were shortly to move.[24] An artist named Tommy Brooks – a friend since their Thorp Arch school-days – was the young man in the centre asking the girl to dance, and Frith used Isabelle's sisters and some of their friends 'rather remorselessly'. His 'intimate friend' Thomas Creswick helped him out with the landscape background. Balancing his investment of time and money in such elaborate works were small pictures painted at ten or fifteen pounds a time for engraving such as those for Edward and William Finden's publication *The Beauties of Moore* (1845–6), a series of female portraits inspired by characters in Thomas Moore's poems.[25] It was easy to sell charming little pictures but, as he told his friend and patron, the Lancashire cotton manufacturer Thomas Miller in 1847, it was important to paint at least one large composition a year 'for the sake of upholding and advancing my reputation'.[26] He had already completed about a third of another large subject, the six-foot-long *An Old Woman Accused of Witchcraft* when the family moved in September 1847 into their first house – 13 Park Village West, Regent's Park;[27] a month later Isabelle gave birth to their second daughter (Jane Ellen, known as Cissie).

The amenities of the two-storey No. 13 included gas lighting, which Frith had laid on in his painting-room (the former coach house), considerably extending his working day.[28] He continued using this studio after the family moved in November 1848[29] to the larger house on the other side – No. 12, distinguished by an Italianate octagonal tower (Fig. 12). The move reflects his growing popularity and income. They used one of the tower rooms as a schoolroom and another may have been the 'rapidly filling' nursery:[30] by March 1851 the Frith household comprised their two elder daughters, a son William (born 1849) and eight-month-old May Louise (born 1850), a nurse, under-nurse, cook and a housemaid. A fifth child was born in the autumn.[31]

Park Village West 'was quiet and retired, yet in half a minute you could see the omnibuses go

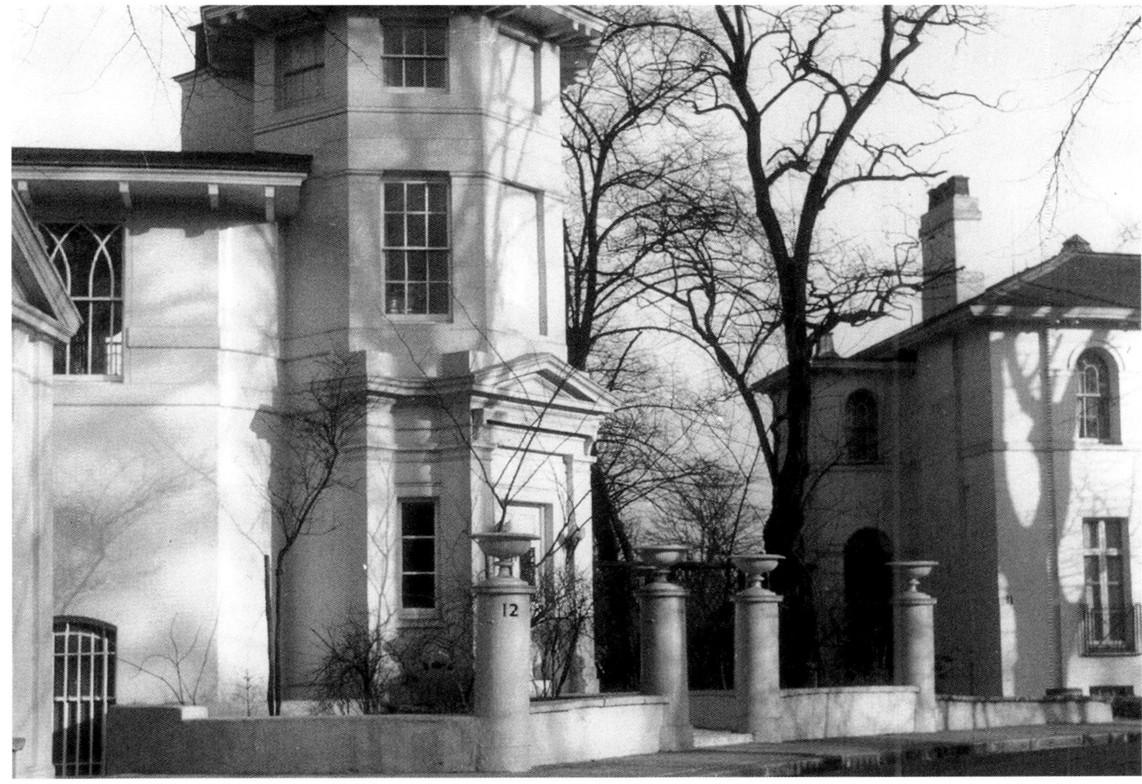

12. Number 12 Park Village West, London. City of London, London Metropolitan Archives.

up and down the street'.[32] The Friths dismissed their young Irish nurse Mary when she took Cissie to a nearby pub, replacing her with a young widow who stayed fifteen years and was known as 'Old Nurse'; she married Joe Wall, a model for Frith since his student days, who also cleaned Frith's brushes and helped his children 'to go to bed and get up in the most unsophisticated manner possible'.[33] Outside, in the long garden sloping down to an arm of the Regent's Canal, the children foraged for snails in the ivy bed alongside Frith's painting room, 'out of which we used to emerge black and odorous, to be raged at by Papa, who could not bear us to scrimmage in his beloved ivy bed . . . I see him, young, lithe, active, wrath personified, yet with a humorous twinkle in his eye and a suppressed smile round his mobile mouth, rush out, palette and mahl-stick [sic] in hand, to chase us away; while we shrieked with mingled awe and delight, the wrath vanishing in a game of romps . . .'[34]

From now on Frith's family life played a significant supporting role in his work. He began *Coming of Age in the Olden Time* in September 1848 (Fig. 13) after his summer holiday in Scarborough, where the weather was so cold that he sat beside the fire making sketches for it.[35] Returning to London via York, he visited Heslington Castle, on which – with Hever Castle in Kent – he based the picture's background (although, never confident about drawing architecture, he used engraved antiquarian book illustrations as the direct source).[36] Frith finished the painting in April 1849 and immediately dispatched it to the Royal Academy (it must have been barely dry) where it was hailed as one of the great achievements of the Exhibition, the *Art Journal* observing that it was 'superior to everything that has preceded it from the same hand. Mr Frith amply maintains his position, and establishes his right to the honour not long ago conferred on him' – a reference to his election in 1845 as an Associate of the Royal Academy.

Increasing success led to a more public social life. In May 1851 he attended a Conversazione held by Lord Londesborough at his Piccadilly mansion, alongside other artists, scientists, army officers and engineers, earls, dukes and marquesses.[37] A few months later he was rubbing shoulders with Londoners from the lower end of the social scale during the family's annual seaside holiday, this time to Ramsgate. The Friths' holidays usually ran from late July to mid-October, and it was Isabelle's job to find suitable rented houses facing the sea. When the children were older they ensured there were London friends going to the same place: at Ramsgate in 1867 the holiday colony comprised the writer C. W. Shirley Brooks, the artists P. H. Calderon, G. A. Storey and G. Du Maurier, and the actors E. A. Sothern and Quintin Twiss, 'each with their overcrowding families of children'. Decanting the London household was a complicated business, with belongings packed in boxes and 'each box sewn up in a wrapper and then corded, the latest "long-clothes" had to have its cradle sewn up and packed, and finally the very last morning the bath was packed with the last oddments, sewn up in its wrapper and corded'.[38] Frith himself 'never travelled without the most extraordinary collection of things, from a portable easel downwards'.[39]

In 1851 Frith's holiday was interrupted when he was summoned back to London and the deathbed of his uncle Scaife. On his return to Ramsgate he spent the first two weeks of September making sketches on the beach and a pencil drawing in preparation for what would become *Life at the Seaside (Ramsgate Sands)* (Fig. 14).[40] His holiday was curtailed completely when he was called to Dover, where his beloved brother Charles was seriously ill with what had been diagnosed as a neglected cold. Frith was back in London by 28 September and a week later visited the Great Exhibition. But Charles died, and Frith tore out of the house with 'mad and uncontrollable grief'[41] to go to him:

> my Brother was quite young & . . . apparently in robust health. Yet a few days severe inflammation of the lungs & I think also of the brain, killed him. We never knew he was in danger till there was no hope of his recovery & I am continually distressed by the impression which

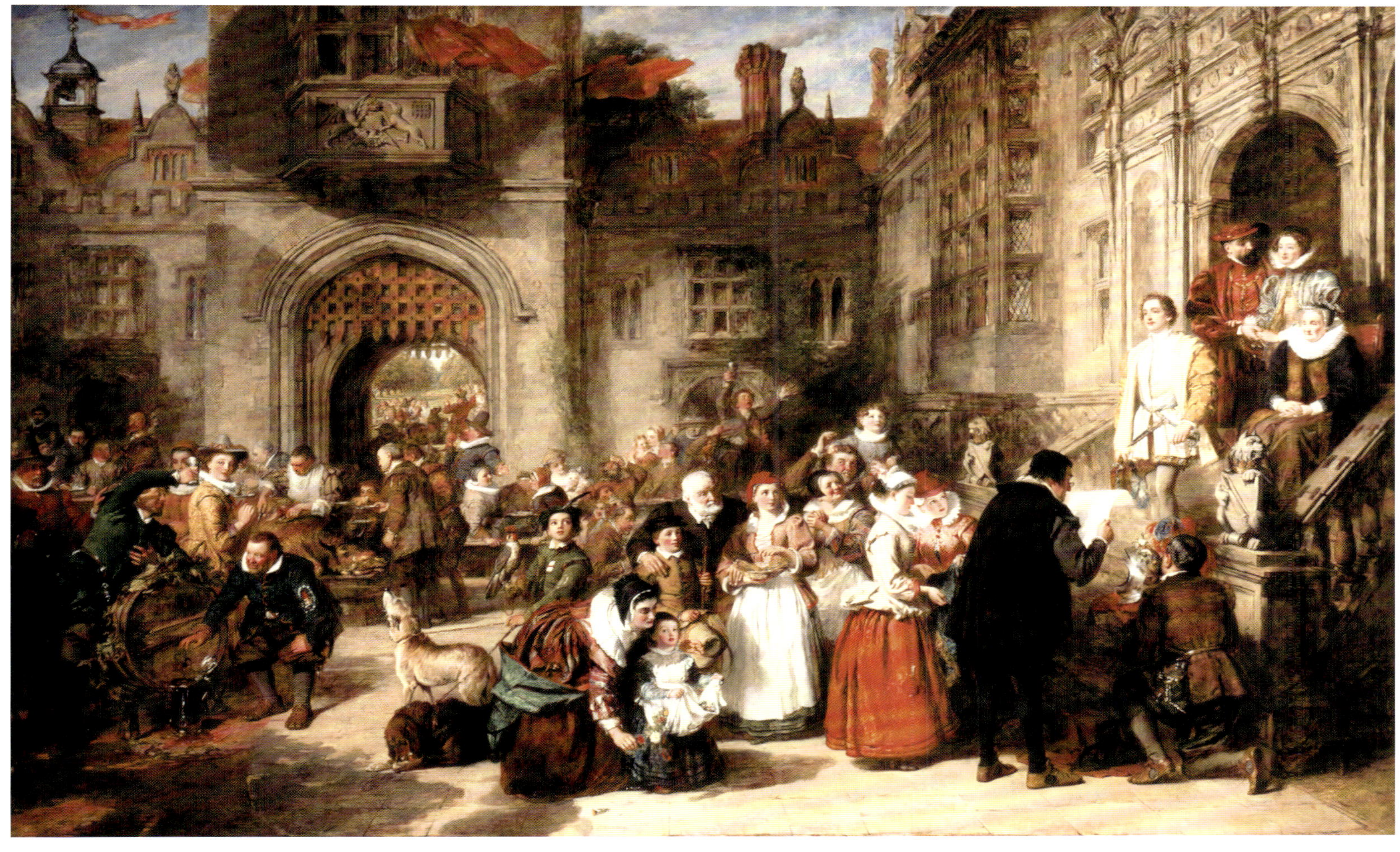

13. *Coming of Age in the Olden Time*, 1849. Private Collection.

will never be removed from my mind, that his case was not understood by the Dover doctors & think if he had been at home he would not have died – they could not have understood the case for they never admitted him to be in danger until he was dying.[42]

The double loss of the brother-in-law to whom they were all close, and her youngest son took its toll on Frith's elderly invalid mother and on 24 November 1851 she too died.

Frith was under a cloud, but it had a silver lining. In addition to a legacy from his wealthy uncle Scaife, with his mother's death he and his sister, the residuary legatees of their father's will, now also inherited his assets. Suddenly William could contemplate buying a property of his own.

Frith's new house was 10 Pembridge Villas, Bayswater, a west London suburb where development flourished from the 1840s following the completion in 1838 of the Great Western Railway's new London terminus at Paddington.[43] Frith already had friends in the neighbourhood[44] but he could also have been attracted by the advertisements for Pembridge Villas properties that appeared in *The Times* from 1850 onwards. The houses were large and imposing, many approached up flights of steps surmounted with porticos; they included libraries and conservatories but also such modern conveniences as water-closets and fully fitted bathrooms with hot and cold running water. When the ground rents of properties in Pembridge Villas (Fig. 15), Chepstow

14. *Life at the Seaside (Ramsgate Sands)*, 1854. The Royal Collection.

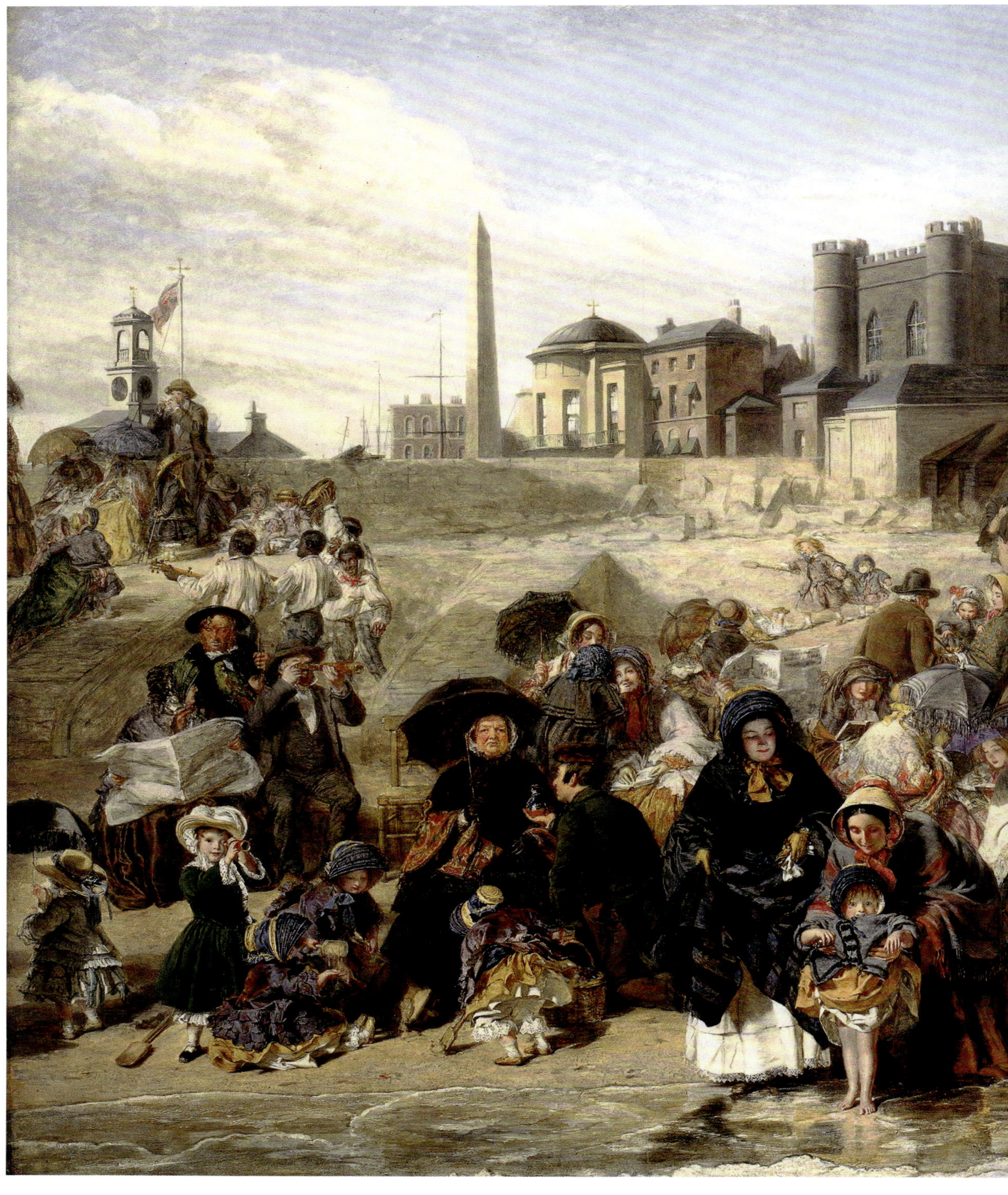

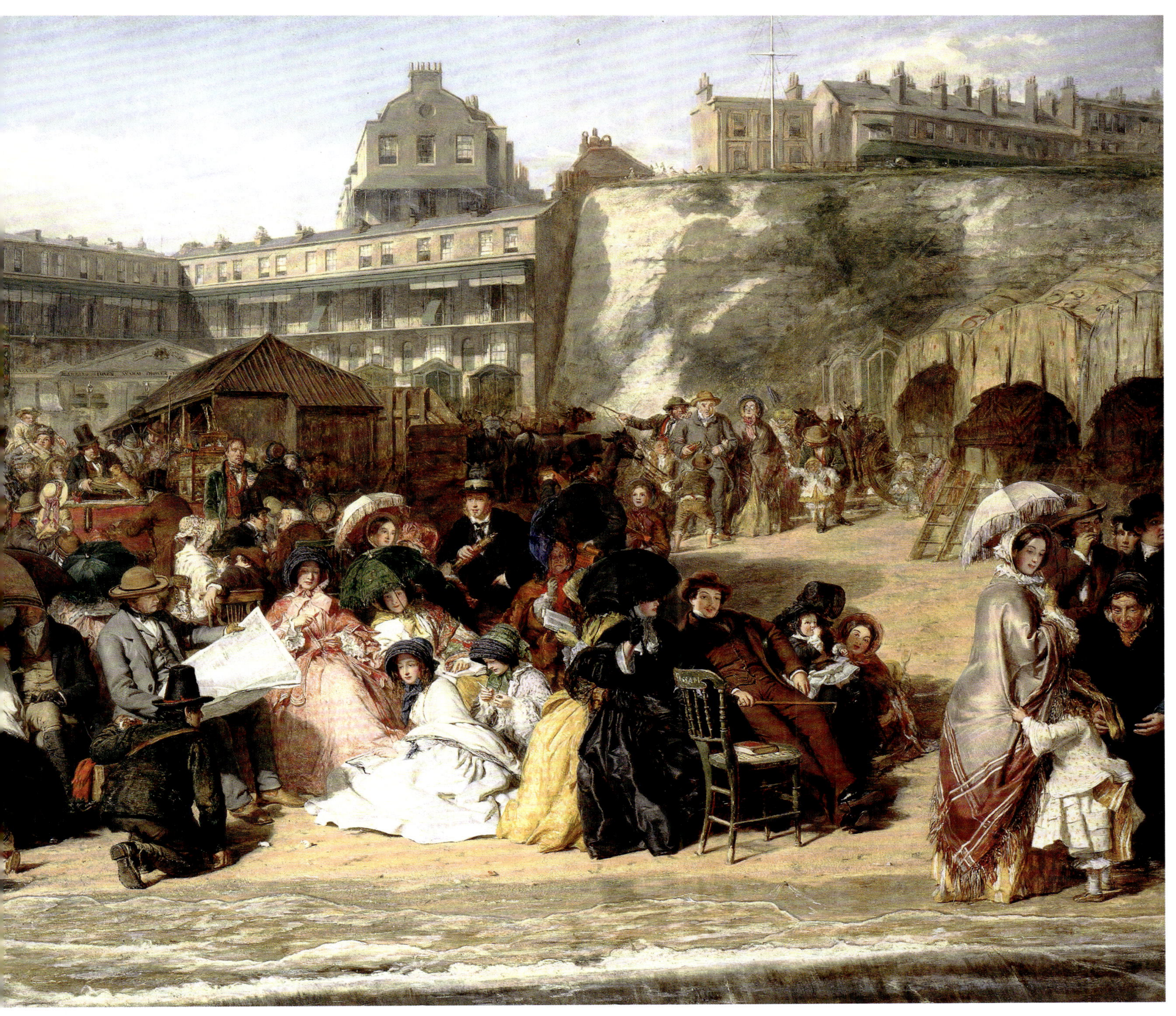

Villas and Westbourne Grove were sold in 1853, the advertisement noted that they were 'greatly sought after' and that the estate had 'been laid out under the most able superintendence and is one of the most improving and fashionable localities of the west outskirts of London'.[45] In the 1860s the adjoining Westbourne Grove would be transformed into a smart shopping street, but when the Friths arrived the neighbourhood was quiet and almost rural. Their own back garden was large enough for them to grow 'salads, currants, and all kinds of fruit and flowers' and to play croquet and tennis. On summer Sunday evenings they ate supper in an arbour made from the branches of a weeping ash, lit with gas laid on from the house, and when Cissie got married in 1869 the Friths celebrated with a garden party held in an 'Arabian Nights sort of tent'.[46]

When Isabelle took the older children to look over the house early in 1852, it 'was in the most fearsome state of dirt and dilapidation, due to its having been inhabited by a family of Greeks. At least, that is what the caretaker said, as she pointed out damaged paint, spoiled boards and walls which appeared to be studded with nails in every available place.'[47] It needed work, and Frith also commissioned an extension comprising a painting-room with another bedroom and a bathroom above,[48] expecting the job to be finished at the end of August 1852 so that they could move in after the family's summer holiday, again at Ramsgate. Normally Frith insisted on a holiday break from painting,[49] but this time he had brought his current picture – *Life at the Seaside (Ramsgate Sands)* (begun on 7 May) – with him 'so that I shall lose no time if I can manage to get models & a good room to paint in – at any rate the background can be done as well or better than at home' (he had hoped to paint the background from photographs, but they were unsuccessful).[50] Building work at the new house took longer than expected[51] and when he inspected it at the end of September it was still uninhabitable. The family returned to London on 4 October after a ten-week holiday and had moved in by 31 October, but the new rooms were damp and Frith had to paint in the drawing-room.[52] He went back to Ramsgate early in November to continue the picture's background, but when he came home his new painting-room had still not dried out, and his occupation of the drawing-room as a studio meant his children were 'obliged to forego their Christmas tree & the rest of the fun'.[53]

15. Pembridge Villas, London, 1905. Royal Borough of Kensington and Chelsea Family and Children's Services, Local Studies. Although Frith's house does not appear in this photograph, taken when the neighbourhood was in decline, it still gives a good idea of the imposing size of Pembridge Villas properties.

Although six potential buyers rejected *Life at the Seaside (Ramsgate Sands)* – one wondering 'how anybody in his senses could waste his time painting such a tissue of vulgarity'[54] – given its size, the number of figures in it and the fact it had already taken up so much of his time and would continue to do so, Frith decided on a price of £1,000 as early as February 1853.[55] He secured this sum (and more) when the print publisher Lloyd Brothers of Ludgate Hill bought it for 1,000 guineas. At the Royal Academy Exhibition in 1854 its fame was assured when they resold it for the same figure to the Queen and it was voted Picture of the Year. In the meantime Frith's regular income came from undemanding but readily saleable small pictures painted for private patrons and for Lloyds' to publish as prints.[56] *Evening Prayers* or *Bedtime* (Fig. 16) was one such picture, begun in March 1852, the first of his 'modern-life' subjects to be exhibited (and the prototype for several versions). A portrait of Isabelle with Cissie on her lap, it was a charming portrayal of familiar domestic life. Frith's later description of the painting displayed an uncharacteristic, even Whistlerian emphasis on its formal qualities: 'The child was kneeling in its mother's lap, with the wandering attention so common to children. The gray and black dress of the mother and the white night gown of the child made a sufficiently agreeable arrangement of negative colours.'[57] Exhibited at the RA with

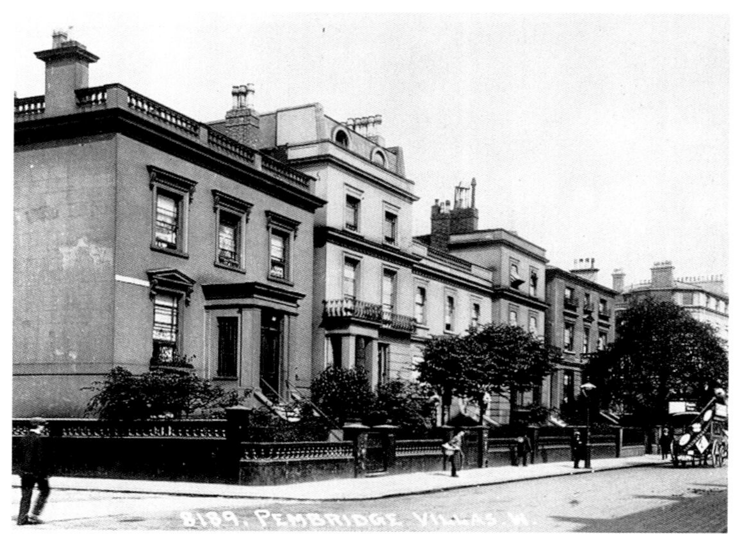

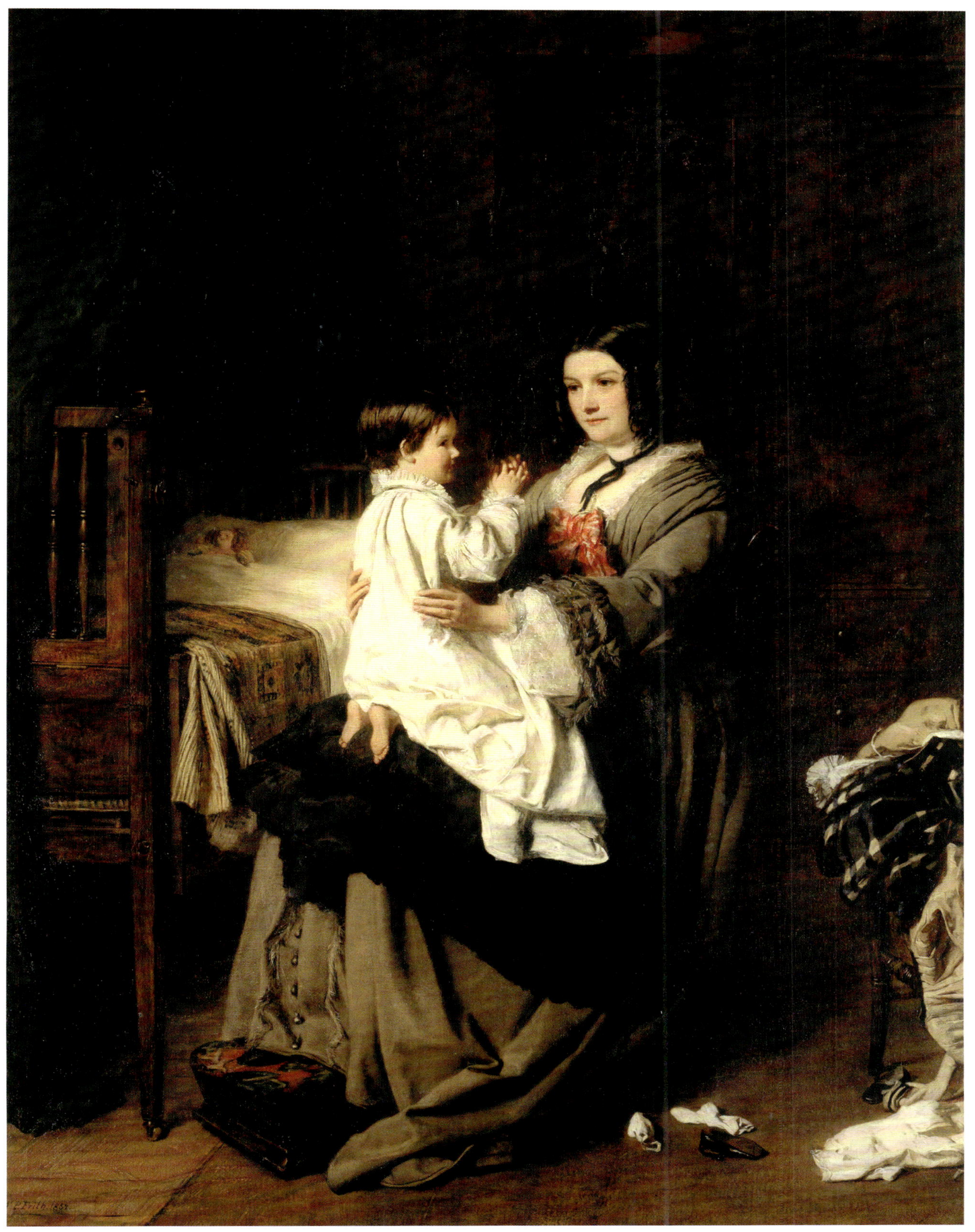

16. *When we devote our Youth to God, 'tis pleasing in His eyes*, 1852. Private Collection.

the title *When we devote our Youth to God, 'Tis pleasing in his Eyes* (from Isaac Watts, *Divine and Moral Songs for Children* (1715), song 12), the composition was unique in Frith's work in having any religious associations. The 'dreadful Sabbatical atmosphere' of his own childhood, in which 'he was taught to love going to church by attendance at long dull services, where, if he did not behave, he was tied to the leg of the kitchen table at home until the time for the next service came round', had made him an 'easy-going freethinker, whose opinion of all Churches [was] small and of all clerics even smaller still'. As a student Frith accompanied the Sasses to church but as an adult rarely if ever went, while insisting on his children's attendance;[58] he gave up painting on Sundays, not from any religious scruples or his mother's objections, but because he 'found the one day of rest an emphatic necessity', better spent visiting his Kensington artist friends in the morning and taking his children out in the afternoon. He told Miller, 'I am wicked enough to see nothing much now in it – don't be shocked, for I don't understand much about spiritual subjects – I never could paint them'.[59]

When Frith moved into Pembridge Villas in October 1852, his lease on 12 Park Village West still had almost a year to run. It was also a more expensive house than the old one, with a gross estimated rental value of £140 and a rateable value of £125.[60] Frith said he would never stoop to court Academicians to secure his own election, but when he was elected RA by a majority of 19 to 6 in February 1853 he was so excited he could not sleep.[61] He was less thrilled when his seventh surviving child (Alice) was born a month later:

> I fear I am not sufficiently grateful for these super additions to my family – I love the little things when I once get them but . . . I am quite satisfied with the present generation & feel disposed to leave to more deserving individuals any future additions in the shape [of] these unmistakeable little blessings – one of which is screaming dreadfully at the present moment. . . . I think 'the new Baby' wouldn't be a bad subject. The expressions of the last of the children were droll in the extreme the eldest girl begins to look dubious when she is told the Doctor brought the baby in a basket. I fear that pleasant fiction won't do another time.

Frith hoped there would not be another time, but in total Isabelle gave birth to at least eleven children.[62]

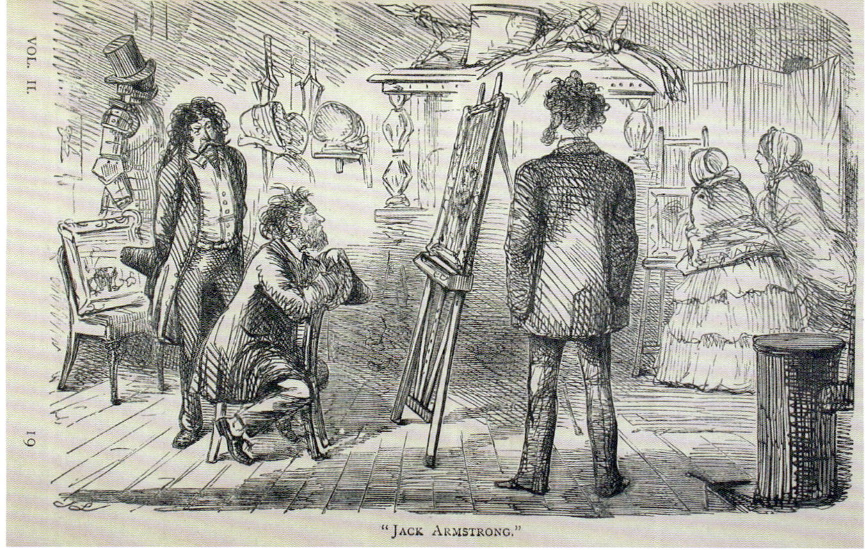

17. John Leech (1817–64), *Frith in his Studio*, 1856. Guildhall Library, City of London.
Two artists came to see *Many Happy Returns of the Day* while John Leech was visiting Frith. They did not know what to make of the picture, and Leech drew the event for *Punch* characterising Frith as 'Jack Armstrong' and the two visitors as 'Potter and Feeble'. When Frith reproduced the sketch in his biography of Leech in 1891, he said that its background, with the suit of armour and the oak-cabinet, perfectly represented his painting-room at Pembridge Villas at the time.

The little group in the centre of *Life at the Seaside (Ramsgate Sands)* of a child coaxed into the water by her mother was only one of many observant and sympathetic portrayals in the painting of children at play. Cissie's memories of their 'dear young father' with his 'never-ending stories' included accompanying him on his habitual after-work walk: 'to all the delightful things he used to tell us were added the romantic glamour of the dusky badly lighted streets, the yellow gas-lamps peering through the low-lying foggy air . . . Does any celebrated artist buy hot potatoes and chestnuts in the street now for his children'?[63] When their friend Shirley Brooks visited, Cissie remembered them all,

> from Papa downwards, steeplechase all up and down the drawing-room, leaping over every obstacle which came in our way in the shape of chairs and until we were too breathless to speak: then we would have a 'quiet' game of cards, animal grab, or some such peaceable pastime, the quietness of which once resulted in a call from the

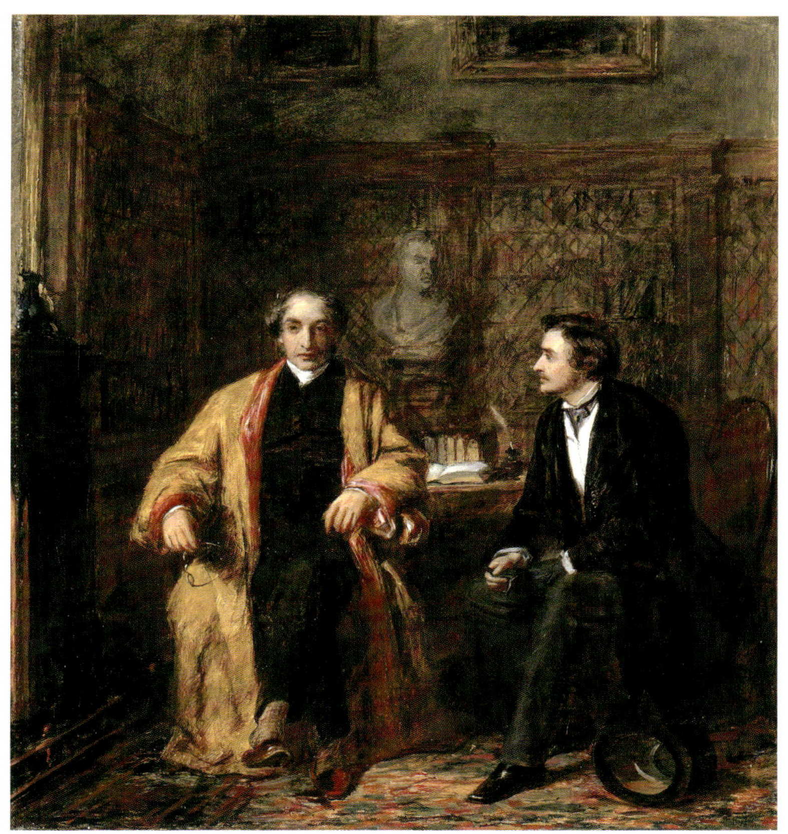

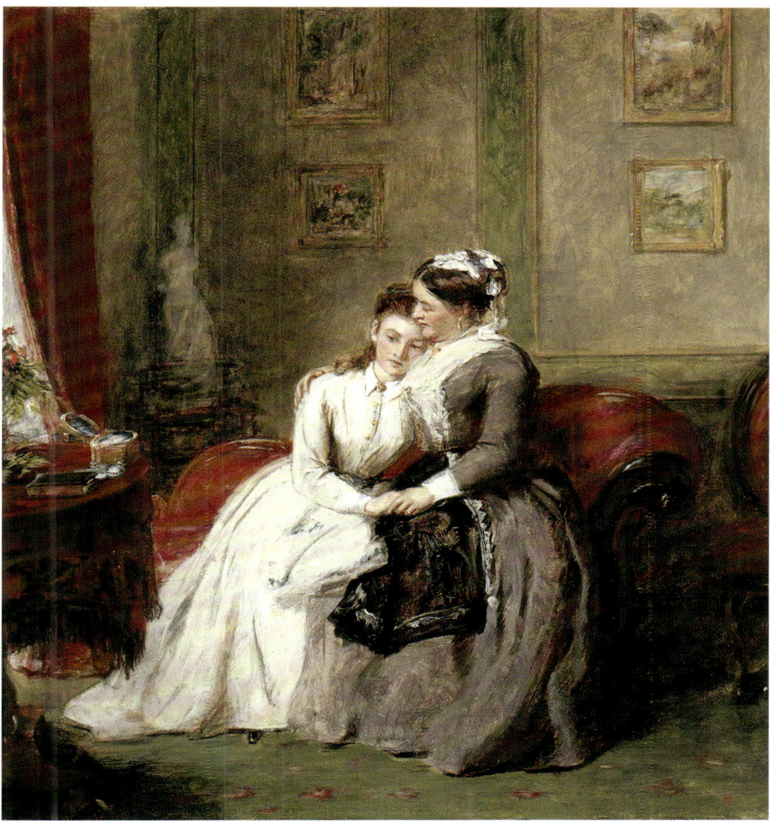

police. This is an absolute truth, because we were all screaming at the top of our voices, and they thought something must be wrong. A half-crown and a glass of something proved to their satisfaction that things were very much all right.[64]

18. *Hope*, 1869. Private Collection.

19. *Fear*, 1869. Private Collection.

Frith's own insistent domestic life now began to appear in his work. *Did You Ring Sir?* (1853; Fig. 21) was the second portrait of one of his servants, behind whom is seen the grained paint Cissie described on the internal doors. She thought the house was decorated 'in a fearsome manner', with 'a heavy dark red flock paper' in the dining room, but in *Many Happy Returns of the Day* (1854–6; Fig. 117) the wallpaper is dark green and is presumably the 'egg gum paper' which Frith had seen in Thomas Miller's and Richard Ansdell's houses and hung in his own in November 1852.[65] (The paintings seen on the wall in this and in later pictures are not easily identifiable, but Frith owned works by, among others, his friends Ansdell, Creswick, Mulready, Egg, Elmore, Landseer, O'Neill, Frank Stone and Louisa Starr, as well as by Constable, Hogarth, J. M. W. Turner, Guardi and Aert van der Neer [80].)[66] Here Frith consumed his regular breakfast of fish, York ham and eggs, toast and marmalade, writing letters as he ate, and reading *The Times* for half an hour afterwards, a routine that was, 'as indeed the whole day's programme . . . sacred and unalterable'.[67] He stopped work at midday for a glass of sherry and a biscuit in the dining-room with his children,[68] and after dinner in the evening he sat for half an hour in one of the dining-room's two leather arm-chairs, reading and smoking his customary cigar. The red velvet sofa in the Hogarthian pair *Hope* and *Fear* (Figs 18, 19) of 1869 may be the one in the dining-room from which Frith's children watched for the arrival of Christmas hampers or distinguished guests; the mother appears to be a portrait of Isabelle, and this picture too may have originated in personal experience – 1869 was the year of Cissie's marriage.

Alice is often said to be the child whose birthday is being celebrated in *Many Happy Returns of the Day*, although as Frith himself said it showed a sixth birthday celebration and Alice would have been only one when the picture was begun and three when it was exhibited in 1856, this may be incorrect. At one end of the table, Frith glances towards the grandfather figure (painted from a workhouse model, even though his own father-in law was alive and living in London). Isabelle sits at the other end beside the grandmother and a young aunt, perhaps modelled by her mother Ellen Severs and one of her sisters, while another one pours a small glass of wine for the eldest daughter. The scene is relaxed: Frith described the 'uproarious brothers and sisters, whose wishes for many happy returns of the day are screamed by half a dozen shrill voices' and remembered his own children being 'small and noisy, as is the habit of such little people', their ' very demonstrative ebullition of juvenile spirits at the midday dinner', and the opinion of his soon-to-be-sacked butler Johnson: 'you have got a pack of noisy, impudent children as deserves a precious good 'iding'.[69] But how far is the painting genuinely autobiographical? 1854 may have been a difficult year. Frith confessed that after the success of *Life at the Seaside (Ramsgate Sands)* at the RA exhibition, 'from one cause or another I wasted a great deal of time . . . I was abominably idle, or occupied on trumpery subjects unworthy of the trouble taken in reproducing them'.[70] He had been prevailed upon to paint a successor to the embarrassingly titled *Sherry, Sir?*, *Did You Ring, Sir?* (Fig. 21) Perhaps also painted at this time was another small picture painted for engraving, *Hot Water, Sir?*[71] It is tempting to imagine that he titled the picture ironically, for Frith found himself in very hot water around this time.

Critical of her parents for not isolating sufferers to prevent the spread of disease, Cissie recalled the scarlet fever epidemic that killed the young families of friends like Horsley and Faed. In 1867 she accompanied four siblings to Brighton to escape the diphtheria that killed their youngest sister, Evelyn Shirley.[72] After whooping cough in 1854 Frith's children were taken to recuperate at Hampton Court with Isabelle's parents and sisters, who 'chased us all through the Maze, bought us heaps of sweets at a lovely shop in Kingston, and were generally delightful'.[73] The party included a nineteen-year-old friend, Mary Alford; the evidence for her affair with Frith is mostly circumstantial (his family destroyed his diaries after his death), but the period when it began is confirmed by Cissie, who linked it with memories of family discussions about the war in the Crimea (1854–6). During their stay at Hampton the party visited the races at Kempton Park and perhaps Mary was the unnamed female friend to whom Frith said 'Here is a scene I'd like to paint – "modern life" with a vengeance.' Despite her belief that it would be impossible to make a coherent picture from the 'groups and tents and sports, the jockeys, course, stands and all the rest',[74] the concept would come to fruition in 1858 as *Derby Day* (Fig. 61).

In 1878, when Frith was appearing as a witness for the defence in the Whistler–Ruskin libel trial and his series *The Road to Ruin* was on view at the Royal Academy, Whistler's counsel noted:

> But Mr Frith could give the Jury a solemn lesson in The Road to Ruin
> in his own life not his own ruin – his Wards [sic]
> He seduced his own ward
> In his own house
> Where lived his own wife
> and his own numerous family[75]

There is no other evidence that Mary was Frith's ward.[76] He was always susceptible to pretty women and Cissie implied it was Mary who led him on;[77] either way their affair resulted in the

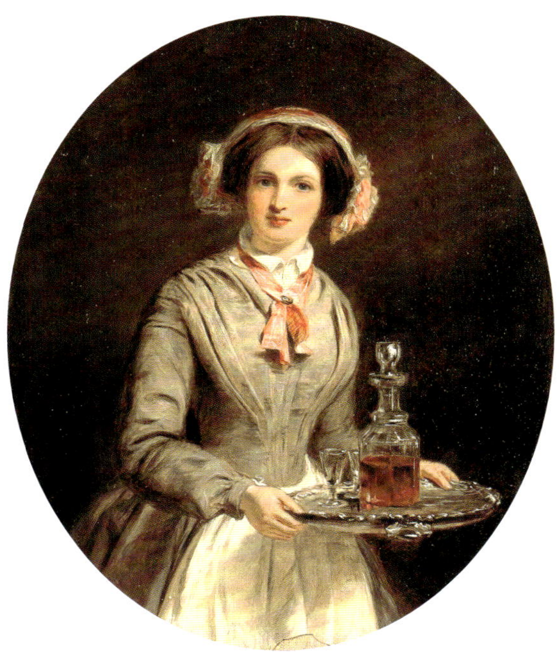
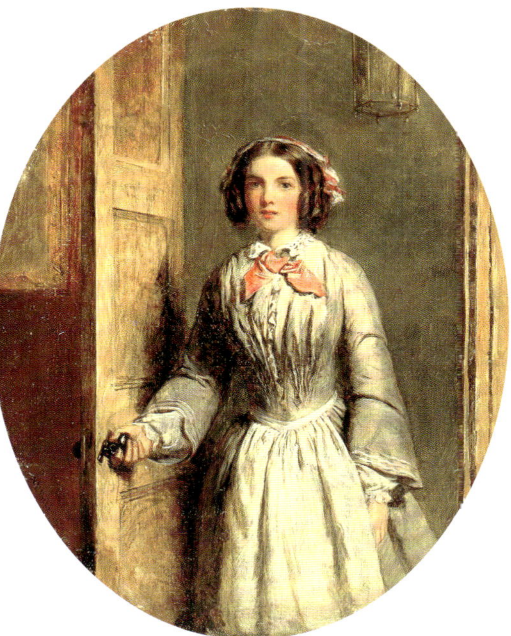
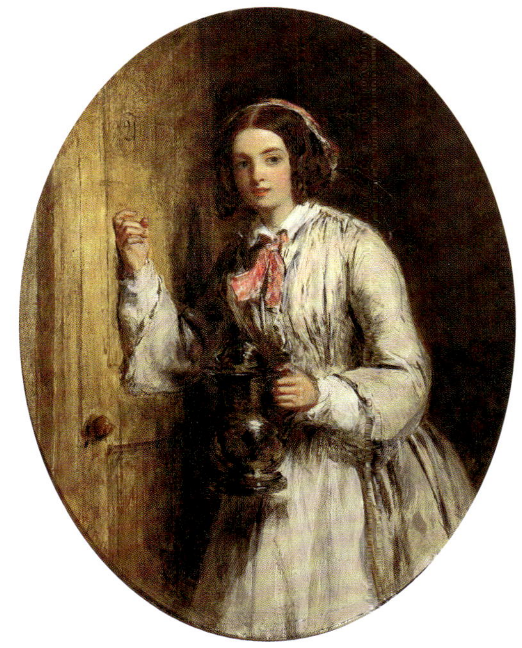

inevitable pregnancy and was public knowledge by November 1855. Frith was nervous of going to vote in the Royal Academy election but he was relieved to meet 'with no unpleasantness whatever – all the men – most of whom must have known my position – treated me with the greatest kindness'.[78] Cissie remembered that at home, 'despite the trouble, the great trouble my father once gave my mother, I never remember the smallest "row" or unpleasant atmosphere in our household'.[79] The baby, Mary Powell Alford, was born a few streets away from Pembridge Villas on 29 December 1855 at the house of a surgeon, Richard King Pierce, 16 Norland Place, Kensington.[80] Mary went on to bear Frith six more children[81] during a relationship spanning twenty-six years until they were finally able to marry in January 1881, exactly twelve months after Isabelle's death.[82] Meanwhile she lived first at 14 Duke Street, St James's and from 1862 at 12 Oxford Terrace (now Sussex Gardens), about a mile from Pembridge Villas and close enough for Frith to visit her under cover of the long walk he took daily before dinner.[83] She shared these addresses with Sophia Dolby, an older friend or more probably a relative, and the two women maintained an apparently independent existence together as lodging-house keepers.[84]

Fortunately for everyone, the period of Frith's greatest prosperity was about to begin. In February 1857 he sold the unfinished *Derby Day* to his old friend Jacob Bell for £1,500, and the copyright in the picture together with a smaller replica for the same sum to the dealer Ernest Gambart.[85] The picture was a sensation when it was exhibited at the Royal Academy exhibition in 1858, *The Times* observing that 'no closer nor completer transcript of a scene of English amusement has been painted since Hogarth . . . all the frequenters of the course will be seeking to identify friends and acquaintances for the next three months'.[86] Bell saw spectators three or four deep 'smelling the picture like bloodhounds'; the policeman brought in to guard it had difficulty keeping them at bay and one Academician made a formal complaint when told to withdraw his head in case his hat brim touched the canvas. Eventually Bell prevailed on the Academy to protect

20. Left: *Sherry Sir?*, 1853. Private Collection.
Frith recorded that this picture was painted from 'a good-looking girl who was in my service as housemaid'. She may have been Matilda Pudfield, born in Somerset in 1834 and recorded as Frith's housemaid in the 1851 census. Frith's friend Jacob Bell bought the picture but the title, which caused Frith much embarrassment, was assigned to it by Lloyd Brothers when they published the engraving by Francis Holl.

21. Centre: *Did You Ring, Sir?*, 1854. Private Collection.

22. Right: *A Maid with a Flagon*, 1858. Private Collection.

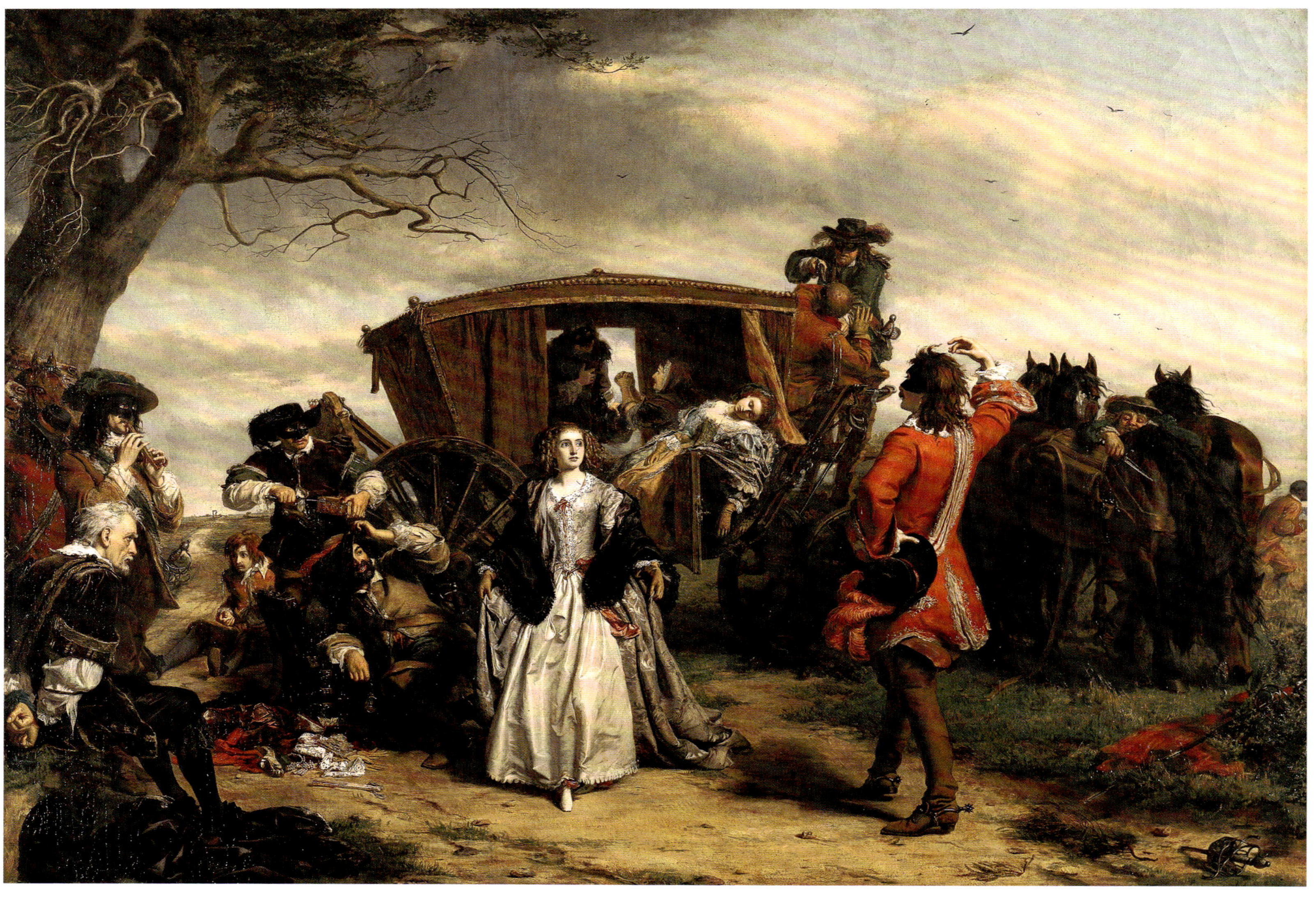

23. *Claude Duval*, 1860. Manchester City Art Gallery.

his picture with an iron railing.[87] Frith's next important picture was smaller and took less time to paint, so it earned him proportionally less: returning to the familiar territory of English history, he began *Claude Duval* (Fig. 23), by making studies for it during his summer holiday in 1858, this time at Weymouth. Frith usually enlisted Creswick to paint the landscape backgrounds in his pictures, but the background in this one was based on his own little oil study (private collection) made at Binegar Heath. His contract with the dealer Louis Victor Flatow gave him £850 for the original painting and £250 for a smaller version plus a separate head of Lady Aurora Sydney, the picture's central female character. The copy for the engraver was begun by an assistant, but Frith was paid £250 to complete it. Flatow bought the copyright for £300, undertaking to give him an extra £50 should he sell it to someone else.[88]

It was also Flatow who commissioned the largest and most ambitious of Frith's modern-life subjects, *The Railway Station* (Fig. 63). Begun in 1860 and completed in March 1862 (Fig. 24) after eighteen months of incessant work, the picture kept him away from the Royal Academy

Exhibition in 1861 (and that year's census; it was easy to evade, simply by not opening the door to the enumerator). He received the unprecedented sum of £4,500 for the sketch, the finished picture and the copyright; and for £750 he resigned the right to send the picture to the Academy so that Flatow could exhibit it for seven weeks at his Haymarket gallery: 21,150 people paid to see it and many were bullied or cajoled into subscribing for the engraving. The picture was exhibited again early in 1863 for a shilling a head admission at 79 Cornhill ('brilliantly illuminated by the patent sun light'), and then went on tour round the country and abroad.[89] On 28 April 1860 Frith had been part of a deputation from the Society of Arts to the Prime Minister (Palmerston) demanding amendments to existing copyright law; Frith himself deeply objected to his pictures being pirated in the form of photographs, and his selling the copyright in them was a means to prevent this. Much has been made of his apparently businesslike attitude. However, Frith was not so canny a businessman as the dealers: he made a total of £5,520 from *The Railway Station*, but Flatow made more than £16,000 when he sold it to the print-seller Henry Graves together with the list of subscribers, and Graves was said to have made more than £40,000 from the engraving alone.

The Railway Station depicted Paddington Station, not far from Pembridge Villas. In the picture's central group of a family seeing off their sons to school – in which his own self-portrait is prominent – Frith again alluded to personal experience: it would have been from Paddington that twelve-year-old Willie and nine-year-old Charles travelled to Frome, Somerset, where they were boarders at a small private school run by the Rev. George Newenham Wright. Frith deplored his own lack of general education and was glad to have been able to educate his own children well.[90] But their upbringing was relaxed: 'thank heaven, we were allowed to grow, we were let alone, we were neither trained nor developed nor interfered with', although Cissie also complained that the girls' education was 'the worst that could be conceived' in that useful crafts like cooking and housekeeping were neglected in favour of sewing and mending.[91] The Friths' first governess, Dadd's sister, was 'a subdued, sad, wearisome creature'; she was soon succeeded by Sarah Wright (born 1831), 'one of the primmest and most particular governesses that could be procured', whom Frith paid £50 per annum. Her main attraction for the Friths – both of whom were good linguists – was that she spoke fluent French, albeit with a bad accent; Cissie claimed 'she did not possess a single certificate and had not one single accomplishment of any sort or kind'.[92] Miss Wright left 'in a fit of pique' in 1861 and was succeeded by Mrs Port, 'a sour-faced widow' with a son whom she inveigled in to the children's meals, and then by a Fräulein Haas who was supposed to speak only German to the children and could not keep discipline. While Frith's eldest daughter Isabelle 'really liked the stuffy schoolroom and the hateful books, and in consequence . . . received all the teaching', Willie and Cissie 'drew rude pictures on our slates, and read what we liked, and came in and went out as we liked, and no one interfered with us at all.'[93] Additional education was provided by a secretive Italian aristocrat (who disappeared after Frith's all too accurate portrayal of him as the 'foreigner' in *The Railway Station*) and at a dancing master's a few streets away. Although the Friths continued to employ a governess until at least 1871, when Cissie was old enough she too was sent away to school at Bath. She came home after a few days and refused to return: Frith grudged having still to pay the term's fees but did not send her back – even as a student he had deplored boarding schools as 'the very vilest things you can send a girl to' and Cissie was useful to him as a model as he only had to pay

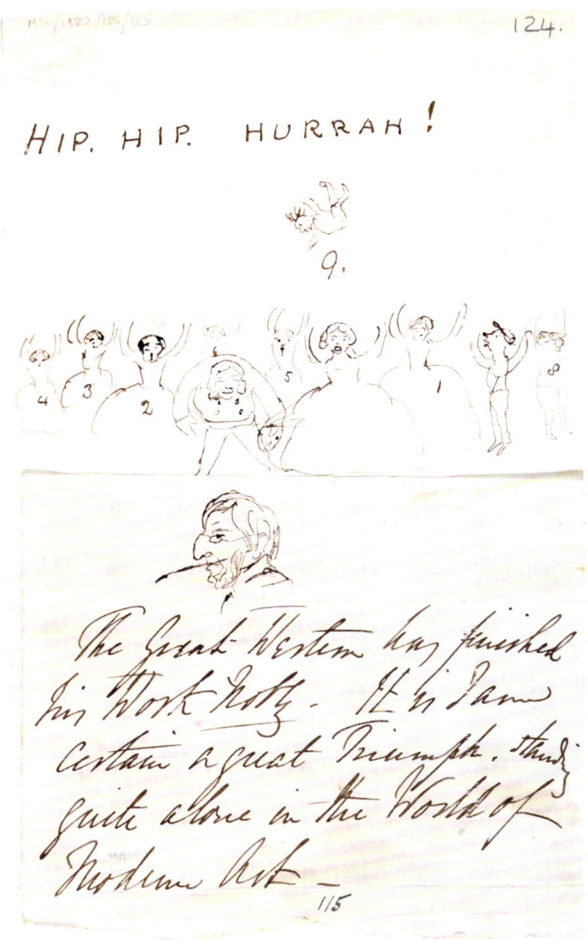

24. Unknown, *The Great Western has finished his work nobly*, *c.* 1862. Victoria and Albert Museum, London.
This drawing celebrates the completion of *The Railway Station*. Alongside Frith (who takes a bow) and his wife are children who may be identified as his daughter Isabelle (b. 1846), Cissie (b. 1847), Willie (b. 1849), Louey (b. 1850), Charles (b. 1851), Alice (b. 1853), Mary Fanny (b. 1855) and Walter (b. 1857), with Philip (b. 1860) the baby being tossed in the air.

her nine pence an hour, threepence less than the professional model's rate.[94] In 1863 she was supposed to stand in for the figure of Queen Victoria in Frith's painting *The Marriage of the Prince of Wales*, but the Queen's dress was too short on her and he had to find a smaller model.[95]

Having declined an invitation in 1857 to paint the marriage of the Princess of Wales, when Frith was asked to paint the Prince of Wales's wedding in January 1863 he felt obliged to agree, even though it meant he had to postpone an agreement with Gambart for the more congenial Hogarthian subjects 'Morning', 'Noon' and 'Night' for which, including sketches and copyright, he would have received £10,000 (Figs 41, 43, 44).[96] His fee for the royal picture was £3,000, while Flatow paid him a further £5,000 for the copyright in it, a sum described by the *Art Journal* as 'the most munificent recompense ever accorded to an artist since art became a profession'.[97]

The royal wedding took place on 10 March 1863 at St George's Chapel, Windsor, and Frith had a seat in the front row in the Household Gallery, on the south of the altar, where he was spotted 'in Court suit and ruffles in the midst of a little crowd of ladies, all desperately coquetting to ensure their portraits figured in the picture'.[98] In April the Queen approved a compositional sketch, and he embarked on the actual ten-foot painting. He painted the Queen at Windsor Castle and other members of the royal family came for sittings at Pembridge Villas (Fig. 25), but he experienced great difficulty in obtaining sittings from bridesmaids and foreign royalty, borrowing dresses and costume to paint from, and – when real models were unavailable – even in obtaining portrait photographs. When the picture was finished, on 28 March 1865 the Queen visited Pembridge Villas to inspect it. Isabelle's youngest sister Vicky dressed up as the housemaid so she could get a good look at the royal visitor, and Frith 'stood at the foot of the steps, bowing profoundly, until the Queen shook hands graciously with him'.[99] Once inside, Frith wrote, 'though I was conscious of the many shortcomings of the picture, and quite aware that they could not escape her eyes, she found little or no fault, and left me under the impression that I had succeeded as well as could be expected, considering the great difficulties of the task'.[100] After the Queen left, 'Papa danced a fandango at the bottom of the steps, while the children rushed tumultuously towards him wanting to know what had happened and if she had made him a lord'.[101] Frith had refused the Queen's first invitation in 1857 ostensibly because he had to finish *Derby Day*. But according to Cissie, the real reason was that his 'sense of the humorous always overcame him too much to be able to take royalty seriously, and he had always refused royal commissions because, as he said, 'he should never be able to behave'. The family were 'raging republicans' and in 1852 Frith had described Prince Albert as a 'thickhead', but he gave no hint in his *Autobiography* of being anything other than pleased by royal attention paid to his pictures.[102]

Up the Friths' front steps passed 'every notable in England' from the Queen downwards, but what the Friths prized more was their friendship with the literary, artistic and musical celebrities of their age. They had a wide circle of old and new friends and entertained often. Isabelle's 'at home' day was Tuesday, and her dinner parties were on Thursdays until their growing number of theatrical and journalist friends made Sunday a better choice.[103] Cissie remembered the glass chandeliers being cleaned piece by piece in preparation for her mother's birthday party, and the loose covers coming off the scarlet silk damask upholstery of the drawing-room sofas for Christmas parties, when Isabelle decorated the house with flowers, cork, holly and ivy. She was a 'past mistress in every womanly art' and even at the height of their prosperity made her own jam and 'creams and jellies and custards'; although he would ostentatiously push his wine glass aside when he came to dine, even the teetotaller (and, Cissie thought, hypocritical) George Cruikshank was happy to consume her jellies made with sherry, port-fortified soup and plum pudding with sauce 'in which one could smell the brandy quite well'. After dinner there were songs and musical sketches and games of Dumb Crambo.[104] Alongside old friends from Frith's student days like

25. John Ballantyne (1815–97), *Frith in his Studio painting Alexandra, Princess of Wales, for 'The Marriage of the Prince of Wales'*, c. 1863. Private Collection.

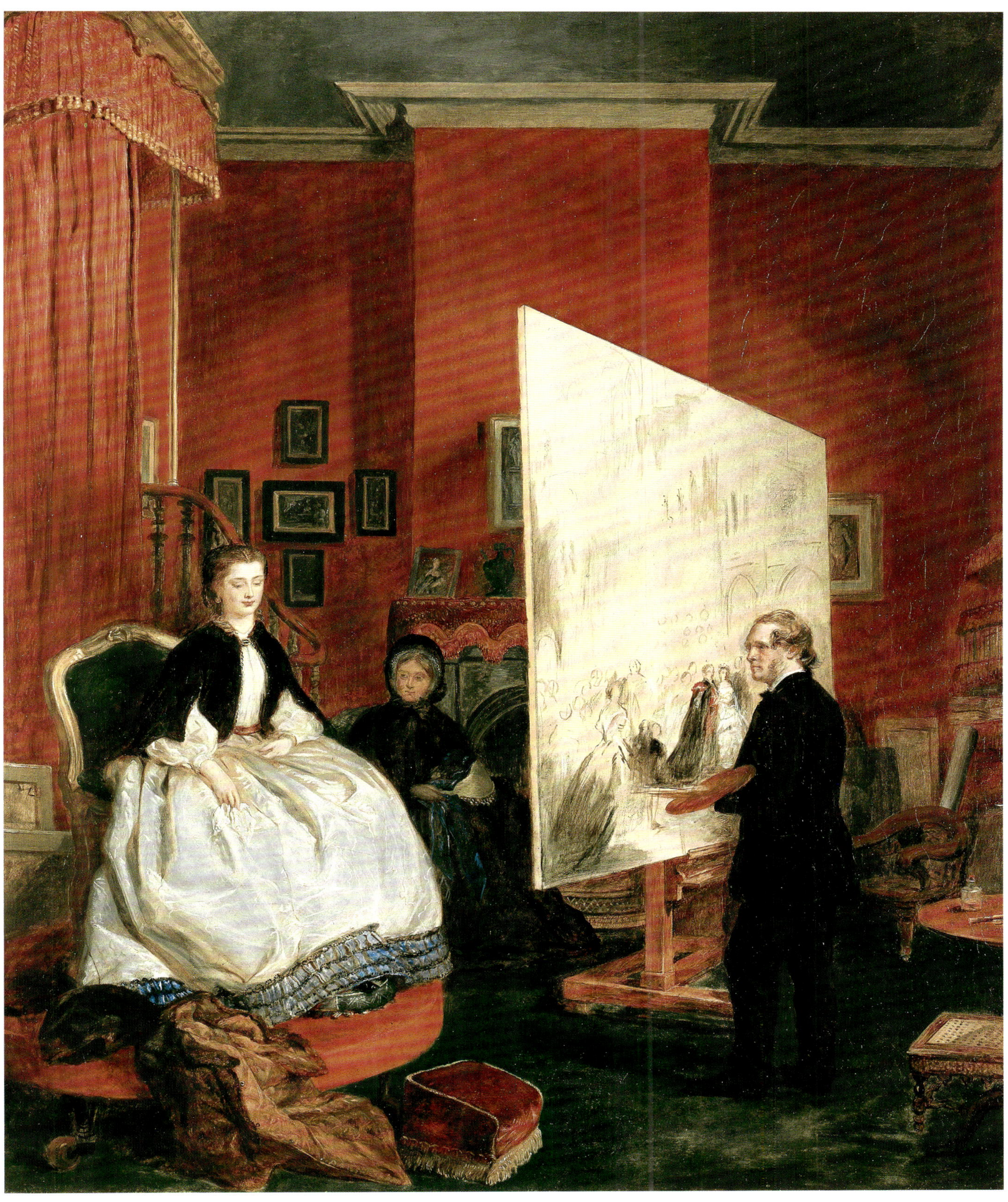

Ansdell, Elmore, Phillip, and Millais (whose nickname at the whist table was 'sixpenny Jack'), dinner guests included Landseer, Leighton and Tenniel. The writers Shirley Brooks, Wilkie Collins – one of Isabelle's 'most appreciative dinner guests'[105] – and Mary Braddon, Amelia Edwards, Dr John Doran, and the Belgian mezzo-soprano Desirée Artot (once briefly engaged to Tchaikovsky) were also close friends and frequent guests. Frith had been a passionate theatre-goer since first coming to London as a teenager, and his family went often to plays, pantomimes and the opera, sometimes occupying boxes paid for by another friend, J. Moses Levy, proprietor of the *Daily Telegraph*.[106] His many theatre friends[107] in the 1860s included Dion Boucicault, whose horse-racing 'sensation drama' of 1866, *The Flying Scud, or a Four-Legged Fortune*, recreated Frith's *Derby Day* on stage at the Theatre Royal, Holborn;[108] and another was Henry Irving, whom they first saw in 1869 in *Dearer than Life* at the New Standard Theatre, making 'several expeditions by the Underground Railway, then a new toy';[109] as the Standard was in Shoreditch, they presumably travelled from Paddington on the Metropolitan Line, opened in 1863. When his friend Wybert Rousby, manager of the Jersey Theatre, eloped with the beautiful Clara Dowse and married her, Frith let him bring her to Pembridge Villas where, captivated ' as he always was . . . by a beautiful woman', he watched her walking up and down the room and unpinning her floor-length hair. Mrs Rousby became a stage sensation of the late 1860s and early 1870s, Frith painting her in 1870 as Amy Robsart and also in character as Princess Elizabeth in *Twixt Axe and Crown*, a play written specially for her by Tom Taylor, which he must have seen on its opening at the Queen's Theatre, Long Acre in February that year.[110] Another close friend was the actor Edward Askew Sothern, an inveterate practical joker, who sometimes enlisted Frith to assist in the deceptive séances he held during the spiritualism craze of the 1860s. Frith also attended 'real' séances conducted by the celebrated medium Mrs Marshall but, unlike Isabelle, remained a sceptic.[111] Frith also enjoyed other kinds of spectacle: he was not a good rider but he enjoyed 'horse-exercise' and rode in Rotten Row to ogle the beautiful girls – some of them high class prostitutes – who also rode there; when recalling his equestrian misadventures in 1887, his description of his horse behaving 'in precisely the same way as the buck-jumpers did at the Wild West Exhibition'[112] suggests that he was one of the two million people who visited Buffalo Bill's Wild West Show, part of the American Exhibition at Earl's Court that year.

A different form of theatre came courtesy of Frith's legal friends, through whom his family attended trials such as that of the Tichborne Claimant (Frith did not himself attend the case but read all the evidence, and turned down a commission to paint the courtroom scene believing the Claimant to be guilty).[113] He painted his lawyer friends William Ballantine and Montague Williams as the barristers in the Old Bailey scene that formed the fourth episode in his *Race for Wealth* series (1880), in which the judge was modelled by another great friend, Baron Huddlestone (their relationship apparently being no barrier to Frith's appearing before him as a witness in two famous libel trials over which Huddlestone presided, Whistler v. Ruskin (1878) and Lawes v. Belt (1882):)[114] Frith had first met Huddlestone's wife, Lady Diana de Vere Beauclerk, when she sat for him for the *Marriage of the Prince of Wales*. When the Belt trial ended, Frith went to stay with them at Ascot, and when he fell ill soon after returning to London the surgeon Sir Henry Thompson diagnosed typhoid from drinking the water in the carafe on the washstand in his bedroom there. Frith refused to have typhoid nurses, while his 'domestic arrangements' – he was now married to Mary Alford – made it 'impossible' for his unmarried daughters to nurse him (for the married Cissie it was simply 'out of the question'). But the diagnosis must have been wrong, as Frith made a rapid recovery and was back at work in three days.[115]

Did Isabelle believe that once Mary had been sent away in 1856 the affair had come to an end? An unsubstantiated story has it that she discovered what was going on when she saw Frith posting a letter near their home when he was supposed to be on holiday in Brighton. In fact he must have seen Mary regularly, and perhaps she was the unidentified 'fellow-student' with whom he fondly recalled making watercolour illustrations in 1871 of scenes in Vanbrugh's *The Relapse*: 'Many were the evenings we spent over this labour of love. We always compared our renderings of the same points, and wondered at the dissimilarity of our conceptions.'[116] Mary was 'as deeply interested in art matters' as Frith himself, and even prouder of his works,[117] and he acknowledged her 'constant sympathy and ever-ready help' in his dedication to her of *My Autobiography and Reminiscences* in 1887. His first family 'one and all detested art . . . Not one of his ten could draw a line',[118] but three of Mary's children grew up to study art or architecture, their materials paid for by Frith from his account with Roberson's.[119] Isabelle died on 28 January 1880 and Frith married Mary as soon as convention allowed, on 30 January 1881, their nineteen-year-old son William Powell Alford being one of the witnesses. Their marriage surely prompted Frith's enigmatic Royal Academy exhibit that summer, *For Better, for Worse*[120] (Fig. 65) and presumably *Honeymooning in Switzerland* (1883), but it may have been kept secret at first: when the 1881 census was taken on the night of 3 April, Mary and all seven of her children were still at 12 Oxford Terrace, albeit her status improved to that of a leaseholder and annuitant as well as a wife, with a cook and two housemaids. But eventually she and the children did move into Pembridge Villas, and Frith's unmarried daughters moved out.

Agnes Alford was married from Pembridge Villas in 1882 and gave birth there to a son in 1885[121], and Guy was still living with his father in 1901, but publicly Frith recognised the Alfords only as 'stepchildren'. Although he maintained a close relationship with most of his first family, Cissie could not tolerate the realisation that throughout their apparently happy childhood he had been leading a double life: she rarely saw him from now onwards, and seems not to have attended his funeral. Yet she was familiar with artists among whom 'there may be, there are, concealed lapses from the strict code of morals prescribed by Mrs Grundy; there is shortness of money, there are debts and difficulties', and there were many among the Friths' close friends whose domestic lives more or less openly diverged from the Victorian ideal. George Augustus Sala's wife 'had not been Mrs Sala quite as long as she ought to have been, but really in those very Bohemian days marriage certificates were taken much as a matter of course'.[122] Wilkie Collins maintained two separate households and was addicted to laudanum. Mary Braddon was cohabiting with the married publisher John Maxwell (separated from his wife because of her mental condition) and had several children with him before his wife's death allowed them to marry in 1874; and after Cruikshank's death in 1878 it emerged that – rather like Frith himself – he had been maintaining a mistress and ten children.

In 1888 Frith gave up Pembridge Villas, probably for pecuniary reasons, possibly because it was now too large for his needs. He had altered it a great deal from its original form. In the 1860s his children had lost their special gardens when he built a schoolroom with a spare bedroom above – 'the disappearance of Willie's onion-bed making a specially sore spot in his heart'[123] – and a night nursery over the leads on which they had played. In 1872 he laid a new drain to connect with the sewer beneath the road outside (the house may have had a drainage problem as later owners applied to the Kensington Vestry for permission to lay further drains in 1888, 1901, 1908, and 1928.[124] At the highpoint of his prosperity and success, in 1875 he converted his old painting-room into a billiard-room, extended his drawing- and dining-rooms with bow windows, added a larger painting-room (which proved impossible to heat) and a model-room, both approached by an external iron staircase so that models should not have to come through the house, a big room for his sons and some servants' rooms at the top of the house.[125] In total Frith may have added at least eleven new rooms, the accommodation ultimately comprising twelve bedrooms, two

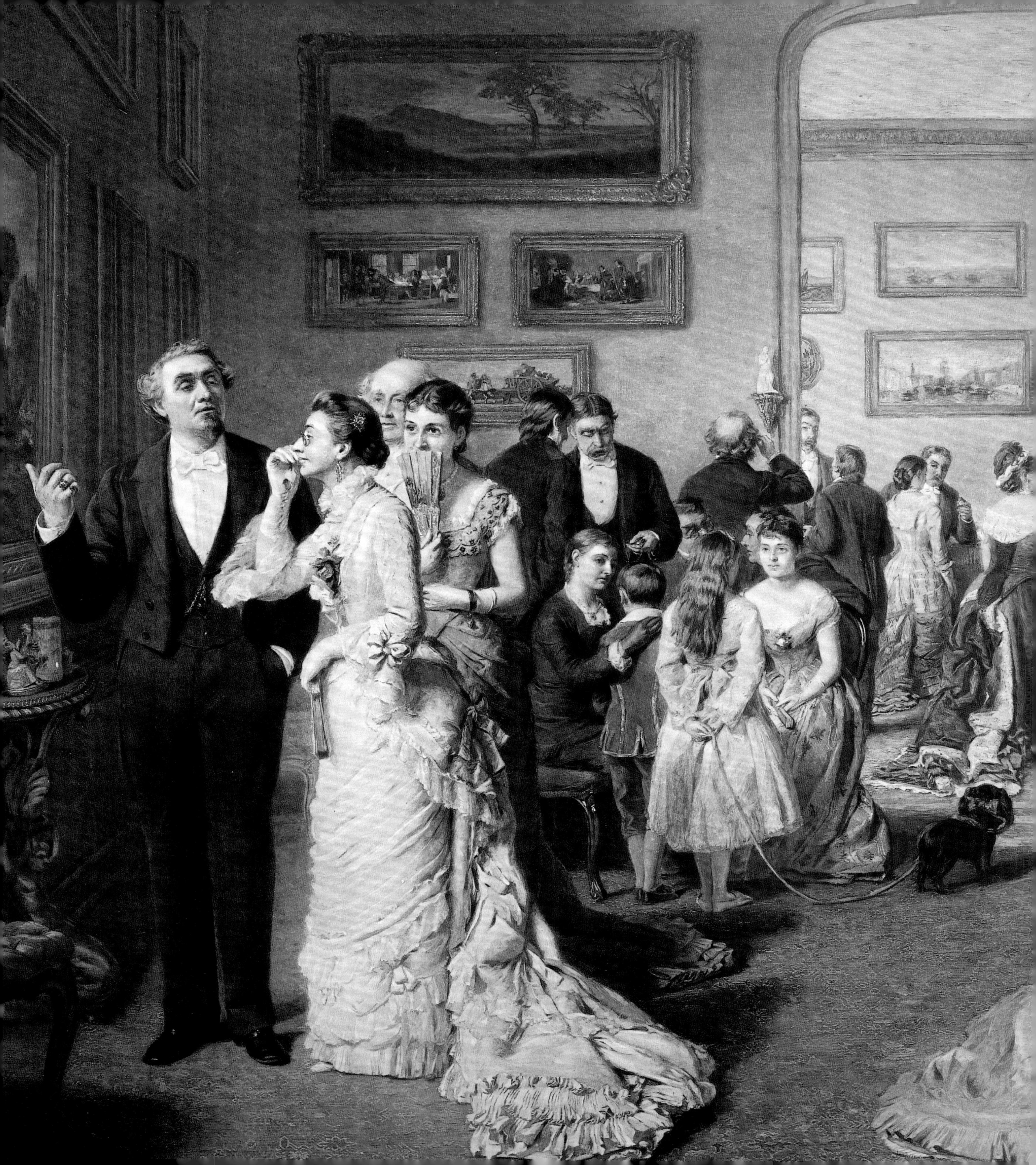

dressing-rooms, a fitted bathroom, a pair of conjoined drawing rooms, a large conservatory, dining room, billiard room, library, boudoir, and an enormous forty-one foot long studio with north-east light. In the basement were a kitchen, scullery, coal cellar, larder, housekeeper's room and bedroom, wine cellar, pantry, storeroom and a cellar beneath the front steps.[126]

Frith used his own opulent drawing rooms as the setting for *The Spider at Home,* the second episode of the *The Race for Wealth* series (1880; Fig. 26), in which the crooked *nouveau riche* financier shows off his wealth to his gullible victims. The series follows 'the career of a fraudulent financier or promoter of bubble companies, a character not uncommon in 1877',[127] and its immediate inspiration was probably the appearance in the bankruptcy courts in 1879 of the dubious company promoter and politician Baron Albert Grant (1831–99). Clergymen and widows were supposed to be particularly numerous among the small investors attracted to speculation in Grant's ventures such as the Emma Silver Mine Company, which crashed in the mid 1870s, and in *The Race for Wealth* Frith also made the principal victim a clergyman and the scam a worthless mine. In Frith's narrative the financier got his just desserts when sentenced at the Old Bailey to a term in Millbank Penitentiary. Grant avoided this fate, but in 1877 both his vast unfinished mansion, Kensington House, and his important collection of modern pictures were put up for sale to pay his builders and creditors. Kensington House failed to sell and it was eventually demolished for its materials in 1881, but there was enormous interest in the art collection which had been stored in the Pantechnicon and never hung, its sale at Christies exciting 'the greatest curiosity and speculation . . . as to the prices likely to be obtained for pictures purchased during the last seven years when modern art has been at its zenith in this respect', with a policeman required to control the 5,000 or more people who attended the pre-sale viewings.[128] Prominently displayed in the centre of a wall in the large room was Frith's *Before Dinner at Boswell's Lodgings,* for which Grant had paid the record price of 4,350 guineas at the sale of Sam Mendel's Manley Hall collection in 1875. When it came up on the second day, it was greeted with loud applause and Agnew started the bidding at 1,500 guineas to gain it at 3,050 – a drop of thirteen hundred guineas in two years.[129] *Boswell* was not Frith's only picture to lose value in the Grant sale, heralding the start of a decline in his prices and popularity. *Sterne's Maria* (1868) had fetched £945 in 1875 but now went for only £525. *The Miniature* (1872), which Grant bought for 1,000 guineas, now realised £378, and *I Know a Maiden Fair to See, Beware!* (1870) had cost him 600 guineas but now fetched only £262. And in 1882 *Altisidora Pretending Love to Don Quixote,* for which Edward Hermon, MP for Preston had paid 2,000 guineas, fetched only £504.[130]

At the height of his career Frith never sent a picture to the Academy that was not either already sold or sold at the Private View: Cissie said he had 'just what he liked to ask, while his enormous family were growing up'. Changing taste in the 1880s and a reaction against high prices for contemporary art affected many artists, but in Frith's case these were allied to a decline in quality of his work which Cissie attributed to his relationship with Mary.[131] Frith's last popular success and the sixth of his pictures to require a rail in front of it was *The Private View at the Royal Academy* (1881), a hit not so much for its formal or other qualities but because 'pictures formed of groups of well-known people are always very popular'. Although he claimed to deplore potboilers and 'the vice of copying', the demand for smaller replicas of his successful pictures sustained him – with his Academy pension – for the rest of his life.[132] It was presumably in order to liquidate assets that he sent twenty-six paintings by other artists to be sold at Christies on 14 June 1884 (see note 66), but the prices were mostly very low; two paintings by Augustus Egg were bought in at only two and eight guineas respectively, the 'Turner' made ten guineas and the sale realised less than £1,200.

Well-known as an excellent raconteur, Frith now took up writing, his gossipy two-volume *My Autobiography and Reminiscences* being heavily advertised in *The Times* from October 1887 onwards

26. *The Spider at Home,* 1882 photogravure, detail of Fig. 54. Museum of London.
The financier demonstrates his bona fides with a reception at his opulent home. In evening dress, he extols 'the merits of a large picture to a group of his guests, one of whom, a pretty girl, shows by her smothered laugh, that she appreciates the vulgar ignorance of the connoisseur, whose art terms are evidently ludicrously misapplied.'

27. Frith with his pupils at Ashenhurst, from 'Representative Men at Home: Mr W. P. Frith at Sydenham', *Cassell's Saturday Journal*, 1890. Guildhall Library, City of London.

28. 114 Clifton Hill, St John's Wood. City of London, London Metropolitan Archives.

and its popularity prompting the publication of a third volume the following year (his biography of his friend John Leech was published in 1891). Frith may have had pupils informally in the past[133] but now he began teaching in earnest, as a visitor at his old friend Mrs E. M. Ward's art school for ladies, and advertising in *The Times* for pupils from 11 May 1887.[134] It is tempting to see a preoccupation with his own diminishing finances underlying his painting *Poverty and Wealth* of 1888 (Fig. 66), the year in which Frith sold 7 Pembridge Villas and moved with Mary and five of their children to a suburban address miles away from the art scene and all his friends. Ashenhurst, 7 Sydenham Rise, Forest Hill was very different from Pembridge Villas, homely rather than 'impressively grand', with 'a pleasant garden . . . very pretty in the summer time with its turfy slopes and winding walks and the smother of roses.'[135] Crystal Palace was nearby and his old friend Millais – up in Scotland – envied him being able to go and see the dinosaurs.[136] Frith converted a wood-panelled upstairs room into a studio, sparely furnished but still housing the old suit of armour that had terrified the gipsy who modelled for *An Old English Merrymaking* (Fig. 11). He continued to advertise in *The Times* until 1894 for pupils 'to whom he proposes to impart a sound art education', with Mary perhaps helping him to run the separate 'ladies class for painting from the living model twice a week', later adding a separate drawing class.[137]

MR. W. P. FRITH IN HIS PUPILS' STUDIO.

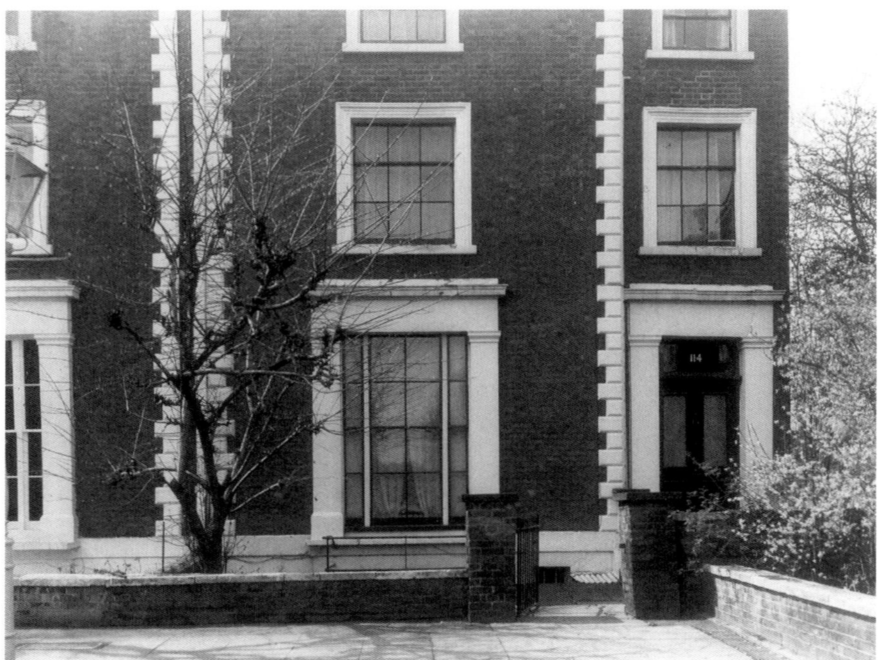

Mary died in 1895, and in 1896 Frith moved to a smaller and plainer property, 114 Clifton Hill (Fig. 28), closer to his artist friends than Sydenham but still some distance away from fashionable Grove Road and the artistic and literary centre of St John's Wood. There was no painting-room and Frith again used the dining-room, but it had (as presumably had Ashenhurst) electric light.[138] The five servants he had employed at Pembridge Villas at the time of his remarriage had dwindled to three by 1891, and by 1901 Frith and his son Guy Alford were making do at Clifton Hill with just a cook and one housemaid. Although contemporary accounts emphasise Frith's excellent health, the household now included a nurse, Sarah Elizabeth Clarke, who lived in Paddington but also had her own bedroom at Clifton Hill.[139] She was still there eight years later, and was perhaps the attendant who, with his son Walter accompanied Frith on the morning of his eighty-ninth birthday to Buckingham Palace, personally invited by the King – whom he had painted forty-five years earlier as the Prince of Wales – to receive the Commandership of the Royal Victorian Order. At the end of his life Frith was said to enjoy sitting in the garden smoking a cigar with friends, recounting his anecdotes or watching a game of bowls.[140] On 29 October 1909 he took his usual walk but fell ill in the night with pneumonia and died on 2 November. His funeral was held three days later at St Augustine's Church, Kilburn, after which his body was cremated at Golder's Green and the ashes interred at Kensal Green Cemetery. Cremation was still comparatively rare at this period, but Frith had specified it in his will (dated 4 August 1908), 'believing that the duty of the individual to his kind includes providing for such final disposal of his body as shall be least detrimental to those who survive him and believing that the modern process of incineration provides the quickest and safest mode of such disposal'. Although not a signatory himself, Frith evidently adhered to the tenets of the Cremation Society founded in 1874 by Sir Henry Thompson with a Declaration signed by among others his friends Shirley Brooks, Millais, Tenniel and Trollope.

On Isabelle's death in 1880 her personal estate had been valued at under £200, and Frith himself now left the surprisingly small sum of £1,380 1s 5d gross (the net value of his personal estate was £1,310 18s 7d – the equivalent of under £100,000 today). His will was brief: his Alford children were not mentioned but each of his children by Isabelle was allowed to choose one picture, his daughters first in order of age (eldest first) and then his sons likewise.[141] The only financial legacies were £500 to his son Charles George and £150 to his nurse Sarah Clarke, who was also left the furniture and contents of her bedroom at Clifton Hill. Frith directed that his real estate and the residue of his personal estate was to be sold and the money used to pay his funeral expenses, debts, legacies and his executor's fees, with any remaining money divided between his children. The contents of 114 Clifton Hill were sold by Phillips, Son & Neale on 13 December; unsold items were transferred to the Furniture and Fine Art Depositories Ltd, Islington and were still being advertised for private sale in 1911.[142]

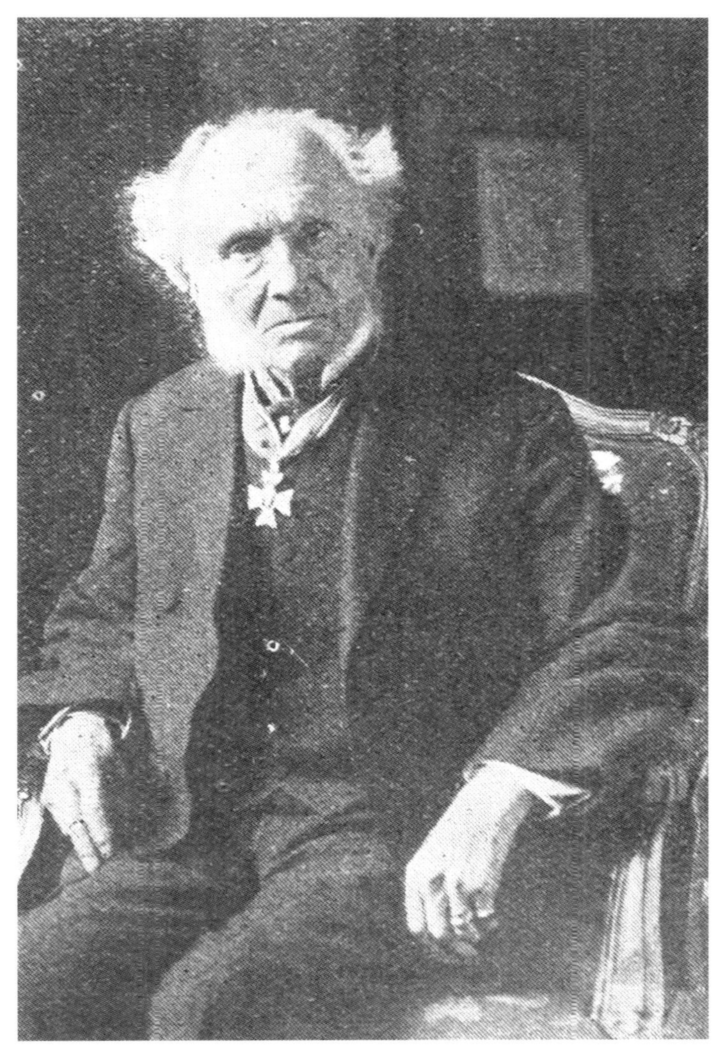

29. Originally published in *The Graphic*, 6 November 1909, this photograph shows Frith with his CVO. Edward VII had conferred the Commandership of the Royal Victorian Order on him the previous year, on his 89th birthday.

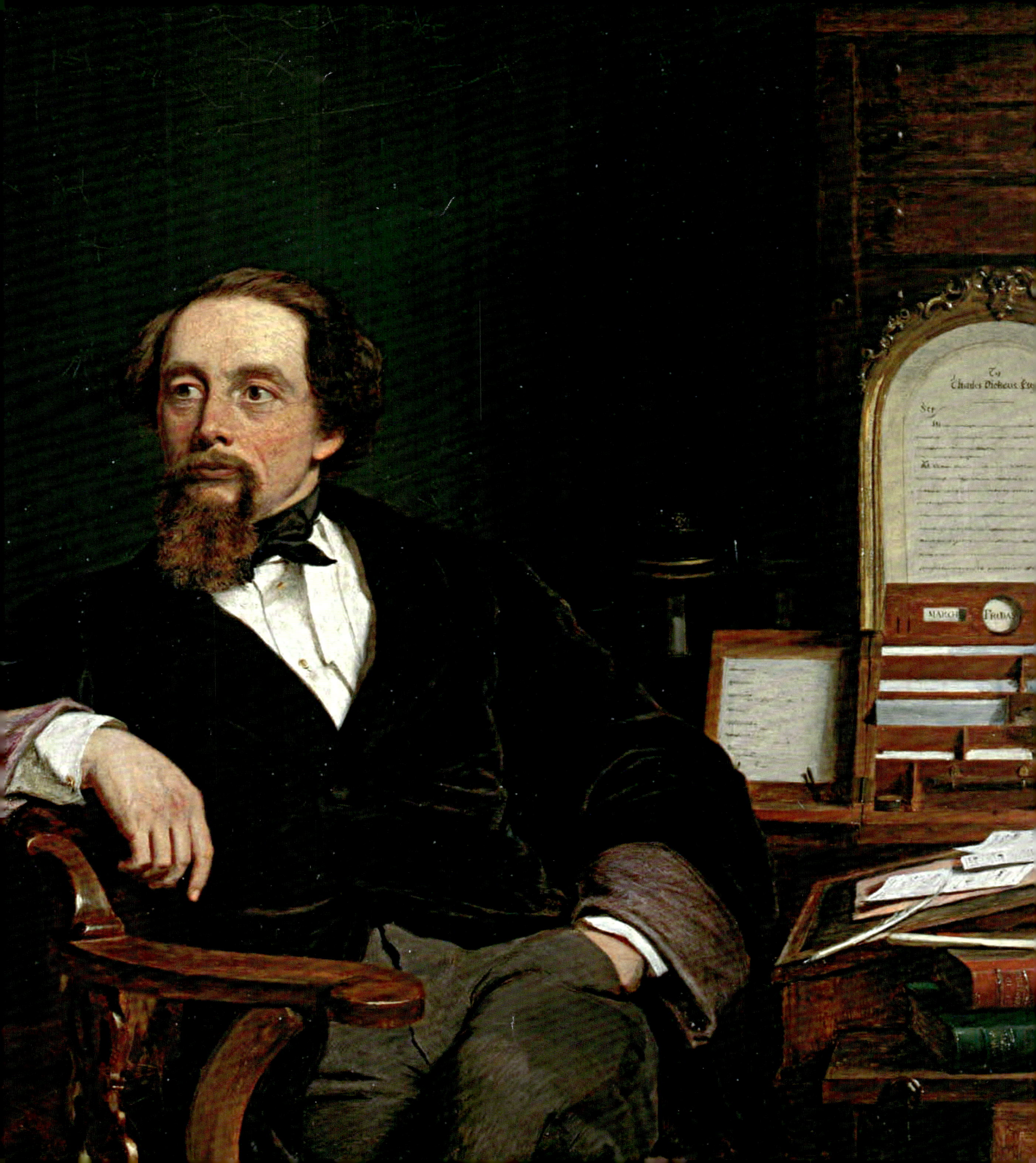
To
Charles Dickens
MARCH

Chapter 2

Dickens and Frith

DAVID TROTTER

Dickens liked painters. In fact, he liked them rather more than he liked his fellow-writers. Among the eminent artists he kept company with, both in the interminable round of banquets and excursions which made up the social life of the Victorian celebrity, and by regular correspondence, were David Wilkie, Clarkson Stanfield, Edwin Landseer, Frank Stone, Augustus Egg, Daniel Maclise, and W. P. Frith. Some of the illustrators of the novels (Landseer and Maclise, but also Marcus Stone, George Cattermole, and Luke Fildes) also found a place in the Dickens circle.[1] Writers, although by no means left out, do not seem to have figured to quite the same extent as a species. Dickens's friendships with painters were often long-lasting and deeply felt. Should the occasion arise, he could usually be relied upon for an affectionate obituary. *Little Dorrit* (1855–7: Fig. 33), one of his most ambitious novels, was dedicated to Stanfield.

In November 1842, Dickens, who had seen Frith's original picture at the Society of British Artists of an exultant Dolly Varden (Fig. 31), the pert lower-middle-class heroine of *Barnaby Rudge* (1841), commissioned two companion pieces: Dolly Varden, again, this time 'tripping through the woods, and looking back saucily at her lover', and Kate Nickleby, from *Nicholas Nickleby* (1838–9). When the pictures were ready, Dickens came round to inspect them. Dickens, of whom Frith stood in considerable awe, turned out to be a pale young man with long hair, a white hat, and a heavy stick. The young man extended his hand 'with a frank cordiality, and a friendly clasp, that never relaxed till the day of his untimely death'. The following Sunday Dickens brought his wife, the party arriving in a carriage with a bright steel bar, of uncertain social and technological function, across the front. The friendly clasp was still active in 1859, when Dickens sat for his portrait to Frith (Fig. 30). His expression then was that, Frith thought, of a man who had 'reached the topmost rung of a very high ladder and was perfectly aware of his position'.[2] Dickens, for his part, merely noted that the portrait was 'a little too much (to my thinking) as if my next-door neighbour were my deadly foe, uninsured, and I had just received tidings of his home being afire'.[3] The friendship proved durable. Frith recalled a visit to Dickens's house at Gad's Hill, in Kent, in July 1868.[4] Frith's memoirs provide plentiful evidence of the ample pleasure Dickens took in the company of artists. But how much pleasure did he take in the company of art?

It is probably not too much of an exaggeration to say that Dickens liked artists more than he liked art; more, at any rate, than he liked contemporary art. To be sure, he took an interest in the visual arts, both classical and contemporary. There is evidence of that interest in essays, reviews, speeches, and letters.[5] He regularly attended Royal Academy exhibitions, and wrote at some length to his friend John Forster about the paintings on display at the Paris International Exhibition of 1855.[6] Where contemporary painting was concerned, however, Dickens's taste had been formed at a relatively early age by his acquaintance with Sir David Wilkie, whose vivid genre scenes he admired intensely: prints from two of the most characteristic of them, *Rent Day* (1809) and *Reading*

30. *Charles Dickens in his Study*, 1859. Victoria and Albert Museum, London. Detail of Fig. 32. Aged nearly 47 and at the height of his fame and popularity, Dickens is shown in his study at Tavistock House in Bloomsbury, with early chapters of *A Tale of Two Cities* on the desk. The portrait was commissioned by Dickens's friend and (later) biographer John Forster in 1854 but postponed when Dickens grew first a moustache (a 'hideous disfigurement') and then a beard. Frith finally began it in 1858, arranging in January 1859 for Herbert Watkins to take photographs to assist him – however he felt the photographs were not a success and did not use them.

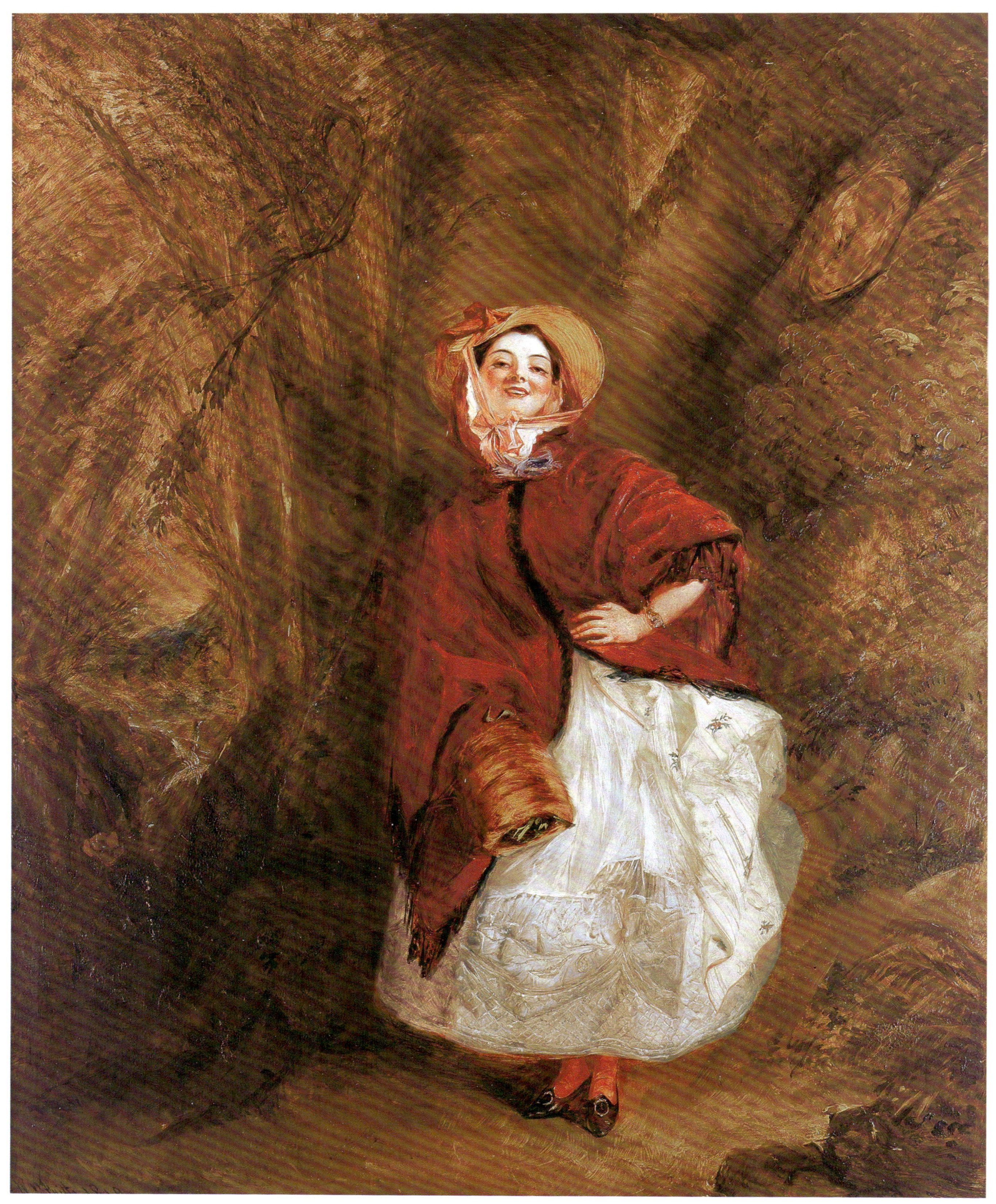

the Will (1820), hung in the entrance hall of his house in Devonshire Place.[7] The contemporary art Dickens liked best of all was literary and historical genre painting. The work by Frith he singled out at the 1855 Paris Exhibition was *Mr Honeywood Introduces the Bailiffs to Miss Richland as his Friends*, from Oliver Goldsmith's comedy of 1768: a costume-piece entirely lacking the scope or vitality of the previous year's *Life at the Seaside (Ramsgate Sands)*.[8] Wilkie's name heads the list of the Royal Academicians whose achievement had been dishonoured, in Dickens's view, by the inclusion of Millais's *Christ in the House of His Parents* (Tate Gallery) in the Royal Academy Exhibition of 1850.[9]

The note of Dickens's commentary on art, classical or contemporary, was one of defensive facetiousness. Any departure from what he thought of as truth to nature, or truth to an idea generally understood, received the stigma of instant derision. Millais's Pre-Raphaelite carpenter's shop got short shrift.

> In the foreground of that carpenter's shop is a hideous, wry-necked, blubbering, red-headed boy, in a bed-gown; who appears to have received a poke in the hand from the stick of another boy with whom he has been playing in an adjacent gutter, and to be holding it up for the contemplation of a kneeling woman, so horrible in her ugliness, that (supposing it were possible for any human creature to exist for a moment with that dislocated throat) she would stand out from the rest of the company as a Monster, in the vilest cabaret in France, or the lowest gin-shop in England.

And so on. What most offended Dickens about the painting was its departure from the generally understood idea of the essential nobility of Christ's sacrifice of Himself in and through His life on Earth. 'Wherever it is possible to express ugliness of feature, limb, or attitude, you have it expressed.'[10] Millais's realism, Dickens probably thought, would have had Wilkie spinning in his grave.

And yet, for all his evident alarm, Dickens did not want to be seen as a dyed-in-the-wool reactionary. The title he chose for his review was 'Old Lamps for New'. He argued that the Pre-Raphaelites had by their insistence on ugliness undone the 'revolution in Art' brought about by Raphael in the fifteenth century. It was they who were the reactionaries, he thought, because they baulked at the intensity of Raphael's devotion to 'what was most sublime and lovely in the expression of the human face divine.' Indeed, so anxious was Dickens to avoid any imputation of conservatism that he concluded by imagining what would happen if contemporary science were to follow the example of contemporary art. A Pre-Newtonian Brotherhood might be founded, to revoke the laws of gravity; or a Pre-Galileo Brotherhood, to arrange for the earth not to circle around the sun. In literature, perhaps, a Pre-Chaucer Brotherhood would restore the ancient English style of spelling, and weed out from the libraries the works of such dangerous innovators as William Shakespeare.[11] The jokes are laboured, and their labour tells a story. Dickens was profoundly ambivalent about change. Ambivalence about change is, I would suggest, the proper ground for a comparison between Dickens and Frith. Both wanted to be modern, with an urgency which everywhere shapes their work; neither quite knew how to be.

Frith made no effort to disguise his ambivalence.

> One of the greatest difficulties besetting me has always been the choice of subject. My inclination being strongly towards the illustration of modern life, I had read the works of Dickens in the hope of finding material for the exercise of any talent I might possess; but at that time the ugliness of modern dress frightened me, and it was not till the publication of *Barnaby Rudge*, and the delightful Dolly Varden was presented to us, that I felt my opportunity had come, with the cherry-coloured mantle and the hat and pink ribbons.

Facing page:
31. *Dolly Varden*, 1842. Victoria and Albert Museum, London.
This picture was commissioned by Dickens's friend the engraver Frank Stone, after seeing Frith's first picture of Dolly Varden exhibited in 1842. He apparently intended to present it to Dickens, but in the event he gave it to the writer's friend and later biographer John Forster, who bequeathed it to the Victoria and Albert Museum in 1876.

The cherry-coloured mantle and the hat and pink ribbons were evidently the aspect of modern life Frith found it easiest to come to terms with. Dickens, too, it seems. According to Frith, his response to the Dolly Varden and Kate Nickleby was, 'All I can say is, they are exactly what I meant, and I am very much obliged to you for painting them for me.'[12] The compliment should not be thought idle, because fidelity to the original conception mattered a great deal to Dickens. In this case, he put his money where his mouth was, paying Frith £40 for the two pictures.

Barnaby Rudge enabled Frith to modernise himself because it was itself both an old lamp and a new one, at once historical and contemporary in reference. The story begins on a blustery March evening in 1775, at the Maypole Inn at Chigwell, in Essex, where the landlord John Willet and his cronies rehearse the story of the murder of Reuben Haredale at the Warren twenty-two years before. Reuben's brother Geoffrey had been the prime suspect, but nothing could be proved against him. A steward, Rudge, was later found stabbed in the vicinity. His son Barnaby, born the day after the murder, has grown up a simpleton. Geoffrey Haredale's niece Emma has fallen in love with Edward, the son of the haughty Sir John Chester, but the fathers conspire to thwart the match. A second romance, between Willet's son Joe and Dolly, daughter of the London locksmith Gabriel Varden, is also going nowhere fast, in part because Dolly is a world-class coquette, and Joe too modest and straightforward (i.e. dim) to call her bluff. Joe enlists in the army, and Dolly becomes Emma's paid companion. She is persecuted by Hugh, the Maypole's brutish ostler, and by Varden's apprentice, Sim Tappertit, a fizzing human cocktail of vanity, resentment, and ambition.

At the end of Chapter 32, after Joe's departure abroad, and Edward's banishment from his father's home, the story breaks off; to resume, in Chapter 33, with the outbreak of the 'No Popery!' riots provoked by Lord George Gordon, leader of the Protestant Association. For a week in June 1780, the London mob took over the city, in what seemed to many a fundamental challenge to the existing social and political order. These momentous events absorb, amplify, and eventually resolve the domestic melodrama, which is the subject of the novel's first thirty-two chapters. The reviewers were quick to spot disparities of scale and intensity between its preoccupation with murder mystery, on one hand, and the pillaging of a capital city, on the other. However, the novel is consistent in its focus on rebellion. From the very outset, the sons (Edward Chester, Joe Willet) seem minded to rise up against the fathers; and with good reason, since the fathers persist in treating them as though they were children. Dickens is clearly on their side. Once the rising up has become general, he allows its anarchic energy to infuse and shape some of the most vivid descriptions of public violence ever written. He was not on the side of the rioters. But he knew that such violence was a subject made for him. Furthermore, it was topical. In the summer and autumn of 1839, violence provoked by the militant Chartist campaign for universal manhood suffrage had brought the Gordon Riots of the 1780s back into the news again.[13]

There was, however, another way in which *Barnaby Rudge*, while remaining historical, had brought itself up to date; through the topicality not of riots, but of a cherry-coloured mantle and pink ribbons. For Dolly Varden had been on the point of freeing herself from the narrative which contained her long before Frith rode to the rescue. In Chapter 19, the Varden family travels down to Chigwell, so that Dolly may visit Emma Haredale at the Warren, to deliver a message from Edward Chester. Their departure from town appears to drive Dickens to distraction.

> As to Dolly, there she was again, the very pink and pattern of good looks, in a smart little cherry-coloured mantle, with a hood of the same drawn over her head, and upon the top of that hood, a little straw hat trimmed with cherry-coloured ribbons, and worn the merest trifle on one side - just enough, in short, to make it the wickedest and most provoking head-dress that ever malicious milliner devised.[14]

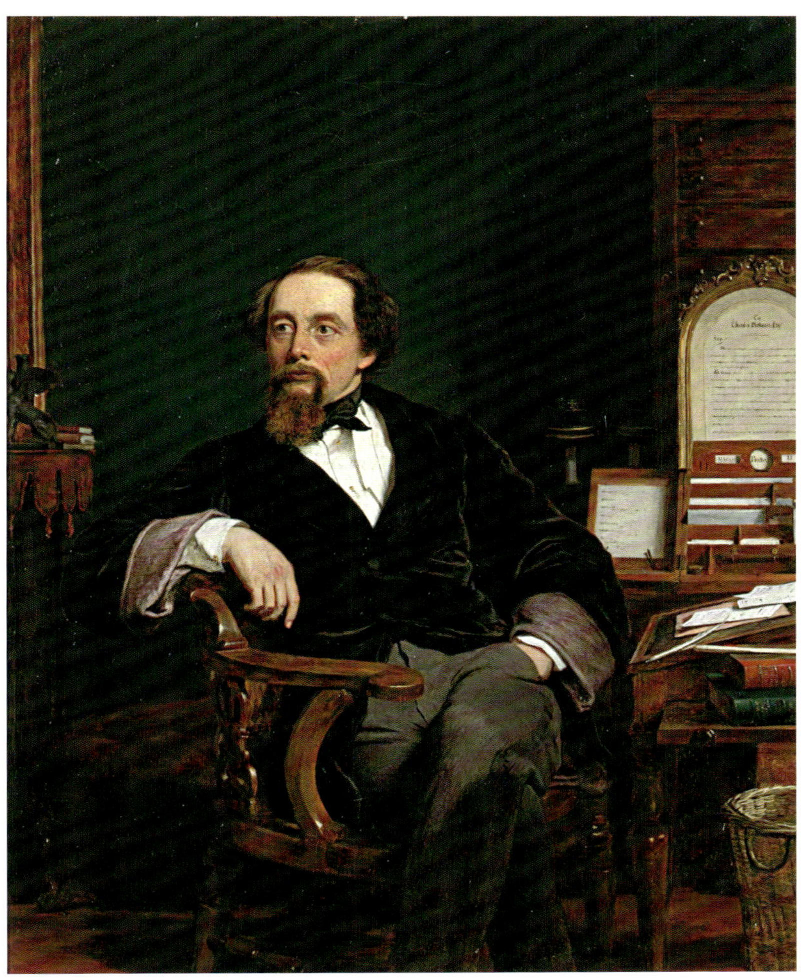

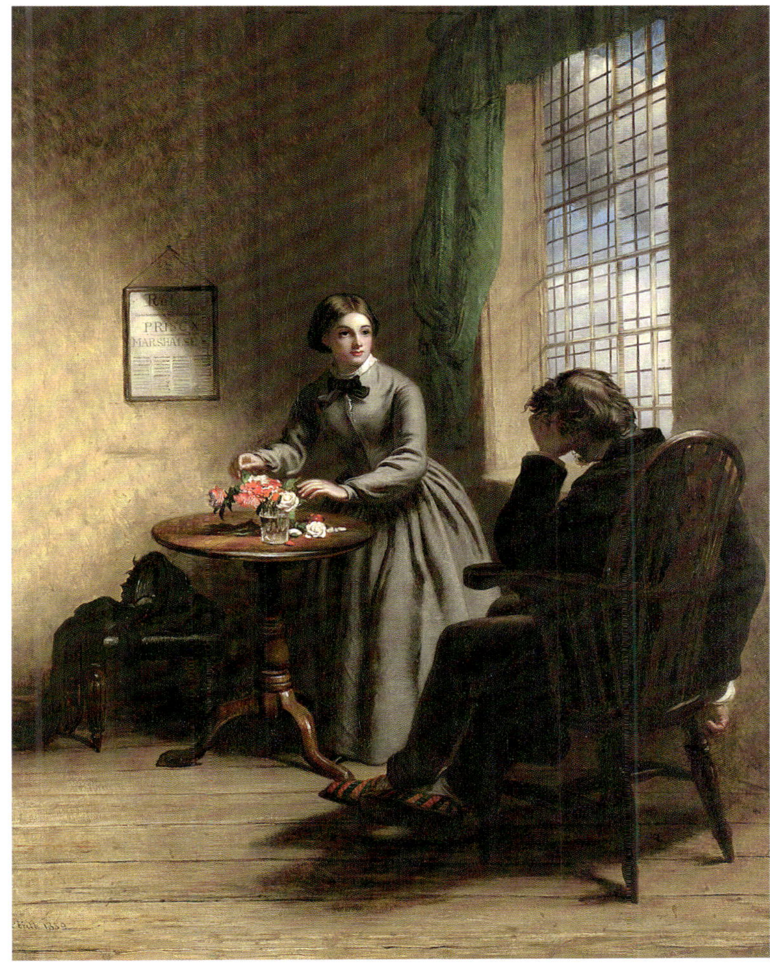

Who, exactly, is in danger of being provoked by this display? In theory Sim Tappertit, who holds the horse's head. But it is hard not to feel that the author regards himself as the main victim of the milliner's malice. A few pages on, in the chapter's final paragraph, he admits as much. The Vardens safely stowed in the Maypole, Dolly sets off across the fields to discharge her mission at the Warren; 'and this deponent hath been informed and verily believes, that you might have seen many less pleasant objects than the cherry-coloured mantle and ribbons, as they went fluttering along the green meadows in the bright light of the day, like giddy things as they were'. Dickens has in effect created a point of view, which is that not of any of the characters, but rather of a phantom 'deponent', or witness, from which alone Dolly can be seen truly, and truly appreciated. From that point of view, the mantle and ribbons thoroughly obscure the mission at the Warren.

Dickens has not done with Dolly yet. She is the most unashamedly sexual of his pretty young heroines; and yet he can only imagine her eroticism fully in and through the threat of rape. He arranges for her to walk back from the Warren along a path through a wood, where she is intercepted by the Maypole's ostler, Hugh, a 'handsome satyr' whose sexual ferocity at once intensifies the deponent's appreciation of her, and retrospectively guarantees its innocence. Worse is to come. During the Gordon Riots, Emma Haredale and Dolly Varden are kidnapped by Hugh and Sim Tappertit, who compete for Dolly's favours. Dolly in distress is a Dolly ripe for something a

32. *Charles Dickens in his Study*, 1859. Victoria and Albert Museum, London.

33. *Little Dorrit*, 1859. Private Collection.
Frith painted this picture and a companion for engraving as illustrations in a library edition of Dickens's works. He recounted that he had 'begged' to be one of the illustrators, his sole motive being 'the great pleasure that I felt in the anticipation of once more trying my hand in realising the characters of the author'.

34. Hablot Knight Browne (1815–82), *A Visit to the Warren* (from Dickens' s *Barnaby Rudge*).Guildhall Library, City of London.

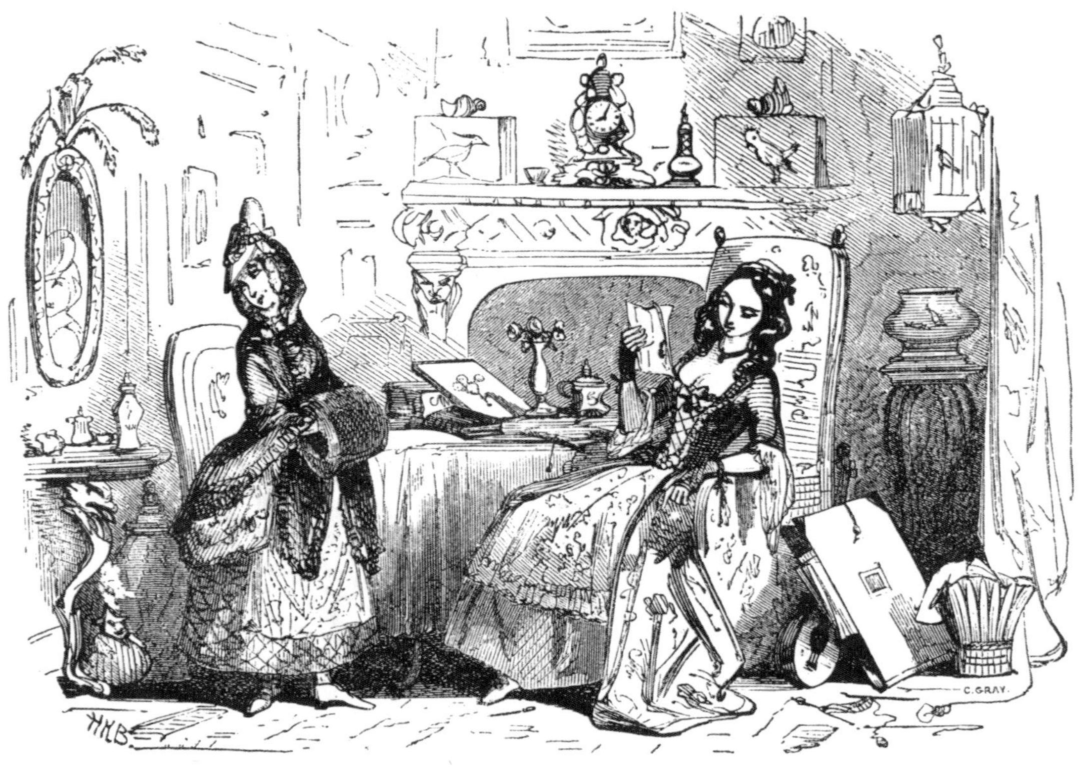

little warmer than appreciation. 'When, forgetful for a moment of herself, as she was now, she fell on her knees beside her friend, and bent over her, and laid her cheek to hers, and put her arms about her, what mortal eyes could have avoided wandering to the delicate bodice, the streaming hair, the neglected dress, the perfect abandonment and unconsciousness of the blooming little beauty?'. Not Dickens's, evidently.

Dickens's 'lip-smacking authorial commentary' on the blooming little beauty might well make us feel uneasy.[15] But there is a further element to it, which complicates the otherwise pornographic picture. Dolly's three suitors, Hugh, Joe Willet, and Sim Tappertit, all take part in the uprising of youth against age. Two of them, furthermore, Joe and Sim, are defined as much by social as by sexual desire. Both are petty-bourgeois aspirants. One aspires nobly, the other ignobly. For both, Dolly represents a social as well as a sexual prize. She is of the same class as them. So marriage to her would not count as elevation. But it would validate their claim to status, because her proven taste exemplifies her ability and her willingness to make something of herself. The millinery matters, in short. Dolly's eroticism constitutes her as an object, of the deponent's gaze; but also as a subject, as someone who spends in order to accumulate. Her sexual forwardness is a social vanguardism. Dickens ogles her because he is on her side. He wills her to be modern.

So strenuous is his advocacy that he creates for her a hapless fourth admirer, in the shape of a young coachmaker whom she had met at a party, and who 'had given her to understand, when he handed her into the chair at parting, that it was his fixed resolve to neglect his business from that time, and die slowly for the love of her'. When the Vardens leave for Chigwell, the coachmaker is to be found on the pavement outside their house, 'looking so genteel that nobody would have believed he had ever had anything to do with a coach but riding in it, and bowing like any nobleman'. The coachmaker's sole function in the narrative is to serve momentarily, as Dolly sets

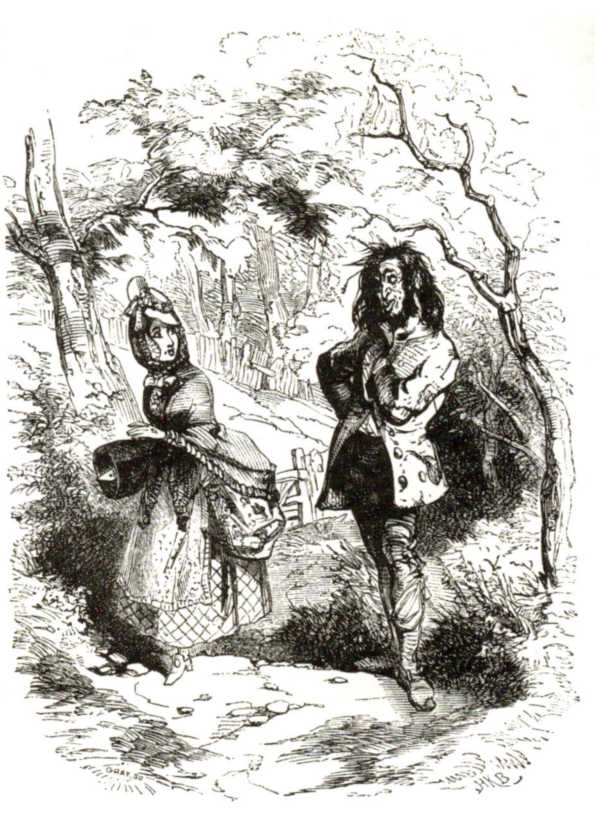

35. Hablot Knight Browne (1815–82), *A Walk in the Wood* (from Dickens's *Barnaby Rudge*). Guildhall Library, City of London.

out on her great adventure, as the figure of social aspiration. His mournful loitering frames the emergence of her sexuality as a social event. When Joe Willet says a stoical farewell to Dolly in Chapter 31, the coachmaker is invoked as someone who under those circumstances 'would have been dissolved in tears, and would have knelt down, and called himself names, and clasped his hands, and beat his breast, and tugged wildly at his cravat, and done all kinds of poetry'. He receives one final mention, towards the end of the novel, as a young man who 'had turned out, years ago, to be a special donkey'. That is the thanks you get for acting as a signpost on the road to prosperity. The significant social change *Barnaby Rudge* foreshadows is the rise not of working-class militancy, but of a sexualised consumerism.

Hablot K. Browne, who illustrated the episode of Dolly's visit to the Warren under Dickens's supervision, chose to show her admiring herself in a mirror while Emma Haredale reads Edward Chester's letter (Fig. 34), and then on the path through the wood, shrinking terrified from Hugh, and the 'coarse bold admiration in his look' (Fig. 35). The images tell a moral tale, of narcissism and its consequences. Frith, by contrast, caught her at a moment of radiant, and rather strikingly amoral, ascendancy. After leaving Emma, Dolly had been intercepted on her way out of the Warren by the forbidding Mr Haredale. The encounter discomposes her.

> The first thing to be done, of course, when she came to herself and considered what a flurry she had been in, was to cry afresh; and the next thing, when she reflected how well she had got over it, was to laugh heartily. The tears once banished gave place to the smiles, and at last Dolly laughed so much that she was fain to lean against a tree, and give vent to her exultation.

36. William Makepeace Thackeray (1811–63), *Miss Horrocks caught ransacking Sir Pitt Crawley's study* (from *Vanity Fair*). Guildhall Library, City of London.

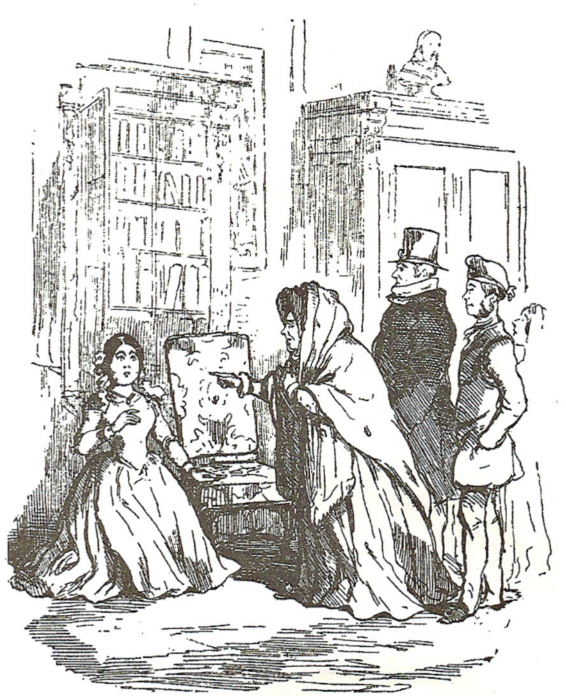

Frith managed to capture her in the first flush of exultation. His Dolly stands out, or stands forward, from her ground: partly through the intensity of the cherry and pink of her mantle, stockings, and ribbon in contrast to the greys, greens, and yellowy-browns of the murky forest path; and partly through the extravagant curve which leaning against a tree has imparted to her body. Relatively little has been left to the imagination, with regard either to the female form, or to the commodities which enhance it. The thrust of Dolly's hip has placed both the standard equipment of 'heart-rending shoes' and 'cruel little muff' and the bracelet just given her by Emma Haredale firmly in the shop window. Her level gaze might be thought to single out and even to confront any lip-smacking deponents among the audience.

If we are to take the measure of this image, we need to find out from the novel why Dolly is laughing. When Mr Haredale intercepted her, her first thought had been that he meant to punish her for carrying messages between Emma and Edward Chester. In fact, he offers her a job: the 'office' of companion to his niece. As Emma's companion, she will attain a social and economic status, not to mention an elegance of milieu, ordinarily far beyond the reach of a locksmith's daughter. The role will enable the novel itself to take her seriously: to have her kidnapped at the same time as Emma, and thus given the chance to redeem herself from narcissism by her conduct in adversity. She is laughing, as she leans against the tree, because she has come good. Her sudden social ascendancy takes the form, in this image, of an eroticism of which she is both subject and object. Frith's achievement was to have captured not just Dolly, but Dickens's own allegiance to Dolly, an allegiance he felt deeply, and could never express directly.

The cherry-coloured mantle and the pink hat-ribbon mattered, in short. When John Ruskin grumpily recalled *Barnaby Rudge*, thirty years after its publication, it was as an 'entirely profitless and monstrous story' mixed up with a 'certain quantity of ordinary operatic pastoral stuff, about a pretty Dolly in ribands, a lover with a wooden leg, and an heroic locksmith'.[16] Dolly's ribbons, it would seem, are by no means the least among the novel's offences. Ruskin cared passionately about ribbons. In fact, he loathed them with a rare bitterness. In a remarkable passage in *The Seven Lamps of Architecture* (1849), he compared the beauty of seaweed, which 'has a marked strength, structure, elasticity, gradation of substance', with the drabness of a ribbon:

> It has no structure: it is a succession of cut threads all alike; it has no skeleton, no make, no form, no size, no will of its own. You cut it and crush it into what you will. It has no strength, no languor. It cannot fall into a single graceful form. It cannot wave, in the true sense, but only flutter: it cannot bend, in the true sense, but only turn and be wrinkled. It is a vile thing; it spoils all that is near its wretched film of an existence.

In Ruskin's view, ribbon was a 'vile thing' because it lacked the organic form which gave even the humblest of natural substances a distinctive structure, a 'will of its own'. The same objection could of course be raised against more or less any of the products of the proliferating commodity culture which had begun to transform British society in its own image. In *The Seven Lamps of Architecture*, Ruskin raised it with characteristic vigour against the new suburban housing-estates around London: 'those gloomy rows of formalised minuteness, alike without difference and without fellowship, as solitary as similar'.[17] Ribbon, Ruskin thought, had the mechanically produced uniformity of all modern substances. It failed to be unlike.

What connects these esoteric speculations to Dolly Varden is the anxiety informing them. To Ruskin, the suburban houses were not just an eyesore. Their existence bore witness to a 'great and spreading spirit of popular discontent'. They were the product of a time 'when every man's aim is to be in some more elevated sphere than his natural one, and every man's past life is his habitual scorn'.[18] By this account, to elevate oneself was to exchange natural difference for a mechanically produced sameness. John Stuart Mill was later to worry that the supposedly all-inclusive social order in prospect in Britain from the 1850s onwards would extinguish 'variety of situations'.[19] Among the instruments of that extinguishing sameness, the ribbon appears to have received as much attention as the suburban house, and not from Ruskin alone. In Thackeray's *Vanity Fair* (1847–8), set during the conclusion of the Napoleonic wars, the decrepit and debauched Sir Pitt Crawley causes a scandal by conspicuously enjoying the company (and no doubt the sexual favours) of the butler's daughter, Miss Horrocks, an 'individual in ribbons'. 'The rise and progress of those Ribbons had been marked with dismay by the county and family. The Ribbons opened an account at the Mudbury Branch Savings Bank; the Ribbons drove to church, monopolizing the pony-chaise, which was for the use of the servants at the Hall. The domestics were dismissed at her pleasure.'[20] Miss Horrocks's reign comes to an end when Sir Pitt collapses, and the dignitaries summoned to his aid catch her in the act of ransacking the study. Thackeray himself illustrated the scene (Fig. 36). Dolly Varden's favourite adornment, fluttering like 'giddy things' along green meadows in the bright light of day, had become the gold-digger's emblem.

Dickens, I have argued, had mixed feelings about giddiness. The novels he wrote at this time took an unrelentingly punitive attitude towards petty-bourgeois chancers whose ambition was, in Ruskin's words, to attain a 'some more elevated sphere' than their 'natural' one: for example, Uriah Heep, in *David Copperfield* (1849–50), or Mr Guppy, in *Bleak House* (1852–3). But these variously loathsome or hapless social climbers, distant descendants of the coachmaker in *Barnaby Rudge*, are all men. Aspiration in women was a somewhat different matter. That Dickens, unlike Thackeray, found easy enough to accomodate; especially if there was a hint of millinery about it. In an essay published in the *Examiner* in 1848, he wrote admiringly of John Leech's readiness to incorporate 'beautiful faces or agreeable forms' into his sketches of fashionable young people.

37. John Leech (1817–64), Autumnal Fashions for ladies (published in *Punch* 'Almanack', 1849). Guildhall Library, City of London.

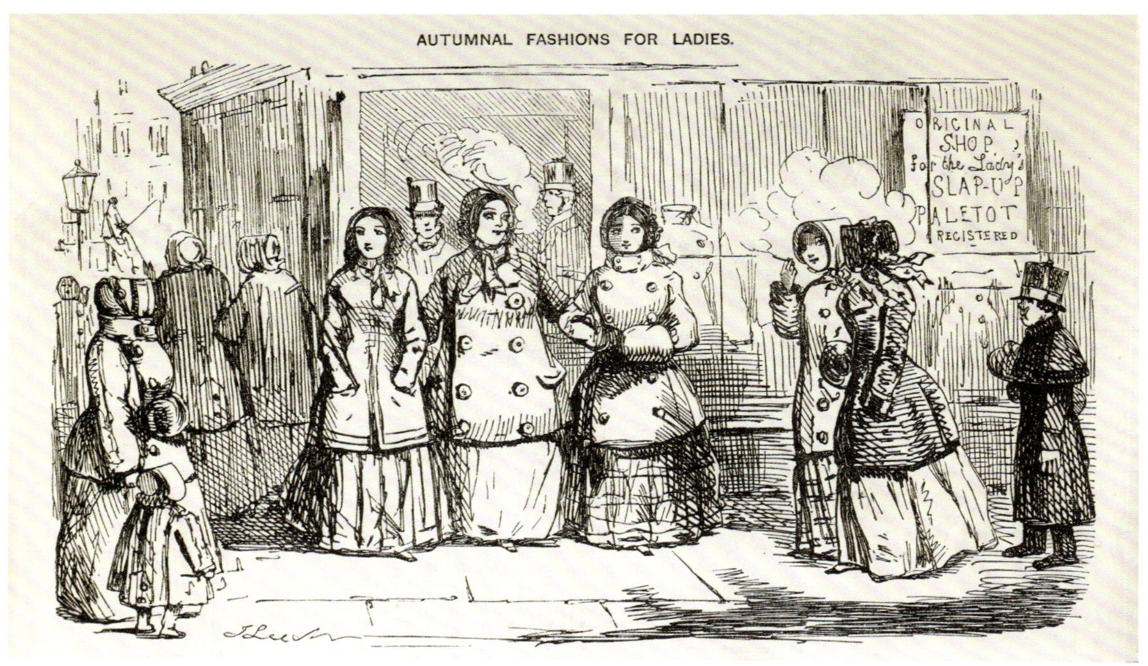

> In Mr Punch's *Almanack* for the new year, there is one illustration by Mr Leech representing certain delicate creatures with bewitching countenances, encased in several varieties of that amazing garment, the ladies' paletot. Formerly these fair creatures would have been made as ugly and ungainly as possible, and there the point would have been lost, and the spectator, with a laugh at the absurdity of the whole group, would not have cared one farthing how such uncouth creatures disguised themselves, or how ridiculous they became.[21]

Dickens badly wants to think that these fair and delicate creatures will redeem themselves from their paletots, as Dolly Varden had redeemed herself from her ribbons. So much so, in fact, that he entirely overlooks Leech's decision to equip two of them with cigars or cigarettes (Fig. 37). *Punch* readers would have considered women ostentatiously smoking in public, if not uncouth, exactly, then unfeminine.

Frith understood, and painted, the profound affinity Dickens felt with social aspiration at its most unapologetic. Joe Willet is as much the aspirant in *Barnaby Rudge* as Sim Tappertit or the hapless coachmaker. Autobiographical David Copperfield is as much the aspirant as Uriah Heep, his repulsive *alter ego*. Dickens, however, did make a habit of apologising for social aspiration. Sim and Uriah are part of that apology. Indeed, it is notable that in *Barnaby Rudge* both aspirants, good and bad, take a beating for their temerity: Joe loses an arm in the wars; Sim's legs (his chief asset) are crushed, and he becomes a bootblack. Dickens made great literature both out of his affinity with social aspiration and out of his long apology for it.

Frith seems to have been less inclined to apologise. The affinity he felt for shameless social aspiration is plain enough in the genre paintings of the 1850s and 1860s. By his own account, he took it upon himself to stiffen Dickens's resolve in that respect. He was upset to discover that when Dickens delivered Sam Weller's humorous observations in public, he tended to lower his voice to the tones of someone 'rather ashamed of what he was saying, and afraid of being reproved for the freedom of his utterances'. He most likely regarded the young bootblack's sharp tongue as

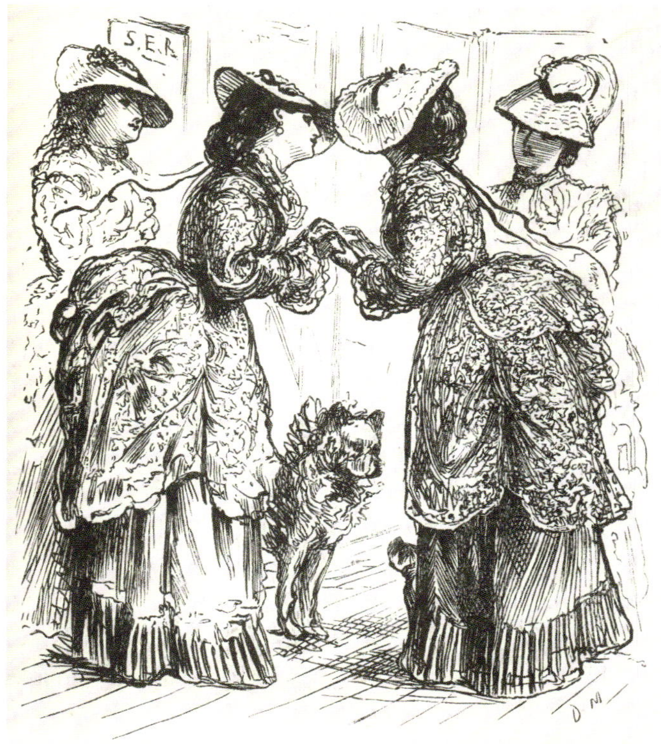

38. George Du Maurier (1834–96), *The Dolly Varden Farewell Kiss* (published in *Punch*, 14 October 1871). Guildhall Library, City of London.

evidence of a desire to improve himself. 'Sam is self-possessed, quick, and never-failing in his illustrations and rejoinders, even to the point of impudence.' He told Dickens as much, and claims that the world's best-known writer thereafter amended his incarnation on stage of one of his best-known characters accordingly.[22]

Dolly Varden herself had the last laugh.[23] When Dickens died, in June 1870, the paintings and prints sent for auction included Frith's view of Dolly Varden tripping through the woods, and looking back saucily at her lover. According to a contemporary report, 'the enthusiasm culminated when the Dolly Varden was put up, and found vent in rounds of applause. The charming "mist of coquettishness" environing this dainty figure, its beauty, its tripping, lightsome step, the innocent playfulness of the fair young face, took the room by storm.'[24] And not just the room. By 1870, the costume of the 1770s had undergone something of a revival. 'Overskirts drawn up to reveal quilted petticoats, piled up hair and tiny hats came back into fashion', Vanda Foster explains, 'and, in particular, the polonaise, an overskirt looped up to form three large puffs over the hips.'[25] This was exactly how Dolly Varden had been dressed by Hablot Browne, and by Frith. 'The novelty par excellence', the *Englishwoman's Domestic Magazine* reported in June 1871, 'is the "Dolly Varden" costume, which is a pretty, coquettish copy of the noted picture of Dolly Varden, which was among Mr Charles Dickens's collection and sold at his death.'[26] A straw hat should be worn with it, trimmed to correspond. A *Punch* cartoon of October 1871 shows the dress and hat in action (Fig. 38). Dolly Varden, already thoroughly modern in the 1770s, as Dickens imagined her, was still thoroughly modern a hundred years later. Frith could be said to have understood rather better than Dickens himself what it was that kept her young.

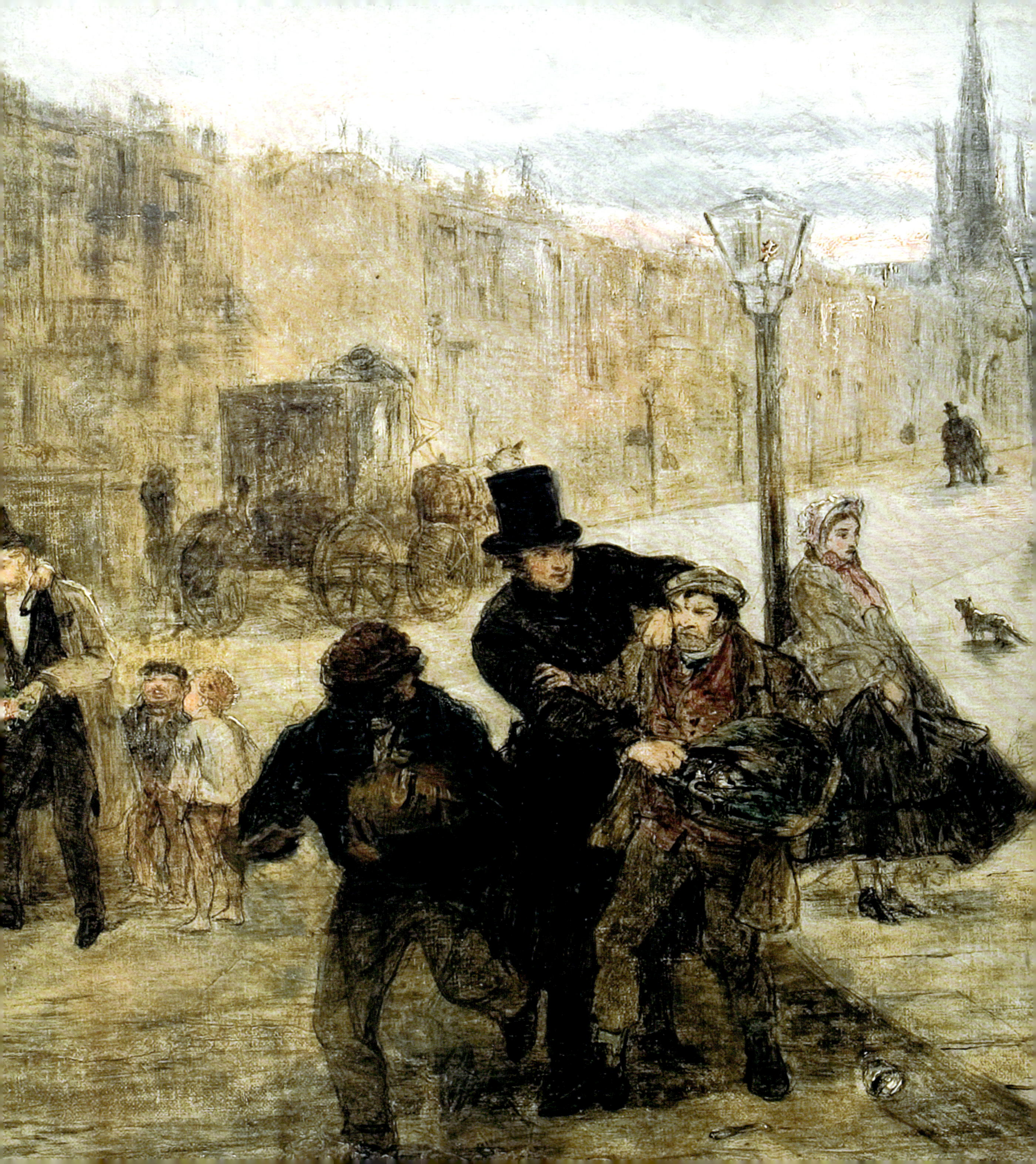

Chapter 3

'The line which separates character from caricature. . .' Frith and the influence of Hogarth

MARK BILLS

Frith, like the majority of his contemporaries, revered William Hogarth as the father of English painting. When Frith wrote that Hogarth 'stands *longo intervallo* above any of his successors', he was reflecting the predominant critical opinion of the nineteenth century.[1] 'It is from Hogarth,' Ruskin assuredly and confidently stated with little fear of contradiction, 'that English painting may be truly said to date.'[2] From Allan Cunningham's *The Lives of the Most Eminent British Painters, Sculptors and Architects* (1829) to Ernest Chesneau's *The English School of Painting* (1885), Hogarth is pre-eminent; originator of a distinctive and characteristic national school, reassuringly and originally British in manners, style and observation. For the Victorians he provided an idealised and archetypal British artist. For the artists who followed him he presented an often chimerical and unachievable ideal, and a *Times* review of 1863 sounded a cautionary note to those who would try; 'Hogarths are not common; and the attempt to wield Hogarthian weapons will oftener prove a snare than a success.'[3] From the Victorian standpoint, Hogarth's paintings represented so many contemporary aspirations in the visual arts: a distinctive and successful national school; a subject that offered narrative, popular appeal, and the possibility of a didactic moral message; and an approach that placed truth in both meaning and depiction above artifice and abstraction. Yet like any age in its understanding and interpretation of the past, it was Procrustean, particularly where the eighteenth-century master was concerned. In certain respects Hogarth appeared to fall short of the Victorian ideal and remained problematic, particularly in the direct confrontation with vice and 'low' life and the unique synthesis of 'high' and 'low' art forms. Paradoxically, while it was felt that he was the genius and ideal of the British school, there were certain 'low' elements of his work, which should be improved upon in the evolution of the national school. 'The enthusiasm excited by Hogarth's first humorous works,' Chesneau writes, 'had a decisive influence on the English school, which even to-day continues to cultivate . . . the ground . . . on which this intelligent adventurer in art . . . planted his tent of observation.'[4]

In Hogarth, Frith saw an artist who was a true antecedent to his own painting, a living influence, whose spirit continued in the nineteenth century. 'In colour, form, composition, and execution, Hogarth's works are a "continual feast" to every true artist.'[5] With the hindsight of his own time, Frith looked upon his forbear with awe, fellowship and the confidence that, were the great master alive in mid-nineteenth-century London, not only would he continue to paint everyday life around him, but perhaps that he would tackle them in the manner in which Frith adopted after his example. Hogarth gave confidence and authority to the subject and approach of Frith's paint-

39. *Morning, Covent Garden*, 1862. Private Collection. Detail. Queen Victoria's commission for a painting commemorating the marriage of the Prince of Wales meant Frith postponed — and ultimately abandoned — his plans for a series of three moralising pictures inspired by Hogarth's *The Times of Day*, which now exist only as preliminary studies. In this detail, his interest in physiognomy is reflected in the coarse features of the 'rough' caught red-handed with a sackfull of stolen silverware, while the exhausted streetwalker is treated with gentleness and sympathy and the early morning light gleams on the cat's fur.

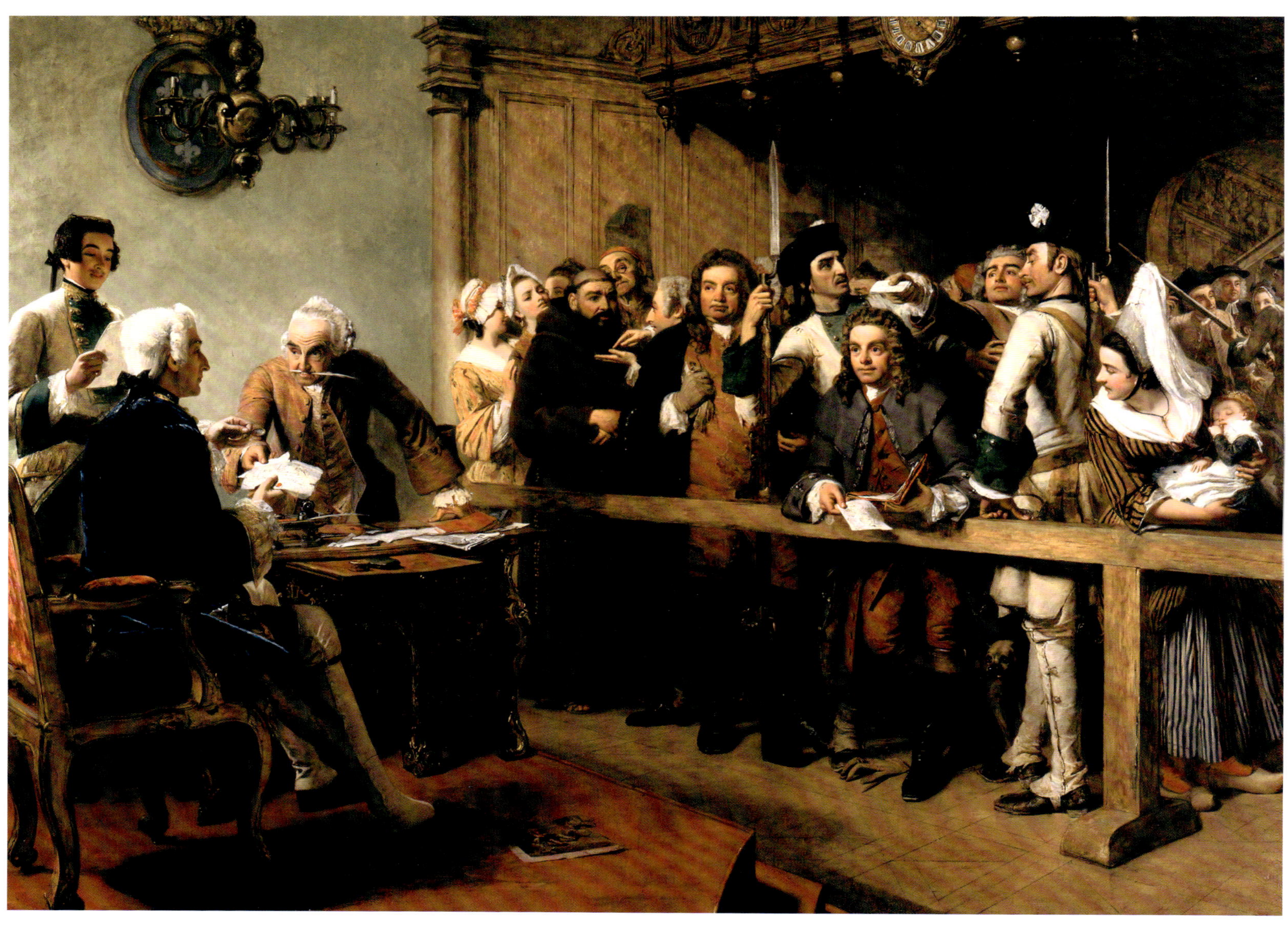

40. *Hogarth Brought Before The Governor of Calais as a Spy*, 1851. Private Collection.

ings. When certain critics and fellow artists expressed concern over his popular and contemporary subjects, looking towards Hogarth gave a critical legitimacy. The influence of Hogarth is evident throughout Frith's work, but this essay focuses upon the paintings in which he most directly and overtly draws from his predecessor. Before Frith turned his hand to paint the contemporary life around him, his work often utilised the costumes and props of Hogarth's own era and included *Hogarth Brought Before the Governor of Calais as a Spy* (1851; Fig. 40), a direct portrayal and homage to the master. After his three great social panoramas he then directly explored Hogarthian ideas (Fig. 42) in a projected series entitled *The Streets of London*, which was to consist of three large paintings, *Morning*, *Noon* and *Night* of which, sadly, only sketches were produced (Figs 41, 43, 44). In 1878 *The Road to Ruin* drew directly on Hogarth's modern moral subjects particularly those of the *Rake's Progress*, which Frith brought firmly up to date with a Victorian rake and the subsequent stages of a life obsessed with gambling. The success and popularity of the series led him to explore the genre in a more contemporary fashion in *The Race for Wealth* (1880). Yet before considering these works further it is worth exploring in more detail attitudes towards Hogarth prevalent in the mid-nineteenth century and the critical framework within which these were understood.

In 1851, William Thackeray delivered his series of celebrated lectures on English humorists at Willis's Rooms, before an audience that was filled with the leading lights of the Victorian world, including Charles Dickens and Charlotte Brontë. One of the lectures concerned Hogarth, and Thackeray explored with clarity and admiration the contemporary relevance of the eighteenth-century artist. The lectures, which focused primarily on writers, emphasised the characteristics and importance of a national school and were in line with art criticism in placing Hogarth at the head of the English painting school. Thackeray's lectures brilliantly reflected the confidence of the period in establishing a precisely discernible history of British art and literature.

Hogarth's appeal to a new generation is more than evident in Thackeray's lectures and it is a remarkable that he chooses to include Hogarth as the only artist in a series of lectures about writers. One clear reason for this is the obvious narrative and literary content of the artist, an increasingly important element in English painting at this time. Another important aspect of Hogarth's art that Thackeray emphasised was its ability to reach a wide audience, an art that was supremely popular. As the author explained: 'It was not by satire of this sort, or by scorn and contempt that Hogarth achieved his vast popularity and acquired his reputation. His art is quite simple, he speaks popular parables to interest simple hearts, and to inspire them with pleasure or pity or warning or terror.'[6] Thackeray is, of course, simultaneously emphasising the importance to his contemporaries of the underlying morality in Hogarth's work, an aspect he shows to be intimately linked with their popularity and one which he saw as of the utmost importance. 'The care and method,' he writes, 'with which the moral grounds of these pictures are laid is as remarkable as the wit and skill of the observing and dextrous artist.'[7]

Morality in painting for the mid-Victorians meant fidelity to truth in both depiction and narrative, truth in terms of morality, and truth also in being an accurate mirror to the visible world around them, a belief in realism above artifice. Hogarth represented for them a cornerstone of this belief and Frith saw this in terms of a 'blunt and truthful rendering of nature'.[8] Consequently Hogarth's paintings were seen as an accurate portrayal of the life around him. 'To the student of history,' Thackeray writes, 'these admirable works must be invaluable, as they give us the most complete and truthful picture of the manners, and even the thoughts, of the past century.'[9] Some thirteen years later, the *Art Journal* responded to Frith's paintings of contemporary life in similar terms, judging them a summation and lasting record of 'people, manners and customs of his time.'[10] 'Hogarth's works show,' commented a reviewer of *The Railway Station*, 'the value of that

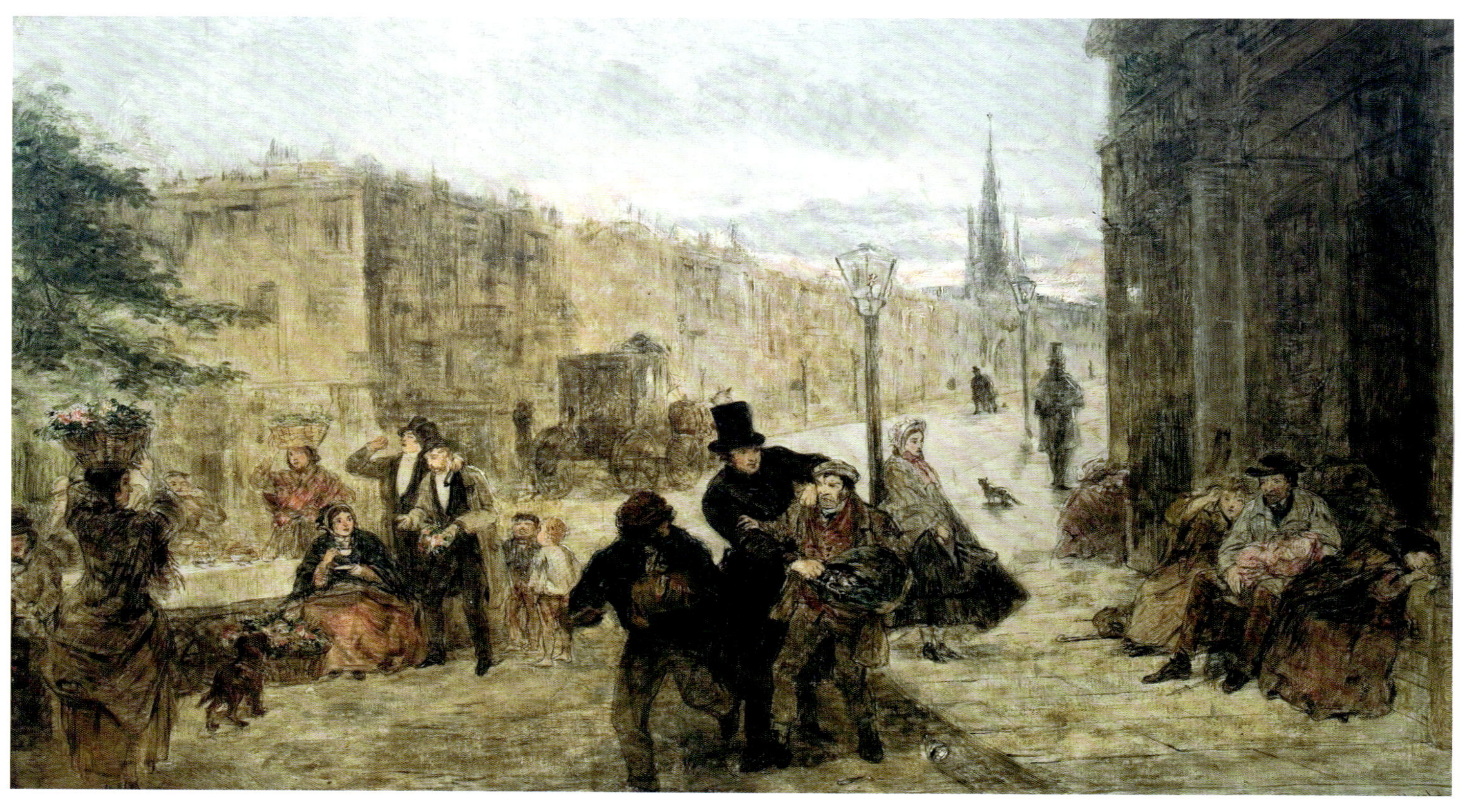

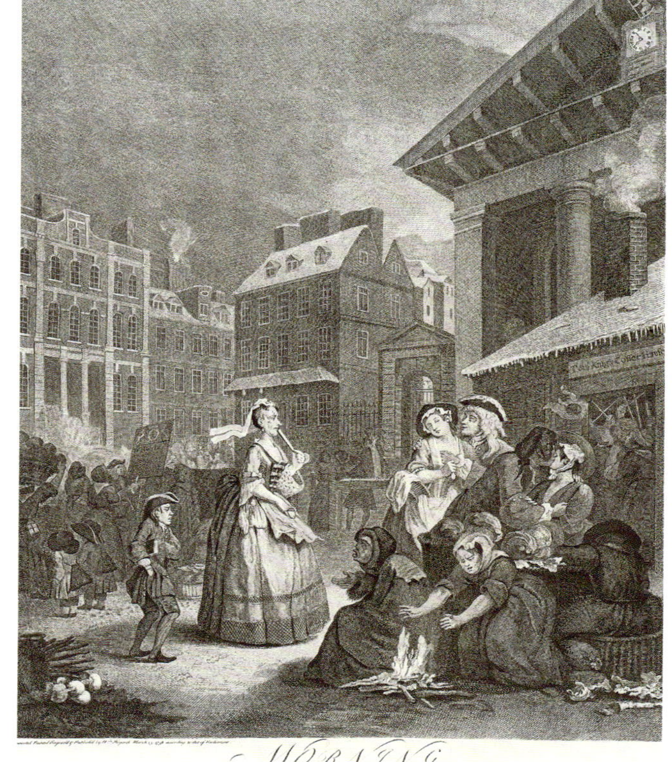

41. *Morning – Covent Garden*, 1862. Private Collection.

42. William Hogarth (1697–1764), *Morning*, from the *Four Times of Day*, 1738. Museum of London.

Facing page
43. *Noon – Regent Street*, 1862. Private Collection.

44. *Night – Haymarket*, 1862. Private Collection.

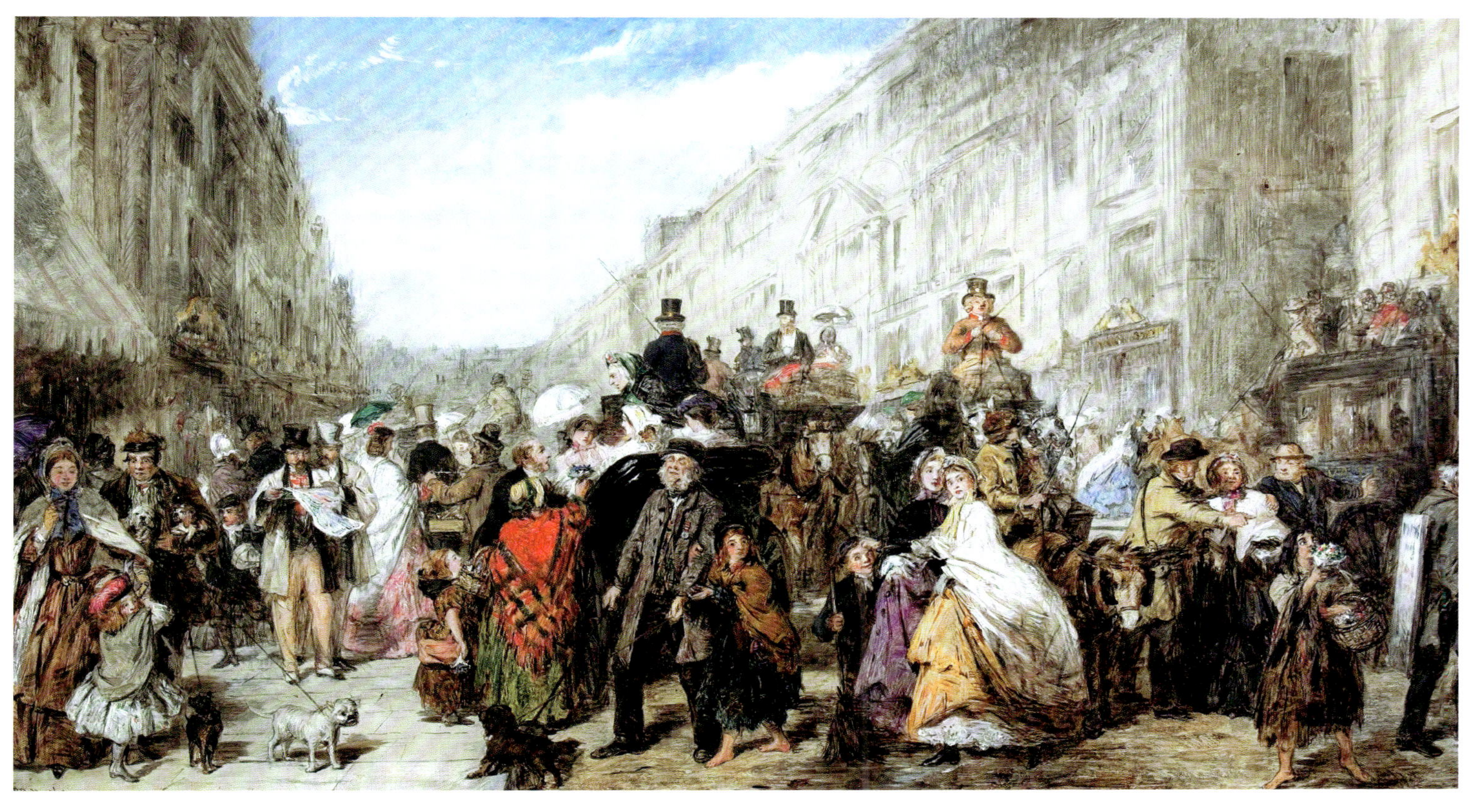

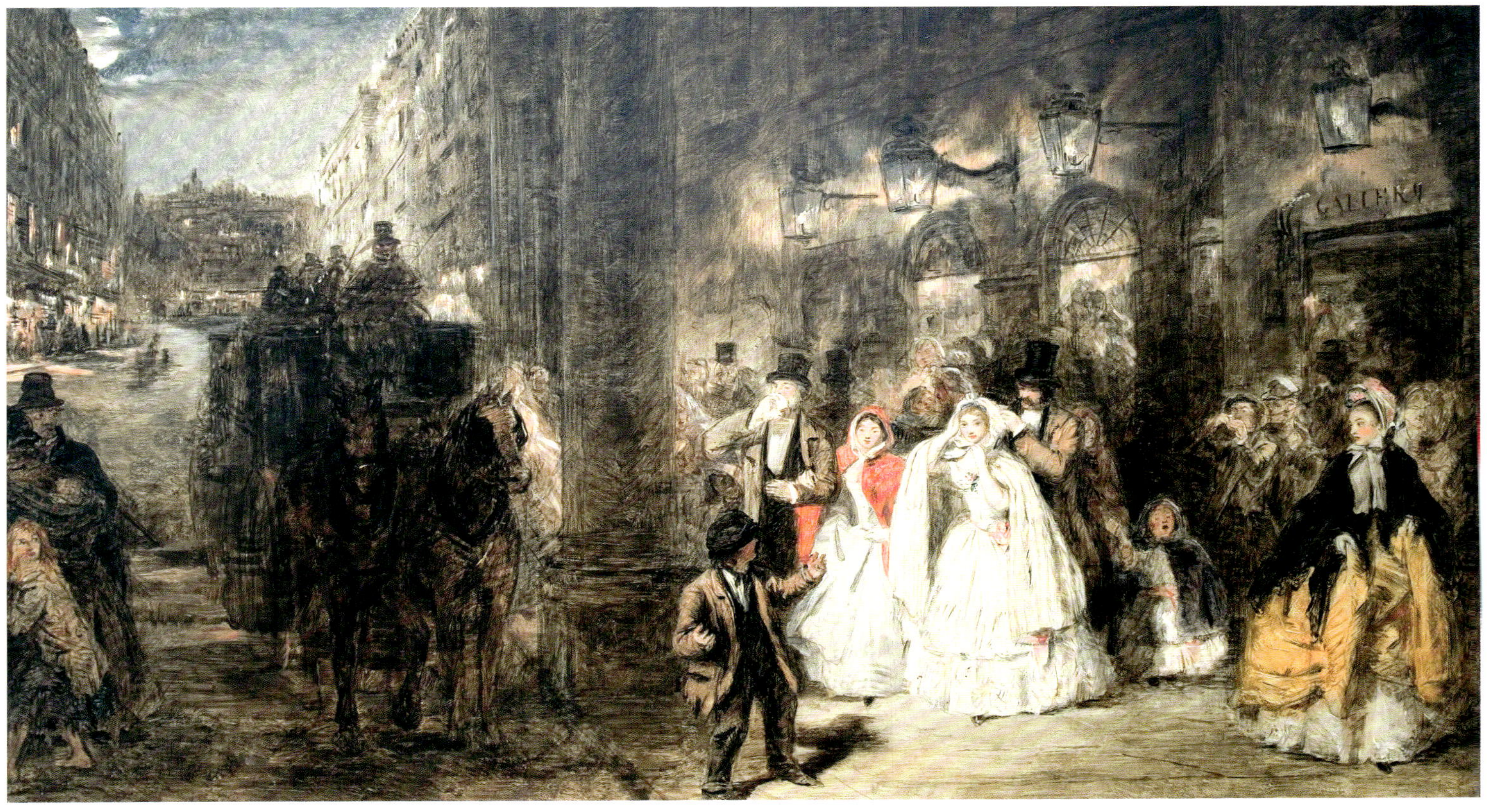

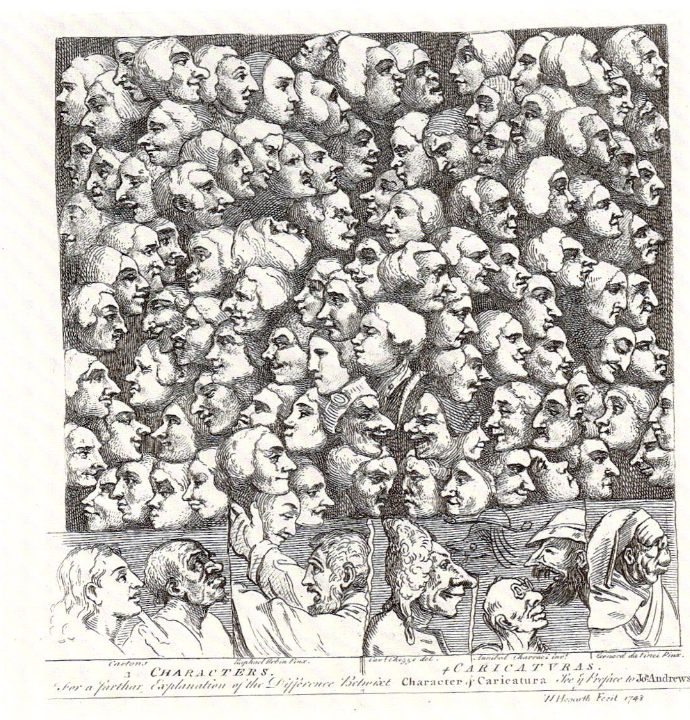

45. William Hogarth (1697–1764), *Characters and Caricaturas*, 1743. Museum of London.

art which records with insight the manners and dress, occupations and amusements, the domesticities and out-door doings of the painter's age. Mr. Frith is helping to do for our time what Hogarth did for his.'[11]

For those who sought to emulate Hogarth's example, the realisation was problematic, particularly in the areas of depicting what was perceived as essentially unpicturesque contemporary life, at the same time avoiding the more candid depictions of vice offensive to Victorian sensibility. 'It is not given to many to handle common contemporary life. Happy those who can,' remarked a critic who added his own analysis of the prerequisite of success. 'To do so with success requires the most genuine appreciation of the human comedy going on about us, united with the nicest taste and the most considered judgment.'[12]

Yet if the choice of subject could be difficult, the most problematic area was one of approach. If Hogarth could move effortlessly between 'high' and 'low' forms of art, the Victorian artist could not. The division between the art of illustration and caricature and the fine art of painting was an unbridgeable gulf, yet there existed a complex relationship of mutual influence, even if there was never any doubt that illustration was a lesser art form. This was clearly expressed by critics in a dichotomy established by Hogarth himself in the distinction between character and caricature, famously expressed through his print, *Characters and Caricaturas* of 1743 (Fig. 45). To Hogarth, 'caricatura' was a deliberate distortion rather than observation, a hobby practised by amateurs.[13] Critics seized upon this distinction, even though the 'caricatura' to which Hogarth referred was very different to the polished observations in *Punch*, and it remains a division in how Hogarth was understood by Frith's generation. Hazlitt used this distinction in reference to Hogarth's own works: 'He gives the extremes of character and expression, but he gives them with perfect truth and accuracy . . . His faces go to the very verge of caricature, and yet never (we believe in any single instance) go beyond it.'[14]

For contemporary critics of modern life painting, the dichotomy remained relevant and the line is drawn time and again. Of Hicks's *One Minute to Six* (1860, Fig. 72), a critic noted that despite the painting being 'executed in perfect good faith, and with Hogarthian seriousness of intention', it unfortunately 'suggests caricature far more than character throughout'.[15] Artists were constantly warned by critics that they 'must be careful to keep on the right side which separates character from caricature'.[16] The desire for a contemporary Hogarth within the framework of mid-nineteenth century criticism, was openly stated 'We sadly want painters of contemporary life who can draw the line between character and caricature and dignify common subjects by conscious treatment.'[17]

The nearest that the Victorians got to this chimerical ideal were on two different sides of the divide between art and illustration: Frith himself and his friend, the comic illustrator John Leech (Fig. 46). The dichotomy of character and caricature applied equally to both artists, one considered a master of whimsy, the other as a leader of the British School of social life painting. It is ironic therefore that in the criticism of modern life painting it is Leech whose name appears most often as an example of good practice. When the *Times* reviewed John Ritchie's paintings at the British Institution of 1858 it noted that: 'Mr Ritchie shows much cleverness, though it is obviously immature, and he has overstepped the line that separates character from caricature. Such subjects are only tolerable under slight and sportive treatment, like Mr Leech's in his inimitable social cuts, and run the risk of looking vulgar and impertinent when elaborated into pictures.'[18] (Fig. 71)

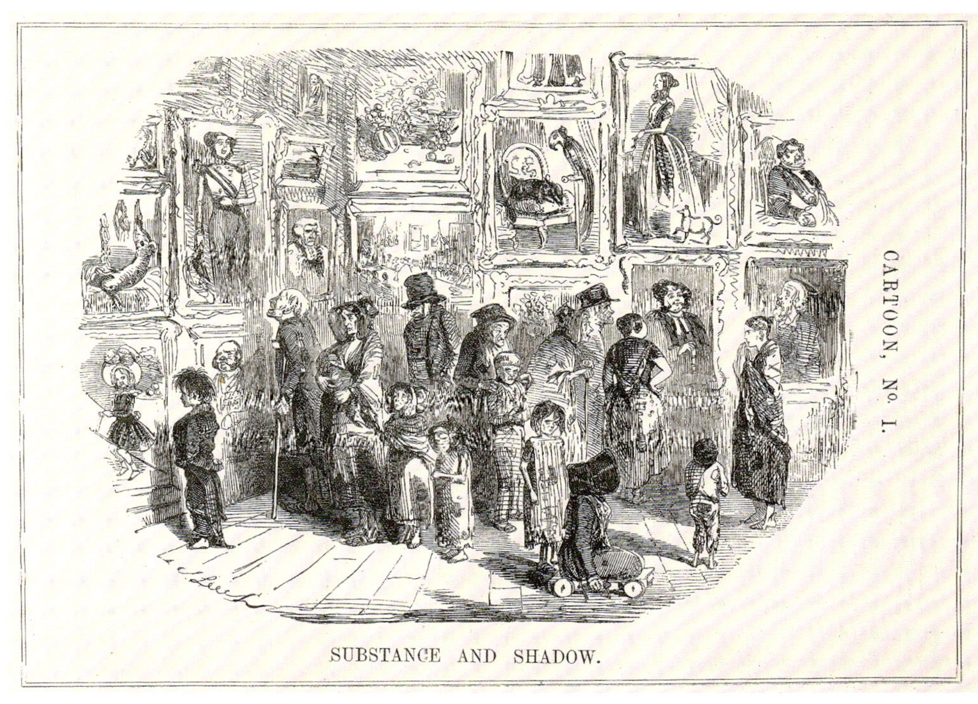

46. John Leech (1817–64), *Substance and Shadow, Cartoon No. 1* (published in *Punch*, 1843). Museum of London.

Frith admired Leech, which is more than evident in his two-volume biography of the illustrator. It is also interesting in being the book in which Frith most clearly expresses his own understanding of Hogarth. 'The name of caricaturist,' he writes, 'is as inappropriate to Leech as it is to Hogarth'[19], as opposed to his opinion of 'immortal' George Cruikshank, whom Frith declares to be on the wrong side of the division: 'I do not agree with those who place Cruikshank above Leech. Cruikshank was essentially a caricaturist; Leech was not.'[20] For all the praise that Frith and his critics bestowed upon Leech it was clear that the illustrator's burgeoning ambitions to be a painter were necessarily doomed to failure. 'Leech was once heard to say that he would rather be the painter of a really good picture than the producer of the "kind of things" he did. I, for one, am very thankful that he never did produce a good picture. . .'[21] The onerous task of a 'high' artist taking on the mantle of Hogarth was one which Frith privately determined to do, even though he modestly eschewed it in public.

Frith's first direct reference to Hogarth, which hinted at this ambition, came in 1851 with *Hogarth Brought Before the Governor of Calais as a Spy* (Fig. 40). Exhibited at the 1851 Royal Academy Summer Exhibition it clearly expresses Frith's admiration for the artist. It is based upon Hogarth's *O The Roast Beef of Old England* (1748, Tate), a painting he knew well and later recommended for purchase, to the then National Gallery. 'I implore,' he wrote to the editor of *The Times* 'the authorities at the National Gallery not to let slip the opportunity – rare in the extreme – of acquiring one of Hogarth's finest works.'[22]

The incident depicted in Hogarth's painting was the starting point of Frith's own composition and made clear in the Royal Academy catalogue of 1851, which quotes the account of the incident given by Walpole: 'Hogarth has run a great risk since the peace; he went to France, accompanied by some friends, and was so imprudent as to taking a sketch of the drawbridge at Calais. He was seized and carried to the governor, where he was obliged to prove his vocation by producing several *caricatures*, etc., such as which would by no means serve the purposes of an engineer. He was told by the governor that, had not the peace been actually signed, he should have hung him immediately on the ramparts. – *Horace Walpole*.'[23]

In his recreation of the scene, Frith uses several of Hogarth's characters in his own work, particular the lanky and comically stupid French soldiers, although any element of caricature is deliberately played down. Despite a comic element, it is a predominantly historical portrayal, akin to Frith's other paintings of this period. The dividing line of the wooden bar gives a dichotomy to the painting, the elegant and not unsympathetically portrayed Governor on one side, the crowd and comedy on the other. Paul Barlow has suggested that Frith is allying himself with the figure of authority: 'Frith, in the position of Governor, observes Hogarth and his audience from the

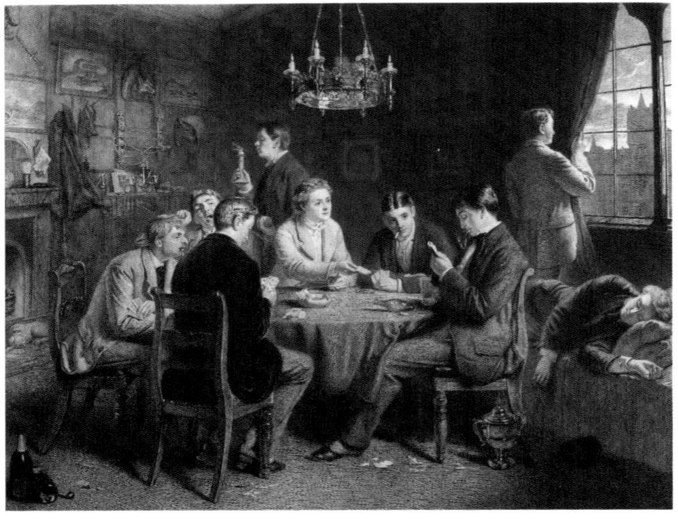

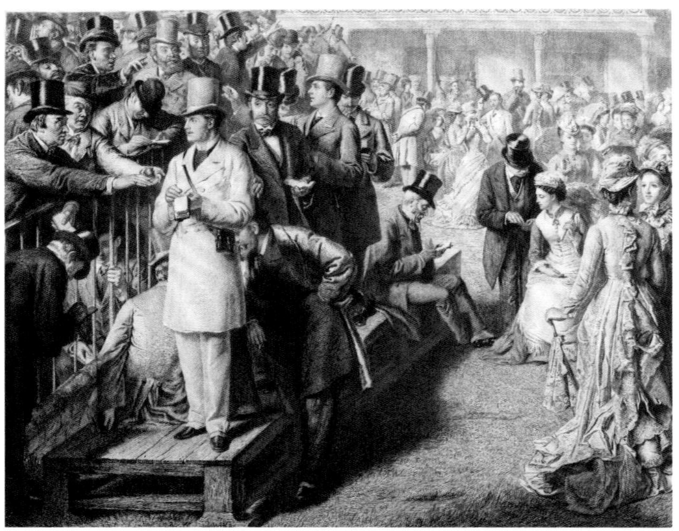

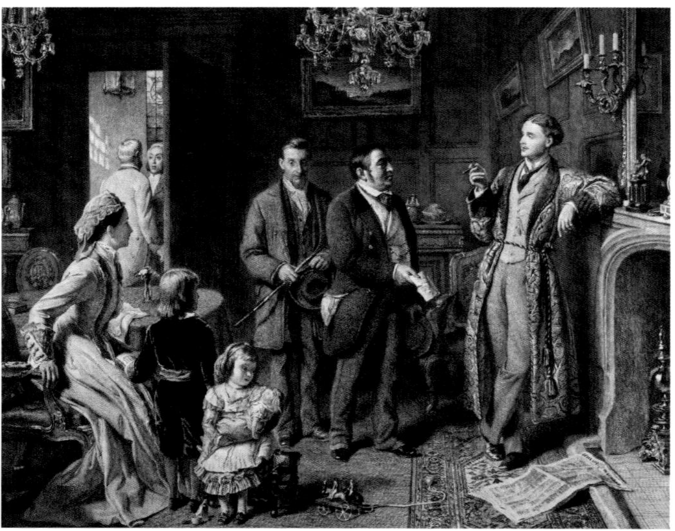

detached position on the other side of the wooden bar which crosses the image. This attitude of vigilant respectability also defines Frith's borrowings from Hogarth's other work.'[24]

Hogarth stands out from the crowd. The British hero is intent in his fixed and penetrating stare, he is resolutely standing by his moral position; yet his imminent danger is not so apparent. In his autobiography Frith records looking for the model who was to play Hogarth in the painting. 'As I could not have Hogarth to sit for me, I had to keep a bright look-out for someone resembling him. After much searching and delay I found a suitable model, not unlike the great moralist in body, but in mind as opposite as the poles.'[25] This delightful, if rather tame, homage was well received throughout his career, one critic calling it 'one of the best achievements of the British School'.[26]

As a delightful piece of costumed history, the painting was Hogarthian in subject rather than approach and it was not until three years later that Frith attempted to manifest Hogarth's influence in a more direct way through a contemporary setting. After the success of *Life at the Seaside (Ramsgate Sands)*, *Derby Day* and *The Railway Station*, Frith was looking for another great social subject. As Hogarthian as these great panoramas may be in depicting contemporary life, Frith looked towards a more direct influence for his next series. 'The great success that had attended my modern life subjects encourage me to further effort in the same direction, and I forthwith arranged compositions for three pictures of London street scenes, to be called 'Morning', 'Noon', and 'Night'.[27] *The Streets of London* clearly echo Hogarth's *The Times of Day*, in which areas of London were illustrated in a visual perambulation around the metropolis. The idea and influence were not entirely new to modern life painting, and George Augustus Sala's literary ramble around London in *Twice around the Clock* (1859) partially inspired George Elgar Hicks's paintings which depicted the scenes described and illustrated by Sala.[28] Essentially journalistic, Sala and Hicks echoed the works of Henry Mayhew, whereas Frith's ambition was to be altogether more Hogarthian and less obviously documentary in his approach.

'How I should have delighted in trying to realise all that these subjects were capable of, no tongue can tell', Frith later wrote[29]; and we too are left to wonder what these paintings might have been. Sketches remain and his autobiography partially transcribes the contract between the artist and the dealer, Ernest Gambart, although the contract itself contains several more important details. Frith was to receive the amazing sum of £10,000, for the paintings to be called 'The Streets of London', works which as well as being ambitions in subject would also be ambitions in size. 'And it is hereby agreed that the said pictures shall consist of three separate parts and pictures and that the figures of the said pictures shall not be of a less size than the figures painted by the said William Powell Frith canvas "The Railway Station".'[30] The contract also reveals interesting details about the works' commercial possibilities, and the preparations that the artist must undertake into preparing them for the engraver: 'That after the completion of the said pictures the said William Powell Frith shall touch up photographs of the pictures in order to assist the engraver in engraving the said pictures and that in case the said William Powell Frith take a longer time than one calendar month in and about touching up . . .'[31]

The burden of a royal commission effectively ended Frith's hopes of realising these paintings and the termination of the contract between Frith and Gambart was widely reported. Fortunately the studies survive in private collections and with Frith's commentary in his autobiography they give us a good indication of the paintings' conception. *Morning*, like Hogarth's *Times of Day*, was set at Covent Garden with drunken rakes, flotsam from the night before, alongside the market stall holders setting up for the day. *Noon* was a crowded Regent's Street, teeming with life, character and variety. *Night* was set at the Haymarket in moonlight with the audience leaving the theatre, a scene which Frith describes in some detail: 'a party is about to enter a carriage, and a gentleman is placing a young lady's cloak closely about her shoulders, in tender lover-like fashion. This is being observed by an overdressed and berouged woman, whose general aspect plainly proclaims her unhappy position; and by the expression of a faded though still handsome face, she feels a bitter pang at having lost forever all claim to manly care or pure affection.'[32] Frith's depiction of a pathetic 'fallen' woman is not that of Hogarth's harlots, although both express a moral tone. In Frith the prostitute is entirely the victim, a surprisingly empathetic portrayal, more obviously Dickensian in its morality.

Although Frith was never to complete *The Streets of London*, Hogarth's influence was to manifest itself even more directly on the artist, in transforming the modern moral narratives of the painting series, *Marriage à la Mode*, *Industry and Idleness*, but more particularly the *The Rake's Progress*, into tales of contemporary life (Figs 47–57). The artist evasively explained that 'Without any pretension to do my work on Hogarthian lines, I thought I could show some of the evils of gambling; my idea being a kind of gambler's progress, avoiding the satirical vein of Hogarth, for which I knew myself to be unfitted. I desired to trace the career of the youth from his college days to his ruin and death – a victim to one of the most fatal vices.'[33]

The idea itself was surprisingly novel as *The Times* pointed out in 1879: 'It is so rare to find a series of pictures by one painter illustrating the "acts" of the same story – though Frith in his "Road to Ruin" last year revived that Hogarthian practice.'[34] Such a series offered Frith a number of hitherto unexplored areas for development. Through it he could be an author inventing characters and getting them to act out the scenes of his own narrative. Perhaps it is not surprising that the opportunity of acting as a popular storyteller appealed to the artist. After all his *Railway Station* was so full of individual narratives, that it had made Tom Taylor's lengthy commentary possible. As *The Builder* commented on how the narratives were eagerly related by popular journalists and art critics alike: 'the pictures have been so fully described in the daily newspapers but we need

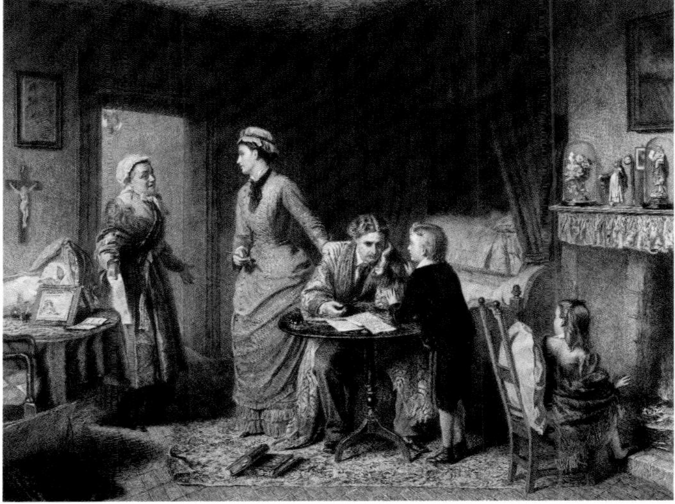

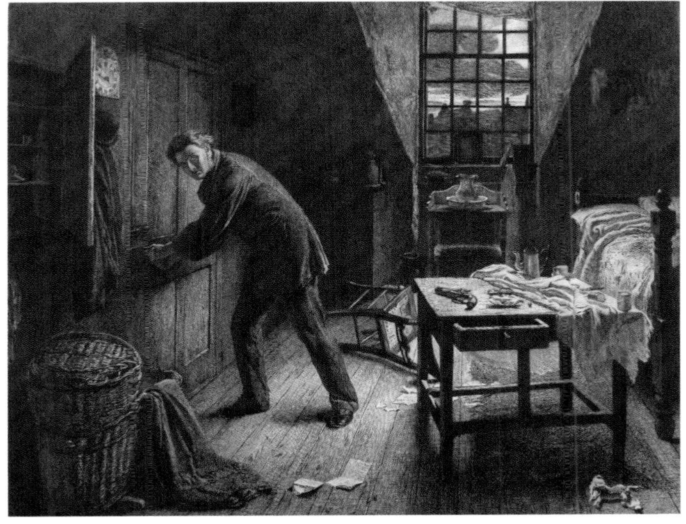

Louis Flameng after William Powell Frith: *The Road to Ruin*, 1878. Etchings published by the Art Union of London, 1878. Museum of London.
Frith recorded that he worked incessantly on the five paintings comprising *The Road to Ruin* (Private Collection) throughout 1877. Commissioned by the dealer L.V. Flatow for £2,000 each, they were exhibited at the Royal Academy in 1878, protexted from the crowds by a rail, and sold at a profit after publication of the Art Union prints after them.

Facing page
47. *College*, top
48. *Ascot*, centre
49. *Arrest*, bottom

This page
50. *Struggles*, top
51. *The End*, bottom

not go over the ground again. Suffice it to say that they contain much able and carefully-studied work, display a large amount of character . . . that tell the story clearly and well.'[35]

A narrative series also offered Frith the opportunity to explore a single theme in further detail. It allowed time to develop a clear moral idea, and the consequences of particular actions. In expounding a single tale he could also plot the development of characters' psychology, particularly as it was expressed in the human face, something which had always greatly interested him. His great social panoramas were a multiple of narratives held together by brilliant composition and even handling. Frith had proved himself masterly in creating a mass of sub-plots held together by one moment in time. In contrast, and a departure for him, each canvas of the *Road to Ruin*, had a central action which every object and actor worked towards expressing, and each part worked towards the central motive. Hogarth's *Rake's Progress* was the model around which Frith was able to construct the *Road to Ruin*, a series filled with Hogarthian details in all the objects placed to echo the central action. The story concerns the progress of a wealthy and educated man gripped by obsessive gambling from his college days to his final demise. Covering a span of around two decades we see the protagonist's family and associates move around him in order to express the consequences of his fatal obsession. The five paintings which make up the series are almost symmetrical in presenting an affluent world and descent into poverty and finally death, the third being pivotal in tottering between action and consequence.

According to the artist, who later recalled the series for a popular magazine, 'It was about 1869, after a visit to Ascot, that the idea first suggested itself for the *Road to Ruin* series. Some rough pen-and-ink sketches were the beginnings of this well-known series, and these were developed into chalk studies for the five pictures.'[36] The chalk drawings, now in the British Museum, were also recalled in his autobiography: 'careful chalk drawings were made, groups rearranged, compositions changed; in fact, all the thinking part of the business was settled before the small oil sketches what made.'[37] Frith's working method for the *Road to Ruin* closely resembled that of his other major works in using models for the main figures of his compositions and photographs for the settings. Fidelity to truth, a trait that he admired so much in Hogarth, was expressed through the accuracy of his paintings' details pursued through long modelling sessions and commissioning of photography. In this particular series, for example, photographs for the first painting were made: 'Mr Frith told me that for this scene he had photographs taken of a college room at Cambridge to ensure the accuracy in the background of the picture.'[38]

Models, crucial to his painting, were a constant aggravation to him. Finding the models appropriate to their ascribed role in the painting and their behaviour in his studio are the subject of numerous anecdotes in his autobiography. He recalled in this case 'the whole of that year being taken up in incessant work at the pictures of "The Road to Ruin". The difficulties in respect of models and material were increased by the variety of men, women, and matter required.'[39] Female characters for the series were provided through 'the kindness of lady friends', which 'rendered the employment of the professional model almost needless in the pictures'.[40] For the main male model and central protagonist Frith used a professional model named Mr Green who stood for many of the figures, a model whom he finally dismissed for his alcoholism.[41] The degree to which he manipulated the facial expression in these dramas is hinted at in an interview with *Cassell's Saturday Journal* where he recalled Green: 'I remember when I was painting that "Road to Ruin" series, I tried to get a model to look as though he was locking the door and going to commit suicide. The fellow struck an attitude and made a grimace just as though he were going to be sick. "Yes, that'll do", I said, as well as I could without laughing.'[42]

The underlying moral message was key to Frith's conception of the series as a whole, and was unambiguously pursued. According to *The Quiver*, the paintings had 'a distinctively didactic

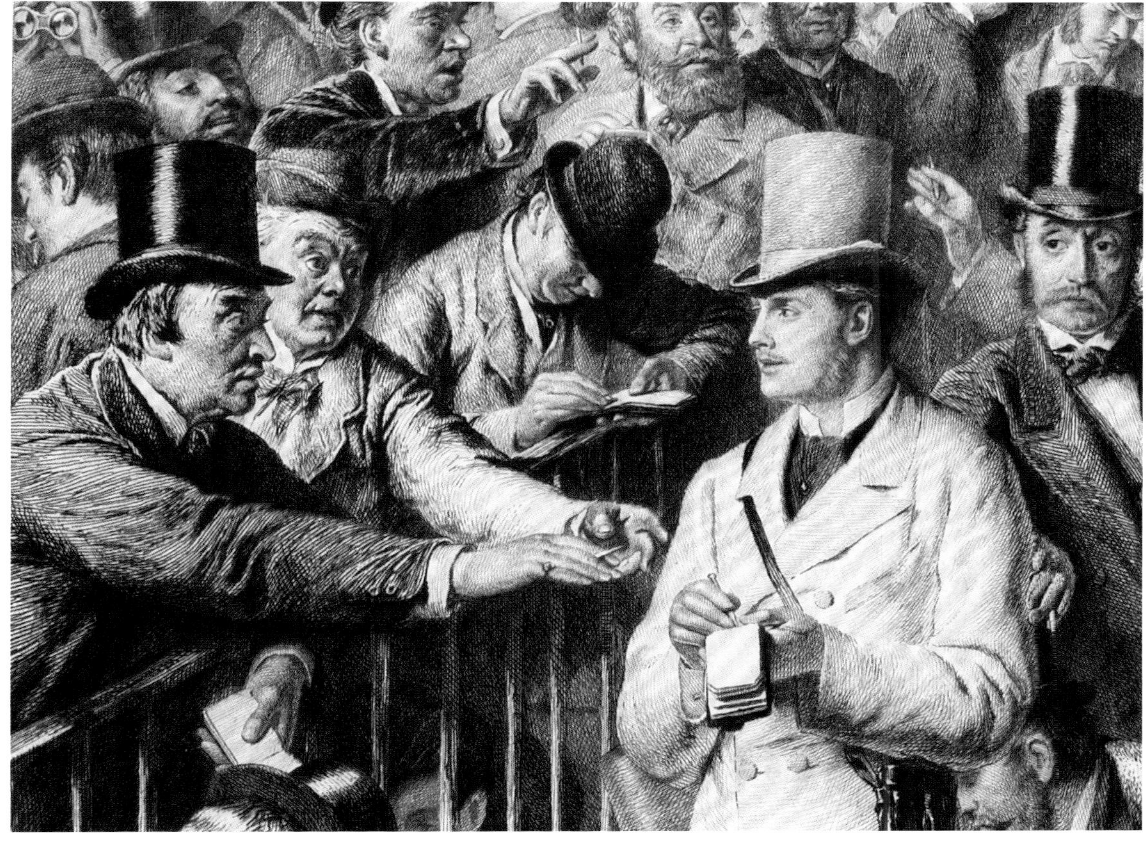

52. Louis Flameng after William Powell Frith: *Ascot*, from *The Road to Ruin*, 1878. Detail of Fig. 48. Museum of London.
The young man is now 'the centre of attraction in the Royal Enclosure at Ascot to a horde of betting-men, who are offering him chance after chance of immediate or prospective ruin'.

purpose: the artist is preacher as well as painter; the pictures are sermons written in paint on the canvas sheet. Simple, but forcible; easily read, but imprinted on the mind with far greater power than many spoken words.'[43] Not surprisingly the works were used didactically, particularly in sermons, although in an unpublished letter of 1889 Frith makes clear the underlying moral motive was sparked by an established hypocrisy. They aimed to 'draw further attention to the anomaly at present existing with regard to gambling which is lawful apparently in one place and subject to severe punishment if it is practised in another. Young men may lose their stakes at Ascot or Epsom, but they may not bet for shillings in London's streets of parks . . .'[44] Clearly it was the central diatribe against the evils of gambling in general that struck a chord with its audience and Frith recalled that 'I have a sermon somewhere which was preached upon them, I forget by whom and they also were the subject of a discourse in Hyde Park by an open-air preacher.'[45] Facts that must have both pleased and amused the artist.

The works were a very public success and when they were exhibited at the Royal Academy Summer Exhibition of 1878, 'the policeman and the rail were again required'.[46] The engraving rights were purchased by the London Art Union who commissioned Leopold Flameng to etch the series. With the release of the prints, the paintings were exhibited once more, this time at the Art Union Gallery in the Strand to stimulate sales.

The *Illustrated London News* was full of gushing praise for Frith's series but referred to its central protagonist as a 'good looking brainless hero'.[47] Within the popular press the paintings found favour, even though they perhaps hinted that a happy conclusion would have been more satisfac-

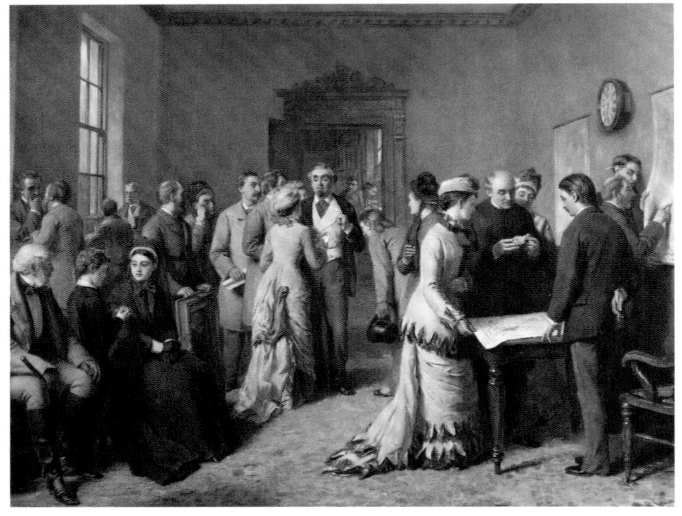

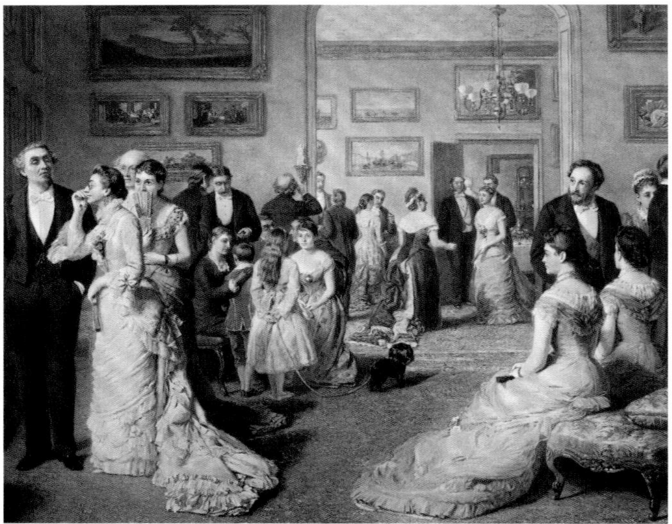

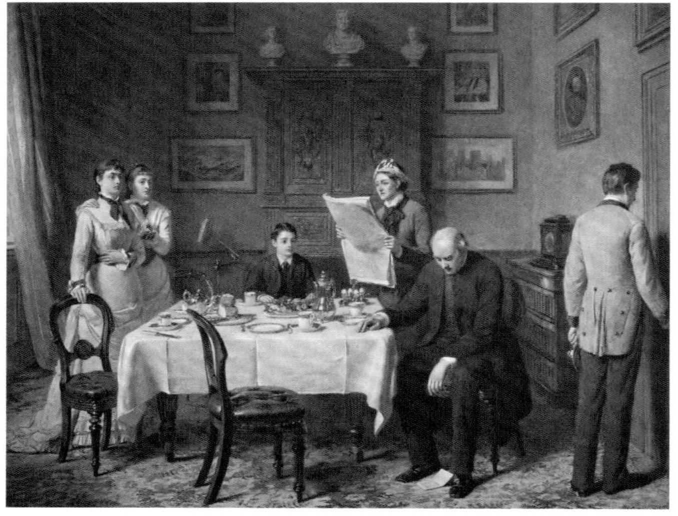

tory. Reform would have been a much more positive message. When *Punch* devoted over a page to the series it was filled with a similar sentiment: 'wishing that the curtain would rise once more, and show a gleam of happiness . . . Believe me, that young scamp has had far more brains than Mr Frith all along has given him credit for.'[48]

If the popular press was full of praise, the *Athenaeum* was fairly damning of the paintings. Their intentions may be 'high' Hogarthian art, but the results were 'low' art, its critic argued: 'Mr Frith, wishing apparently to emulate Hogarth, sends a series of five small pictures . . . A painter may have no grander object that to teach a moral lesson in his work; but there are two ways of doing this: the one, as with Hogarth in his 'Rake's Progress', where he expressed his intention its dignity and an impressive power making all things subservient to the motive for his work; and the other, a trite, tame, commonplace method, carrying no weight except with those ignorant of Art, and impressing only the superficial and thoughtless . . . a monument of misapplied Labour.'[49]

Such criticisms did not deter Frith's ambitions but may have affected his approach. Characteristically he focused upon the very public success when he wrote of his intention to continue the Hogarthian method:

> Encouraged by the success of the 'Road to Ruin', I immediately embarked in a new venture: a series of five pictures representing the career of a fraudulent financier, or promoter of bubble companies; a character not uncommon in 1877, or, perhaps, even at the present time. I wished to illustrate also the common passion for speculation, and the destruction that so often attends the indulgence of it, to the lives and fortunes of the financier's dupes.'[50]

The success of *The Road to Ruin* allowed and encouraged Frith to explore the Hogarthian genre further and it was clearly a form that he felt had far more potential for contemporary subjects, than he had hitherto explored.

After the acclaim of *Life at the Seaside (Ramsgate Sands)* and *Derby Day* at the Royal Academy, Frith had decided that his next major work, *The Railway Station* was to be exhibited at a private gallery, presumably for greater commercial possibilities. Similarly for his next Hogarthian progress, *The Race for Wealth*, he made the decision to exhibit them for the first time at a commercial gallery in King Street. As with *The Railway Station*, the dramatist and humorist, Tom Taylor, was once more called upon to expound the works in a rich narrative catalogue.

Frith had learnt a great deal from his last series and in his new work, with the initial technical problems overcome, he experienced a greater freedom in the exploration of his new subject. He chose to depict a series that dealt with speculation, a different kind of gambling, which allowed him to draw in related ideas, themes and sub-plots. Consequently it was more sophisticated in its narratives, layers of meaning, critiques of society and, perhaps more importantly for Frith, its varied depictions of character.[51] The story of the series surrounds a central protagonist, a fraudulent financier, described in the titles as the 'spider', whose narrative is portrayed from his selling shares for a bogus investment to his subsequent trial at the Old Bailey and punishment at Millbank Penitentiary. The first two scenes show the 'spider' confidently defrauding his 'flies', the final two his trial and punishment. Like *The Road to Ruin*, *The Race for Wealth* uses the central painting as the pivotal work in the series, in this case depicting the effects of the 'spider' on his victims through a 'foolish clergyman'.[52]

Within the paintings, realism continued to be an important factor. As Frith had suggested in his letter about *The Road to Ruin*, although gambling was its primary target, the hypocritical anomalies of the law in part inspired the work. In *The Race for Wealth*, the subject criticises the financial world in general through a very obvious fraud, although Frith strongly suggests there are other such 'crimes', if we can call them such, that were legal or escaped prosecution. Indeed if the realism of these paintings were questioned it would be in respect of a main protagonist who did not successfully escape justice. The magazine *Fun* produced its own series of five images after Frith's entitled *Odds on 'The spider'*, in which the final scene depicts the 'spider,' in a rich carriage with two footmen, raising his hat to the defrauded clergyman who has become a crossing sweeper.[53] Frith saw the paper and he commented:

> In the comic paper called *Fun*, the admirable artist of that journal, Mr Sullivan, laid hold of my puppets and make them play a different game. He represented the clergyman as ruined, it is true; but he declined to punish the swindler, who rolls along a street in his carriage accompanied by his vulgar wife, without the least display of sympathy for the poor parson, who is reduced to sweeping a crossing over which the carriage has just passed. I will not dispute the probability of the truth of my friend Sullivan's version, for I know instances of it; but, naturally, I prefer my own.[54]

The accuracy of the settings of each of the scenes were determinedly recreated by Frith, the locations of the Central Criminal Court and Millbank Penitentiary, for example, being explored in great detail. A later interview relates that: 'Mr Frith tells me that the trouble and Labour connected with the working out of this series were very great. The court is an exact representation of the Central Criminal Court at the Old Bailey, necessitating several photographs being taken of the building. Mr Frith stood in the dock and tried to realise to some extent the feelings of a criminal waiting the sentence.'[55] Recreating the rooms of City stockbrokers offices proved more of a problem. It seems clear that the criticisms of the financial world implicit in the paintings caused City companies to hesitate allowing Frith access to their offices. They did not wish to be associated with fraudulent practice, nor in the public imagination with the immorality of high finance. As Frith pointed out: 'With a view to truthfulness, I visited several offices in the City – stockbrokers' and others, – in order that my swindler's surroundings in his place of business should be *en règle* but I found so strong an objection on the part of my stockbroking friends to any of their offices being used on my purpose, that I was obliged to call one out of my inner consciousness.'[56]

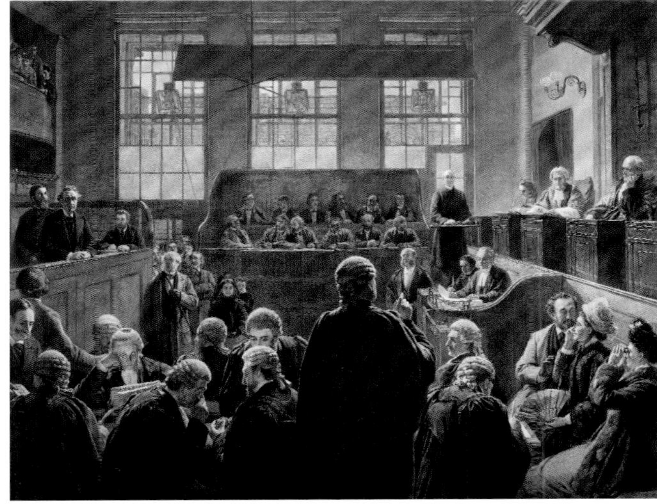

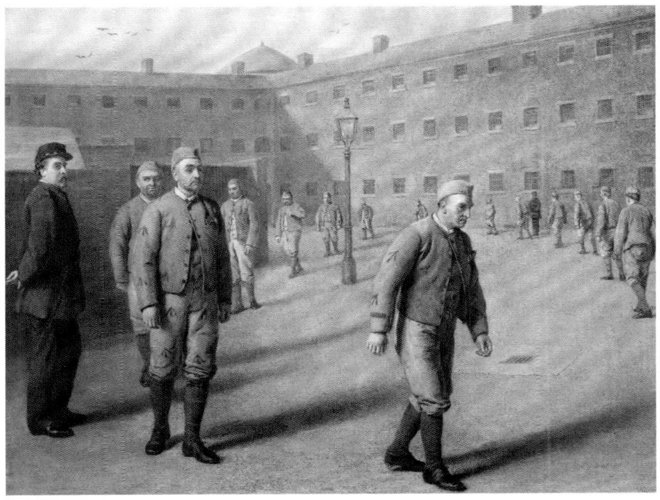

After William Powell Frith: *The Race for Wealth*, photogravures, 1882. Museum of London.
According to Frith, 'The pictures were translated by photogravure, but whether from the faults of the pictures, or the method in which they were reproduced, the result was far from satisfactory.'

Facing page
53. *The Spider and the Flies*, top
54. *The Spider at Home*, centre
55. *Victims*, bottom

This page
56. *Judgement*, top
57. *Retribution*, bottom

Criticism of commercial life was voiced by reformers and by the Church. In 1878 a leading clergyman, Canon Barry, had spoken out against its immorality, which was widely reported. As the *Times* reported: 'Canon Barry . . . a concluding appeal . . . The sermon was an earnest protest against the divorce of Christianity from commercial life, as exhibited in adulteration, short weight, dishonest commissions, fraud, over speculation . . .'[57] Frith himself is less likely to have had sympathy with the clerical perspective and the pages of his autobiography and those of his daughter Mrs Panton, make clear his critical attitude towards the Church. The central character of the parson, although sympathetic, hints also at the hypocrisy of his own position and one cannot help but reflect upon the similarity of motives for speculation with those of the 'spider's': the *Morning Post* crudely but accurately noted 'the skill with which the artist has depicted the besotting influence of avarice upon the human intellect'.[58] How interesting to find that in October 1880 after its exhibition at King Street, the paintings were then moved for display into the City, the heart of London's financial district, at No. 62 Cheapside, daily from 10 to 6 o'clock for an admission price of sixpence.[59]

In contrast to *The Road to Ruin, The Race for Wealth* series was a critical success as well as being popular with the public. The *Art Journal*, alongside the popular journals such as the *Morning Post* hailed that '. . . Mr Frith has never produced anything better, whether for conception of character or masterly execution . . . Nothing he has produced can be placed on a par with the Race for Wealth.'[60] Even the *Athenaeum*, which had been so damning of *The Road to Ruin*, found words of praise for the series: 'Let us say at once that in the works before us,' it wrote, 'Mr Frith has re-established himself in a position which he had not for a long time occupied, and has produced a series of works almost as good as the Derby Day.'[61] There was general recognition that in these paintings, Frith had taken the Hogarthian form and produced works that were a sophisticated contemporary equivalent. The drawbacks and difficulties that had been so often warned against were reiterated in the *Times* review of the series: 'familiarity of type, incident, and character, and unpicturesqueness of costume are heavily against him. Hogarth is for us of the past in all these points. If he in his own time traced the former, the costume of his day was highly paintable.'[62] In all of Frith's work that were so unambiguously Hogarthian in intention and method, did critics recognise the difficult balance between taste, decency, satire, character and caricature. *The Builder* commented, 'He does not, like Hogarth, revel in the grotesque, nor has he that master's power of what may be termed caricature, but he hands down to our successors pictures which must always be of great value, pointing as they do a moral and likewise showing boldly parts of the life of the latter end of the nineteenth century.'[63]

The question of taste, viewed by critics as central to the updating of Hogarth, was alluded to in the second painting of the series, *The Spider at Home*, where the fraudulent financier is clearly a vulgarian. In the painting, Frith is also referring to breakdown in social restrictions, something at the heart of eighteenth-century satire. As *The Builder* wryly noted, 'here we have a capital picture of a scene in modern society, showing how wealth, with management, can get all kinds of people into a drawing room.'[64] The fine line of taste and form was seen to be successful and the paintings as well as being widely popular also attracted a more exclusive and fashionable audience, an indication of their less obviously didactic purpose and simplicity of story telling. *Vanity Fair* even listed the exhibition as a fashionable thing to do.[65]

Of all the paintings in the series, the final scene 'Retribution,' was least liked by critics largely because of its unpalatable subject matter. In it the 'spider' tramps anonymously around the exercise yard of Millbank Penitentiary. *The Academy* wrote that 'the last picture, – "Retribution" – is certainly not amongst Mr. Frith's happiest efforts.'[66] To disguise prisoners' identities and emphasise anonymity and temporary equality, each prisoner shares almost the same face. The bleak background and lack of interaction – although highly effective in evoking the spirit of late nineteenth-century penal service – was not, according to critics, the basis of a good painting. In this approach, Frith was more obviously departing from Hogarth's example, yet as a whole the series was almost universally praised. It was, perhaps, the closest that the Victorian art world got to having a contemporary Hogarthian series.

For Frith, Hogarth gave the underlying tradition and model for the development of his art. He provided a critical legitimacy to the subjects that Frith chose to paint, linking him with a clear tradition of English painting, a tradition manifestly understood by critics. In Hogarth, Frith also found a popular icon, an artist that he could associate with and was also understood by his popular audience, in particular Hogarth as the personification of 'Britishness', remaining solid in the face of foreign influence and artistic innovation. He stood for the importance of the subject, a contemporary and relevant subject and an approach that opposed aestheticism and the effeteness of rarefied critics. Hogarth's feet were seen to be very firmly on the ground, and in the mind of his nineteenth-century admirers, he was a Victorian at heart. Frith drew even more directly from Hogarth in providing inspiration in both subject and approach, a fact immediately recognised by contemporary critics. A Victorian Hogarth could only really exist in the imagination of a Victorian, it jarred too much with the eighteenth-century Hogarth, but Frith came closest to the realisation of this ideal, a masterly assimilation of Hogarth through Victorian eyes.

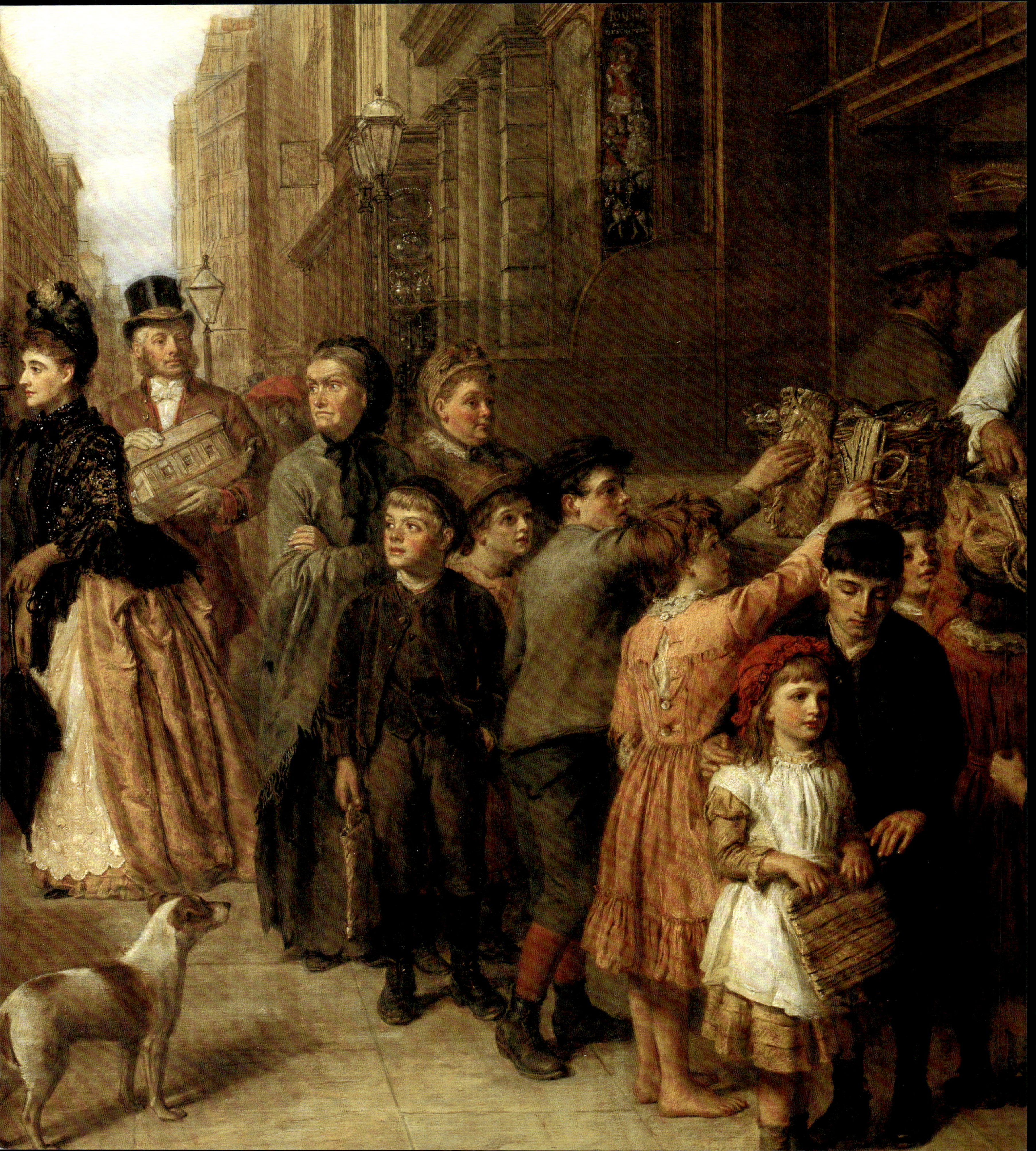

Chapter 4

Frith and his Followers: Painters and Illustrators of London Life

MARY COWLING

In 1854, a painting which had been dismissed as 'a tissue of vulgarity', and 'a piece of vulgar Cockney business unworthy of being represented even in an illustrated paper' was shown at the Royal Academy.[1] *Life at the Seaside (Ramsgate Sands)* (Fig. 14) was the first of the modern life panoramas which brought fame to William Powell Frith, an ambitious young Yorkshireman who had moved to London to train as an artist at the age of sixteen. Frith staked his reputation on this new venture, and his gamble paid off. *Life at the Seaside (Ramsgate Sands)* was proclaimed the picture of the year, and its purchase by Queen Victoria proved that Frith had caught the mood of the moment.

In 1837, the year Victoria came to the throne, Frith began his formal training at the Royal Academy Schools where teaching was based on the assumption that History Painting marked the summit of the artistic hierarchy: the final challenge to any artist worthy of the name. As the *Art Union* put it in 1840, with uncompromising frankness: 'The object of art is not to gratify the taste of tinkers and cobblers', but as the critic proceeded to explain, through a judicious choice of subject and treatment, to elevate and improve the national mind.[2] But some younger painters had other ideas. Frith had never aimed to be an artist of the 'High' variety, preferring to grapple with real life rather than abstractions, and much of his training bored him. In his *My Autobiography* he openly admitted his failure to master the 'dreadful science' of perspective and soon parted company with anatomy; since both were unnecessary to his own chosen route in art.[3] In 1840 Frith formed The Clique with Augustus Egg, Henry O'Neil and other like-minded artists. Recognizing that changing demands were at odds with established academic taste, the young painters opted instead for accessible subjects, with the emphasis on character and incident, detail and high finish.

Having established his reputation with literary and anecdotal historical subjects, Frith made his greatest and most original contribution to British art with his panoramas of contemporary life. These would always court controversy. As the social observer Henry Mayhew admitted, 'A London crowd is an awful thing, when you reflect upon the number of infamous characters of which it is necessarily composed';[4] but modernity, novelty and the appeal to familiar experience were potent forces in the new art market. To the majority of people, Frith's scenes were irresistibly attractive: a veritable mirror of their own times. Predictably, they gave rise to a host of imitations, all of which are now prized as uniquely informative records of the Victorian scene.

Frith's ambitious portrayals of the London crowd illustrate a new element in contemporary art and illustration, which had evolved in parallel with the rapid growth of the urban population.

Facing page
58. *Poverty and Wealth*, 1888. The Leicester Galleries, London. Detail of Fig. 66.

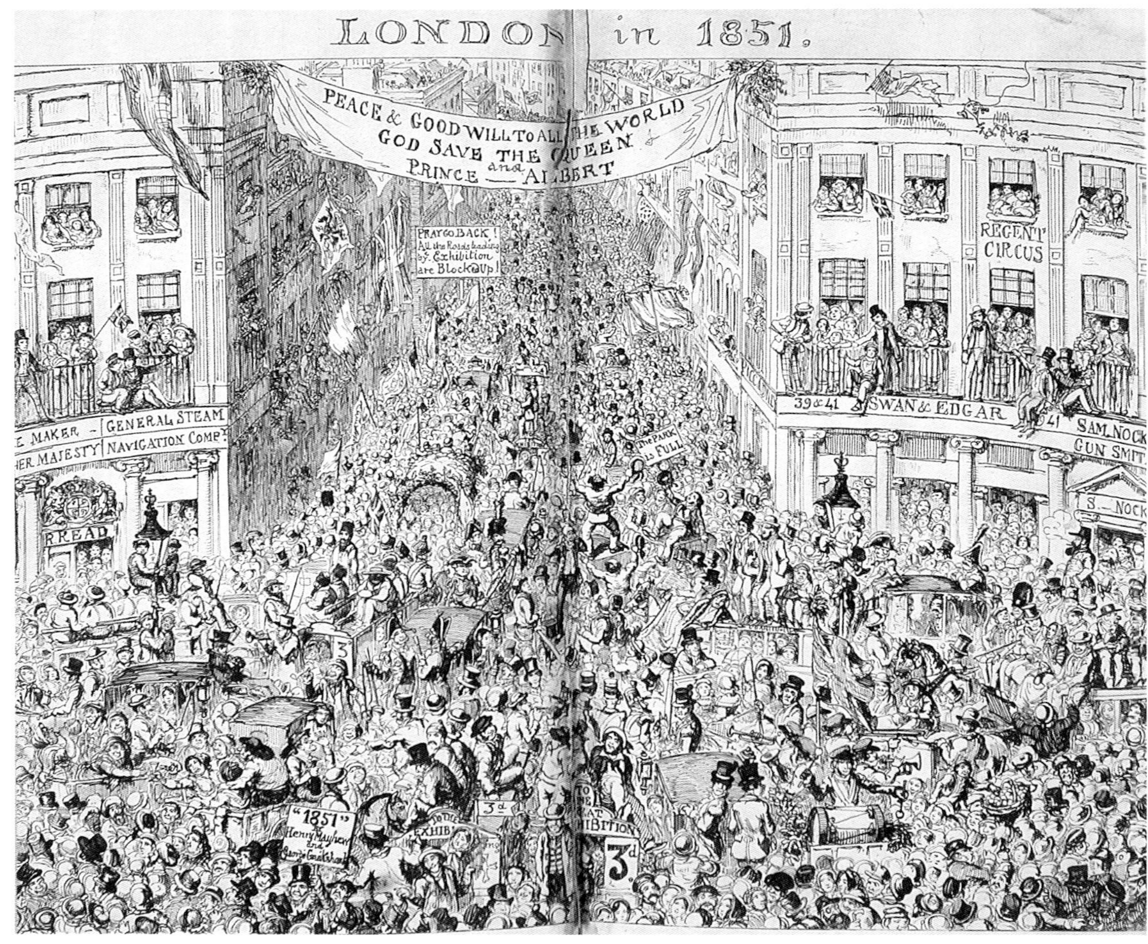

59. George Cruikshank (1792–1878), *London in 1851* (from Henry Mayhew, *London in 1851; or the Adventures of Mr and Mrs Sandboys*), 1851. Guildhall Library, City of London.

Already the largest industrial and commercial city in the world, London experienced a six-fold increase in population to more than 6.5 million during the first half-century. The London crowd was acknowledged as an extraordinary phenomenon. Foreigners reacted to it with amazement, but residents like Mayhew and John Binny could not take it for granted either. It was the extreme contrasts of the crowd as well as the size which struck them, and which, they noted, distinguished London 'from all other towns and cities in the world'.[5]

The attraction was what Victorians called the 'Anthropology' of the London crowd: its diverse physical make-up in terms of race, class and individual type, and the unlimited scope it offered for the student of human nature. In the Victorian age, Physiognomy or the study of character from external features was an absorbing business, and one which was practised by professional anthropologists as well as amateurs like Charles Dickens and Frith himself. Faces were there to be 'read' in the most literal sense, and the London crowd supplied the greatest variety. This physiognomical interest is clearly expressed in Dickens's *Boz* and other *Sketches*, in which the writer travels through the city, observing and classifying familiar human types. These were illustrated by George Cruikshank (1792–1878), one of the most prolific of all portrayers of London life, and Dickens's other main illustrator, Hablot K. Browne (1815–82), who adopted the pseudonym of 'Phiz' – short for physiognomy – in order to emphasize his main purpose. During the 1850s especially, places of work and entertainment, such as Billingsgate Market, Covent Garden, Cremorne, railway stations, international exhibitions – anywhere where crowds congregated – increasingly attracted the attention of artists and writers (Fig. 59).

Frith had broken new ground with his portrayal of ordinary families in their drab everyday dress, lounging and amusing themselves on Ramsgate sands; but his two subsequent panoramas were much more challenging. His choice of Derby Day (Fig. 61) for his second subject was a stroke of genius; for in Victoria's day the Derby was the major national holiday of the year, when even Parliament closed down to join the exodus to Epsom Downs. In the words of the *Illustrated London News*, the Derby provided 'the most astonishing, the most varied . . . and the most glorious spectacle that ever was or ever can be, under any circumstances, visible to mortal eyes.'[6] Frith felt the attraction of what he called the 'kaleidoscopic aspect of the crowd'[7] as strongly as the majority of the British public did. He was an avowed physiognomist, describing the face as 'a sure index of character',[8] and he determined to paint 'the infinite variety of everyday life' which Epsom Downs presented.[9] Every year, illustrators such as John Leech (1816–64) and Dickie Doyle (1824–83) responded enthusiastically to the occasion, and the degree to which their characters correspond with Frith's suggests how truthfully they all recorded the habitués of the scene (Fig. 60).

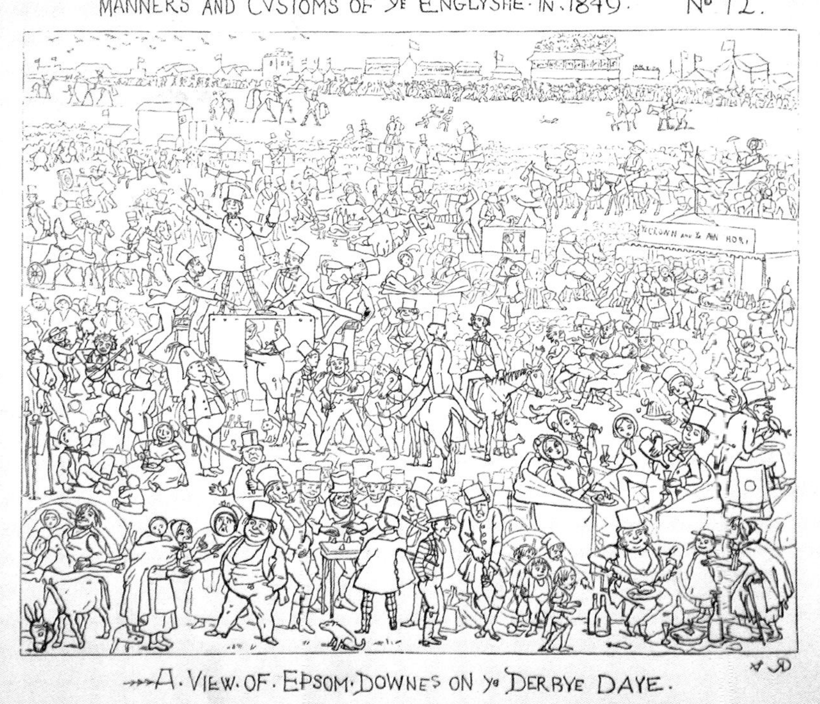

60. Dickie Doyle (1824–83), *A View of Epsom Downs on ye Derbye Day* (from *Manners and Customs of Ye Erglyshe in 1849*), 1849. Guildhall Library, City of London.

It was a Bacchanalian occasion on which respectable Victorians, even ladies, got drunk and misbehaved, and Frith included elements which led moralists to censure the painting. On top of the carriage in the centre, a group of dishevelled gentlemen quaff champagne with prostitutes; and various criminal types and other representatives of the *demi-monde* appear within the crowd. In the background, a man lies comatose, his top hat over his face, and a fight breaks out over a gaming table. The innate raffishness of the occasion was further enhanced by the fact that conventional class barriers were entirely abolished for the day. This 'temporary saturnalia of social equality', as the *Illustrated London News* described it, was the one occasion of the year when people were prepared to 'positively hob and nob with those palpably inferior to them in station . . . Liberty, equality, and fraternity' being qualities 'very strongly insisted upon on the Derby Day'.[10] Derby Day was a unique event: 'the great leveller'; the day when 'poverty elbows pride, and wretchedness stalks cheek-by-jowl with wealth . . . the snob pushes by the gentleman, and the cad insinuates himself amongst the cream of the land.'[11]

Derby Day presented a virtual microcosm of contemporary society, and Frith exploited this to the full, in a jostling, meandering crowd of almost ninety figures organized in groups, each with its own dramatic focus. Every person is individualised in terms of character and class: itinerant acrobats, gangs of gypsies and pickpocketing boys, policemen, and fraudsters with their gaming tables. Especially striking are the neglected mistress, whose bored lover – a 'vicious voluptuary'[12] – lolls against their carriage, and the foolish youth in top hat and checked trousers who has lost his money, watch and shirt studs to a gang of thimble riggers similar to one which had almost fleeced Frith on his first visit to the Derby two years previously.[13] The trick of these 'heartless

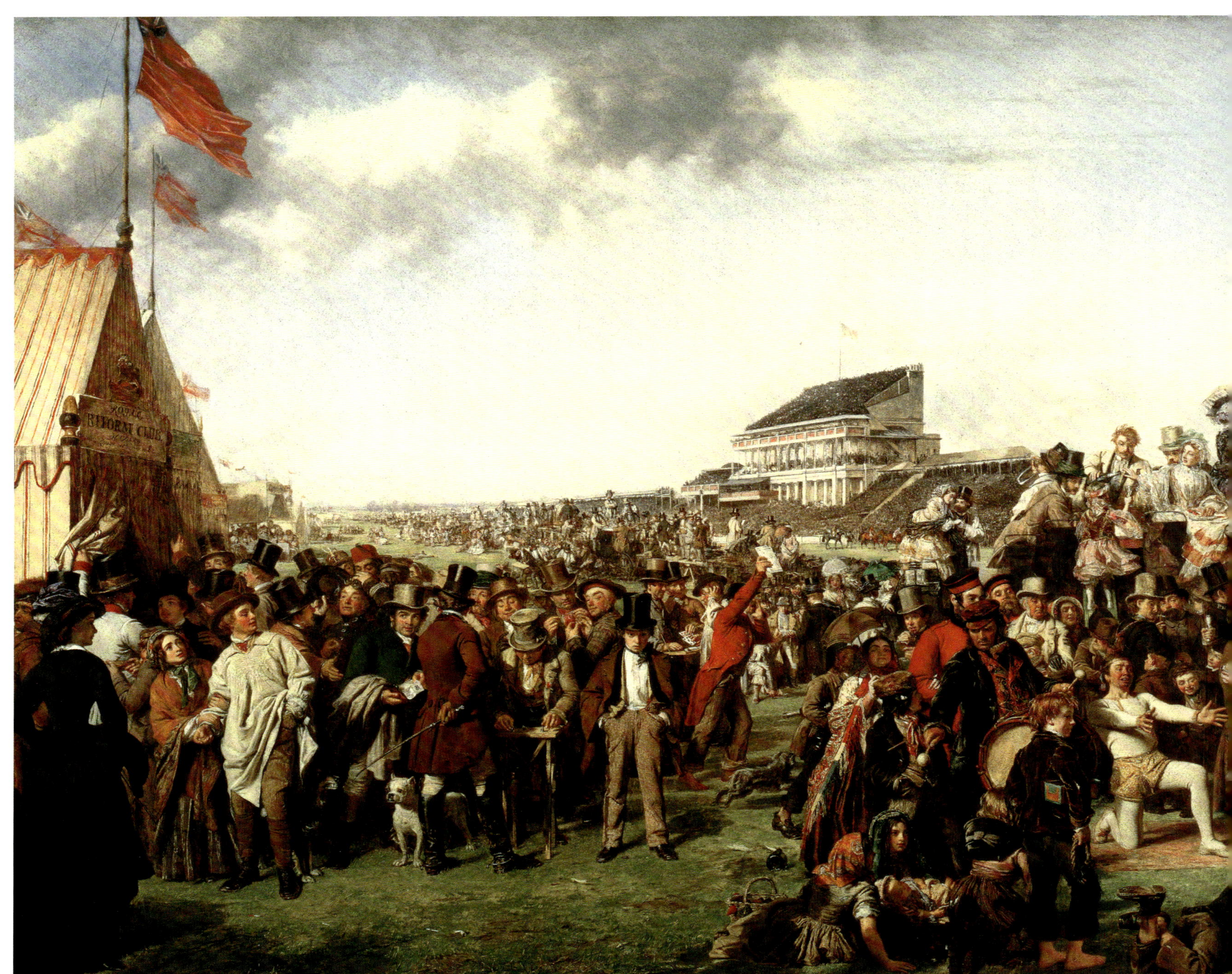

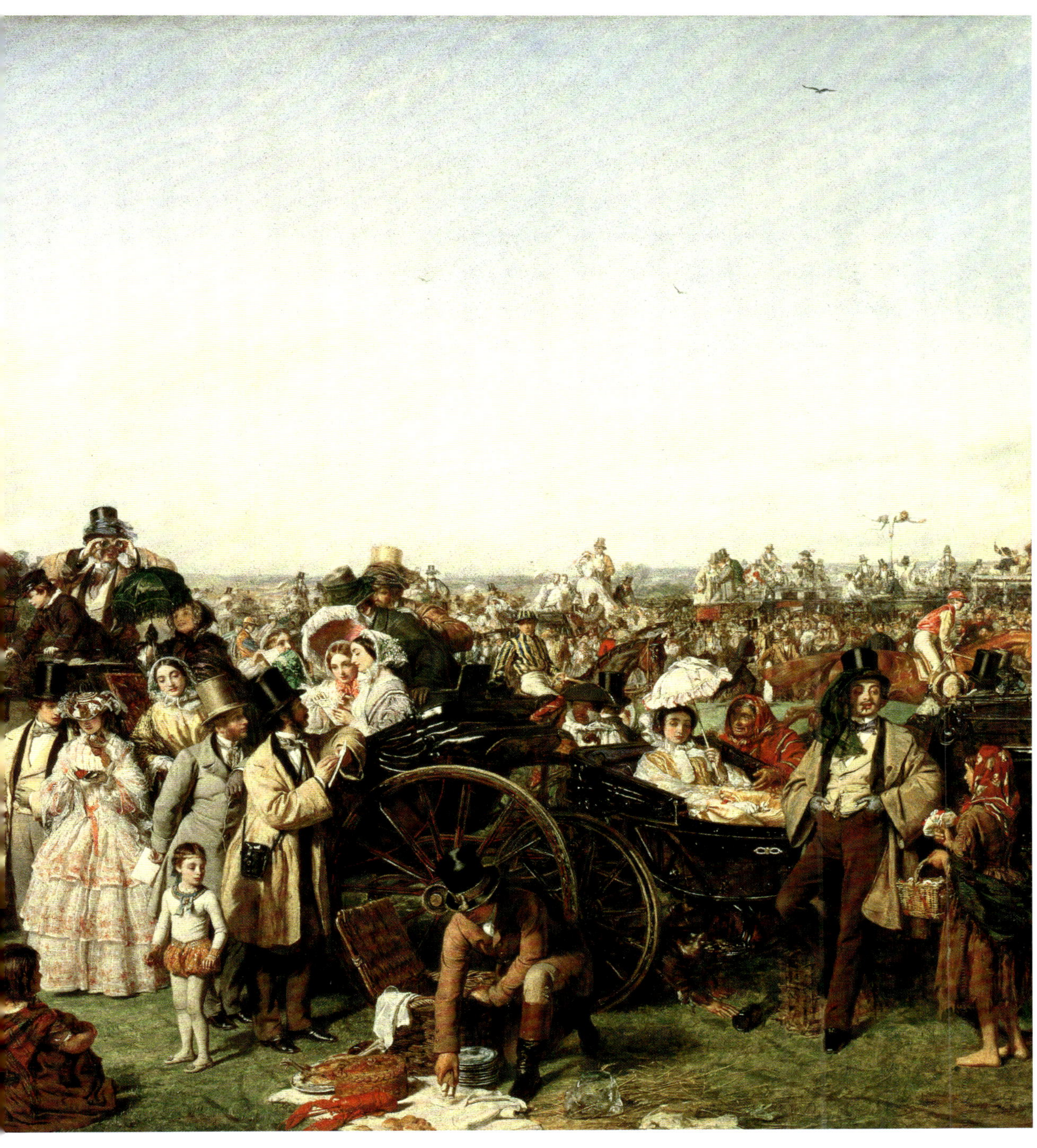

61. *The Derby Day*, 1858. Tate, London.

62. William McConnell (1833–67), *The Railway Station* (from George Augustus Sala, *Twice Around the Clock, or The Hours of the Day and Night in London*), 1859. Guildhall Library, City of London.

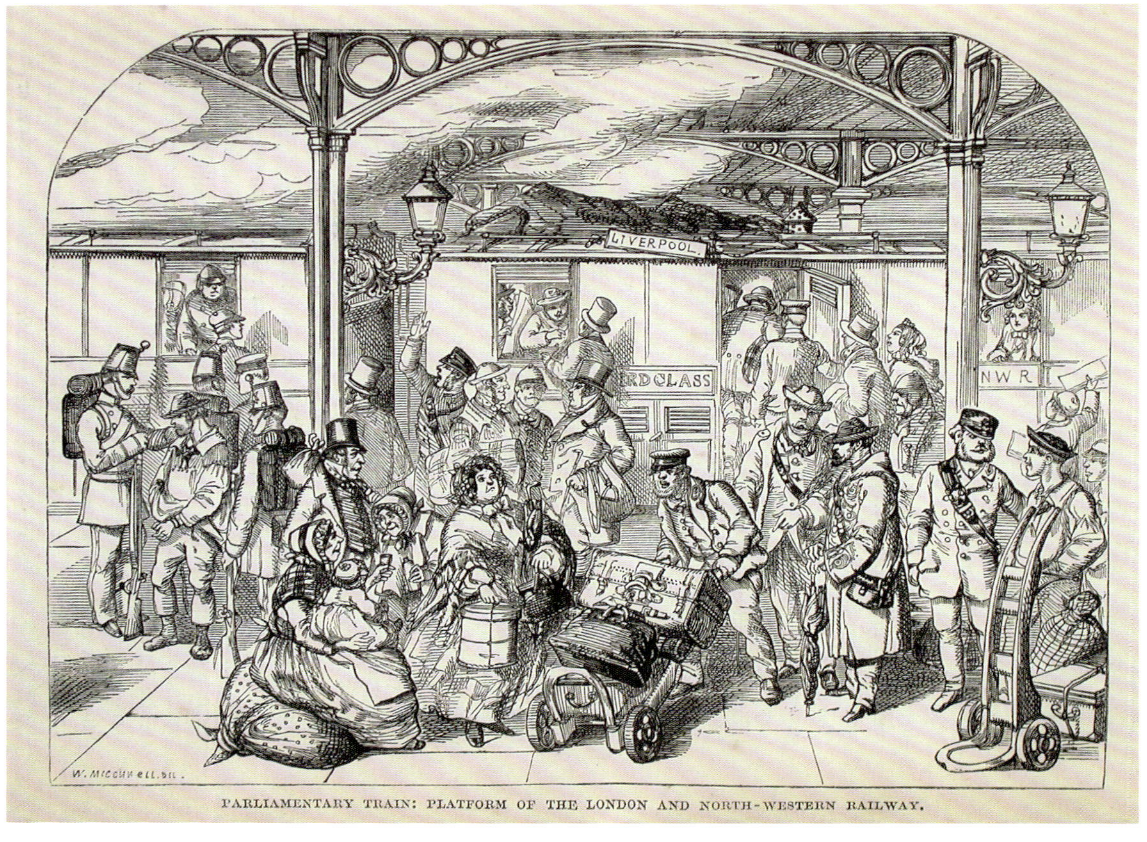

bloodsuckers' and 'ghouls'[14] was to use a false pea, made from a piece of rolled bread which could be picked up on the edge of the thimble. Episodes such as this were already history by the time Frith finished the picture, for all gaming tables had been banned by 1858.

Few paintings have ever earned such universal acclaim. It was recognized as a unique historical record of a significant social event, and critics marvelled at its fidelity. A policeman was called in to stand guard at the Academy, and a protective rail set up to control the spectators: the first of six which would advertise Frith's huge popularity over many years. He wrote delightedly of the 'invidious . . . distinction' thus granted him and the fact that 'thirteen of the elderly Academicians took to their beds in fits of bile and envy'.[15] In recognition of its importance, its purchaser, Jacob Bell, bequeathed the painting to the National Gallery; but although he died in 1859 its arrival was delayed for six years. As part of a massive publicity campaign organized by the owner of the copyright, Ernest Gambart, *Derby Day* toured the provinces and visited Europe before moving on to the United States and Australia. As late as 1922, it remained, according to Walter Sickert, 'the most popular . . . [and] the most unaffectedly enjoyed' picture in the collection.[16]

Derby Day was a hard act to follow, but Frith found a worthy successor in *The Railway Station* (Fig. 63), possibly suggested to him by one of William McConnell's illustrations to G. A. Sala's celebrated book on London life (Fig. 62). McConnell's platform crowd is confined to the third class, and includes, like Frith's, a group of soldiers with a raw recruit, a pair of foreigners, a sailor, a rather less helpful porter than those Frith shows, oblivious to the overladen woman who almost runs into him; and various other people whose physiognomies reflect their low social status.

The Railway Station setting reflects that affirmative response to industrial progress which had been celebrated in the Great Exhibition of 1851, but which was scarcely to outlast the decade. Included in the picture is the small figure of Louis Victor Flatow (conversing with the engine driver) – the print dealer who planned every part of the painting with Frith in what was a carefully calculated business deal. The main appeal is, again, to the interest in contemporary human types, all of them identifiable, and described in detail in a lengthy pamphlet written by the journalist Tom Taylor in collaboration with Frith. Taylor suggested that the painting itself should be examined in just the same way 'as we might scan some actual crowd on a railway platform, if time and train would stay for us'.[17] All town dwellers would feel an affinity with this scene: with its types, its incidents, its dramas; 'for who has not', as the *Art Journal* critic asked, 'some time or other, watched the varied groups assembled at a railway station?'[18]

The urban ugliness of the railway station made the setting a more daring choice than Epsom Downs. The lofty pillars and roof girders of Paddington station and its handsome glass lanterns (painted for Frith by a young architect, W. Scott Morton) soar above the crowd gathered on Platform One. It was not until Gladstone's Cheap Trains Act of 1844 that third-class passengers were allowed to travel in covered coaches and with the first and second, instead of being attached to goods trains; and it was not until about 1860, two years after Frith's painting was exhibited, that third-class passengers were allowed to use the faster trains timed to leave Paddington at reasonable hours of the day.[19] These recent developments gave added topicality to Frith's choice. Exhibited singly, *The Railway Station* caused as great a sensation as *Derby Day* and was equally successful commercially.[20]

The London art world had been tantalized for two years by news of *The Railway Station's* progress, which had been reported in *the Art Journal* and elsewhere as part of an advance publicity campaign engineered by Flatow. When it went on show at the Haymarket in April 1862, it fulfilled all expectations. More than 21,000 people paid to see it,[21] and it was reviewed at great length in every newspaper and magazine. It was subsequently exhibited at a gallery in Cornhill before touring the British Isles for several years.

Flatow's aim was to outdo *Derby Day*, and *The Railway Station* is considerably larger. Frith was at the height of his technical powers, and he ensured that every single face and figure yielded its full burden in terms of physiognomy and expression. With supreme artistry the crowd is arranged in interlinked groups. To the far left, a huntsman prepares his setters for the dog-wagon, and a respectable elderly lady who is hoping to smuggle her precious Maltese terrier into a carriage, is ordered to follow his example. On the other side, a bride who is at the centre of an aristocratic wedding party, bids her sisters goodbye; her bright future providing a dramatic contrast with that of the ashen faced man arrested just as he is about to board the train. Educated, well-dressed and respectable in appearance, he is clearly a 'superior' type of criminal who has committed a crime which requires some intelligence – forgery or perhaps some financial fraud, and more the result of weakness than of innate evil (Fig. 64). In this he is distinguished from the 'born' criminal: the coarse-featured, low-class villain just behind them, who has been recruited by the army, and whose widowed mother weeps on his shoulder. Frith's criminal conformed exactly with popular preconceptions as to what constituted 'a dissipated vagabond of the true London breed',[22] and the critics responded accordingly. As the *Daily News* sternly proclaimed: 'In the hardened roguish face, the yellow unwholesome complexion . . . "fast" shooting-jacket . . . and velveteen cap, we seem to read "town-scamp", "betting-man", "blackleg", and "sot".'[23] Conceived with the same regard to physiognomical expectation, every other figure in the painting was guaranteed the response which Frith intended.

For the two detectives arresting the superior criminal, Frith turned to the real world, recording

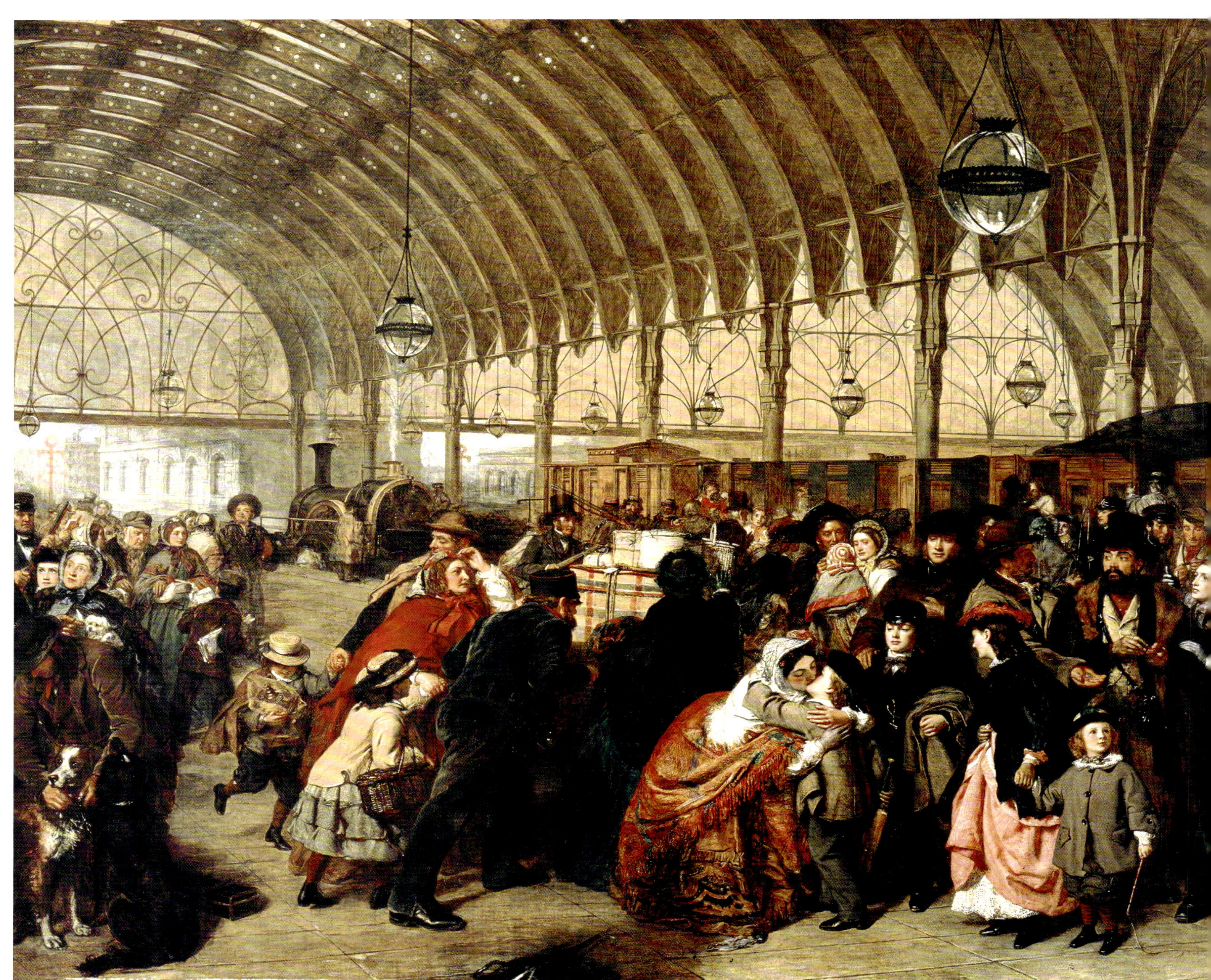

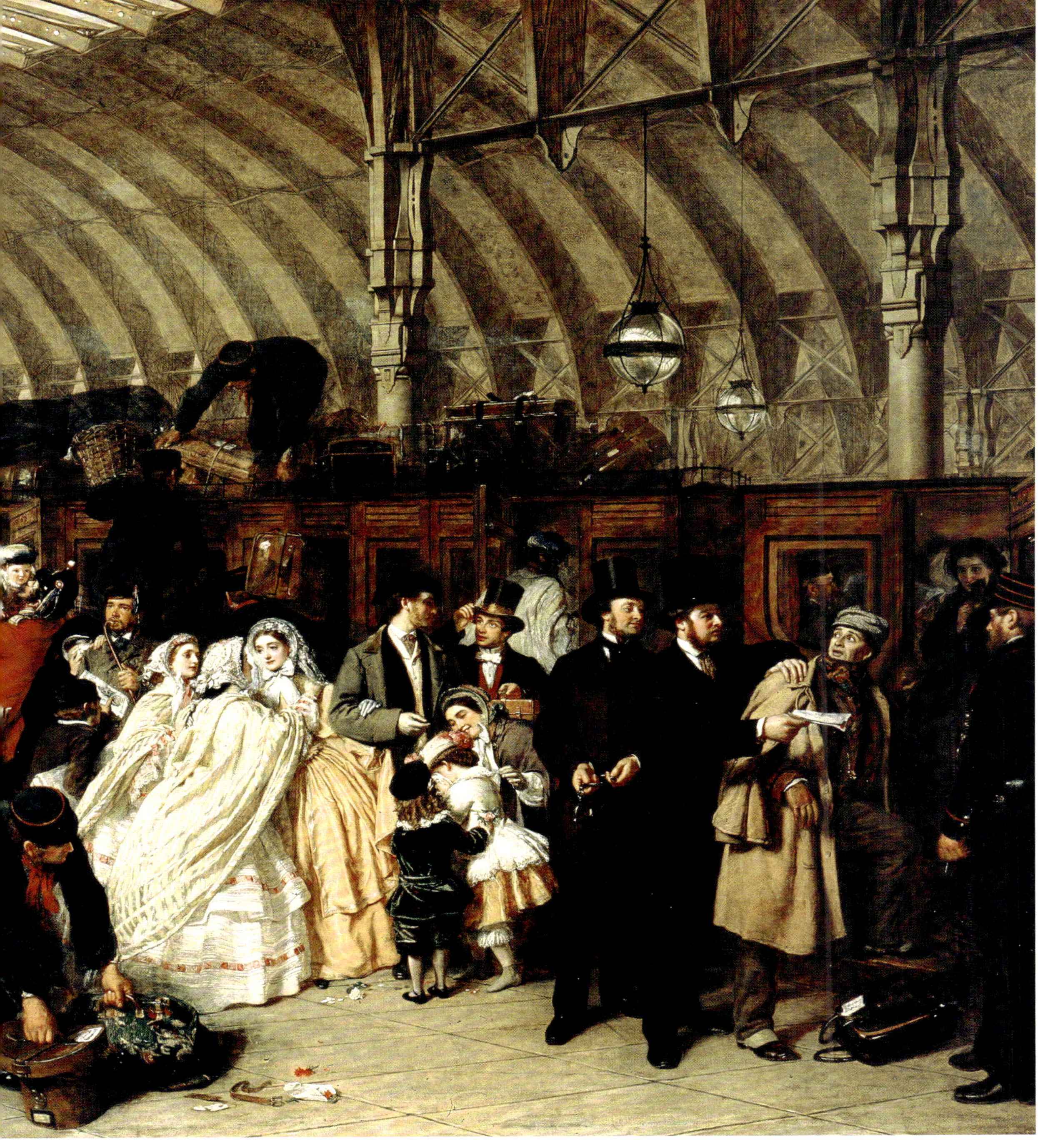

63. *The Railway Station*, 1862. Royal Holloway, University of London.

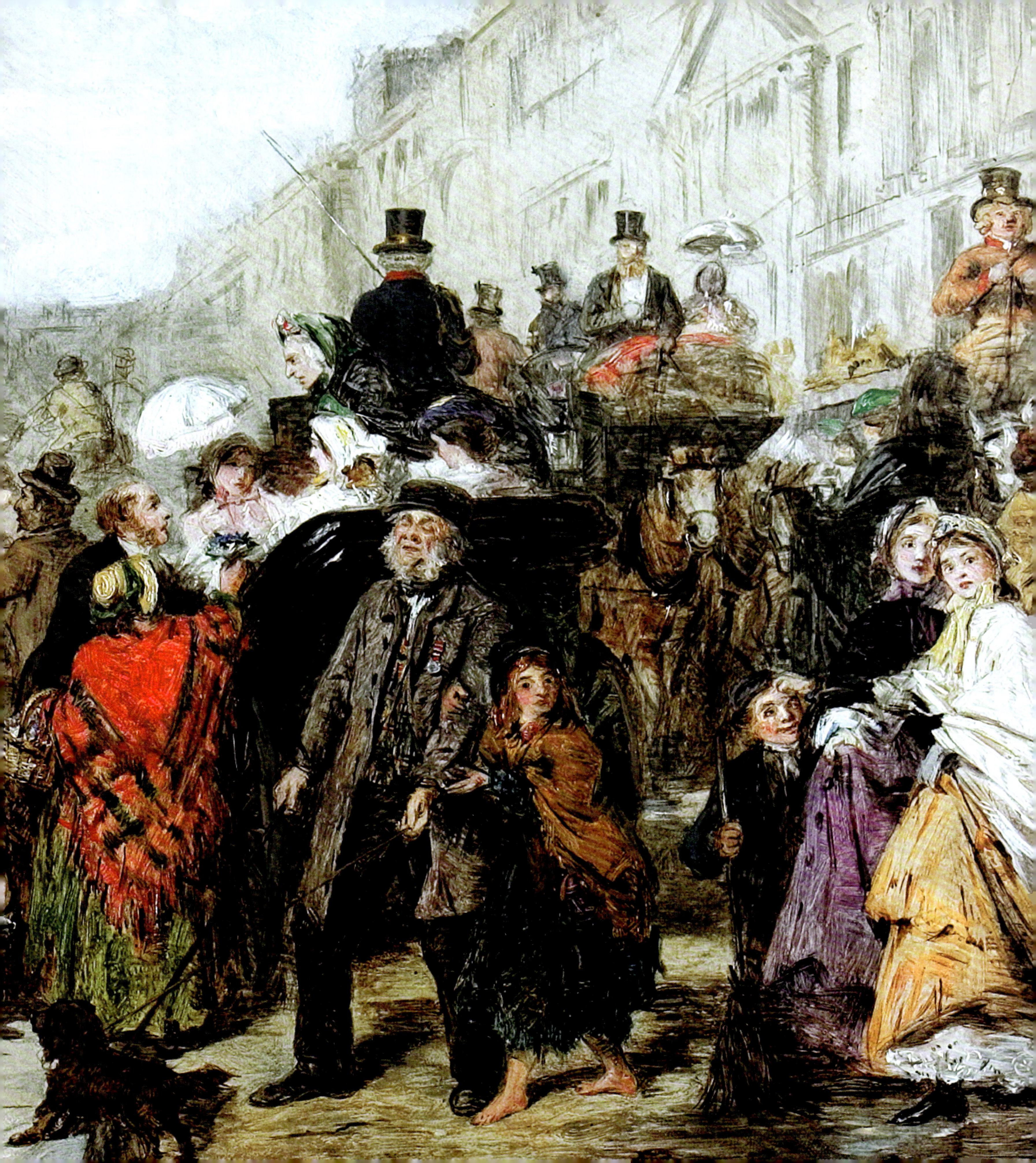

for posterity the appearance of two detective-sergeants of the City of London Police, Michael Haydon and James Brett. Frith was assiduous in seeking out models whose every feature fitted his preconceived characters, sending out scouts with strict instructions as to exactly which shape of nose or other feature he required: 'Fair or dark, long nose or short . . . Roman or acquiline, tall figure or small'.[24] Haydon and Brett epitomize the ideal lower middle-class type. They were as Taylor said, exactly the kind of 'comely, well-dressed, well-appointed persons' who might be depended on to maintain law and order.[25] Of a higher rank are Frith and his family who appear at the centre of the picture, proudly representative of the class which formed the backbone of Victorian Society. He did not hesitate to make fun of a family of a lower rank – the disorganized tradesman's bustling in from the left and colliding with a luggage trolley, in that flurry of 'haste and disquietude' which was associated with people of their rank.[26] A self-made man who could afford later to send his own sons to Harrow, Frith chose to show his family in various states of emotion as the two boys set off for the start of a new term; but he was not quite the virtuous paterfamilias that he would have us believe. Already he had a mistress and three illegitimate children; and indeed he created a veritable crowd of his own in the seventeen surviving children he fathered in total.

The lower levels of society are represented by soldiers, sailors, sportsmen, and visitors from the country. Of the more obtrusive, the cabby – a coarse, belligerent English 'bull-dog' type – thrusts himself amongst his social superiors, demanding further payment from a nervous foreigner and his more combative wife. A boy selling copies of *Punch* is similarly assertive, while the railway officials make a more respectful foray amongst them. The result was judged to be a faithful selection from London life: 'just the mingled classes which may be seen every day at our chief railway stations – and every one of them extraordinarily true to life.'[27] Frith's *Railway Station* was never to be equalled, although in the 1870s George Earl (1824–1908) produced a pair clearly inspired by him which are now missing, and reworked the same theme in *Going North, King's Cross Station* (1893) and *Coming South, Perth Station* (1895), now in the National Rail Museum, York.[28]

Regrettably, another important project, three further London scenes, commissioned by Ernest Gambart in 1862 for the huge sum of £10,000, only reached the sketch stage (Figs 41, 43, 44); for at the Queen's request Frith was obliged to paint the wedding of the Prince of Wales, an uncongenial task, which occupied him until 1864.[29] But despite the lack of hard-edged detail in the sketches, Frith's gifts for characterization and the organizing of a series of incidents into a convincing narrative are abundantly clear.

The first of them, *Morning*, shows Covent Garden still occupied by drifters from the previous night. A homeless family camp under the portico to the right, and a lone prostitute leans against a lamppost; young swells gravitate to the coffee stall and two burglars undergo dramatic arrest in the centre. *Noon: Regent Street* is the busiest scene with its mixture of carriages and pedestrians, who include a dog-seller, a beggar girl with her blind grandfather and a crossing sweeper (Fig. 64). The characteristics and costumes of the figures are clearly distinguished; as in, for example, the dog-seller's furtive expression, his 'fast' fur cap and side whiskers, the cheeky smile of the little crossing sweeper, and the belligerent attitude of the burly cab driver. In *Night: the Haymarket*, a poor bare-footed family are contrasted with an upper-class group towards the right, and a prostitute enviously observes the tender care with which the women are treated by their husbands.

Frith's interest in London street life also emerges in two smaller examples, *For Better, For Worse* (Fig. 65) and *Poverty and Wealth* (Fig. 66), both of which attracted considerable attention. The first of these was suggested by a wedding which Frith saw in Bayswater, and he worked hard to assemble sufficiently diverse types to make up what the *Times* described as 'the regular street crowd' which inevitably gathers on such occasions.[30] The unpredictability of the married state,

Facing page
64. *Noon – Regent Street*, 1862. Private Collection. Detail of Fig. 43, the blind beggar with his granddaughter, and the crossing sweeper.

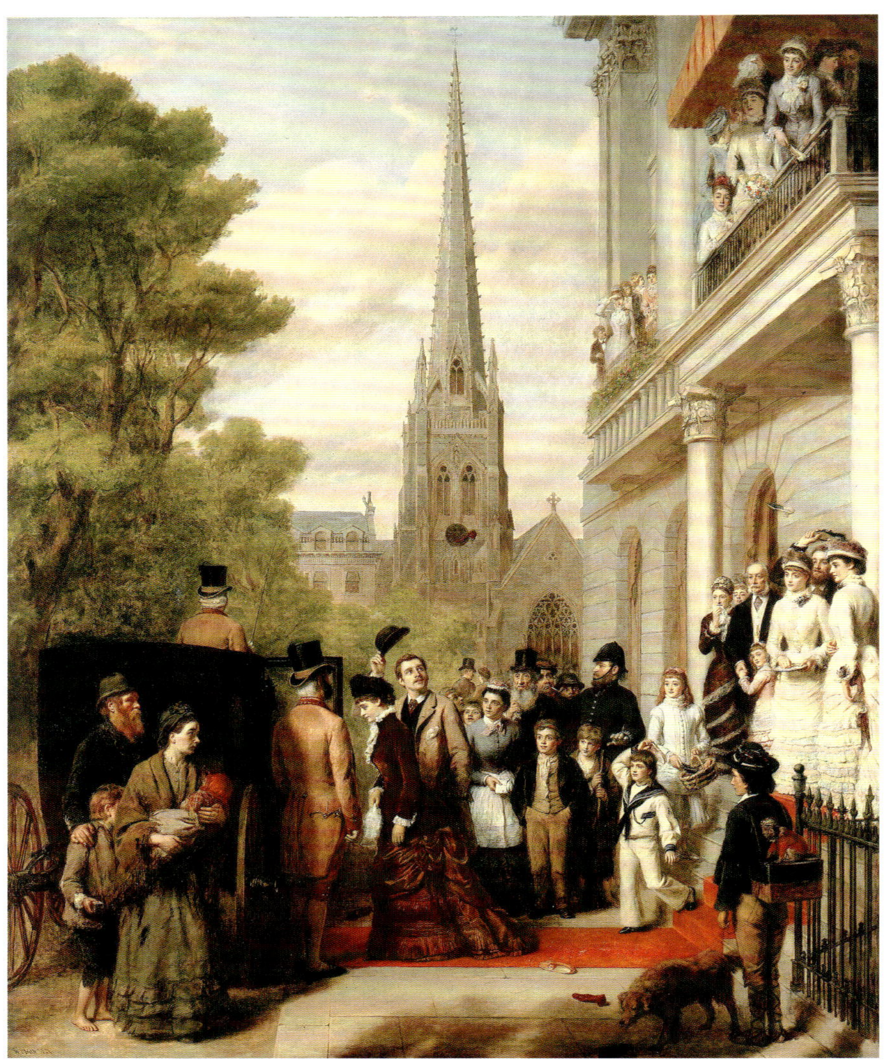

65. *'For Better – For Worse'*, 1881. Private Collection.

and its varying consequences for rich and poor, is suggested in the contrast between the affluent couple, departing for their honeymoon from a large house close to Christ Church, Lancaster Square, and another couple with two children who have been reduced to beggary. With mixed emotions, members of the family watch the final departure of a beloved daughter and sister, while a policeman maintains order amongst an inquisitive audience which includes a servant girl, a bearded Jewish clothes seller, a coarse-featured oaf smoking a cigarette, and a young Italian organ-grinder, whose monkey gave Frith infinite trouble and even attacked his picture.[31] The prospects for happiness would have been much on Frith's mind as he painted it, for in January of 1881, after his first wife's death, he had married his long-term mistress, Mary Alford.

In *Poverty and Wealth*, which was prominently hung at the Royal Academy, affluent adults and children in an open carriage in Bond Street are contrasted with a queue of poor people, waiting to acquire unsold fish cheaply at the end of the day. *The Times* dismissed it as 'one of those pictures of facile contrasts and obvious sentiment which this artist commonly prefers',[32] but the *Athenaeum* critic, who noted Frith's penchant for contrasting 'various social grades', thought the

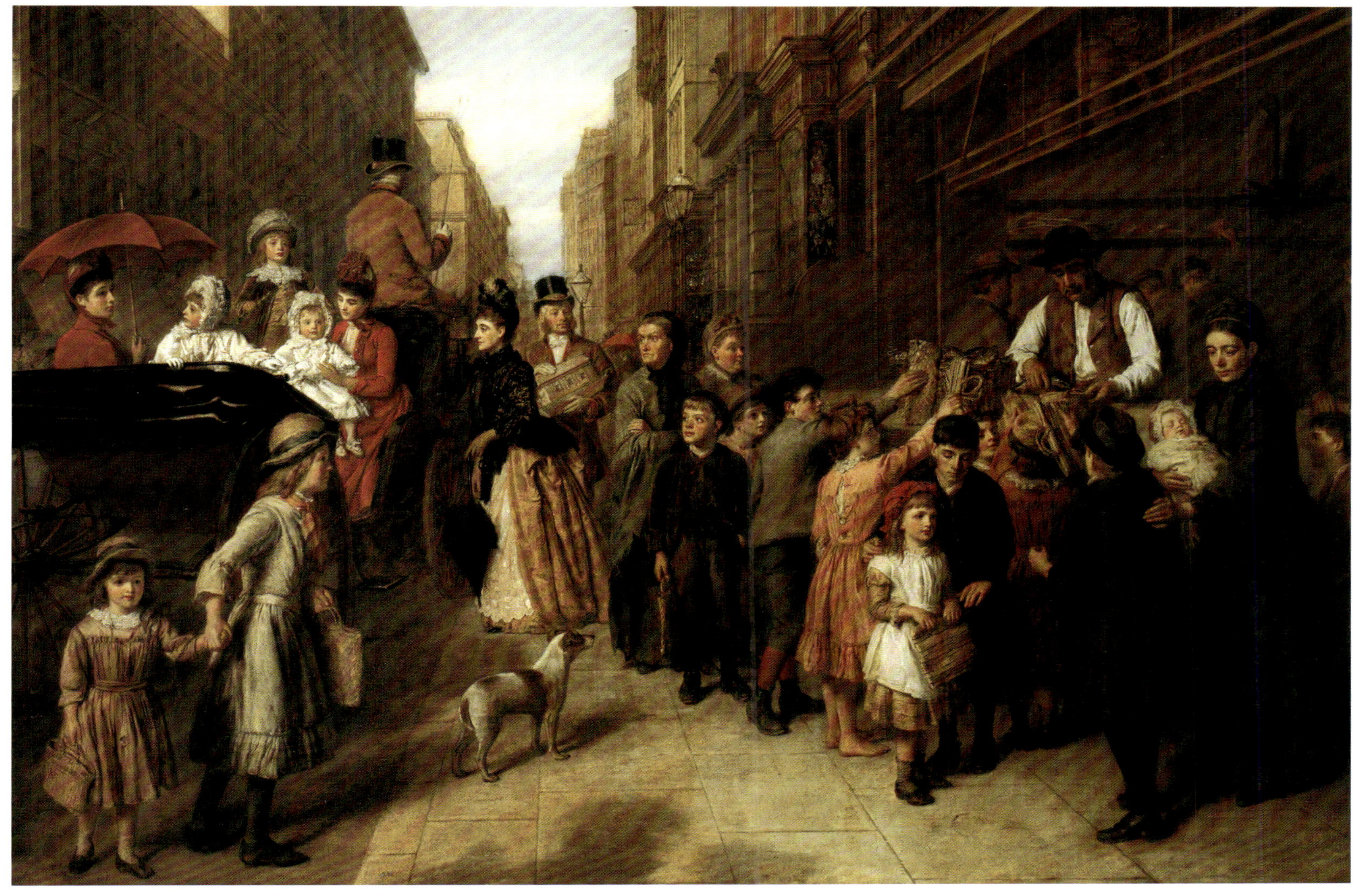

66. *Poverty and Wealth*, 1888. The Leicester Galleries, London.

subject well-chosen. While complaining that his ladies looked vulgar and his babies overdressed, the critic concluded that Frith had seldom done better than with the 'dingy urchins and dishevelled women', who include an 'elderly widow (not innocent of gin)' to the right, a number of girls, and an 'ill-fed, but still pretty boy in the middle'.[33]

The last major London crowd scene which Frith produced was a marked departure from his previous ones. *The Private View of the Royal Academy, 1881* (Fig. 67) was a satire on the contemporary Aesthetic Movement, which – also in 1881 – had provided the subject of Gilbert and Sullivan's satirical operetta, *Patience*. It was of sufficient topical interest to earn Frith his sixth and final rail at the Academy of 1883. Oscar Wilde, Lily Langtry and Ellen Terry are included as worshippers of 'The Beautiful', while John Millais and Anthony Trollope as well as Frith himself, stand for good old-fashioned Common Sense. Piqued by Frith's portrayal of him in *The Private View*, Wilde got his revenge by mocking Frith as both author and artist in one of his wittiest dialogues; and elsewhere credited him with having 'done so much to elevate painting to the dignity of photography'.[34] For Wilde and others, including John Ruskin and J. A. M. Whistler, he would always

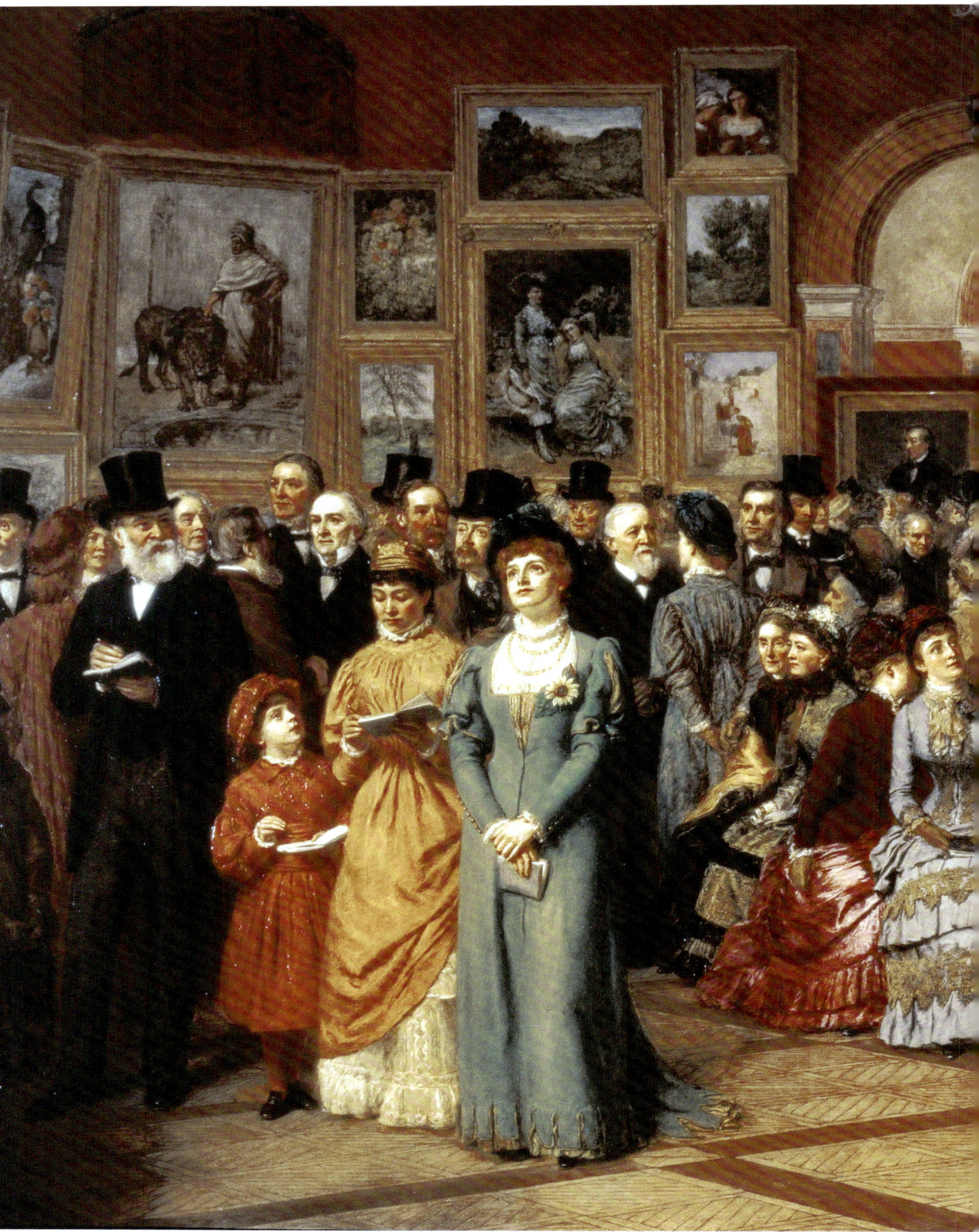

67. *Private View at the Royal Academy, 1881*, 1883. Private Collection.

Among the identifiable figures is 'the homely figure' of Trollope on the left with top hat and exhibition catalogue, looking at an aesthetically dressed child and two women (the one with the sunflower was modelled by Miss Jenny Trip, a professional model whom Frith dismissed for unpunctuality); behind them stand Gladstone and (between the two women) Tenniel and Du Maurier (although in his Autobiography Frith lists them as being on the other side of the picture). In the centre, Leighton talks to Lady Londsale (seated on the ottoman, with Frith himself in the background directly above her) and to their right stand the Archbishop of York and Lily Langtry. Oscar Wilde is the focus of the group on the right, which includes Ellen Terry, Henry Irving, G. A. Sala (in the white waistcoat) and Millais in the top hat on the extreme right.

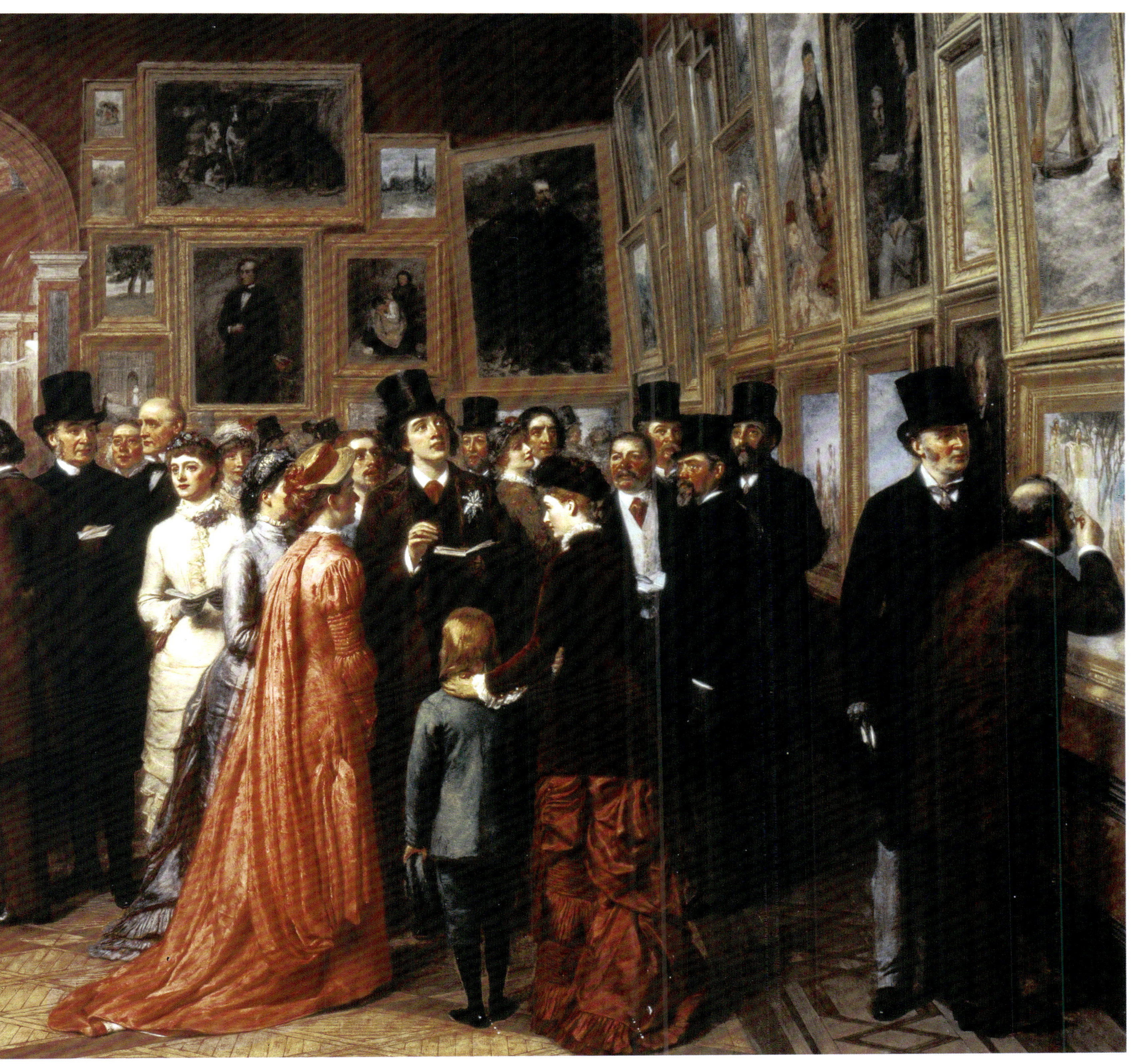

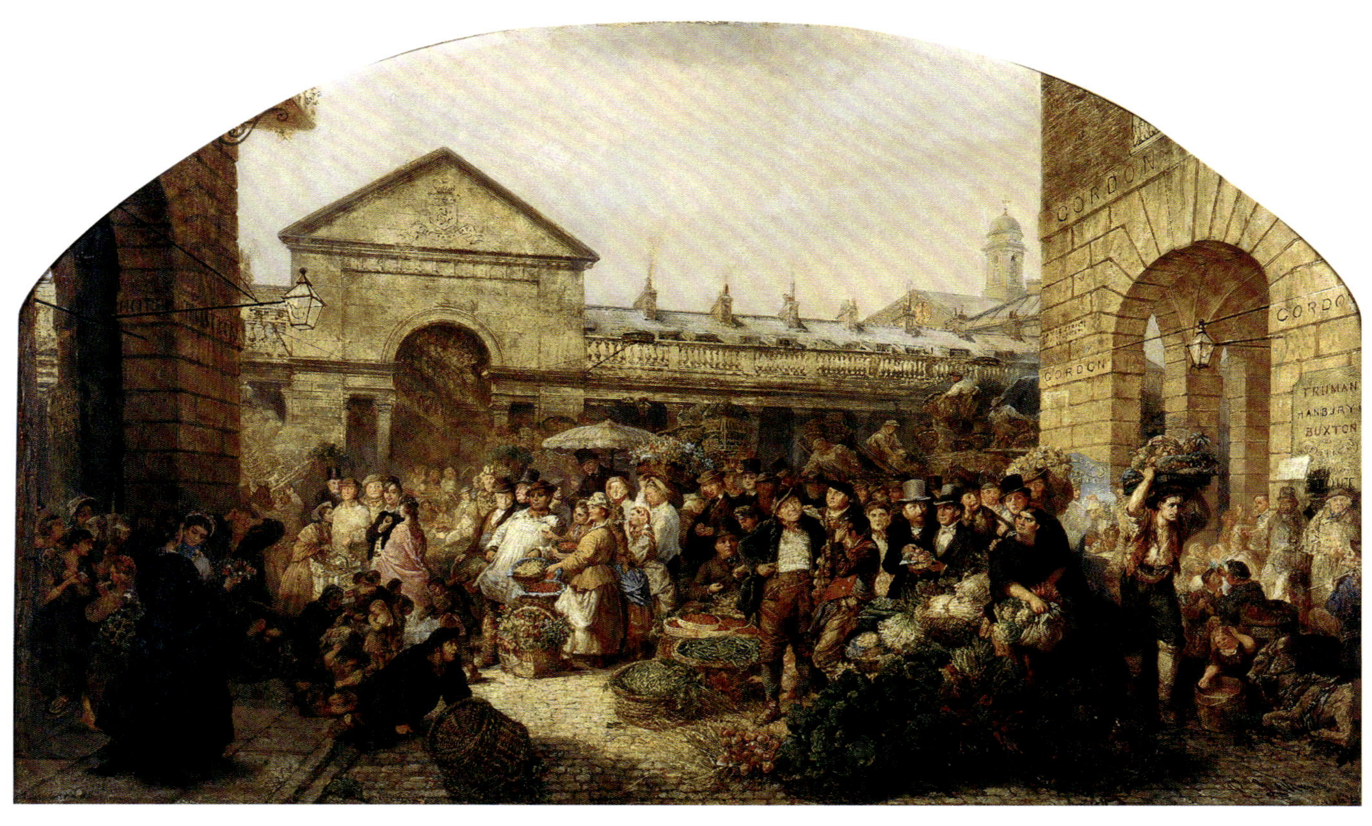
TRUMAN
HANBURY
BUXTON

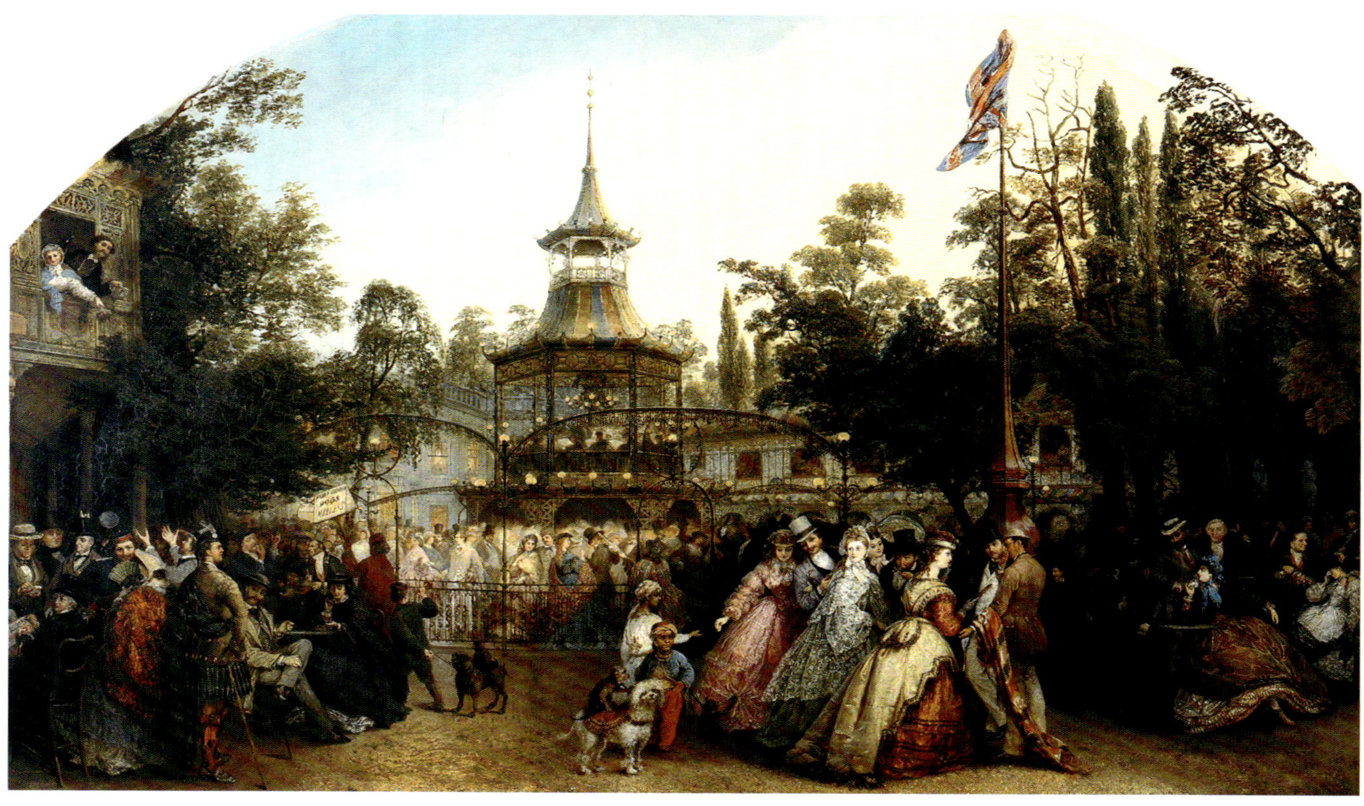

remain the touchstone of artistic philistinism. Frith proudly asserted his reactionary opinions in the books and articles he wrote in later life. To him Aestheticism was pretentious nonsense, and Pre-Raphaelitism 'a ridiculous movement' of no lasting importance. He dismissed the works of the Impressionists as 'constant outrages on popular prejudice',[35] and classed French Realism and its British version as 'the fungi on the tree of [modern] art'.[36] Far removed from the artist in his ivory tower, Frith saw himself as a man of the people. It is significant that he appears as a member of the crowd in three of his panoramas, – to the far right of *Ramsgate Sands* as well as *The Railway Station* and *The Private View*. Not only as witness to, but also as an enthusiastic member of the London populace, Frith was able to relate to his audience in a way that guaranteed his success.

Facing page
68. Top: Phoebus Levin (fl. 1855–78), *Covent Garden Market*, 1864. Museum of London.

69. Bottom: Phoebus Levin (fl. 1855–78), *The Dancing Platform: Cremorne*, 1862. Museum of London.

FRITH'S FOLLOWERS

Among the artists who followed Frith, the German born Phoebus Levin (fl. 1836–78) included disreputable elements of the London crowd in his view of *Covent Garden* looking towards the central arcades from James Street (Fig. 68). To the far left are figures ravaged by poverty and a flighty looking prostitute with a bouquet; a little further back, a raffish youth in a jaunty cap suggestively offering an apple to another prostitute; to the right against the wall, a blind negro; within the arcade, a long-haired woman being ejected, fighting, from a pub; and in the foreground, a large, gypsy-ish, low-browed market woman who sullenly responds to the foreman's orders. Almost all of the Covent Garden buildings which Levin depicts are clearly identifiable today, but nothing remains of Cremorne Gardens, a notorious nightspot which he also depicted (Fig. 69). As the brother of one habitué, Dante Gabriel Rossetti, described it: 'a place of demi-reputable entertainment – dancing, music, fireworks, and assignations, with all their accompaniments and sequels.'[37] A contemporary illustration from *Fun* (Fig. 70) gives a clearer view of the supper boxes which Levin also includes and which catered for the assignations Rossetti mentions. In both painting and illustration the band is in full swing, and prostitutes and prospective customers are busily negotiating with each other. Levin's scene includes, in the right foreground, a group of flashily dressed prostitutes who have already acquired male escorts, one of whom gives money to a pair of Indian boys whose monkey is mounted on a large dog. Another Indian with an elephant appears in the illustration. On the dancing platform in Levin's painting, a stout wife knocks off the hat of her husband whom she has caught with another prostitute, and to the far right, a young woman collapses at a table in a drunken stupor.

One of several such scenes by John Ritchie (fl. 1858–75), *A Summer Day in Hyde Park* (Fig. 71), is much more sedate. The bright sun throws flickering shadows over a group of people gathered by the Serpentine. A flirtatious soldier exercises his charms on a young woman on the bench, to the disapproval of an elderly female; to the far left, a top-hatted gentleman reads a newspaper report of the Indian Mutiny, while a brutish looking child pickpocket hovers dangerously close. A mixture of poor and rich children play in close proximity – the former on an improvised rope swing; one man fishes; a family embark in a dinghy, and beyond the fence fashionable people in carriages and on horseback exchange greetings.

George Elgar Hicks (1824–1914) was a significant recorder of the London crowd, with scenes such as *Dividend Day. Bank of England* (1859), *Billingsgate Fish Market* (1861) and *The General Post-Office: One Minute to Six* (Fig. 72). The frantic race to catch the 6 o'clock post at the central office of St Martin's-le-Grand was a daily occurrence in

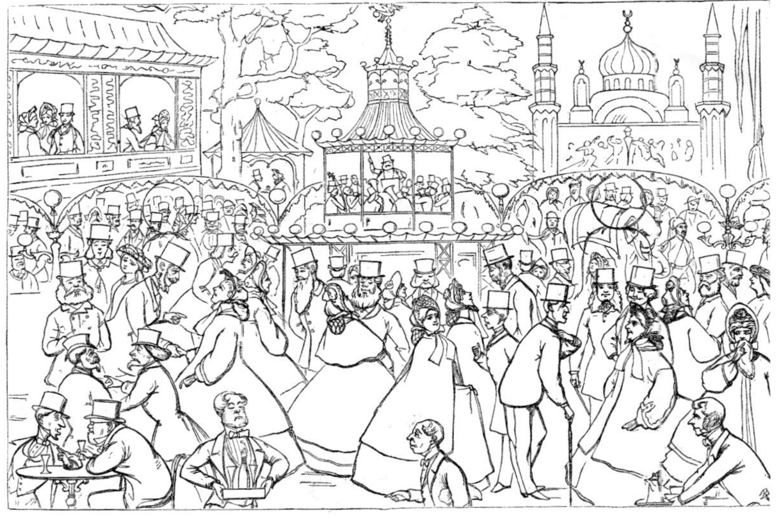

70. Anon., *A Visit to Cremorne*, published in *Fun*, 14 June 1862. Private Collection.

71. John Ritchie (fl. 1858–75), *A Summer Day in Hyde Park*, 1858. Museum of London.

72. George Elgar Hicks (1824–1914), *The General Post-Office: One Minute to Six*, 1860. Museum of London.

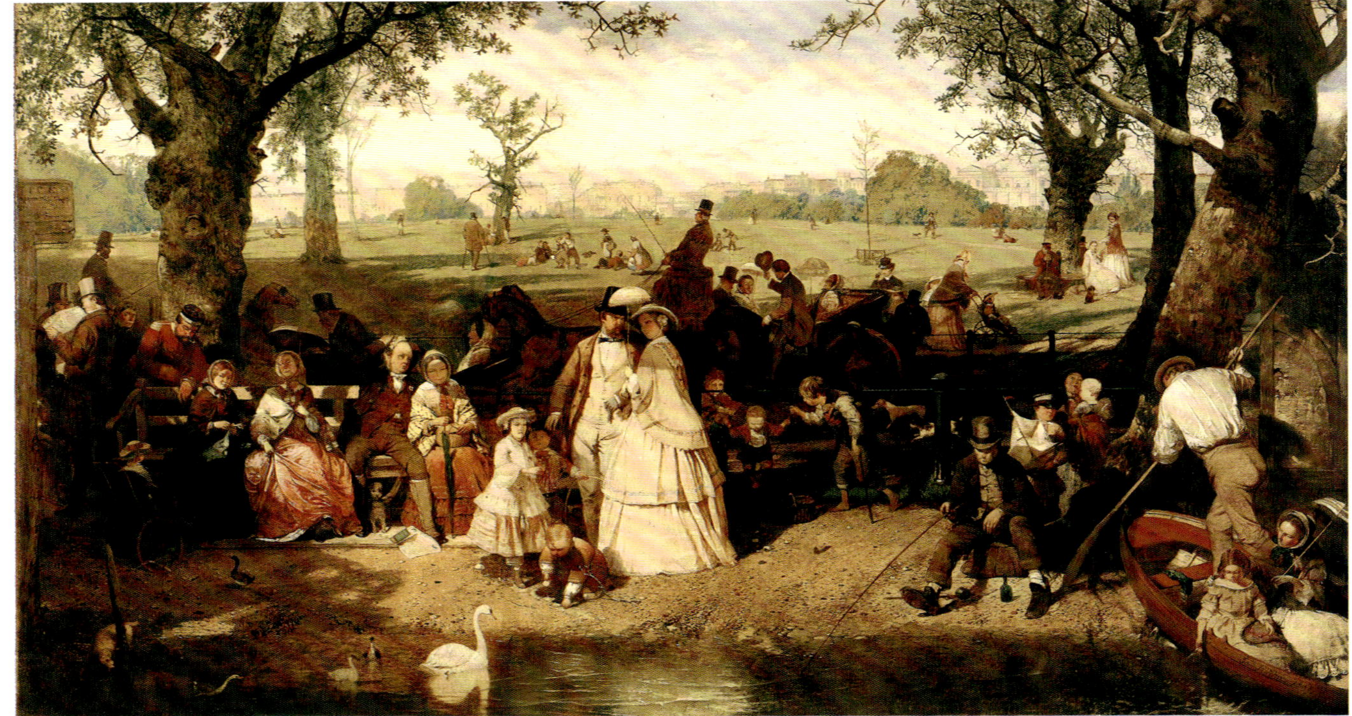

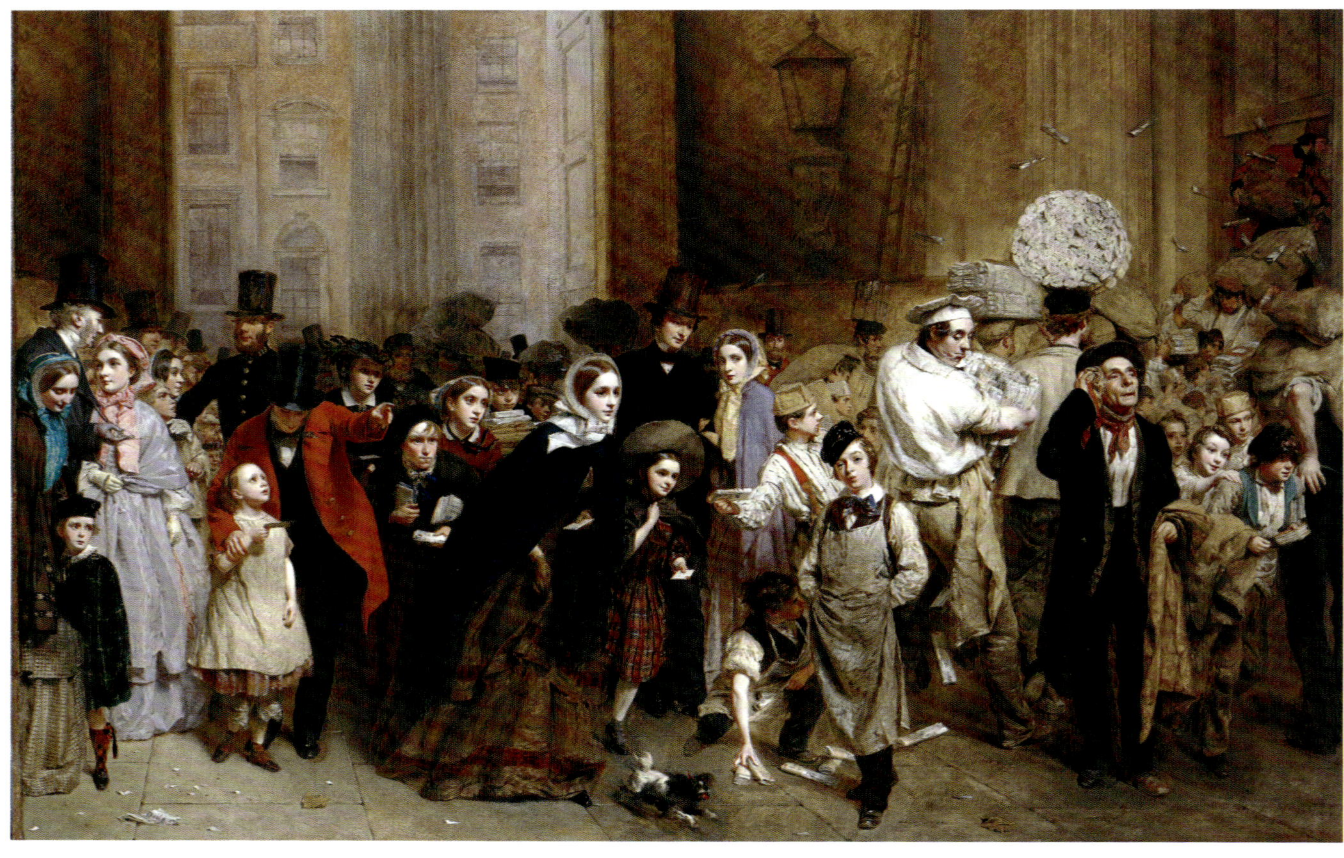

London and 'a mid-Victorian tourist attraction';[38] but no other painter recognized its potential. William McConnell's illustrations of this and other scenes were almost certainly an inspiration to Hicks. Charles Manby Smith's vivid account of the rush for the final post at St Martin's, and Dickens's description in *Household Words* of the busiest postal occasion of the year: St Valentine's Day, when 'a torrent of boys, and . . . a torrent of newspapers came tumbling in together pell-mell' are also likely sources.[39] Refined well-dressed ladies, gentlemen and children – even a small King Charles spaniel – mingle with a mild chaos of officials, urchins and servant girls, as items are hurled through openings to the far right, before the shutters close on the stroke of six.

Each individual face is minutely discriminated. Hicks's attention to physiognomy is clearly articulated in his *Guide to Figure Drawing* (1853) where he discusses the meaning of various forms of head shape. 'The erect *forehead* being peculiar to man, more than any other feature distinguishes him from the brutes', he wrote. 'Its elevation is indicative of intellectual power, a projecting one of idiotcy [sic], and a low and receding one of deficiency in intellect.'[40] Hicks applies these principles in his own work. All of his working-class boys have thin cheeky faces with turned up noses and low foreheads; and the inevitable pickpocket to the far left, caught by a vigilant policeman as he sidles up to a well-dressed woman, also has the exaggeratedly protruding jaw which identifies him as a criminal type (Fig. 73).

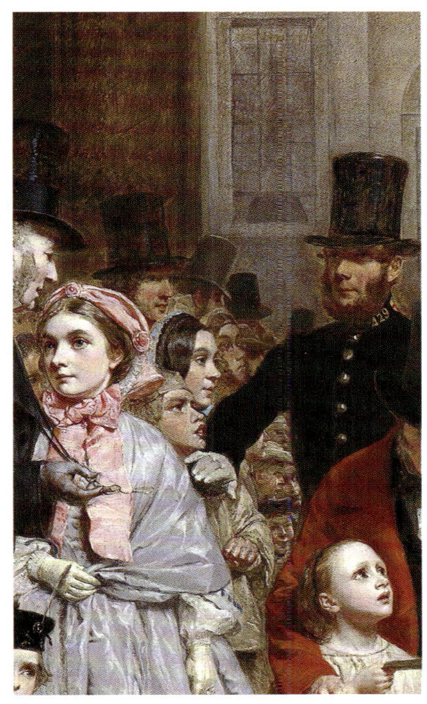

73. George Elgar Hicks (1824–1914), *The General Post-Office: One Minute to Six*, 1860. Museum of London. Detail of the policeman and the pickpocket.

Some painters of the London scene incorporated references to important contemporary events. Among the most memorable are *Eastward Ho! August 1857* (1858) and *Home Again* (1859), by Henry O'Neil, like Frith a former member of The Clique. O'Neil shows the impact of the Indian Mutiny on ordinary families during embarkation at Gravesend and the almost equally fraught return home (Figs 74 & 75). The first picture, described by the *Illustrated London News* as 'almost a national epic',[41] earned O'Neil 'a popularity almost unimpaired by criticism . . . It drew tears, it made pulses beat faster', and attracted a crowd throughout its exhibition.[42] The French critic, Ernest Chesneau, acknowledged the invaluable record of everyday life which British artists were assembling in their genre works; marvelling at O'Neil's scrupulous honesty in registering every feature and detail of his 'rough, coarse' characters, and even accessories such as 'faded tartans, checked handkerchiefs and washed-out dresses'. He found the result 'intensely pathetic' as well as of great historical value.[43] In *Home Again*, most of the main figures reappear. The bearded sergeant is on crutches; the widow embraces her son, now a junior officer. The young rifleman has returned with the Victoria Cross, and another soldier kisses his young baby for the first time. But one Highlander is greeted with bad news, for the legible words on a letter suggest that his wife has abandoned him.

This type of narrative painting, with its hard-edged drawing style and minute detail, was at its peak in the 1850s and 1860s. In the latter decade it was increasingly challenged by the rise of Aestheticism and the new Classicism school headed by artists of the calibre of Whistler, Burne-Jones, Leighton and Albert Moore. Although crowd painting continued, the majority of its practitioners adopted a more objective, unsentimental approach, and a freer technique which shows the influence of French Realism and Impressionism. *St Martin-in-the-Fields* (1888, Tate Britain) and *9th November, 1888* (Fig. 76) by William Logsdail (1859–1944) illustrate the greater sophistication with which the crowd was perceived and represented in the later years of the century.[44]

For many a twentieth-century critic, the work of Frith and his fellow painters of contemporary life summarized everything that was anathema to the modernist spirit. Roger Fry, an enthusiast of Cézanne and other Post-Impressionists, regarded Frith's modern life panoramas as the nadir of British art. In Fry's opinion, *The Railway Station* was 'an artistic Sodom and Gomorrah' from which more poetic painters had understandably 'fled . . . to save their souls by escaping at all costs . . . from the hideous present' which *The Railway Station* so shamelessly glorified.[45] But although,

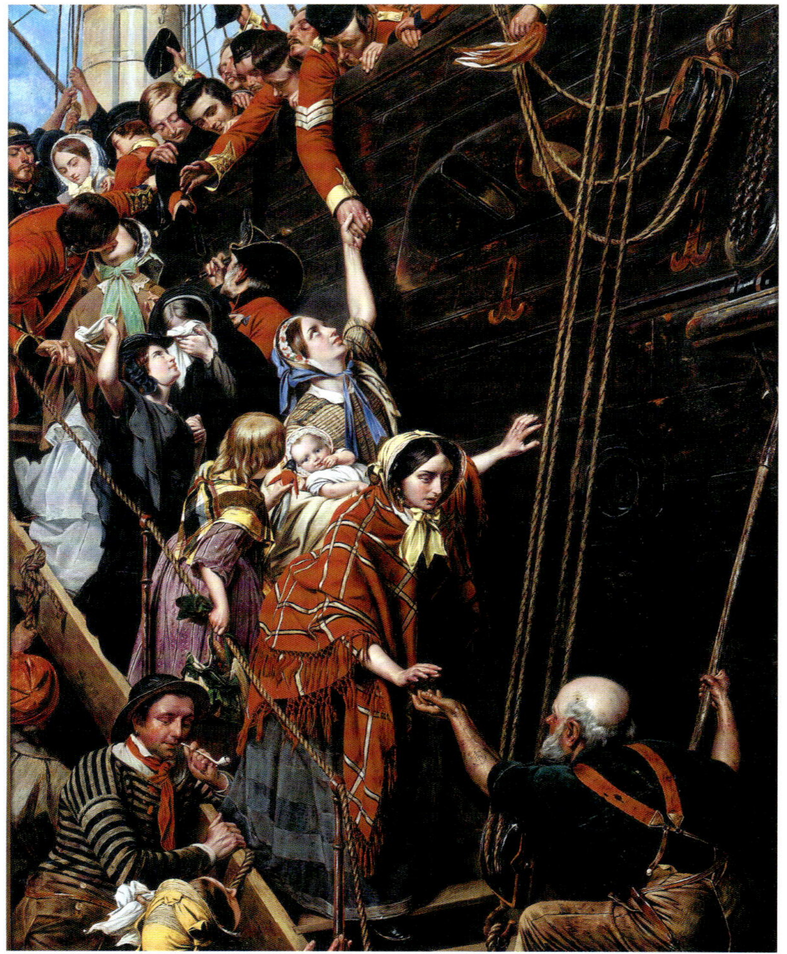

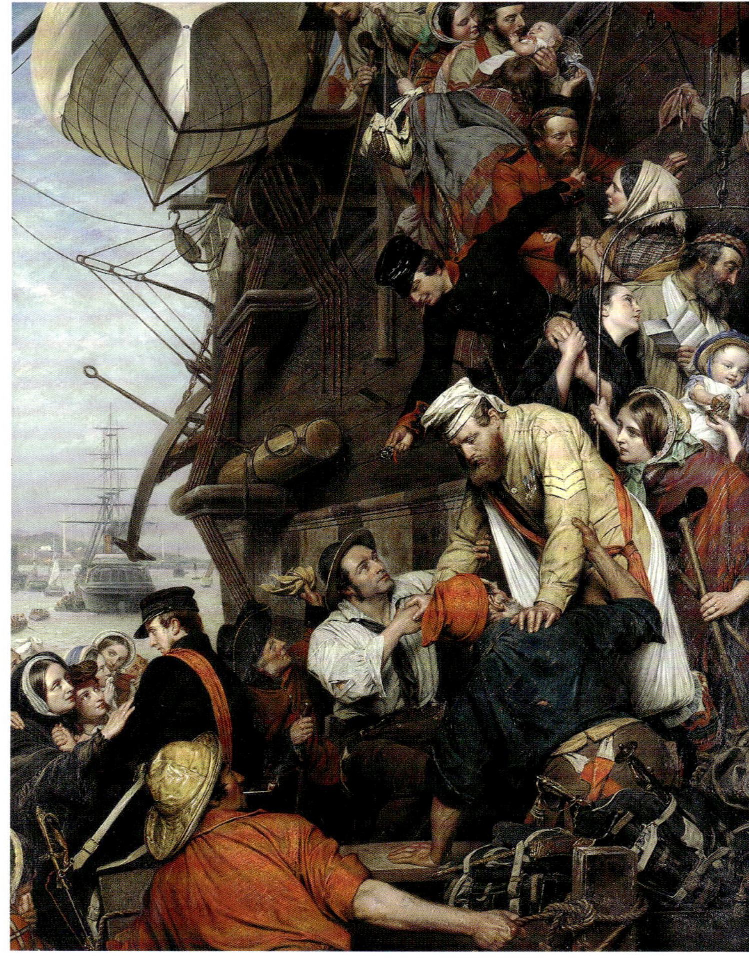

74. Left: Henry O'Neil (1817–80), *Eastward Ho: August 1857*. Museum of London.

75. Right: Henry O'Neil (1817–80), *Home Again*, 1859. Museum of London.

as Frith himself would have agreed, his paintings are far from being aesthetic objects, they are of incalculable historical interest.

The value of genre painting as a record of contemporary history was something which was recognized at the time. As early as 1811, in an essay on William Hogarth (1697–1764) Charles Lamb had objected to the way in which

> We call one man a great historical painter, because he has taken for his subjects kings or great men, or transactions over which time has thrown a grandeur. We term another the painter of common life . . . an artist of an inferior class, without reflecting whether the quantity of thought shown by the latter may not much more than level the distinction which their mere choice of subjects may seem to place between them.[46]

This claim was made increasingly in the Victorian period itself. Frederick Wedmore was convinced that future generations would pronounce 'our historical, our worthiest . . . [even] our most imaginative painting [as that which] dealt seriously and honestly with the life of our own times.'[47] John Ruskin made the same point, insisting that 'the only historical paintings worth a straw' to the future would be representations of the artist's own day.[48] W. M. Rossetti was another who recognized that the only age which any artist is uniquely qualified to paint is his own. Only

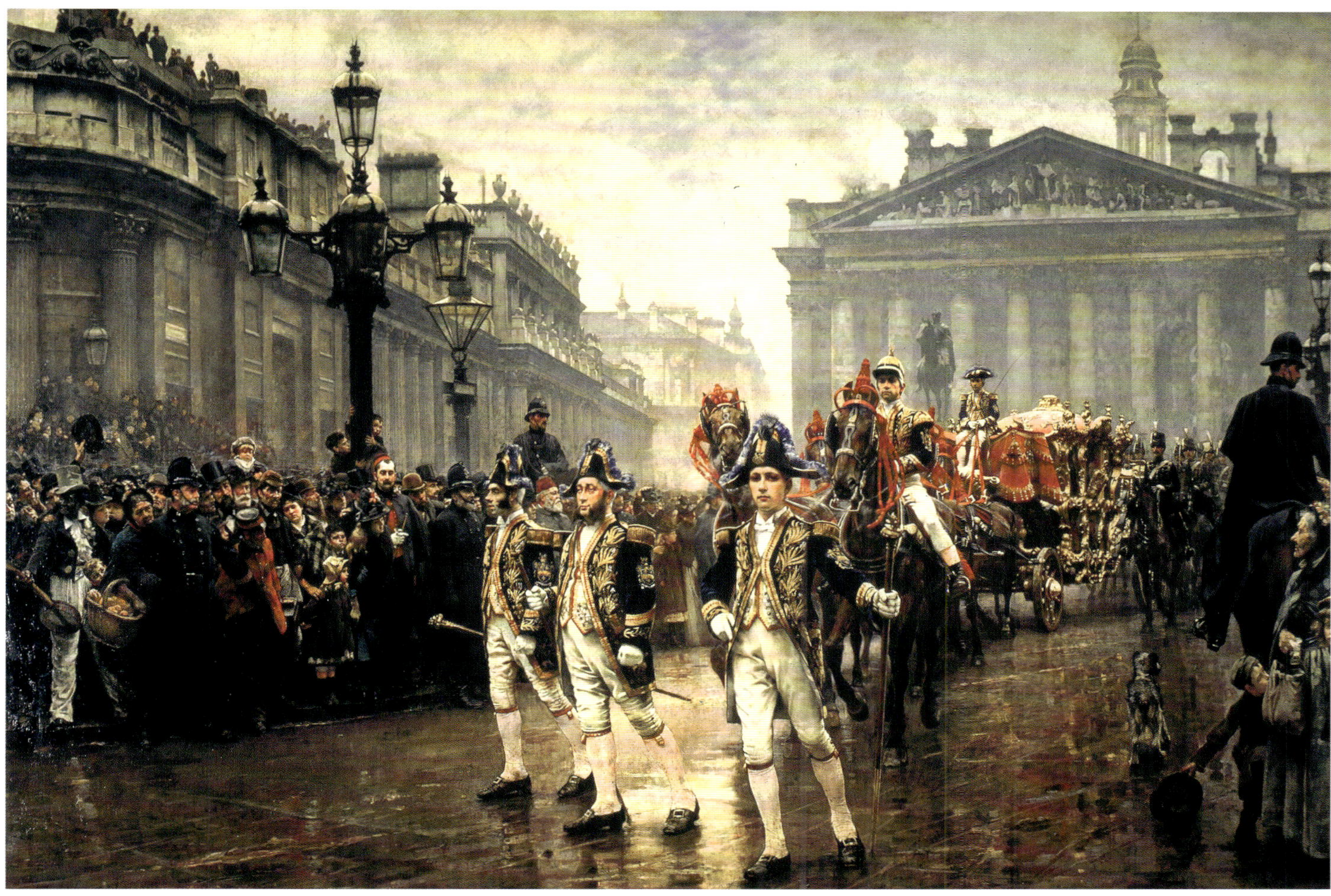

76. William Logsdail (1859–1944), *The Ninth of November, 1888*, 1890. Guildhall Art Gallery, City of London.

of this can he provide an eye witness account, and it is this which makes his work of unique value. No-one can do it afterwards.[49]

Rossetti wrote of *Derby Day's* 'chief real value' as 'the undistorted picture of actual life' which it would provide for future generations.[50] This was Frith's belief too. He wrote that 'pictures of contemporary life and manners have a better chance of immortality than ninety-nine out of every hundred of the ideal and so-called poetical pictures produced in this generation.'[51] He was being somewhat hard on High Art, but his argument is valid. In the year before his death, Frith was hailed as the unrivalled 'historian of his own age',[52] and that reputation continues to increase with time. The contemporary life paintings of Frith and his fellows, are valued by historians as visual social documents; not only as records of fashion and other details, but also as important repositories of ideas and beliefs about society and its individual constituents. Hence their lasting importance to posterity.

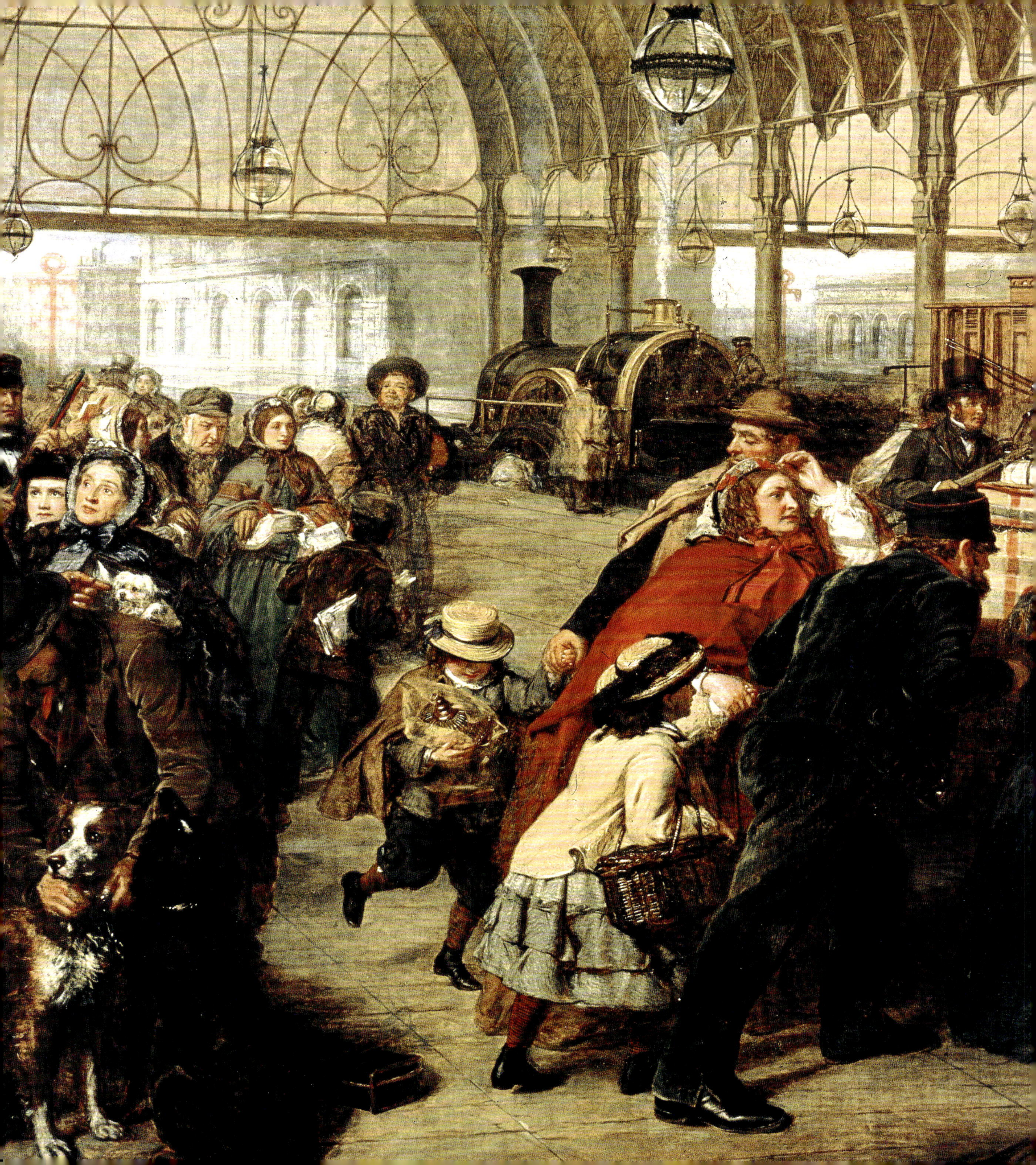

Chapter 5

William Powell Frith's *The Railway Station*: Classification and the Crowd

CAROLINE ARSCOTT

The Railway Station (Fig. 63) is the most celebrated of William Powell Frith's multi-figure genre scenes set in modern-day locations. It was conceived following the success of *Life at the Seaside (Ramsgate Sands)* (1854; Fig. 14). Frith completed *The Railway Station* as a commission for the dealer Victor Louis Flatow (also known as Flatou), negotiating separately over the picture itself, the engraving rights and the exhibition rights. For Flatow the value of the picture was much enhanced by the two latter categories. He was able to arrange for the picture to be exhibited on its own as a single-picture show rather than allowing it to be hung in the Royal Academy, calculating correctly that the work would, in its own right, pull in the crowds. While the picture was on display he was able to sign up visitors to the list of subscribers for the engraving, thereby making profits from admission tickets to the exhibition, catalogue sales at the exhibition and from sales of the engraving in one streamlined operation. Such moneymaking would not have been possible had not Frith lighted on a formula which caught the imagination and piqued the curiosity of the exhibition-going and print-buying public. The depiction of the metropolitan crowd in settings that represented the public spaces of modern Britain was, for a brief period from the early 1850s to the mid-1860s, the most fascinating subject imaginable for exhibition-goers and print-purchasers, and Frith gladly assumed the identity of the originator and foremost exponent of a mode that was also explored by Ford Madox Brown, John Ritchie, George Elgar Hicks, Charles Rossiter and William Maw Egley.[1] A picture such as *The Railway Station* offered a compendium of observation, social commentary, comedy, pathos, adventure and moral reflection that perfectly fitted the appetites and expectations of the middle-class viewing public. The contrasts afforded by the composition: joy and sorrow, virtue and vice, elegance and plainness, were particularly well-suited to the translation into black and white in the elaborate large-scale engraving (Fig. 78) completed by Francis Holl and published by Henry Graves and Co. who purchased the picture, exhibition rights and copyright and took over publication of the engraving in 1863.[2] The tonal contrasts between bright wedding costumes, for instance, and darker street-wear, facilitated the picking out of separate incidents. The definition of detail in the medium of engraving matched, and in portions was more easily legible than the definition offered by Frith's painting, for all its tight, careful brushwork. It is evident that Frith envisaged the translation into graphic form from the outset of the project.

During the early Victorian period, from the 1830s to the mid-1860s, we see many instances of artists turning to urban subjects in an effort to celebrate the achievements of industrial society. The new buildings and busy centres of the metropolis, and of burgeoning cities in the north such

Facing page
77. *The Railway Station*, 1862. Royal Holloway, University of London. Detail of Fig. 63.

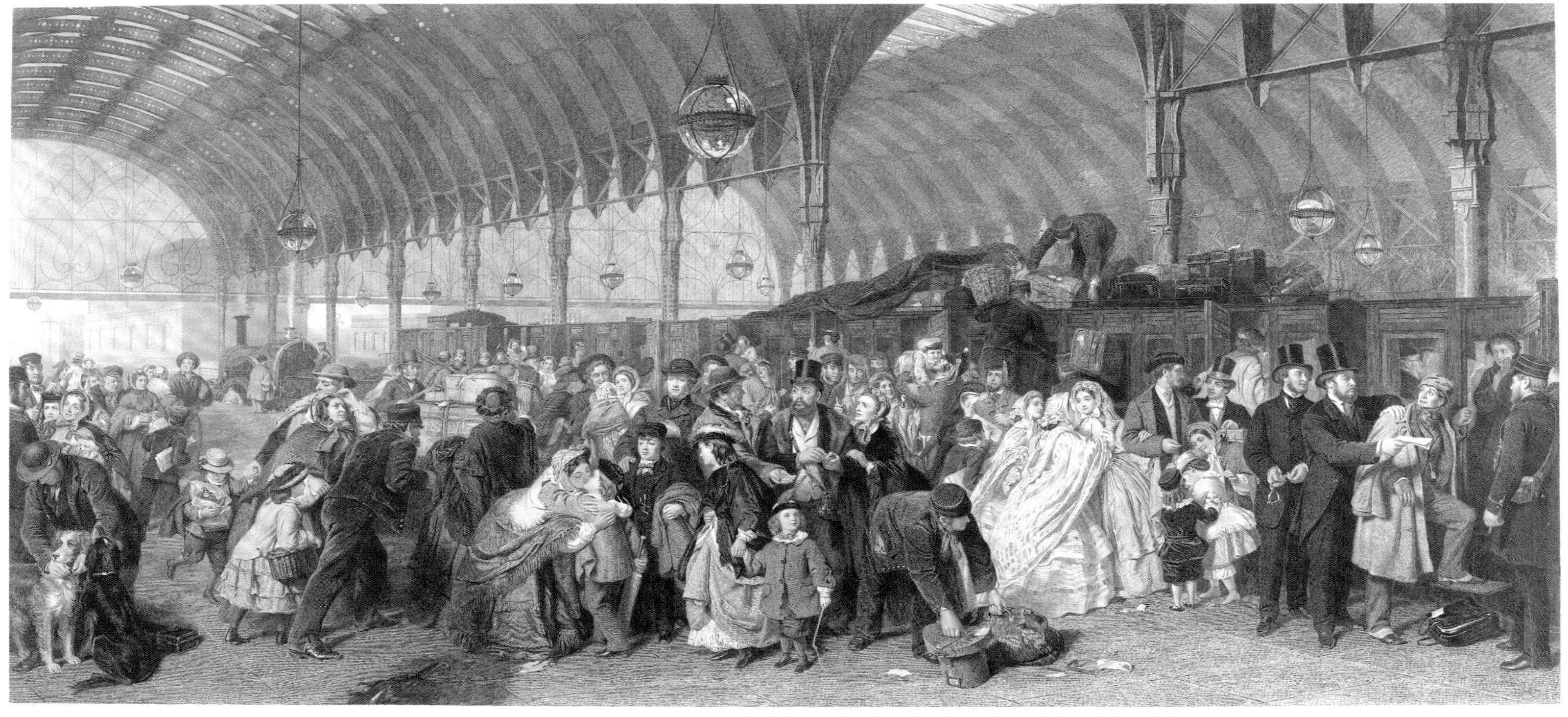

78. Francis Holl (1815–84) after William Powell Frith, *The Railway Station* engraving (published by Henry Graves & Co. 1863). Museum of London.

as Leeds and Manchester, were represented in fine art and graphic media.[3] In modern life scenes such as those undertaken by Frith many small figures were packed together in compositions with public urban settings. These pictures contemplate the nature and constitution of the crowd and offer a celebratory commentary on modernity. For Victorian commentators the city street was a risky place and the urban crowd a volatile and worrisome phenomenon. Middle-class observers were ready to thrill to the unparalleled concentration of human energy and activity in the modern city street, or in the public spaces of park, market or railway station, but there was always an accompanying unease. Assemblies of workers were associated with political protest; the densely populated working-class localities of the modern city were associated with stench, disease and immorality. Public spaces, such as the railway station platform, where there was no guarantee of exclusive middle-class occupation brought together a mixture of classes.[4] Entering crowded spaces involved every chance for middle-class excursionists of proximity to probably dirty, possibly diseased, immoral or criminal members of the working class. Equally upper middle-class citizens of some distinction could find themselves pushed together with lower middle-class people whose demeanour and manners might be offensive. Victorian modern-life painting found ways to neutralise these negative associations without entirely obliterating them. It was necessary, if the exciting novelty of environment and milieu and the thrilling, unprecedented scale of projects and facilities were to be communicated, for representations to incorporate some elements that evoked unease. It could be argued that artists of this 1850s and 1860s phase of modern-life painting sensationalised modern experience by incorporating alarming elements into their representations but tempered that sensationalism by installing components or frameworks that acted in the opposite way, offering reassurance for their predominantly middle-class audiences. As a result the ideological positioning of the works was secured; they served the interests of the existing social elite, riding on the back of thrilling fear and horror to generate enthusiasm for current social arrangements.

It is apparent that time is thematised in Frith's *The Railway Station*, as it is in the modern-life scene completed two years earlier by George Elgar Hicks, *The General Post Office, One Minute To Six* (1860; Fig. 72). In both cases the rapidity of modern communications is featured: rail and postal systems emphasise social linkage and democratic access to benefits of industrialisation. To left and right of Frith's painting a newsboy dash in amongst the crowd, bringing the latest off the press and indicating that the montage of incidents on the canvas is equivalent to the assembly of items on the typeset page. He elaborates this by showing one newsboy on the right holding up the comic weekly *Punch* in one hand and gripping the bundle of serious daily papers under his arm. The painting offers contemporary life in comic and in serious guise, each equally keyed in to the rhythms of modernity. The gentleman in the carriage on the right-hand side of the picture spreads out his newspaper, we see it extending from the window to the open doorway of the compartment. Consequently the dramatic incident of an arrest that takes place on the platform in front of him is overlaid, by a trick of perspective, onto the area of the newspaper, like an item inserted into the daily news.[5] The rush of passengers across the railway station, emphasised on the left of Frith's canvas, corresponds to the unrelenting sense of urgency experienced in a world where time divisions were regulated by industrial factors rather than by nature or the church, to the pace of change in the increasingly technological environment of Victorian England and to the speed of movement enabled by the steam engine whether in transport or industrial production. Frith and Hicks offer pictures about progress but they do not just show evidence of modernisation in the form of girders or newsprint, they give us the movement of the crowd as analogous to the movement of progress in the modern age. They achieve this in different ways; there is an important contrast between the neat segmentation of action in Frith and the way human matter slides and collides in Hicks, much in the way that the parcels of newspapers do. In each case there is a careful delineation of the personnel in the scene; particular class positions and social roles are indicated.

Frith was proud of his ability to group a large number of figures by building up a number of distinct incidents each forming a pleasing subgroup within a rhythmically organised composition. A central pyramid of figures in *The Railway Station* is formed by a combination of three groups; at the apex the father in top hat embraces his wife in the doorway of the train, below this, the right-hand side of the pyramid is formed by the group showing a cabby demanding a fare, the moustachioed, foreign-looking passenger hesitating to pay, his wife leaning on his arm and the porter leaning over to pick up a hat box and carpet bag. On the left-hand side of the pyramid the triangular group of the family taking leave of their sons, who are going to school, stands as a reduced version of the bigger shape. On the right of the picture two important groups echo each other: the wedding party and the detectives arresting a criminal. The wedding party offers a trio where the bridesmaids detain the bride with affectionate words, one putting her hand on the bride's shoulder. The right-hand portion of the same group, in which the bridegroom and the servant receiving instructions about luggage gesture to the right, leads the bride towards the departing train through the linkage of her arm with the bridegroom's. The group at the rightmost side of the picture shows a fraudster in the equivalent position to the bride. However, here, the hand on the shoulder definitively interrupts his rightwards movement and his effort to enter the train to join his wife. He is being arrested just in time, before the departure of the train, by two police officers. In a passage of his autobiography where he recalls the sculptor John Gibson's imperfect vocabulary, Frith mentions Gibson's praise of the variety of 'incidencies' in *The Railway Station* and Gibson's view that Frith was indebted to 'the Greeks, as he called them, for the power

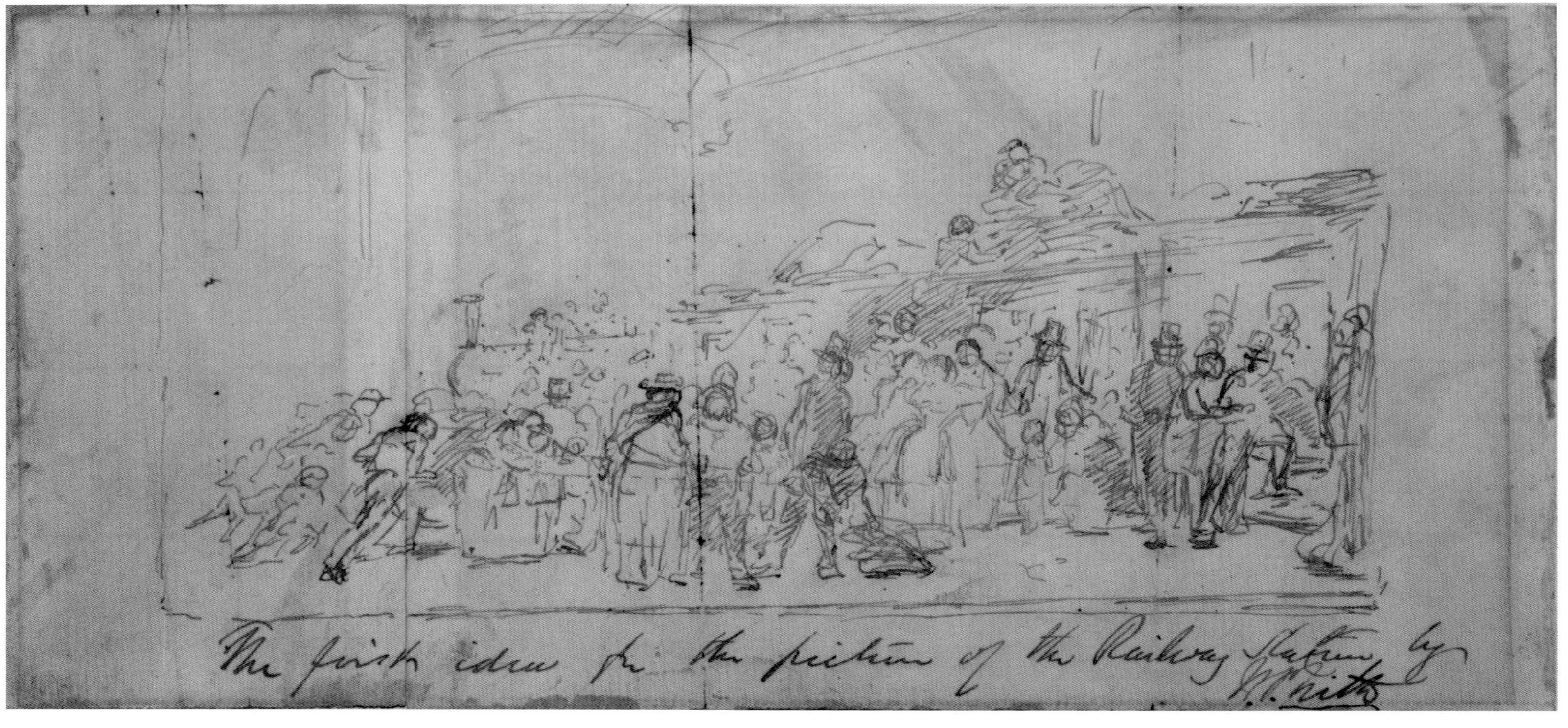

79. Study for *The Railway Station*. Ironbridge Gorge Museum Trust, Elton Collection.

to group the figures'.[6] In this picture by Frith, as in Hicks's *General Post Office*, the collective human energy and the overall shape of the action is presented as the summation of modernity. For Frith modernity is tempered by a sense of pattern and stability that recalls the classical tradition.

A comparison between the final composition and the pen and ink sketch, inscribed 'the first idea for the picture of the Railway Station by W. P. Frith' (Fig. 79) along with one of the oil sketches for the painting (Fig. 80), (two oil sketches remain untraced), reveals that the installation of a central pyramid was a late decision in the process of devising the composition. The earlier oil sketch positioned the red-jacketed recruiting officer lifting his baby at the centre of the composition, and gave more space to the wedding party and arrest scene on the right. It divided the family group with schoolboys from the cab driver and his passengers by showing the cabby from behind so that his back forms a barrier close to the picture plane. The effect of the changes realised in the final painting is that the normative middle-class family, comprising dignified, upright father, affectionate, bending mother, three sons and a daughter, is installed as part of the central, stable, geometric shape. This allows their important ideological role to tally with their pictorial placement. Frith modelled these figures on himself and members of his own family. Additionally the viewer is given an increased sense of the depth of the platform on the left-hand side in the final composition and therefore the crowd is read as a wedge-shape, moving from the left the to the narrow point of the platform on the right, rather than as a flat procession, lined up against the train. The separate groups are understood as overlapping rather than as sequentially arrayed and this is important for Frith's project of presenting not just the variety of modern society but a sense of the integration and interconnectedness of its different elements.

The sub-units of the composition, the little incidents that engage and amuse the viewer, temper the sense of an unmanageable throng. They also introduce other notions of time to counter the sense of uniform, mechanically-derived, industrial or 'railway' time. The time-span of human life

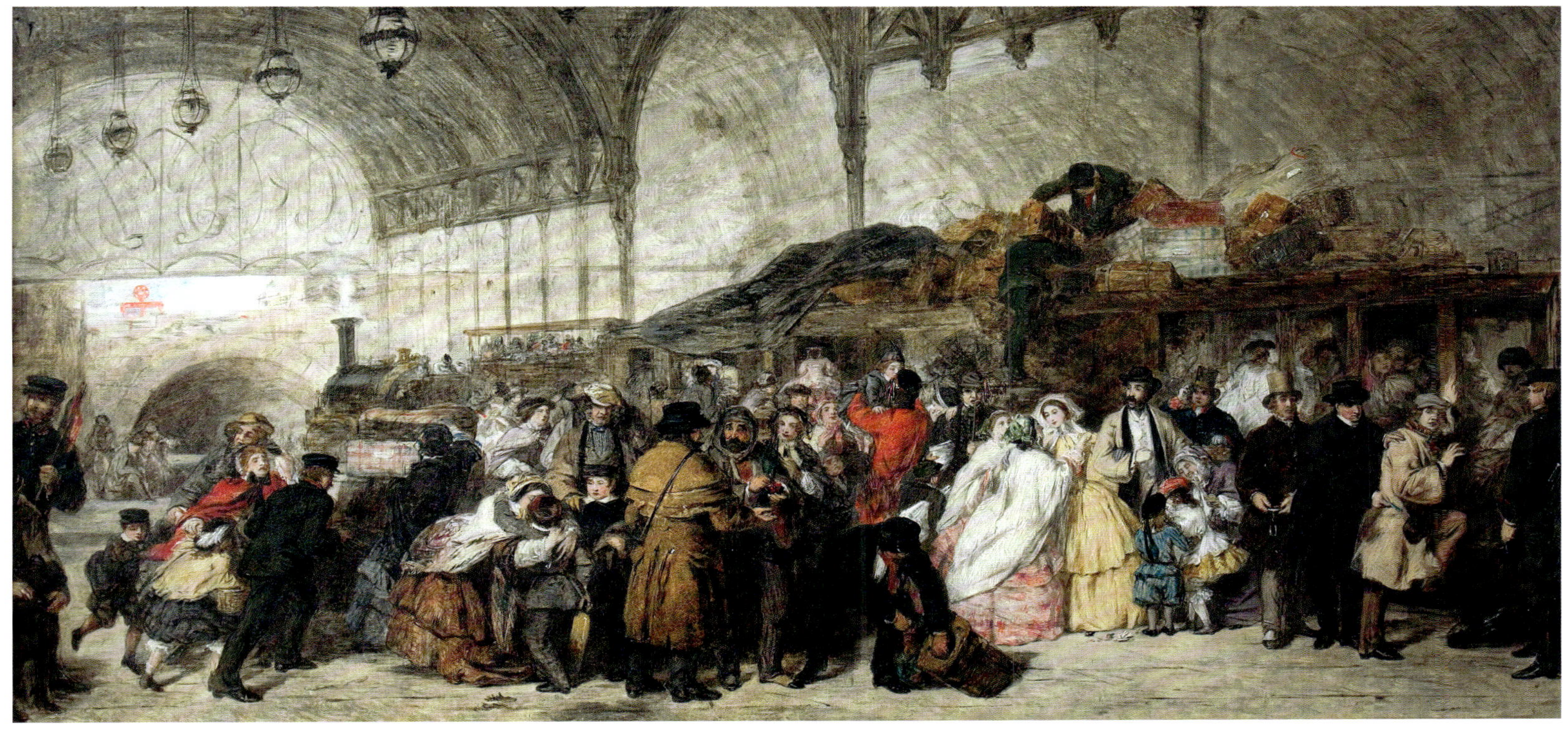

80. Oil study for *The Railway Station*. Private Collection.

is suggested by the three differentiated stages of blithe, emotional and restrained boyishness shown by the three brothers in the family group where the elder boys are leaving for school; the oldest one is most buttoned-up, only betraying his emotion by one tear that slides down his cheek, a detail that is more noticeable in the engraving after the painting than in the painting itself. The bridal group shows the crucial transformation from the girlish dependence on affectionate ties between unmarried sisters to the womanly experience of love in marriage. The destiny of adult subjects is suggested in various ways: Frith signals the pleasure of sport, showing figures with fishing rods or hunting dogs, shows the new recruits to the army embarking on a new venture, draws attention to honest sailors', volunteers' and professional soldiers' valiant dedication (perhaps to the point of sacrifice of their lives), and to the potential or actual wrongdoing of the criminal types such as the fraudster being arrested and the recruit of criminal appearance whose mother weeps on his shoulder.[7] The final stage of life and its necessary progress towards death is introduced by the elderly man who is carefully guided along the platform by his two daughters to the left-hand side of the composition. In the oil sketch for the painting (Fig. 80) Frith rendered this group more melodramatically, setting them apart from the other figures on the left, and showing the old man sitting down and anxiously attended by the female figures as if his strength had failed. In conjunction with the inclusion of a dark tunnel beyond the railway shed, the grim accent and the intimations of death were considerably greater in the sketch. Tom Taylor, in his lengthy account of the picture written for the catalogue on sale at Flatow's Haymarket Gallery exhibition in 1862, was alert to the thematic dimensions of the picture relating to life's stages; he gave much attention to the prospects and activities of the individual figures and pointed out the puff of steam to be seen behind the train, which shows that a train has just arrived at the other platform.[8] Partings are balanced by arrivals, life's fresh ventures by life's final terminus.

In nineteenth-century Britain, and particularly in the early Victorian period, it seemed to be important to envision a crowd that was differentiated rather than made up of the massing of identical units, the blades of grass, or drops of water of the mobs or hordes referred to in Canetti's 1960 study of the crowd.[9] Most often the kind of congregation invoked to sum up the dynamism of modern society was a miscellaneous one. Observers fastened not on gatherings of kin, neighbours or colleagues (where each person carried more or less identical markers of social identity and could be expected to recognise and accept the others in the group) but on assemblies of strangers where each individual had his or her own trajectory and agenda. The buzz of modern urban life was located in the commercial and recreational spaces of the city where separately agitated and cross-cutting units jostled together. An array of occupations, ages and class positions seemed to be a guarantee of the representative nature of the crowd and made it possible to view it as a fragment of a social whole. In this way the accidental juxtapositions of the public hall could be taken to represent the unity in diversity of the modern democratic social order, while the pulse of busy activity summoned up the vitality, inventiveness and resourcefulness of Britain as the pre-eminent industrial and trading nation.

The vision of the crowd as a miscellaneous phenomenon can be differentiated from an alternative vision of grim homogeneity. In visual art we encounter indistinguishable masses in certain versions of the industrial sublime.[10] From the late 1860s spectral, disintegrating, barely human forms crowd the plates of Doré and Jerrold's *London: A Pilgrimage* (1872) or huddle in alleys in Annan's photographic survey of Glasgow (1868–77), or people the foggy streets of Grimshaw's, Fildes's or John O'Connor's oil paintings.[11] In the earlier Victorian period oil painting, in particular, dealt with urban dirt, ugliness, anonymity, fear and immensity in an altogether cheerier and more optimistic way. The troubling issues were indeed vivid to artists and other commentators on urban experience, even at that date, but there was a compensatory belief in the potential of industrious energy. The assumption in genre painting of the 1850s and into the 1860s is that the crowd can be subdivided, enjoyed and inhabited by its viewer. But in *The Railway Station* the optimistic enjoyment is inflected in a new way by certain indications of the breakdown of satisfactory subdivisions.

The issue of subdivision was a complex one since it depended on the allocation of individual figures to types or categories. Mary Cowling has written extensively about the Victorian enthusiasm for phrenology and she points to the ready identification by pictures' viewers of character types, on the basis of the physical characteristics indicated in the depicted figures, in particular the shape of face, head and neck. Frith was a devotee of phrenology, the quasi-scientific study of such features, and it makes sense to consider his presentation of the crowd in terms of readily classifiable types. Certainly Tom Taylor presented the scenario of *The Railway Station* in these terms in the exhibition catalogue, and reviewers in the periodical press followed suit. However, Frith had an interest in the illegibility of the crowd that accompanied his investment in its legibility. Indeed the twin effects of excitement and reassurance that he sought to establish required that he negotiate between these two modes of connecting with the throng. Excitement and instability were necessary if the picture was to convey the thrill and exhilaration of modernity and to suggest its dynamic nature. Reassurance was necessary to instil the conviction that the population in these circumstances was governable and the financial risks entailed in participating in modern developments not too hazardous. In presenting the crowd as a series of identifiable characters Frith drew on a mode of classification that was well established in genre depiction, and one that was consonant with the parcelling out of character attributes in phrenology. Alongside this he dallied with another mode of presentation in which classification broke down. This was a novel way of perceiving and representing the crowd, which started to have an impact in the 1860s.

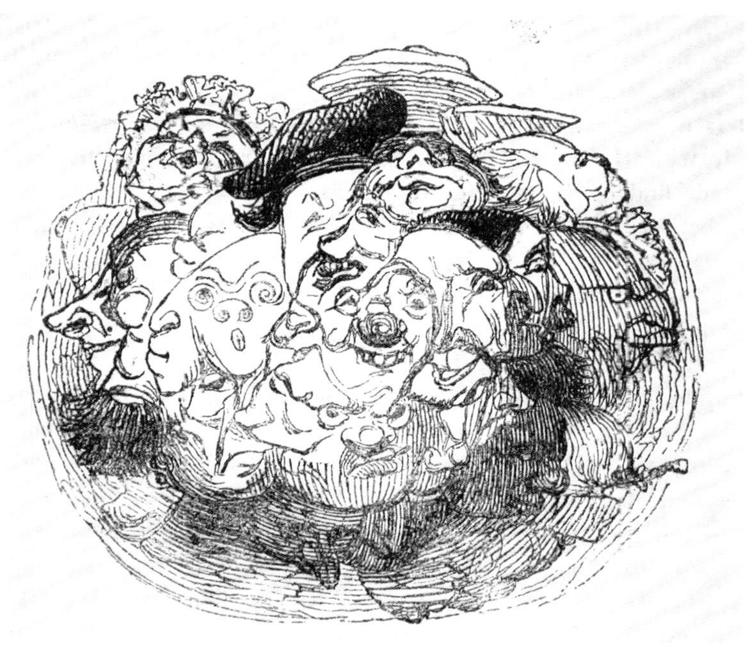

81. Engraved by John Orrin Smith after Kenny Meadows (1790–1874), *Amalgamated heads*, from *Heads Of The People, or Portraits of the English* (Robert Tyas, London, 1840). Guildhall Library, City of London.

The premises of classificatory engagement with the crowd can be explored in a publication dating from 1840. *Heads of the People, or Portraits of the English* was based on drawings by Kenny Meadows engraved by Orrin Smith. This illustrated book set out to present a characteristic figure from a hundred different trades or callings from chimney sweeps to high court judges, thus giving an overview of the modern population. The 'Heads' presented were not actual portraits but genre figures who summed up the traits and foibles of each calling. A single engraving was accompanied by a humorous or campaigning text, several pages long. Liberal authors such as Douglas Jerrold, William Howitt and Richard Henry Horne contributed the texts. The Preface to the second volume asked how the portraits could avoid the charge of inaccuracy since every calling comprised a range of different individuals. The aim was 'to concentrate in individual peculiarity the characteristics of a class' (class being understood here as category of activity not social class), and this concentration would involve the melding together of different existing people to produce one representative type. This literal-minded way of considering genre depiction, aiming to wed it to a kind of empirical survey became the norm in the Victorian

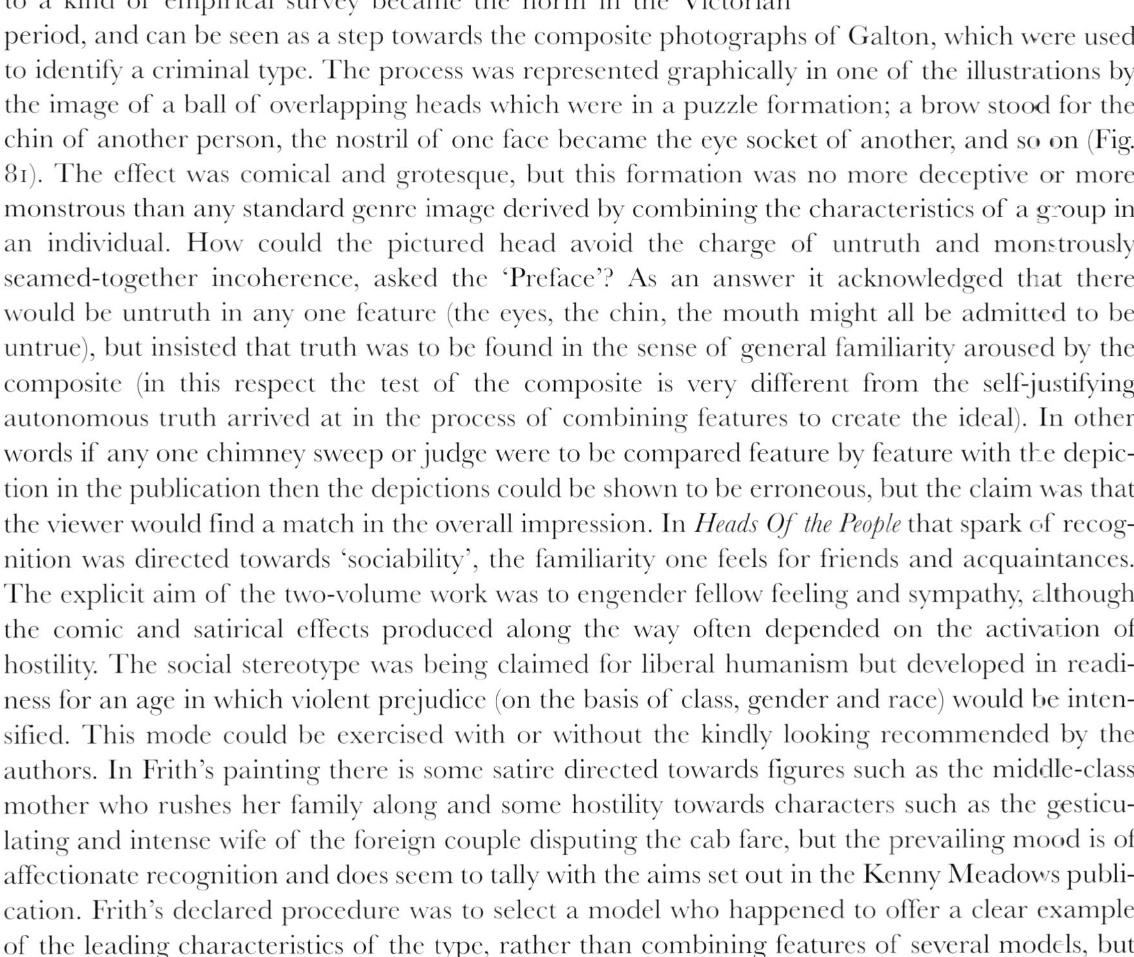

period, and can be seen as a step towards the composite photographs of Galton, which were used to identify a criminal type. The process was represented graphically in one of the illustrations by the image of a ball of overlapping heads which were in a puzzle formation; a brow stood for the chin of another person, the nostril of one face became the eye socket of another, and so on (Fig. 81). The effect was comical and grotesque, but this formation was no more deceptive or more monstrous than any standard genre image derived by combining the characteristics of a group in an individual. How could the pictured head avoid the charge of untruth and monstrously seamed-together incoherence, asked the 'Preface'? As an answer it acknowledged that there would be untruth in any one feature (the eyes, the chin, the mouth might all be admitted to be untrue), but insisted that truth was to be found in the sense of general familiarity aroused by the composite (in this respect the test of the composite is very different from the self-justifying autonomous truth arrived at in the process of combining features to create the ideal). In other words if any one chimney sweep or judge were to be compared feature by feature with the depiction in the publication then the depictions could be shown to be erroneous, but the claim was that the viewer would find a match in the overall impression. In *Heads Of the People* that spark of recognition was directed towards 'sociability', the familiarity one feels for friends and acquaintances. The explicit aim of the two-volume work was to engender fellow feeling and sympathy, although the comic and satirical effects produced along the way often depended on the activation of hostility. The social stereotype was being claimed for liberal humanism but developed in readiness for an age in which violent prejudice (on the basis of class, gender and race) would be intensified. This mode could be exercised with or without the kindly looking recommended by the authors. In Frith's painting there is some satire directed towards figures such as the middle-class mother who rushes her family along and some hostility towards characters such as the gesticulating and intense wife of the foreign couple disputing the cab fare, but the prevailing mood is of affectionate recognition and does seem to tally with the aims set out in the Kenny Meadows publication. Frith's declared procedure was to select a model who happened to offer a clear example of the leading characteristics of the type, rather than combining features of several models, but this should not obscure the status of the generic figure as composite entity, brought out so clearly in the vignette of amalgamated heads.

The cheerful and companionable vision recommended by Kenny Meadows required a particular kind of looking which can be best understood by taking one example, that of the bus conductor. The article on the bus conductor, written by Leigh Hunt, opens by stating 'the conductor is a careless-dressing, subordinate, predominant, miscellaneous, newly-invented personage of the stable-breed order'.[12] It discusses the range of kinds of conductors, 'the most noticeable varieties of the class'. These are introduced in turn: the half-civil half-sulky fellow, a staid and pretentious individual, a weak-faced drunken boy, and the precocious know-it-all boy.[13]

Concerned to negotiate between typical subcategories and the definition of the calling as a whole the description moves back from the 'varieties' (we should notice the language of natural history here, at other times the language of ethnology is chosen) to overall category (perhaps the species) itself, and returns attention to the engraving that is placed at the start of the article (Fig. 82). 'To return to our Conductor *in the aggregate*, [who is wiser than the know-it-all boy] . . . You may see his class, with its rain-dress on, depicted in the figure at the head of this article. He is a good average specimen of his tribe . . .'[14] A paradoxical list of opposites is offered as the summary of his character: health in his outdoor vocation but unhealth in his liking for pubs; civility and rudeness; restraint and violence; honesty and dishonesty. The implication throughout this section is that the negative qualities are the truer indicators of his nature. He will overcrowd the bus, squeezing in market girls of his acquaintance passed off as 'ladies' who should be accommodated out of courtesy; in the competition for fares he will bully truly genteel women into riding on the bus, he will pocket the sixpenny fare himself or gain a fare by misrepresenting the route.[15] But the comedy of the article depends on holding on to the key idea of the average or mean. That notion relates to the idea of the omnibus itself as 'miscellaneous', a container of all social levels, and, drawing on the idea at the end of the article, Leigh Hunt allows a mellower picture to be offered of the conductor who is not too much of a blackguard, and doesn't have an innate tendency to petty larceny and so is 'reasonably honest' (considering the temptations) and can be said to accumulate wisdom through his contact with the world. In this view the conductor becomes a container like the bus of different values and levels. At this point Leigh Hunt evokes the passenger's eye view of the conductor's chest or midriff which is lodged close to the window, potentially a view that is offensive to the gentleman passenger/author, given the odour of the stables, shabby appearance and rough manners of this worker, but the writer is willing to look in detail: 'Our eyes are willing, as he there stands to grow intensely intimate with his waistcoat.' At this moment of close scrutiny there is the adoption of a generous estimate. We are asked to believe, after all, that this is a 'good, civil, reasonably honest, intelligent, ungrammatical, father-of-a-family sort of Omnibus-Conductor'.[16] Looking at the waistcoat gives the viewer an inkling of domestic virtue; '[we] rejoice to see how well his wife has mended the buttons.' Proximity is shown to bring the closeness of understanding rather than disgust and alienation. It is a closeness where there is an exchange of knowledge. The conductor has after all 'had all those experiences of right and wrong, both in himself and others' and has earned the right to pronounce on life.[17] The act of aggregation on the part of the author and artist that formed this fictive conductor is echoed in the mix that is said to have formed him, his experience and the contacts with the crowd. He is an agglomerate of all the crowd, and for that reason the gentleman passenger/observer is led to view him kindly. The observer does, after all, form part of his substance. With this move the method of producing composite generic figures is allied to the ideological imperatives of strengthening social bonds, engendering charitable response and identifying a national community. Frith's railway station also acts as a container for diverse experience and the exchange of knowledge, here too, can be envisaged as the basis of collective identity. Close sympathetic looking, down to the level of buttons and ribbons serves to mediate between silks and homespun.

In 1870 Henry Mayhew published a collection of essays, *London Characters: Illustrations of the Humour, Pathos and Peculiarities of London Life*. Mayhew muses on the question of similarities and differences in the crowd. 'They are all so much alike, and yet so widely different; their stories are so wonderfully similar in their broad outlines, and yet so strangely unlike in their minute particulars. Just as one man's face is like another's, so is the story of his life: no two faces are exactly alike, yet all have many points in common.'[18] The issues are just those which Kenny Meadows and Leigh Hunt encountered in 1840. But Mayhew has a different set of strategies. He takes the case of a demonstration for the extension of the franchise in Hyde Park, a monster Reform gathering ('monster' was the favourite designation of the rally organisers in this period). Enumeration is the first resource; thirty thousand people are there, at one specific time – 8pm on a day in August 1867. He tries calculating probabilities; if a bet had been laid in 1837 on any selected member of that crowd being present at the same event thirty years later as some other member of the demonstration in 1867 the odds would have been incalculable. The divergence of individuals, the possible variations that their lives and activities can take, is immense, almost infinite. The chances of convergence are statistically remote, so that where there is a crowd every conjuncture of one individual with another can be seen as an almost fully random event. This governs the way in which the crowd is experienced, undermines the potential for that familiar sympathetic looking and locating of the self in the other that Leigh Hunt undertook. In the context of Mayhew's example (the build-up to the Second Reform Act of 1867, which enfranchised large sections of the male working population) the vision of a collective where there is no affinity or kinship – the vision of a collective that is generated by random conjunction and multiplication – is a bleak vision of the modern democratic order. For Mayhew the infinite difference of individuals paradoxically produced an erosion of difference. The stability of social position was affected. In the crowd, on the street, elevated personages could be jostled by lower-class people. Mayhew put it like this; 'The Streets are strange levellers. They form a common ground upon which all ranks meet on equal terms'[19] and so a senior civil servant can be told to look out when he bumps into a costermonger or an omnibus conductor can address a countess: 'the indiscriminating busman invites countesses into his conveyance'.[20] This is merely circumstantial, the crowd forces different social ranks together into the same physical space and the appropriate manners and address are neglected. But there is a deeper kind of levelling in Mayhew's vision of the crowd which has to do with moral identity.

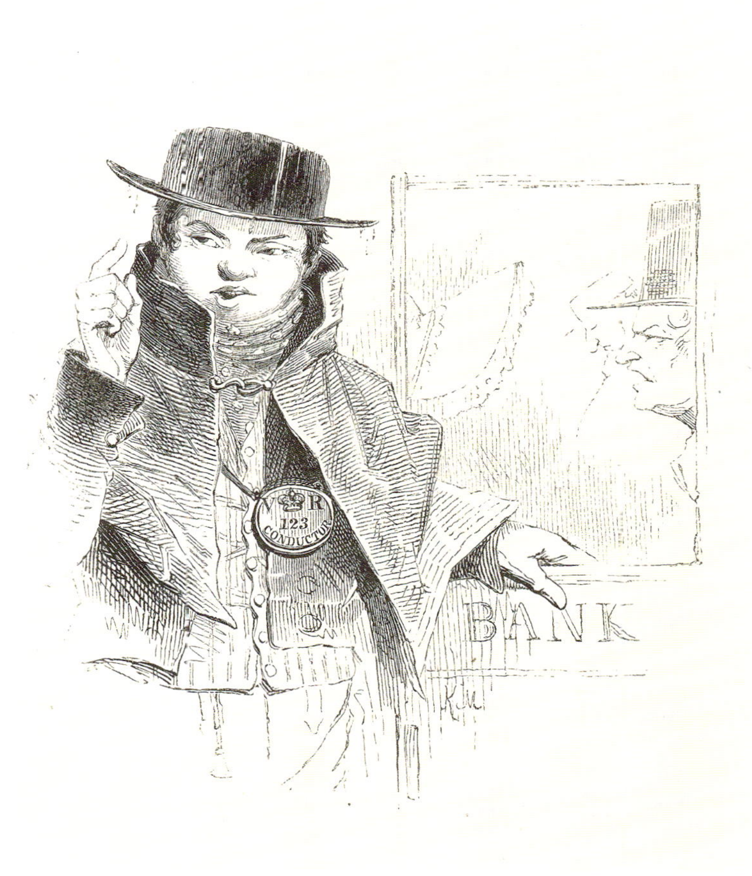

82. Engraved by John Orrin Smith after Kenny Meadows (1790–1874), *The Conductor: By me they goes it now into the city DANTE TRAVESTIED* (from Robert Tyas, *Heads Of The People, or Portraits of the English*, London, 1840). Guildhall Library, City of London.

For Mayhew the crowd creates circumstances in which the ability to arrive at a secure assessment of an individual's character is threatened. His ruminations on the crowd occur in a section of the book called 'Thumbnail Studies in the London Streets' and the mode of isolating a figure from the crowd and giving a brief outline of his or her appearance and habits is very close to the presentation of generic pictures in the earlier *Heads of the People*. The comic or entertainment

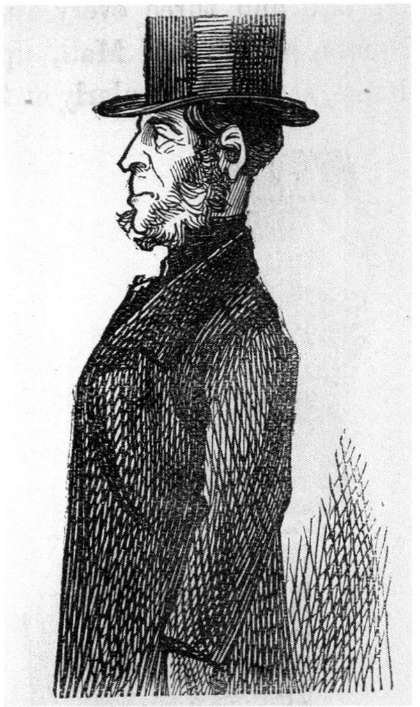
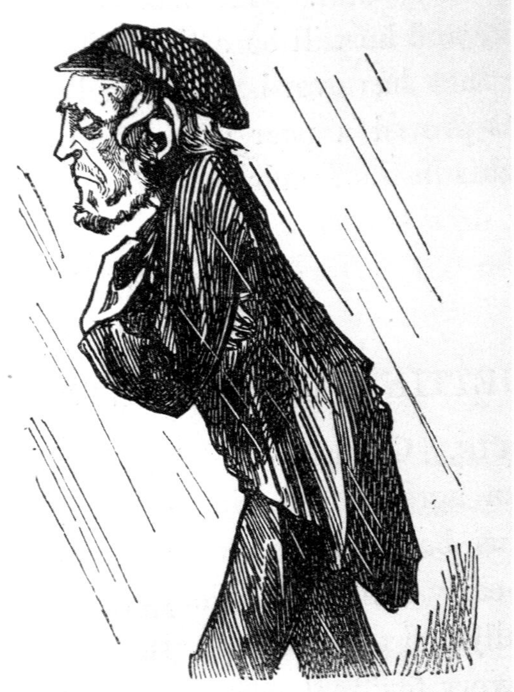
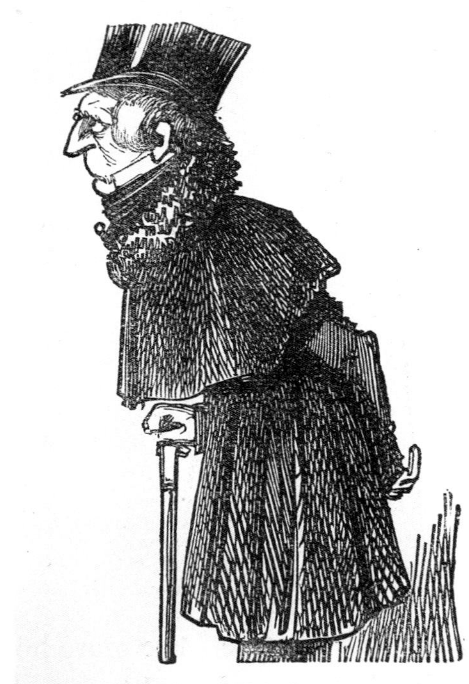

Henry Mayhew (1812–87), Left to right:

83. Plain clothes policeman
84. Poor man/thief
85. Eccentric bachelor

(from *London Characters: Illustrations of the Humour Pathos and Peculiarities of London Life*, new edition, 1881). Guildhall Library, City of London.

potential depends on a response of the reader of recognition ('oh yes, how typical'). In relation to the policeman (Fig. 83) the text reads as follows: 'here comes a tall, soldierly man in civilian clothes. He is soldierly in his carriage, only he has no moustache, and his little black eyes are quick and restless'.[21] The plain-clothes policeman thinks he is in disguise and might pass as a shop-keeper, clerk or yokel depending on his disguise but the narrator can identify him straight away, 'the more he disguises himself the more he will look like a policeman in plain clothes, and as long as he continues in the force his official identity will assert itself'.[22] The pleasure for the viewer is in registering the tell-tale features and naming the familiar type. Equally the thief (Fig. 84) is, the text tells us, unmistakeable, and here the liberal Mayhew emphasises the wretched circumstances forcing such a man along that path. 'He is of course a thief; who in his situation would not be? He is a liar; but his lies are told for bread. He is a blasphemer; God help him, what has he to be thankful for?'[23] The viewer's pleasure in familiarity is rerouted from ridicule into sympathy and outrage. Mayhew is clear that such familiarity is threatened by the sheer numbers of the modern crowd; misrecognition is as possible as recognition. Therefore the sympathetic communality proposed by Leigh Hunt is impossible. He makes the statistical case; first he estimates that one in every forty adults in London is a professional thief. These habitual criminals might dissimulate, but, nevertheless, an alert viewer could perhaps spot them, so that statistic does not in itself disrupt the operations of genre.

The idea of the ubiquitous professional thief is followed by the discussion of those malefactors who commit one-off crimes that may never be detected. Here crime occurs as an aberration: passion, temptation, provocation or desperation could lead to crimes being committed by people who were by no means primarily defined as being criminals. Mayhew gives examples of jealous husbands committing murder, a young girl with an illegitimate baby committing infanticide, a person in a heated moment committing an assault, well-liked clerks being tempted to embezzlement or forgery, and wife-beaters ill-treating their partners. Returning to the assembly of thirty thousand he asks just how many scoundrels will be among the crowd if all the past and future crimes of the participants are counted. What if you added in non-criminal lying and debauchery? A statistical answer is not attempted but the implication is that it would be far above the one in forty for professional thieves. The more important implication is that the occasional criminals or wrongdoers would not be visually distinct from the securely virtuous members of the crowd. All the thumbnail sketches, with their imagined details of the habits and outlook of the figure are retrospectively offered as guesses. Mayhew indicates that he may have been wrong. He tells us that clues may be assembled if the individual is followed and observed detective-style. Some characters are more transparent than others and their identity can be established with relative certainty. But much of the time the 'thumbnail sketcher' glances, hazards a guess, and is ready to acknowledge that he may have misjudged the person. This undermining of the genre distinctions is completed by the presentation of a character who is acknowledged as a complete enigma (Fig. 85). A reclusive old bachelor with set habits and a discreet manservant who will not give any information, 'he is supposed by some to be a fraudulent banker, by others a disgraced clergyman, by others an escaped convict of desperate character, and by the more rational portion of his observers as a harmless monomaniac'.[24] Eccentricity, or just anonymous individuality could hide wrongdoing or it could be innocent.

Significant differences separate this attitude from the method employed by Kenny Meadows in 1840. Mayhew removes the representations from their status as genre figures. The sketches are offered as derived from actual people for whom we can only posit identities. They no longer have the truth value of the 1840 publication (untruth vis-à-vis the specific but true vis-à-vis the category and so including all specific instances). Mayhew severs the specific instance from the category. The posited identity is not any longer the encompassing definition of a social role or position. The singular instance being tracked has truth value as a singular instance but does not necessarily yield up general truths. The mode stands somewhere between reportage and genre depiction. The reader is being offered this new phenomenon of the *enigmatic* as a form of entertainment alongside the *recognisable* (the joys of detection and free-wheeling speculation take their place alongside the comedy of the familiar and expected). One does not displace the other, although the two forms of representation are based on different premises. Instead they are both kept in play, and representation itself, as a result, is radically destabilised. The crowd is the forum in which the balance shifts towards vision that, whether kindly or not, can only extract clues, which cannot secure judgment. The very magnitude of the crowd is what is starting to pull the monstrous amalgam of genre apart into its constitutive singular instances.

Another way of articulating this is to return to genre representation's finessing between genus, species, variety and specimen. By deploying the tree structure of natural history the author or artist assures the reader or viewer that any variation between actual (real-world) examples can be set aside by moving up the tree structure to the next layer. Alternatively the entertainment can be expanded by moving down a layer and giving a range of sub-types. Genre gains its strength from its ability to move in both directions. It splits and joins its categories. The new vision does not; it only offers the possibility of a match between the overarching category and the infinite number of instances, or the equally intriguing possibility of a non-match. A mathematical problem ensues: if there is an infinite range at the level of reality, but the instances are to be grouped together as types, say groups of ten similar items, then how many categories would you need? The answer is infinity since infinity divided by 10 is still infinity. The prospect ensues that the strategy of producing categories to cover multiple instances will be ineffective since it will be necessary to have an infinite number of varieties to group together the specimens, and then an infinite number of species to group together this infinite range of varieties and so on; a pyramidal structure never emerges. Of course, Mayhew with his bent for statistics did not think that the population of the country was infinite, but the crowd is not just a sample of the population (which would give you a fixed number of people, say thirty thousand at a demonstration or eighty-odd figures on a railway station platform), it is the crossing of paths, each of which is determined through time by a vast number of factors, some of which are pure chance. If the members of the crowd are conceived of as dynamic and following unpredictable paths then the issue of infinity is vivid. The fantasy structures of bourgeois society in an era of capitalist expansion are shaped by the thrills of speculative investment.[25] Sensation fiction and the detective novel emerged as popular forms in the 1860s and anonymity, chance, disguise, and suspicion were key components of this kind of literature from Wilkie Collins's *Woman In White* (1860) to Arthur Conan Doyle's Sherlock Holmes tales of the 1890s.

Frith's painting shows us what happens when portraits of individuals are introduced into a scheme that attempts to give a tree-like classification of types. It could be claimed as the perfect match for the category, as his own face and those of his family might be said to be for the category of respectable middle-class family sending boys off to school, or it could be the element that undoes the representation's ability to work with the classificatory structure. The knowledge, in genre painting, that a model, or someone from the artist's circle, was the sitter for a supposedly typical figure can be assimilated to the idea of the perfect match. The artist may be supposed to have located the quintessential representative of the species.[26] Frith certainly did operate in this way, where the model is understood to sit to the artist for a typical figure. However he also drew on the opposite mode, which is one we can associate with Mayhew's idea of infinite variety, in which the model sits to the artist for the production of a portrait representing his or her unique self.

These issues become vivid in relation to the figure of the foreign visitor disputing a cab-fare at the centre of Frith's picture. This figure was, Frith tells us, painted from an émigré nobleman who taught Italian to Frith's daughters. The sitter is reported to have been anxious, for political reasons, that his face should not be recognised by his Italian opponents 'who might come to England'. Frith claimed that he had to promise not to make the portrait recognisable but confessed that he reneged on the promise because 'unless I caught the character of the face, I knew my model would be useless to me'.[27] This reported tension between Frith's purposes and the model's requirements enshrines a tension between the two ways of interfacing with reality. Private and anonymous in one context this figure was supposedly notorious and hunted in another. As a private and anonymous figure he could be employed as the perfect match for the category. As a notorious individual he could only stand for himself. Frith told the anecdote in his 1887 memoirs, in his self-serving way, because he wanted to claim the objective truth status of reportage as well as claiming the overarching truth of the generic representation. It is hard to resist the association of the story told by Frith about the model with the fictional character of Count Fosco in Wilkie Collins's novel, *The Woman In White*. The fat, Italianate, bewhiskered man was substituted for an outlandish figure looking something like an explorer, who argues with the cabby, in the oil sketch. Whether Frith's model for the foreign man was indeed a count caught up in political intrigue we cannot know; in any case it seems likely that Frith drew inspiration for the inclusion of such a loud, emphatic figure with his contrastingly thin-lipped, precise wife from Collins's thrilling story of deception and disguise.[28] The novel does not just turn on Fosco's anxiety about his true identity being discovered by his Italian political opponents but also on the switching of one young woman for another, using physical resemblance to usurp social identity and legitimate inheritance. There are many passages in the novel that meditate on instances where appearance is utterly deceptive, and the hero Hartright takes on the role of detective as he tries to sort out the mystery. The inclusion of a Count Fosco-style character in *The Railway Station* is an indicator of Frith's interest in the thrills to be derived from an occlusion of identity; it shows that in the early 1860s he was discovering an alternative to the classificatory certainties of genre.

Another place in the picture where these issues surface is in the incident on the right, where two plain-clothes policemen arrest an embezzler. The pamphlet to the 1862 exhibition of the picture referred to these police officers as well-known, mentioning their initials B. and H. and describing them in the following terms. 'These detectives are not the conventional types of their class, but the real men, studies from two of the most active and distinguished members of the force.'[29] This states clearly a point that I have sought to establish, that there is a contradiction between a figure standing as a representative of a category (or 'class') and a figure standing for a particular person. The detectives were celebrities of the day, identifiable as Detective-sergeants John Brett and Michael Haydon from the City of London Police. These were not the policemen on the beat in ineffectual disguise lampooned by Mayhew but distinguished members of an elite squad with only six first-class sergeants in the detective section at Great Scotland Yard by 1869. An article of the 1860s describing these officers stressed their specialist skills, subtlety of operation, intelligence and independence of mind and indicated that they were primarily concerned with cases of forgery, complex murder cases, crimes connected with national security such as the 'Fenian outrages', and the tracking of international criminals.[30] That final category of criminals, men wanted by foreign governments, was described in the following terms, 'some of these foreign criminals are very dangerous men – of desperate and subtle character – who need constant surveillance'.[31] The elite detectives shown in Frith's picture are concerned with an embezzler or fraudster, but the idea is permitted that they might equally be concerned with the foreigner disputing over the cabby's fare (Fig. 86). Tom Taylor, in his pamphlet, associates the figures of the detectives with the fame that is brought by the press, as he imagines one of them anticipating the news report of their clever arrest.[32] The logic of mass production of papers, the rhythm of daily items and bulletins, for ever replacing each other, and the patchworking of disconnected items on a news page all link the context of the newspaper to the infinity of dissimilar instances to be found at the level of empirical reality. There is a paradox here, in that celebrity is the thing that pulls the instance out of the typical, marking it as unique, but, marked in that way, the instance is associated with the infinite set of other empirical occurrences. The knowability of the famous face ushers in the unknowability of the mass of faces. Frith's painting encourages the viewer to make discriminations on the basis of appearance and this classificatory activity has its analogue in the pictorial motif of the neat and efficient stowing of luggage. However, the luggage label carefully shown on the fraudster's bag may offer a false identity. Prominently placed in the foreground of the picture on an area of empty platform between the foreigner and the fraudster there is a broken luggage strap and, lying beside it, a detached luggage label. This signals that the world on show is not one where identities are wholly secure.

The inclusion in Frith's painting of portraits that were identifiable by the general public punctures the assemblage of genre types just at the point that discrimination and judgment were invited from the viewer. 'Is this truly the type of a forger?', we are asked as we look at the man being arrested, 'does he show himself as such in his features and demeanour?' The picture's mixed mode of visual attention and knowledge allows for the possibility that appearances would not yield up the answer in a straight-forward way, as was expected in genre. It is certainly the case that the picture is packed with physiognomic indicators of character, and intellectual and moral capacity. In many ways the picture shows us a reassuring social whole through the pyramidal classification of genre, utilising such signs, but it also undermines that summation by rupturing such

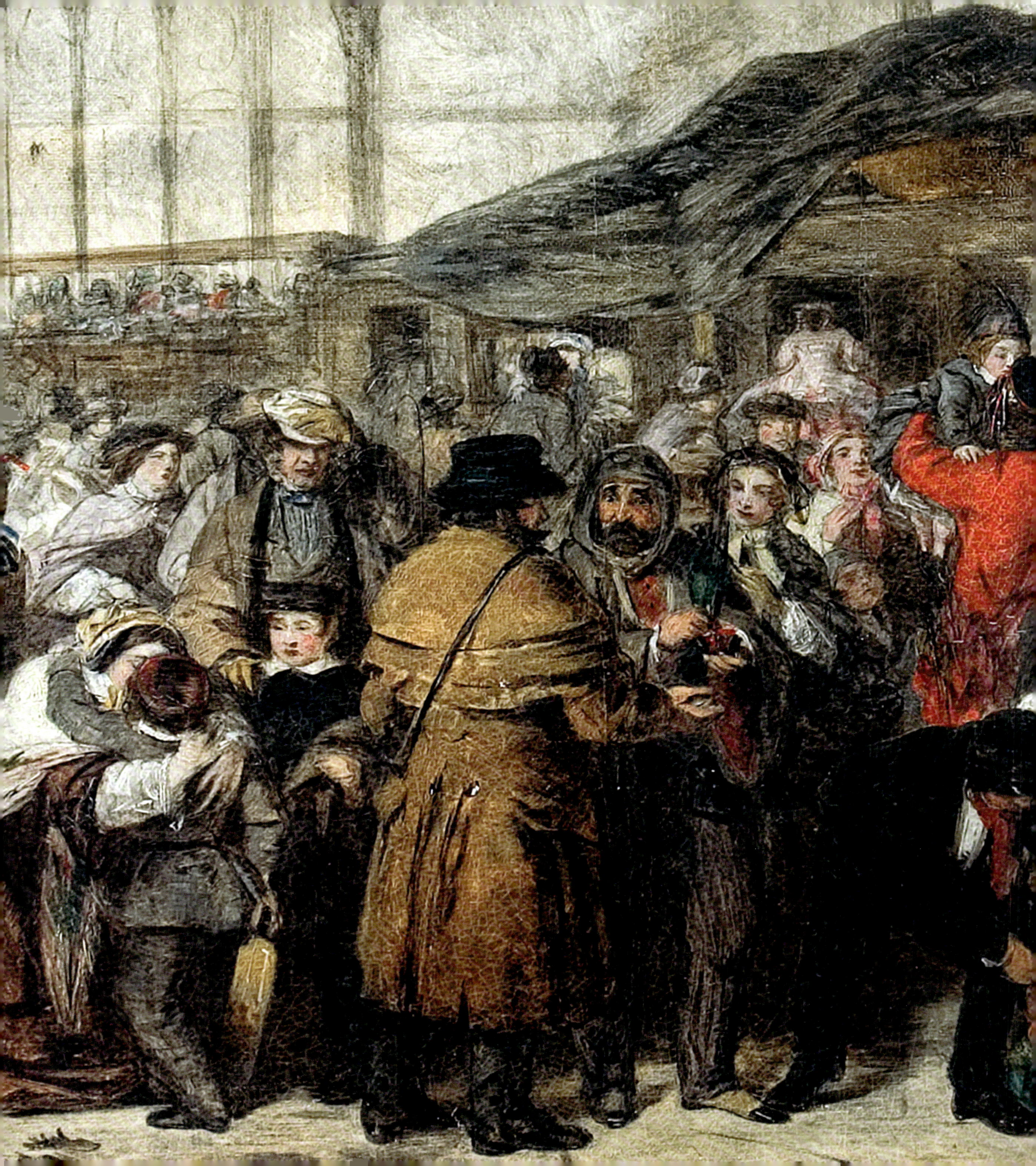

a classificatory system and proposing a different vision of the crowd. According to that vision the picture could be taken to suggest that criminal acts might be committed randomly just as the crowd assembles in a random way; that criminality might not be physiognomically apparent prior to the crime; that clues to behaviour and outlook might be subtle and themselves fragmented; that the number of miscreants in the crowd could be immense and so watchfulness is required; that the person in the crowd if not known to you personally is perhaps unknowable. You might conclude that the best you can do as a viewer is to be alert, let your eyes move rapidly, take on the persona of Mayhew's plain-clothes police detective with his quick and restless little black eyes. Such a mode of attention leads to a distinctly modern experience of the crowd and by prompting such a mode of attention Frith introduces a revised vision of the social order in the decade of the Second Reform Act.

Facing page
86. Oil study for *The Railway Station*. Private Collection. Detail of Fig. 80, the cabby disputing the fare with the foreigner..

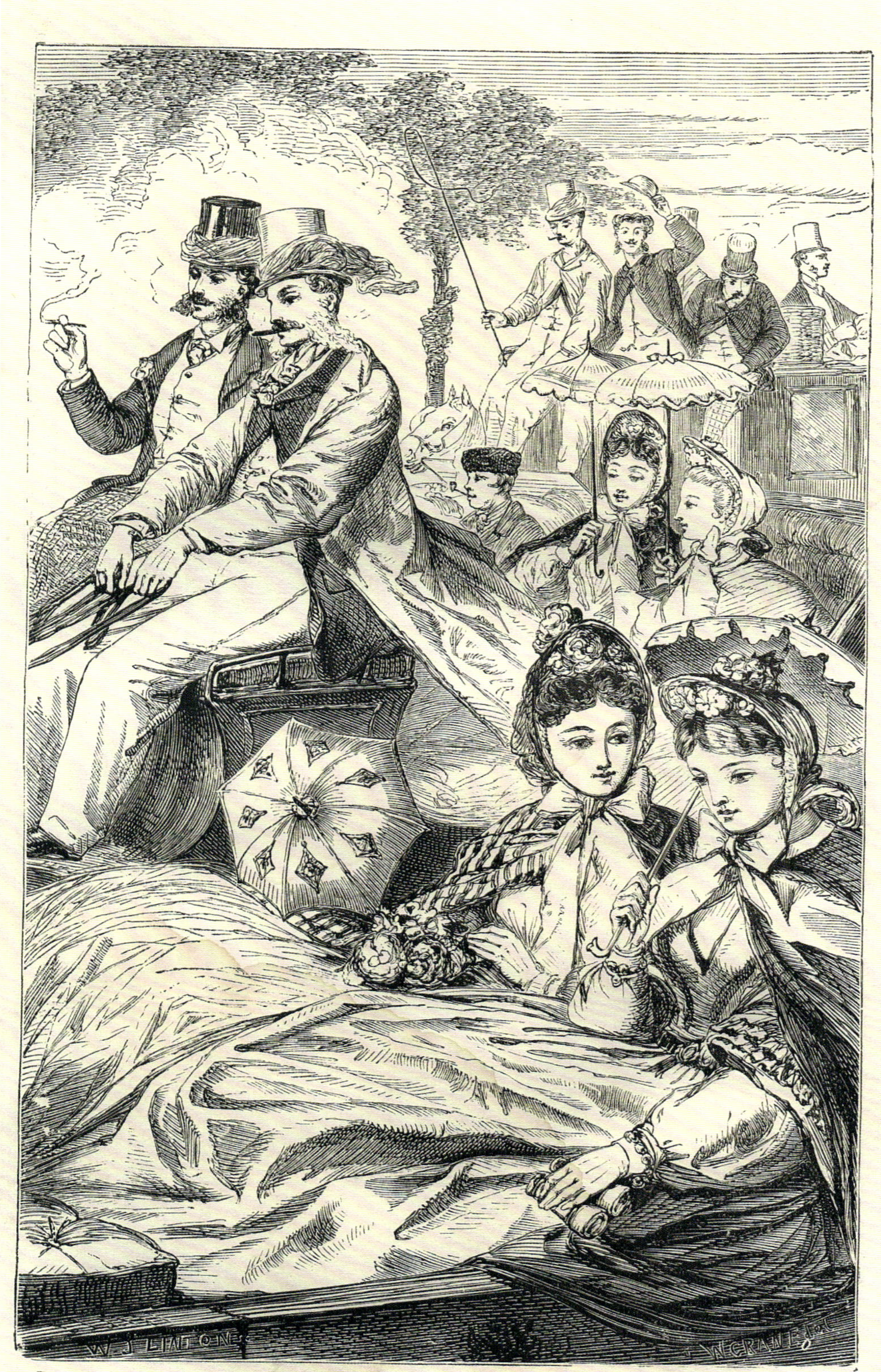

Drawn by Walter Crane. See "The Blue Riband of the Turf."

THE LONDON CARNIVAL.

Chapter 6

The *London Society* magazine and the influence of William Powell Frith on modern life illustration of the early 1860s

ALEX WERNER

When a number of artists in the 1850s chose to paint modern life scenes, they took their lead from Hogarth, the acknowledged founder of British art. For painters like Frith, Hicks and O'Neil, there was a clear tradition beginning with his paintings and engravings, leading on to the genre works of Wilkie, Mulready and Leslie.[1] In the 1820s and 1830s, there were relatively few paintings of urban contemporary life. Major events were recorded such as the opening of a new bridge or the holding of a royal banquet. Yet, the depiction of the life and manners of modern society was rarely attempted. In the genre of history painting, many famous events were set within an urban context and showed what every day life was like in the past. Modern domestic or interior scenes were presented in genre painting but these were confined to bucolic settings where a village tavern or a farmhouse kitchen became the backdrop for the treatment of some sentimental theme. A change took place in the late 1840s and 1850s when urban modern life settings became popular subjects within the tradition of genre painting.

In graphic art, the depiction of contemporary views of every day life and events was well established. From the early 1840s, popular illustrated magazines such as the *Illustrated London News* and *Punch* presented their readers with virtually everything that was new or noteworthy in society. It is clear that these magazine wood engravings had some influence on the development of modern life painting. Whether as straight reportage or caricature, such graphic work portrayed many of the subjects that Frith, Hicks, O'Neil and other artists selected to paint.[2] By the mid-1850s, once modern life painting had established itself as a type of genre art, so it in turn began to impact on popular magazine illustration. Frith's ground-breaking works, *Life at the Seaside (Ramsgate Sands)*, *Derby Day* and *The Railway Station* contributed to this change. A similar influence can be felt also in the illustrations of modern life novels that were published in part form in magazines of the period. The best illustrations charted the inner drama of the main characters as the novel unfolded. Mood and atmosphere were conveyed through the shading and cross-hatching of the lines, often dependent on a successful collaboration between artist and engraver. Even more important was the grouping or pose of the figures and their finely observed facial expressions. A good example was Anthony Trollope's novel *Orley Farm*, first serialised in the *Cornhill Magazine* in 1861–2 with illustrations by John Everett Millais, engraved by the Brothers Dalziel.[3] The novel is largely set in the country though legal London impinges on the main narrative of the work. Two thirds of the forty illustrations are interior scenes, many with just one or two characters present.

87. W. J. Linton after Walter Crane, 'The London Carnival', from 'The Blue Riband of the Turf; or Society at the London Carnival', from *London Society*, July 1862.

88. Left: 'There was sorrow in her heart, and deep thought in her mind'.

89. Right: 'Lady Mason leaving the court'.
Engraved by Dalziel after J. E. Millais for Trollope's 'Orley Farm', *Cornhill Magazine*, 1861–2.

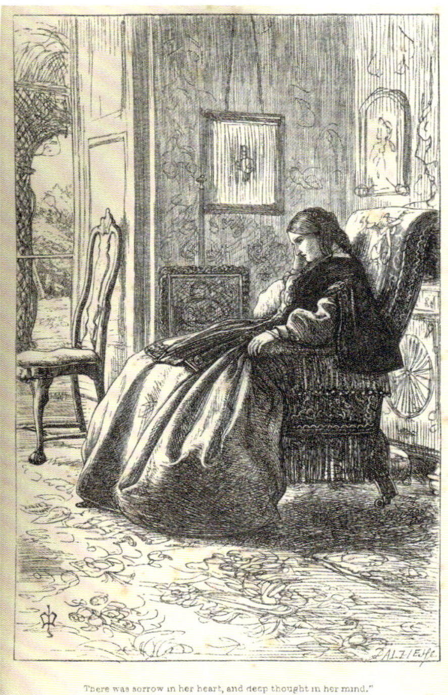

"There was sorrow in her heart, and deep thought in her mind."

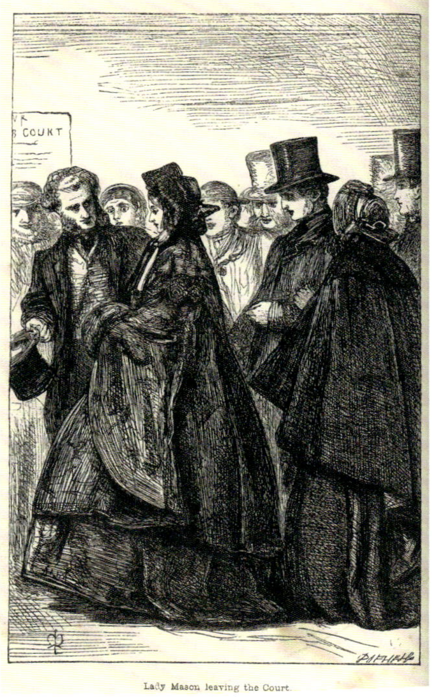

Lady Mason leaving the Court.

Some of them could have been easily worked up as genre paintings in their own right, especially those that portrayed Lady Mason alone as she contemplated her predicament or confessed her crime of forgery (Fig. 88). Only a handful of the forty illustrations, move beyond the sense of confined chamber works to include a wider world. In some, one senses a direct influence of *Punch*'s humorous prints such as the illustration of blind man's buff in the schoolroom at Noningsby with the children catching hold of Judge Staveley's coat tails. However, it is in the three engravings devoted to the trial scene that one catches the influence of modern life painting and illustration as the view widens out, setting the characters in a broader social context, though even here it is the relatively limited world of the law court and its environs (Fig. 89). In the realistic depictions of public spaces of a town or city, artists began to depict the richness of modern life. Painters who were also illustrators, such as Millais, Arthur Boyd Houghton and George Thomas, contributed to the broadening of the subject matter of such genre art. It was easier for the graphic illustrator to stray into areas that had been generally off limits to the painter. Such new attention to modern life subjects can be evaluated in the illustrated magazine *London Society* that was launched in February 1862.

By the early 1860s, there was no shortage of popular illustrated magazines. The success of titles such as *Once a Week*, the *Cornhill Magazine* and *Good Words*, as well as the *Illustrated London News* and its new rival the *Illustrated Times*, demonstrated the public's insatiable appetite for news, literature and art. Billed as offering 'light and amusing literature for hours of relaxation', *London Society* was particularly noteworthy, however, for its fine wood engravings of genre and modern life scenes. George Du Maurier reported that the magazine's programme was 'to move & interest the RANK, WEALTH, WIT and BEAUTY of the Capital'.[4] He was approached by Dalziel, the engravers, to create a series of sketches of London life for the new title. James Hogg, the editor and founder of the magazine, claimed in 1867 that the proprietors had invested 'a large expenditure' to secure 'the very flower of English draughtsmen and engravers'. In the first eleven issues, there were illustrations by, among others, J. D. Watson, M. J. Lawless, George Thomas, F. R. Pickersgill, Frederick Walker, George Du Maurier, Walter Crane, William McConnell, Arthur Boyd Houghton, E. J. Poynter, J. E. Millais and Florence Claxton. The most reputable engraving firms were employed, such as Dalziel, Evans, Harral and Linton. The very wide range of subject matter covered in *London Society* suggests that it was aimed at all sections of respectable metropolitan society. Male and female readers were catered for with articles on sport, fashion, art, the opera, guns, travel, history, flowers and animals. The editor, Hogg, maintained that *London Society* had been 'from the hour of its appearance, one of the most successful works of the day.'[5] This assertion seems to have some elements of truth as a second edition of the first issue of the magazine was being advertised less than a week after its launch.[6]

While the authors of 'the tales', 'miscellaneous papers' and poetry of *London Society* remained largely anonymous, the half yearly index identified nearly all the artists against the title of their work, not just the full page illustrations but also the half or quarter page engravings. Only occasionally was an author named and only then when he or she had sufficient fame, such as the poet Thomas Hood. Sometimes, initials appeared at the end of a piece giving the reader a clue to the author's identity. This avoidance of referencing the authors was perhaps because the magazine set out to be 'light' in character. Nevertheless, some of the pieces were competently written and had no accompanying illustration. Anonymity was a feature of popular magazines of the period but comparing *London Society* with the popular weekly *Once a Week*, which was launched three years earlier, in 1859, as 'an illustrated miscellany of literature, art, science, & popular information', a much higher percentage of its authors were credited while its illustrators were listed simply in the index against a page number, their works lacking either a title or description. The magazine had if anything an even more celebrated list of artists including Hablot K. Browne (Phiz), Charles Keene, John Leech, John Everett Millais and John Tenniel. Some of its wood engravings have a power and dramatic intensity very rare in the popular weeklies and monthlies of the period. However, it did lack the overall focus on contemporary life that made *London Society* stand out from its rivals. The clear acknowledgement of its artists both in the index and alongside the engravings made *London Society* noteworthy and possibly reflected one of its main considerations – the illustration of modern life or society both in text and image. Commonly, in the 1850s, the illustrator had been even more marginalised than the writer in popular magazines. The *Illustrated London News* rarely identified its team of gifted illustrators. In other comic magazines such as *Punch* or *Fun*, the reader was left to identify the small monogram or distinctive style of a Keene or Cruikshank image, with the overall content of the magazine being viewed as of greater importance and value than the work of any one illustrator. One wonders how often the names of the engraving workshops such as Swain and Dalziel that appeared commonly at the lower edge of popular magazine illustration were mistaken for that of the artist. Credit did lie with the engraver's skill, copying and embellishing the artist's work. The best engravers were able successfully to interpret the illustrator's intentions, either from a supplied drawing on paper or the chalked lines on the actual wood block to be cut. However, many artists claimed that engravers only succeeded in wrecking their work.

By the mid-1850s, modern life and genre paintings by artists such as William Powell Frith were drawing large crowds at the Royal Academy and private galleries. Art critics on the whole disliked the new style, even *London Society*'s reviewer (C.L.E. – probably Charles Lock Eastlake, the author of *Hints on Household Taste*) was grateful to find Henry O'Neil 'for once forsaking the "sensation" school of modern incident' at the 1862 Royal Academy exhibition.[7] He noted how the subject matter of Hicks's work *Past, Present and Future*, 'an after-marriage breakfast scene, in which the bride and bridegroom, a pretty widow, and another youthful couple flirting in the

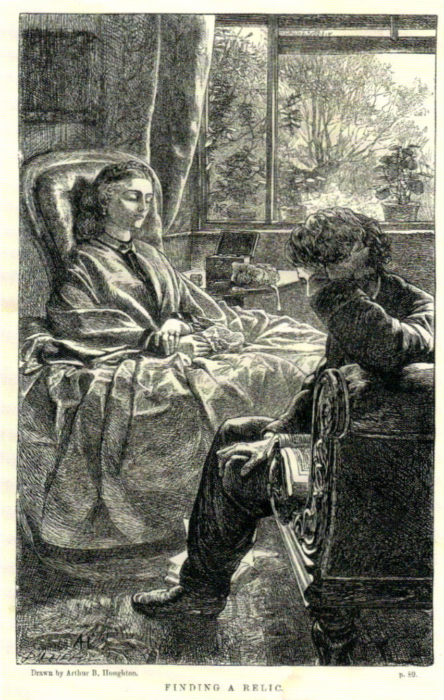

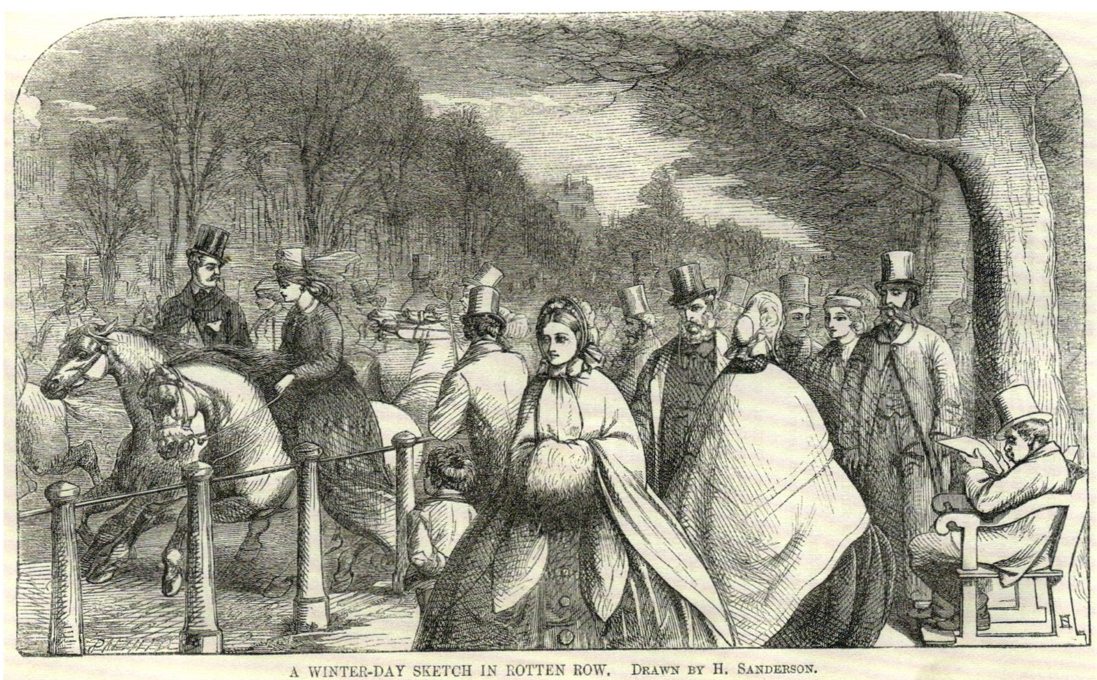

90. Left: Engraved by Dalziel after Arthur B. Houghton, 'Finding a relic', from *London Society*, July 1862.

91. Right: Engraved by Dalziel after H. Sanderson, 'A winter-day sketch in Rotten Row', from *London Society*, February 1862.

background', attracted 'the attention of half the young ladies in the Exhibition'. This was an indirect criticism of the choice of modern life scenes that treated subjects such as love and matrimony in a modern way. It was natural that the popularity of such works should be reflected in illustrated magazines. Illustrations were beginning to be seen as art. More ambitious than before, sometimes panoramic in style, they aimed to copy the subjects and approach of 'modern life' artists. Publishers quickly took account of this fashion and incorporated such scenes within their magazines.

The classic studies of book and magazine illustrators of the 1860s by Gleeson White and Forrest Reid tended to play down the modern life scenes.[8] When such surveys were written in the late nineteenth and early twentieth century, the genre of 'modern life' art had ceased to be fashionable. Reflecting the perceptions of their age, they dismissed such illustrations and concentrated more on what they deemed to be artistic subjects, such as engravings that had a Pre-Raphaelite style. White rejected the modern life illustrations in *London Society* as 'ephemeral', following 'slavishly the inelegant mode of the sixties' and 'lacking lasting qualities', though to his credit, he did suggest that the magazine was a 'document not without interest to the social historian'.[9]

The illustrations in *London Society* fall into two main categories. Firstly, there are the fine genre drawings that illustrate the stories and poems of the magazine. The works by artists such as Arthur Boyd Houghton, F. R. Pickersgill, J. E. Millais and J. D. Watson stand out and reflect the quality of the illustration in *London Society*. Houghton's *Finding a Relic* (Fig. 90), engraved by Dalziel, is a good example where the drawing focuses on an interior scene with just two figures.[10] The pensive woman is bathed in a gentle light while the man in partial shadow has his back turned away from the window. They seem to occupy two separate spaces. This is indicative of the subject matter of the accompanying poem (attributed to L. C.) about a silver thimble (the relic) that had

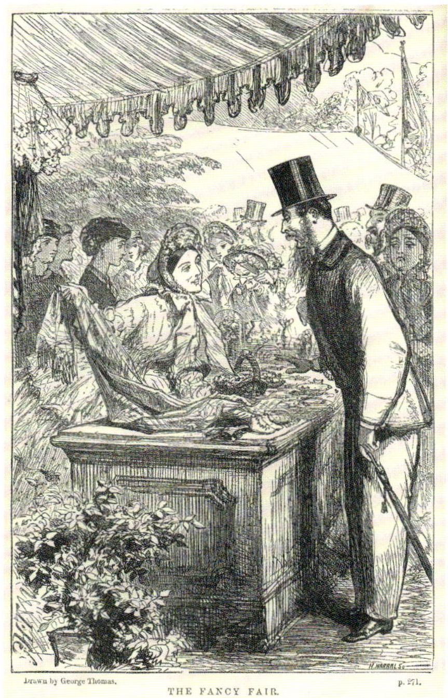

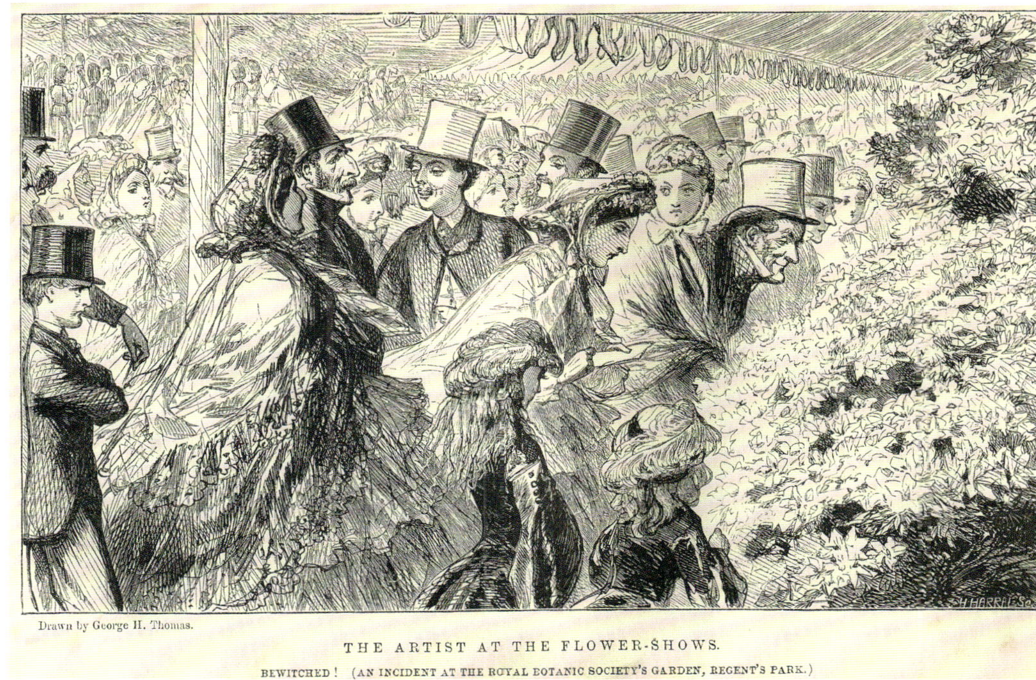

92. Left: Engraved by H. Harral after George Housman Thomas, 'The Fancy Fair', from *London Society*, April 1862.

93. Right: Engraved by H. Harral after George Housman Thomas, 'The Artist at the Flower-shows', from *London Society*, August 1862.

belonged to a childhood sweetheart. The reader interprets the owner of the thimble as the man in the foreground. His reflective pose suggests that he is not reading but staring into space, recalling his sad memories.

The second category in *London Society* is the genre of modern life illustration. From the very first issue, it is clear that the social geographies of the city are to be a feature of the new magazine. There are a short series of illustrations with titles such as 'fashionable promenades', 'the artist in the London Streets' or 'London Societies'. The texts often act as a commentary to the images, supporting the investigation into the mixed cast of London types that occupy and move through the main urban spaces. The first modern life image to appear in the magazine, *A Winter-day Sketch in Rotten Row* (Fig. 91), by H. Sanderson, focuses on one of London's main fashionable sites, with its riding track, drive and promenade.[11] The essay, entitled 'A Stroll in "the Park"', that accompanies it, refers to the fact that, 'here are assembled representatives of all classes – of "all" save "stout peasantry" of England, who with quilted "smocks", and heavy, weather-reddened complexions have no call here. Poverty and wretchedness come here often enough to look at their betters, but it is not "rural" poverty and wretchedness.'[12]

Sanderson's drawing, however, consists of just aristocratic and middle-class figures. *London Society* was not alone in spotlighting Rotten Row. In July 1862, the *Illustrated London News* featured George Housman Thomas's panoramic painting *Rotten Row* that had been displayed recently at the Royal Academy. In this work, showing what was described as 'our truly national promenade', a wider cross-section of society is on view, including a navvy smoking a pipe, a life guardsman, a group of children playing and a 'seedy' swell.[13] Thomas's illustrations for *London Society* include *Is it Friendship? Is it Love? An episode of the Ball-Room* (February 1862), *The Fancy Fair* (April 1862) (Fig. 92) and *The Artist at the Flower-shows – Bewitched! (an incident at the Royal Botanic's Society Garden, Regent's Park*) (August 1862) (Fig. 93). The latter two drawings are examples of subjects that were taken up

94. Left: After Robert Barnes, 'The street singer', from *London Society*, August 1862.

95. Right: Engraved by W. Thomas after F. J. Skill, 'She is My fate!', from *London Society*, December 1862.

96. Below: Engraved by H. Harral after F. J. Skill, 'The Artist in the London Streets: Regent Circus (Oxford Street)', from *London Society*, June 1862.

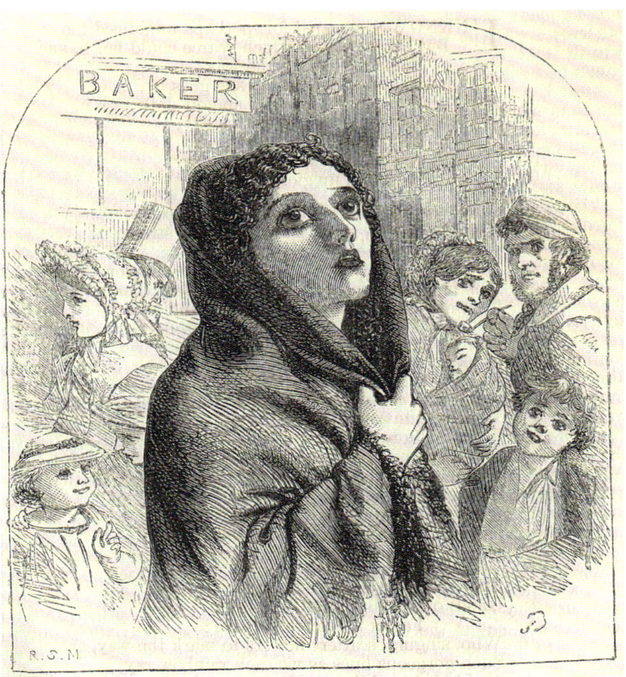

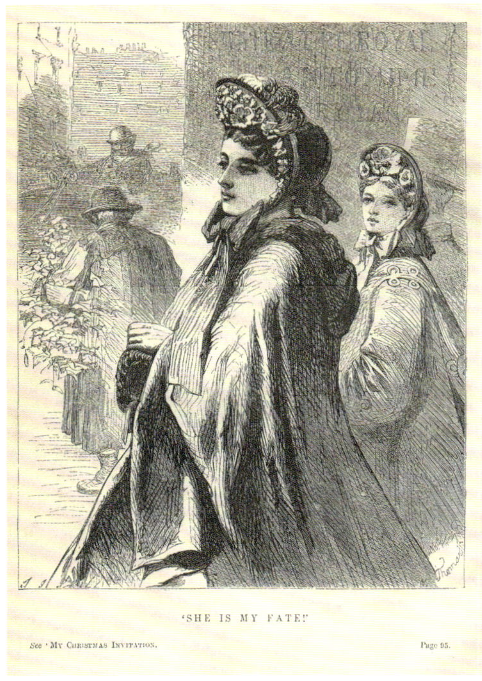

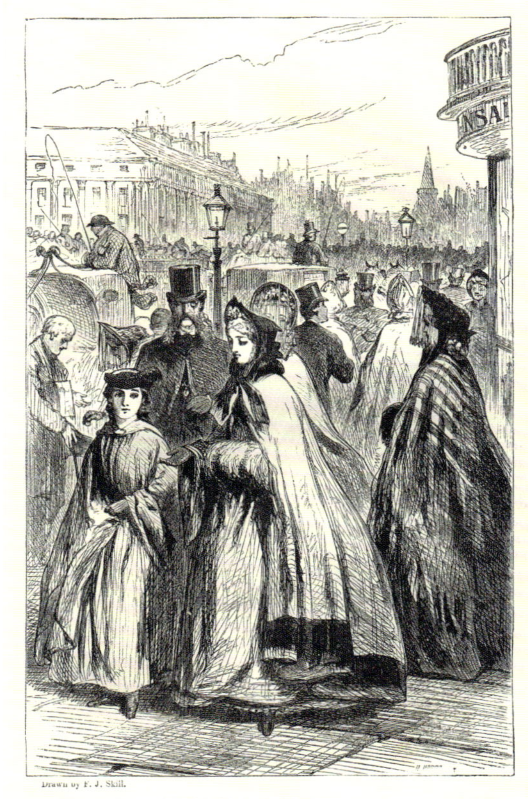

by painters. In 1865, Frith selected to paint one of the attractive 'belles' at a fancy fair.

The majority of the magazine's illustrations depict the fashionable pastimes and events of respectable society. Only a few focus on the street life of the city and the poor make only fleeting appearances in these drawings. A half-page sketch by Robert Barnes illustrates a poor Italian street singer (August 1862; Fig. 94). In the street views, one of the main objectives appears to be portraying attractive women such as in *Fair Faces in the Crowd* by Louis Huard (February 1862), part of *The Artist in the London Streets* series, and *She is My Fate* by F. J. Skill (December 1862) (Fig. 95). Another illustration by the latter artist of *Regent Circus (Oxford Street)* (June 1862) (Fig. 96), one of *The Artist in the London Streets* series, centres on the well-to-do walking along this fashionable shopping street. The hustle and bustle of the scene is suggested by the number of vehicles in the background and the crowded and confined space of the pavement. On the right, a veiled woman stands alone. Perhaps, she has just emerged

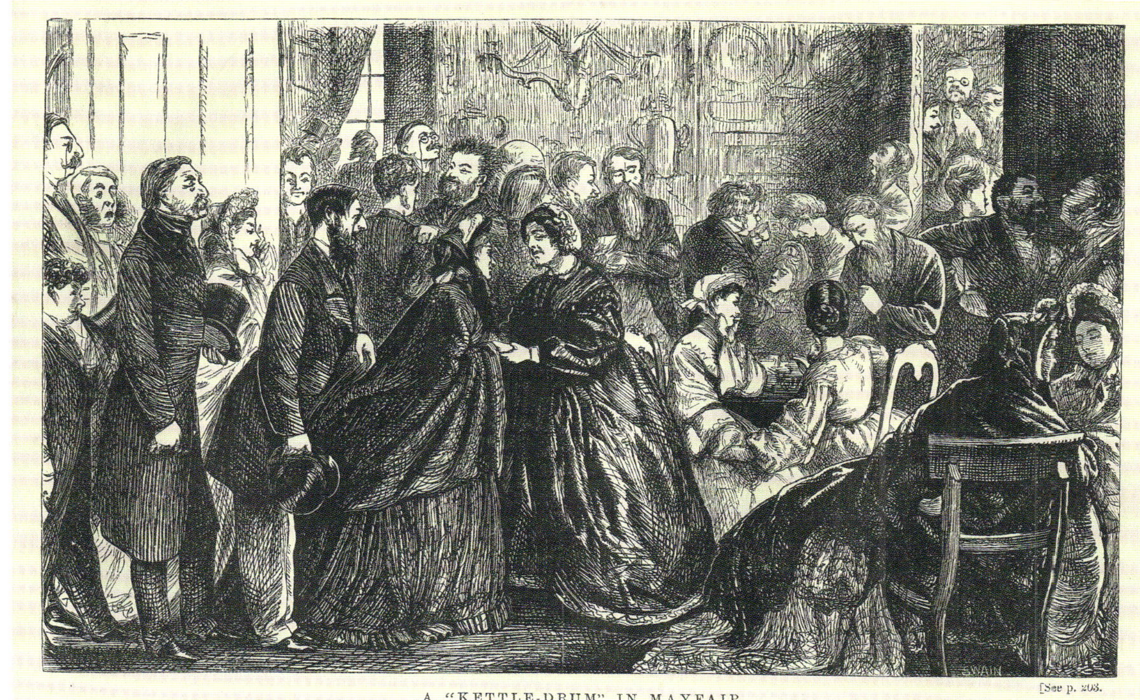

97. Engraved by Swain after George du Maurier, 'A "Kettle-drum" at Mayfair', from *London Society*, September 1862.

from a shop and awaits a gap to emerge in the passing stream of people, before continuing on her way. On the left, a blind street beggar is receiving money from a woman. The blind man is a common social type found in illustrations of the London streets.[14] Here, his position on the edge of the pavement does not hinder the passing figures. He is identified by his stick, hat, board with information about his blindness, and his open palm appealing for alms. The wealthy stop to give out charity, taking pity on his blindness, as he stands vulnerable and alone in this place of movement and activity. Frith's blind man in the centre of his study for the unrealised painting *The Times of Day, 2: Noon – Regent Street* (1862) (Fig. 43) is helped across the street by a bare-footed girl. In this instance, the poor and the blind are shown navigating their way through an unmindful and uncaring city. The tentative approach to illustrating low life in *London Society* is matched by the selection of modern life interior scenes. The engravings of a choral performance, a conversazione at Willis's Rooms and a Parisian drawing room present only a select social class. George Du Maurier's *A 'Kettle-drum' in Mayfair* (September 1862) (Fig. 97) is no different but the work does evoke skilfully a fashionable tea party hosted by one of Mayfair's 'ladies'. The artist noted how the illustration had been 'much praised by artist critics and newspapers'.[15] Du Maurier, along with William McConnell, illustrated scenes at exhibitions for *London Society*. Both artists have an ability to capture the manner and behaviour of people when they are in a public space, among a crowd or as part of a group.

Frith's influence on the subject matter and the style of modern life illustrations can be followed through *London Society*'s pages, in the images of the seaside and the racecourse. Both of these scenes feature regularly in the magazine's first two years. The impact of Frith's *Life at the Seaside (Ramsgate Sands)* (1854) was still being felt on popular illustration and journalism in the 1860s. The subject matter remained very relevant as the urban population took to the seaside in greater and greater numbers, even the working classes. McConnell provides a small sketch of the *London*

Left: 98. Engraved by Anderson after William McConnell, 'The "London Ordinary". – a Sketch at Brighton', *London Society*, July 1862.

Right: 99. Engraved by Swain after Charles Altamont Doyle, 'What we did at the Seaside – Nothing!', from *London Society*, November 1862.

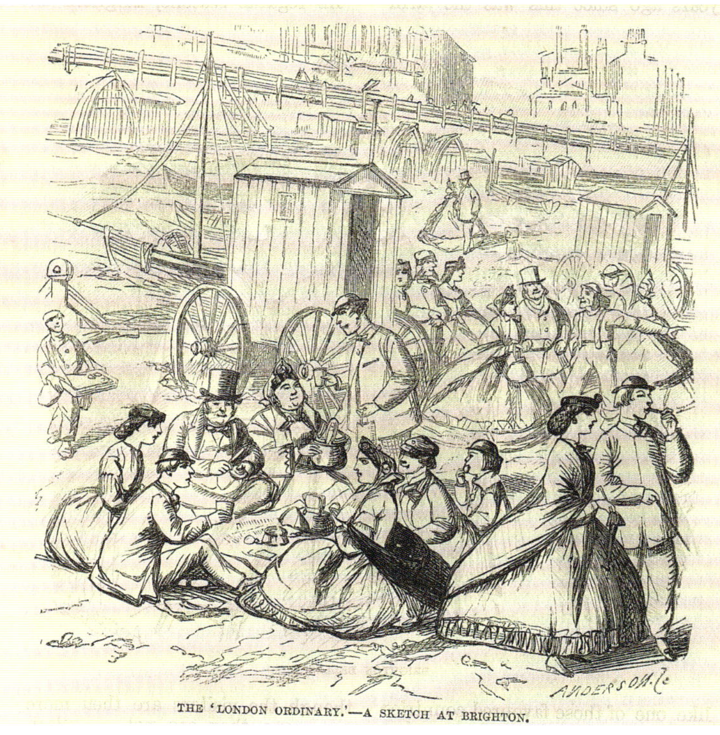

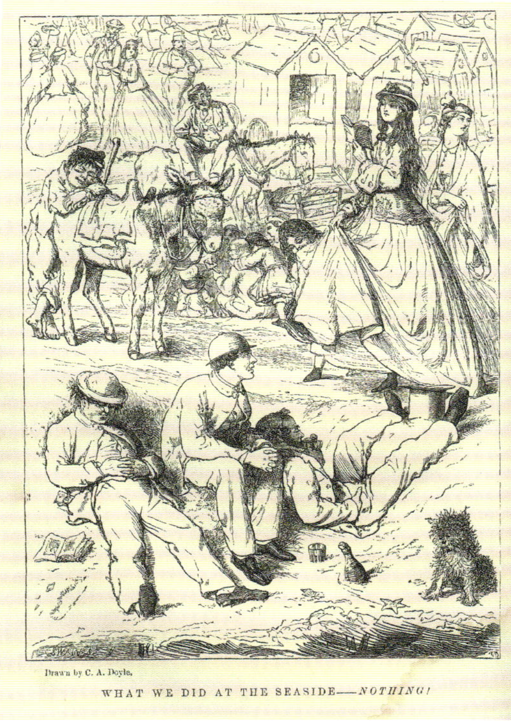

Ordinary (July 1862; Fig. 98), engraved by D. J. Anderson, that shows an extended working-class family having lunch on the beach at Brighton having travelled there by train for a day out. All society was to be found at the seaside, making it a fitting subject for modern life illustrators. In the 1862 September issue of *London Society*, an article entitled 'Dippington: or Society on the Sea-shore' examined how 'the symptoms of Seasidina' exerted itself on the public. Poetry and song were noted as helping to bring the seaside to people's minds or 'a photograph of Ryde Pier or Scarborough Cliffs' or 'Frith's picture of Ramsgate Sands'.[16] The anonymous author described the main characteristics of the seaside such as the bathing machines, lodging houses, walks along the promenade or cliff top, the hiring of a chair on the beach, enjoying the sea air and the view out to sea:

> It is the worthy citizens in the *dégagé* dress, the extraordinary straw hats, and buff slippers we come to study; it is the good natured wives who collect shells and seaweed; the children who build sandcastles, and dig little puddle graves for soft little crabs, whose honest pleasure we come to share in.[17]

The fascination of observing and studying the range of society on holiday was a constant draw, with the viewer becoming a type of voyeur.

The seaside illustrations in *London Society* divide into a number of distinct types. Some images stem directly from the pages of *Punch* and offer a satirical view of the subject. In the late 1840s and early 1850s, John Leech had drawn many amusing seaside scenes such as *Mermaids at Play, or a nice little water party* (1848), *Valuable Hint* (1849) ('always bolt the door of your machine after bathing'), *A Bath at Boulogne* (1853), *A Sketch at Ramsgate* (1852) (here a young girl plays a joke on her short-sighted aunt as they stand by their bathing machine – her aunt mistakes two archery targets

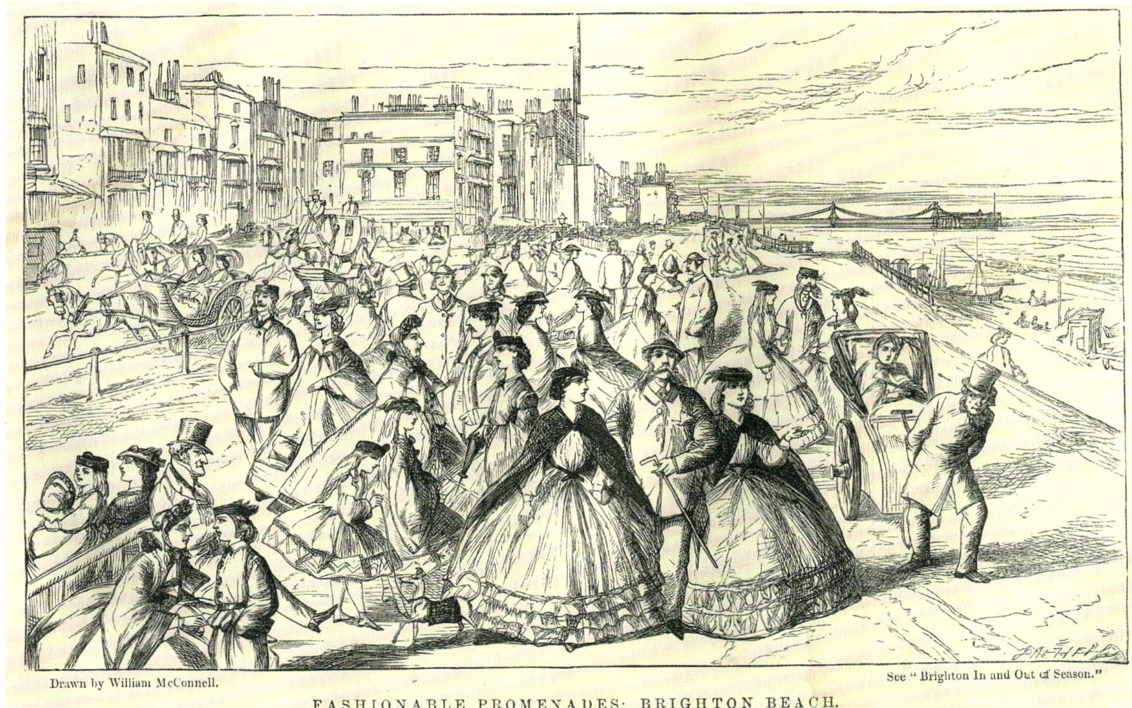

100. Engraved by Dalziel after William McConnell, 'Fashionable Promenades: Brighton Beach', from *London Society*, July 1862.

made up to look like soldiers, she objects to them staring as they bathe) and *Overtaken by the Tide – Margate* (1848). All these works appeared before the immense success of Frith's painting in 1854. In Leech's subsequent cartoons such as *Sea-side – the Bathing Hour* (1855) he continues in the same style, though it is likely that *Punch* readers will have remembered *Ramsgate Sands* with its acute and detailed observation of society at the beach, where everything was set out for all to see and study. In Charles Altamont Doyle's illustration *What we did at the Seaside – Nothing!* (Fig. 99), the frontispiece for the November 1862 issue of *London Society*, the viewpoint is similar to Frith's work; in the lower foreground the sea laps at a sleeping man's feet and in the distance the bathing machines and the donkey rides can be glimpsed.[18] The image stands alone with no accompanying essay. Its portrait format necessitates a different type of arrangement from Frith's wide panoramic approach. The eye moves up the image from three men on the left to the two women walking on the right, back across to the boy on the left leaning against the donkey and then up again to the man resting on one of the ponies employed to drag the bathing machines out into the sea. The sketched-out background with just the outline of some strolling figures and bathing huts completes the image. There are elements in Doyle's illustration that are well observed such as the dog eyeing a starfish in the sand, the pose of the lower three men (one sound asleep, the second resting and smoking a pipe and the third admiring the attractive young girl walking past as she reads a book), the face of the mischievous child poking her head round the skirt of the young girl, and the boy taking a nap while leaning against the hind quarters of his donkey. Doyle's style has elements of satire. The subject's title turns the normal frenzied activity of seaside life on its head by focusing on those asleep and at rest. The linking and grouping of the figures sets up a narrative which balances the central theme of inactivity against suggestions of the beach's normal hustle and bustle, something that is implied by the family group playing in the sand, sketched

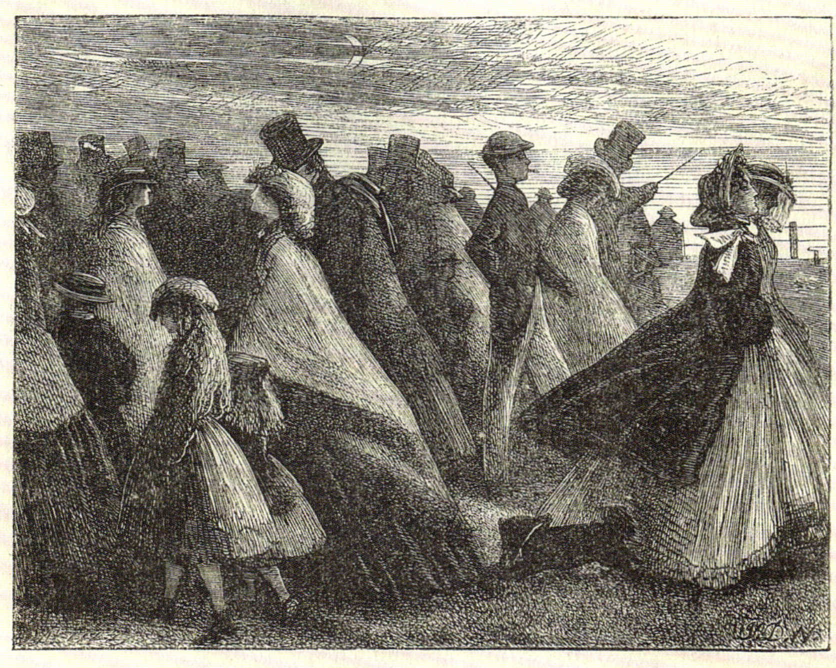

101. After John Dawson Watson, 'Moonlight on the Beach: a Sketch at Ramsgate', from *London Society*, October 1862.

between the donkey's head and the girl's skirt, and the promenading and donkey-riding in the distance.

In contrast, William McConnell's *Fashionable Promenades: Brighton Beach* (Fig. 100) in the July 1862 issue of *London Society* moves closer to the panoramic viewpoint. It illustrated (along with two smaller supporting engravings, one by D. J. Anderson), an essay entitled 'Brighton – In and Out of Season'. McConnell was best known for his fine and very influential illustrations to George Augustus Sala's *Twice Round the Clock* (1859) that showed London life at different times of the day. A feature of many of these engravings was the large number of people depicted in a relatively small work. He supplied such a piece for the 1862 Christmas Number of *London Society*. A short essay entitled 'My Christmas Piece' describes the experience of an author reading his burlesque script in front of the manager and cast. McConnell fills his illustration with twenty-seven characters, each one with a different facial expression. He clearly drew inspiration from Doyle's line illustrations of manners and customs of the English, published in 1849, where many London places and events were featured. These images have the feeling of almost frenzied movement, filled with hundreds of massed caricatured faces and postures. Rather than focusing on just one small scene or group of characters, McConnell filled his drawings with a range of people, often from different walks of life. This type of approach stems partly from the standard wood engravings in the *Illustrated London News* or *Illustrated Times* where the opening of a new building or the visit of royalty was recorded with a large urban crowd on hand to watch the event. The artists and wood engravers employed a shorthand style whereby the scene was full and busy but the detail of the crowd only vaguely sketched out, following a strict stylistic formula. Many of the figures have their backs to the viewer and therefore the groupings and profiles are key to the structure of the scene. Such approaches were necessary as wood engravers had to work quickly to meet strict deadlines. McConnell worked for such titles and knew this style well. Another clear influence on him was modern life paintings such as Frith's *Life at the seaside* (*Ramsgate Sands*). Clearly, the overall character of his illustrations is very different to such works, lacking their realism and attention to detail. However, his adoption of a broad viewpoint, the observation of human interaction matched by the recognisable definite location confirms this as a modern life scene. Here, the composition focuses on the promenade with the roadway and the town's fine houses overlooking the sea on the left and on the right the suggestion of the beach and in the far distance the pier. There is considerable social activity taking place on the central promenade. It is possible to criticize the rather stilted gait and facial outlines of his characters, not something that can be blamed directly on the engraver Dalziel. Nevertheless, McConnell does manage to convey the interaction and movement of a group of people within this public space. In the left foreground, a mother speaks to her son and behind a seated respectable gentleman contemplates the scene. On the right, an elderly man has left off pulling an infirm lady in a perambulator and has stepped forward to stare across at the attractive young woman. Some people have stopped to talk while others walk on past. One notices especially the fashionable central group, the ladies with their wide crinolines and the gentleman's long moustache. While more detail could have been given to

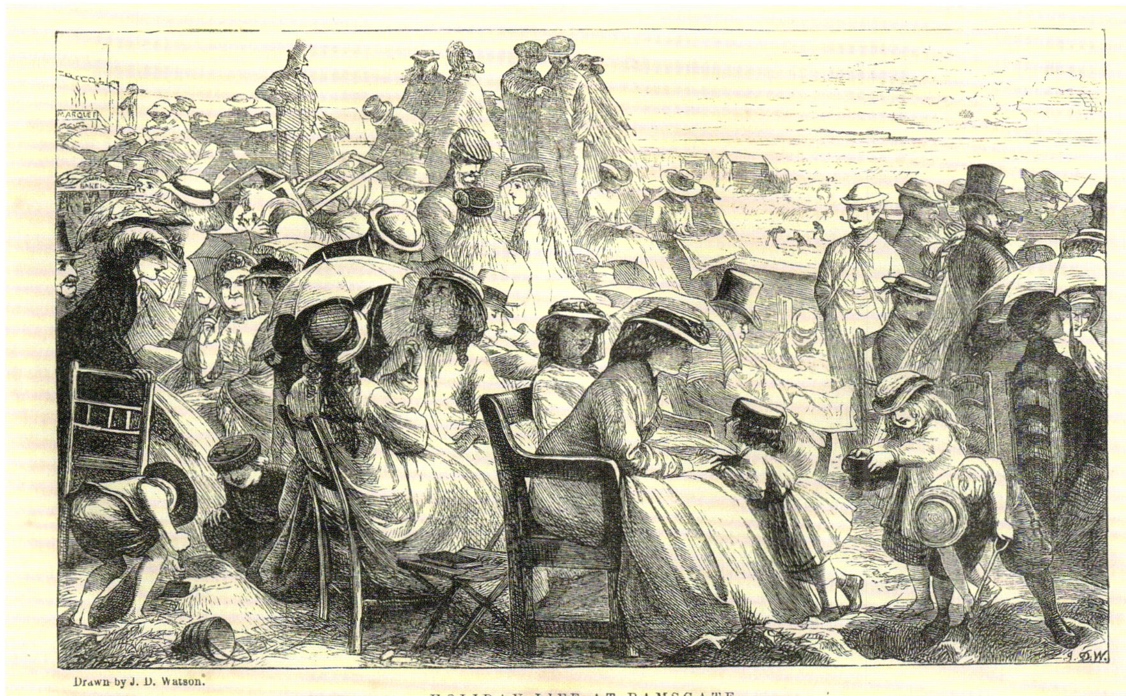

102. Engraved by Dalziel after John Dawson Watson, 'Holiday Life at Ramsgate', from *London Society*, October 1862.

the scene one has to acknowledge that McConnell has succeeded in his commission of illustrating Brighton's promenade. The scene is portrayed in his accustomed style, mixing caricature with a degree of illustrative realism.

Another well-known artist, John Dawson Watson (1832–92), was also charged with interpreting modern life at the seaside in the October 1862 issue of *London Society*. He was perhaps the magazine's star illustrator during its first year, supplying eleven drawings, including the frontispiece to the first issue. He appeared on the scene in 1861 when the Dalziels were approached by the publisher George Routledge to find someone to illustrate their new edition of *Pilgrim's Progress*.[19] A few of his *London Society* genre images were featured by White and Reid in their surveys of the 1860s illustrators, though his modern life illustrations were ignored. His small seaside images present unusual viewpoints on the seaside experience. In *Moonlight on the Beach: a Sketch at Ramsgate* (Fig. 101) a group of people walk along the seaside in near darkness. This mysterious image where the figures almost seem to be sleep-walking brings to mind the work of Arthur Boyd Houghton, another contributor to *London Society*. The moonlight is cleverly picked up on the ladies' shawls and dresses, perhaps a mark of the skilled engraver, in this case the Dalziels, interpreting the artist's sketch.

The subject of Watson's *Holiday Life at Ramsgate* (Fig. 102) was clearly inspired by Frith's interpretation of the seaside, seeming almost like a detail extracted from his painting. One notices how each artist differentiates the spatial planes within the composition. For Dawson, the foreground is given over to the seated figures and the children playing in the sand. The middle distance has a mêlée of people on the move on the left, a tall man talking to two young girls in the centre and on the right a band plays with a man looking away through binoculars and another figure with his hands in his pockets smoking a pipe and eyeing up, almost certainly, the pretty girls in the centre. In the distance, the figures are just sketched out against a background

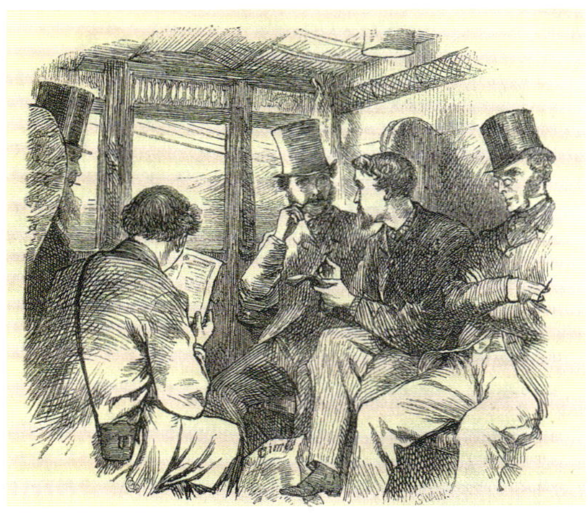
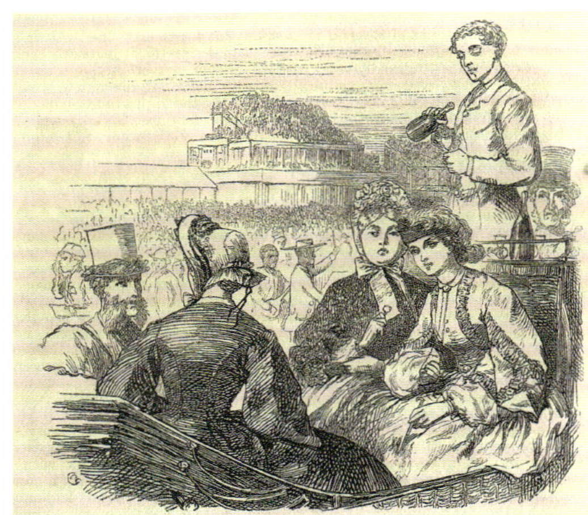
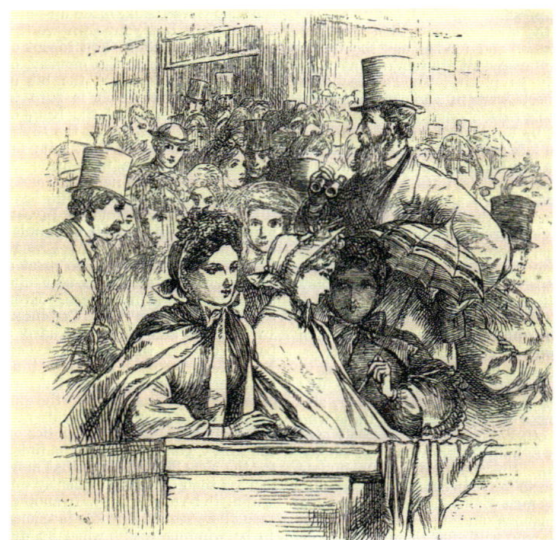

Left to right:
103. *Race-goers Travelling to Ascot*
104. *On the Racecourse*
105. *In the Grandstand*
Engraved by Swain after an unknown artist. From 'Men, Women and Horses: A Study at Ascot', *London Society*, August 1862.

of the cliffs and sea with bathers, bathing machines and even a steamer on the horizon. For Frith, the viewpoint is reversed from the sea to the cliffs, promenades and buildings. Both works have a similar focus on the seated figures, their postures and costumes, though for Dawson there is more dialogue among the different groups and less inner quiet and rest. Frith's mastery of structuring and balancing a massed group of figures is more evident, especially the linking of the foreground to the middle distance. The colour and variety of the costume leads the eye from one character to another whereas with the limits of black and white shading and hatching, the illustrator has to differentiate each group or individual in a shorthand style. Dawson succeeds especially in the foreground female figures with their parasols, bonnets and nets. There is much to admire, here, in the observation of the mother and child in the centre, where the child leans against her mother's legs and the mother bends forward and lovingly touches her child's hand. Such a scene compares with Frith's acute depiction of the little girl's first experience of the sea. Held tightly by her mother, clothes ruffled up, we view the child's two white legs being dipped into the water. The child's face expresses wonder and fear combined. Dawson's other children build sandcastles with fervour and intensity that shuts out everything else that is taking place around them. In both works, the modern life at the seaside has been presented in rich detail. Dawson's drawing is a less satisfying and complete viewpoint than Frith's. It can be seen almost as a snapshot with its edges cut off and the artist's full vision not fully expressed. However, the illustrator succeeds in showing movement, even commotion, of the seaside through a shorthand style where distance is foreshortened and incidents merge together. Frith, on the other hand, overpowers with his detailed focus on the crowd of seated and perhaps over-dressed holiday-makers. Any activity, whether in the foreground with the children playing in the sand or in the distance, is muted by this massed group.

Frith's other great panoramic modern life painting, *Derby Day*, also had a great impact on popular illustration. Whereas *Ramsgate Sands* shows the urban middle class enjoying their seaside holiday, *Derby Day* reveals the whole spectrum of society from gypsies and working people through to the wealthy and fashionable elites of Victorian society, on a day out from the city, enjoying the fun and spectacle of the races. Working from engraved versions or even photographs of the painting, artists drew inspiration and mimicked its vision and observation. *London Society* featured both Derby Day at Epsom and the Ascot race meeting in its early issues. The illustrated article on the latter event was entitled 'Men, Women, and Horses: A study at Ascot', and the writer observed that it still remained 'Ascot the Aristocratic, although two or three railways now carry the million thither'.[20] Unusually for the magazine, the illustrators of the three drawings are not identified, despite the images having been commissioned in advance of the text. This is clear from one reference to the image of an interior of a South-Western Railway carriage (Fig. 103): 'We travelled, by that line of tea-urn coloured engines and solid-wheeled carriages, possibly in some such company as that whose characteristics have here been hit off by the artist.'[21] George Somes Layard, in discussion with a writer employed by *Once a Week*, found that it was common for the text to be 'written up to the pictures, not, as is usually the case, the illustrations prompted by the letterpress'.[22] The second illustration has elements drawn from Frith's painting, depicting three women in an open carriage at the race-course, a man standing up pouring wine from a bottle with the grandstand visible behind (Fig. 104). The final illustration moves within the grandstand itself, showing the range of society men and women watching the races (Fig. 105). The illustrated essay examining the Derby was entitled 'The Blue Riband of the Turf; or Society at the London Carnival'. Walter Crane supplied the full page drawing of the London Carnival (Fig. 87) showing wealthy people on the way to the races. In the right foreground two fashionable ladies are seated with their voluminous dresses filling the inside of their carriage. Like in Frith's painting, Crane gives as much attention to his figures' costumes and accessories as to their pose or physiognomy. For the women, he features their parasols and bonnets tied with large bows and decorated with flowers, and for the equally dapper 'swells', smoking away with their moustaches and sideburns, he shows off their top hats with 'puggarees'. The men seated on top of the far carriage suggest a more boisterous group arriving at the carnival. The society on show here is very limited with only one working class figure visible, his identifiers being a flat hat, a clay pipe and a low brow. Set within the text, A. W. Cooper provides two smaller illustrations, one of a dark-skinned gipsy fortune-teller reading the palm of a lady and the other of a jockey and horse on the way to the weighing station.

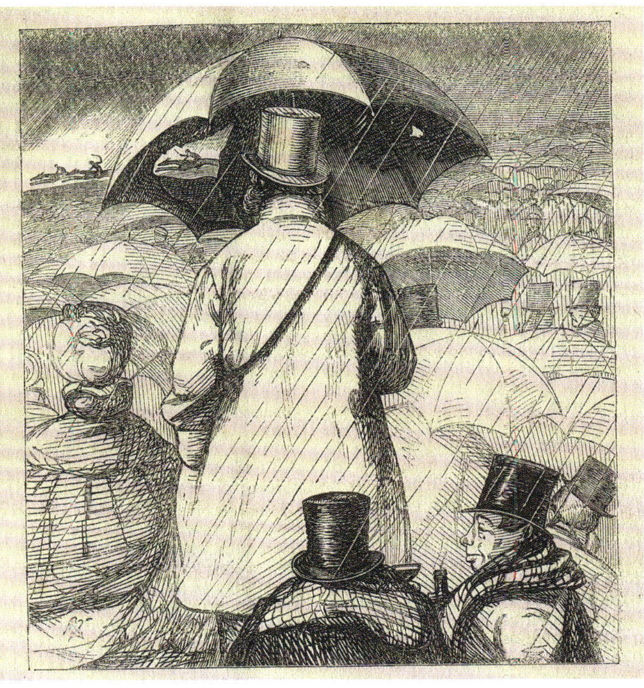

106. Engraved by Ferrier after William Brunton from 'The Derby Day under an Umbrella' *London Society*, July 1863.

In the following year, *London Society*'s July 1863 issue again treats *Derby Day*. Two drawings by William Brunton (Fig. 106) accompany an amusing article, 'The Derby Day under an Umbrella', signed by one 'Jack Easel'. The text has all the light chit-chat to delight readers of the 1860s, such as the information about the author's 'parapluie', its construction, cost and maker ('Issacson's celebrated warehouse in Regent Street'). On leaving town, the author muses on the growth of London, its monotony of new streets, squares and terraces 'which no one but their inhabitants ever see except on Derby Day'. As crowds line the way to watch the stream of carriages passing by, the spotlight briefly falls on a *London Society* reader: 'If you, dear Miss de Browne Browne, who may be conning over this page in Mayfair – if you, I say, lived in Laburnum Villas, or Acacia Cottage, with a serious aunt, for three hundred and sixty-four days in the year, you too would be glad to see a little life on the three hundred and sixty-fifth.'[23]

Ironically, it was just as likely that those living in Laburnum Villas and Acacia cottage would have been keen readers of *London Society*. The magazine was advertised at suburban railway stations and was clearly aimed at a middle-class audience. For the author, the fun and liveliness of Derby Day is somewhat tempered by the rainy conditions and the minor races pall in front of the main event of the day, the Derby Stakes. They are compared to 'the genre pictures and portraits of a "gentleman" . . . hurried over at an exhibition until we stand before the work of Frith or Millais'.

Facing page:
107. Engraved by Swain after Matthew Morgan, 'The Quarter before the "Derby"', from *London Society*, July 1863.

With Matthew Morgan's gate-fold illustration, *The Quarter before the 'Derby'* (Fig. 107), the largest yet featured in the short life of the *London Society* magazine, a bold attempt is made to capture the panoramic scene, in a way comparable to Frith's painting. In fact many of the drawing's details are lifted directly from this work. The viewpoint is slightly higher than Frith's, though the grandstand occupies a similar position in the distance. Morgan endeavours to show a broad cross section of society as low-life figures surround and interact with the respectable classes in their carriages. Closer to satire than realism, the foreground shows a gentleman pouring champagne into the mouths of three frenzied-looking 'urchins', possibly gypsy children. This scene had been adapted from the 'dissolute' upper class group at the centre of Frith's work. Here, the gentleman offers a girl acrobat on stilts some champagne while his female companion tries to hold him back.[24] Another similarity is the depiction of a degenerate aristocrat. Frith's figure leans against the carriage on the right of the painting and faces the viewer, whereas Morgan's gentleman is found within the central low-life group in the foreground. He is shown lighting a cigarette and eyeing up the attractive acrobat girl. The whole foreground in Morgan's drawing is alive with activity with many of the standard character types found at the Derby. A group of figures lays siege to the carriage with the dissolute aristocrats including the sellers of race cards and wooden toys or lucky charms. On the extreme right, a brutish policeman has arrested a gypsy woman holding her baby, possibly for begging, and on the left a bookie is taking a bet from a customer. Overall, the illustration gives a feeling of movement and exuberance. Again this aspect is easier to convey in illustration than in the detailed realism of Frith's painting. In Morgan's image the spaces between the different groups are sketched poorly, just rough hatching filling the gaps. In contrast the distant view is well observed, perhaps owing something to photographic images for the handling of the perspective as employed by Frith.

Whether out of town or in the city, the illustrators commissioned by *London Society* in the early 1860s successfully portrayed many of the incidents of modern life. Their drawings are assured and confident, matching the authority of the modern life painters. The works of artists such as Frith prompted some of their subjects. A few of their illustrated scenes break new ground in the observation of society in public and private spaces. George Du Maurier writing in the *Magazine of Art* in September 1890 explains that

> the illustrator in black and white . . . must not hope for any very high place in the hierarchy of art. The great prizes are not for him! But if he has done his work well, he has faithfully represented the life of his time; and for that reason alone, his unpretending little sketches may, perhaps, have more interest for those that come across them in another hundred years, than many an ambitious historical or classical canvas that has cost its painter infinite labour, imagination, and won for him in his own time the highest rewards in money, fame, and academic distinction.[25]

The engravings in *London Society* have been largely ignored by historians. Taken as a whole, these works are worthy of some attention.

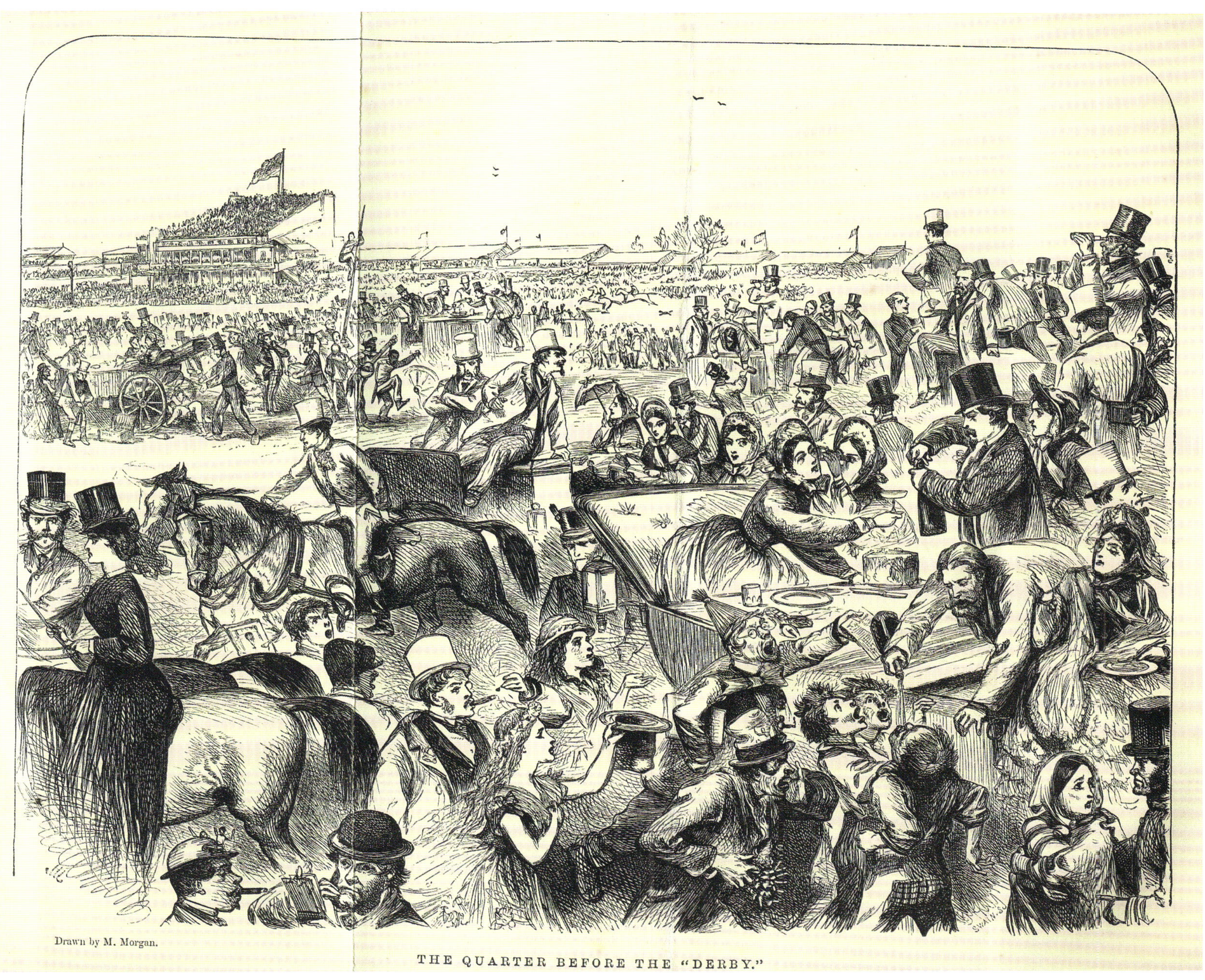

Drawn by M. Morgan.

THE QUARTER BEFORE THE "DERBY."

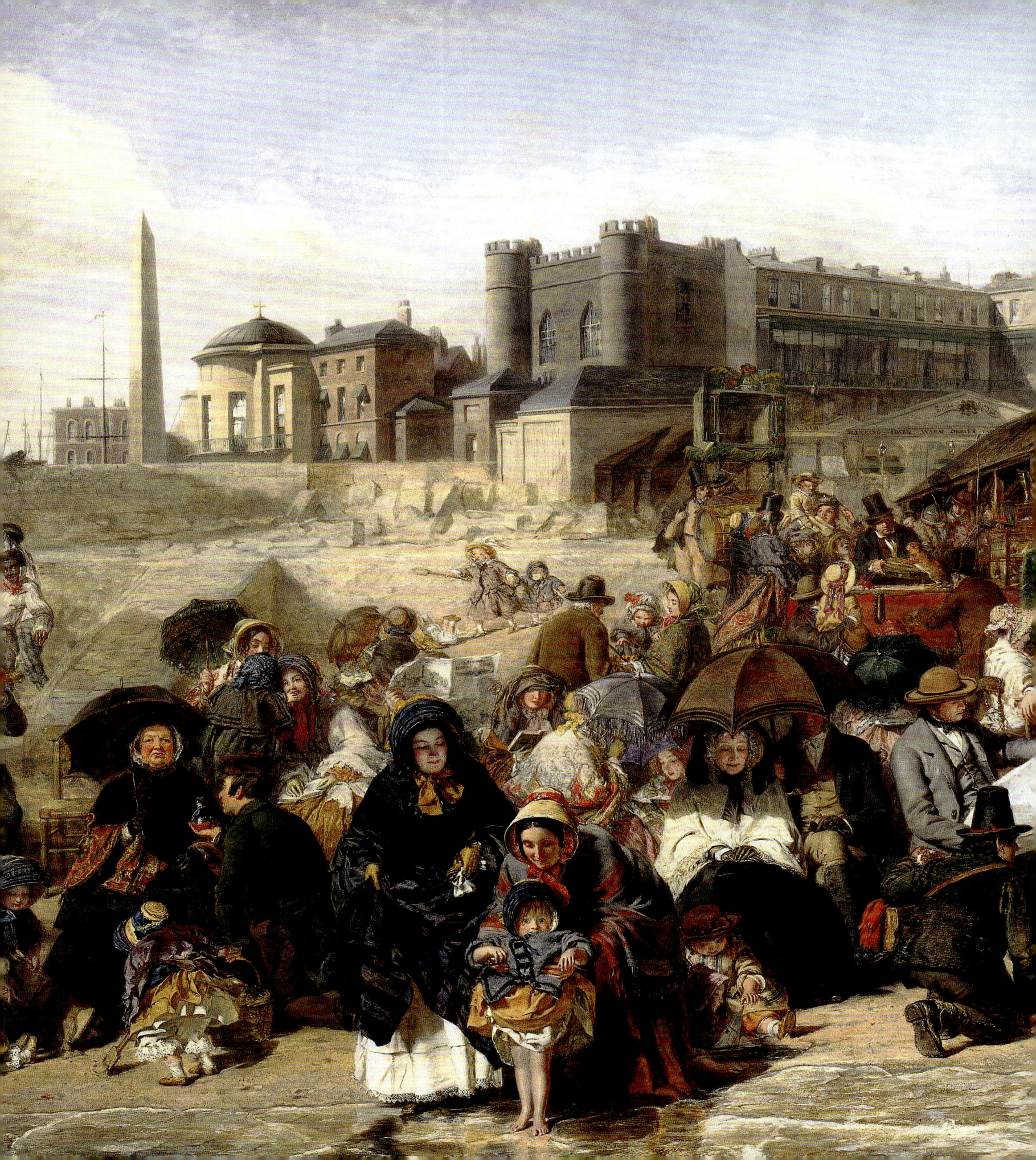

Chapter 7

Frith and Fashion

EDWINA EHRMAN

'Weary of costume-painting, I had determined to try my hand on modern life, with all its drawbacks of unpicturesque dress.'[1] With this brief, phlegmatic statement William Powell Frith marked a turning point in his career. At last he felt he had found a contemporary subject of such compelling human interest that he could risk a 'hat and trousers picture', one that he could make so enthralling that the spectator would 'forget' the clothes worn by the 'actors in it'.[2] Frith understood his audience, and contrary to the predictions of some of his fellow-artists who professed to be bewildered by his subject or shocked by its low, 'Cockney' vulgarity, *Life at the Seaside (Ramsgate Sands)* (Fig. 108) was a huge success with the Victorian public. Frith's observation and humour, his skilfully drawn characters and the many sub-plots in his narrative captivated them. The reviewer for the women's magazine *The New Monthly Belle Assemblée* found the painting

> . . . replete with nature. To each group the gazer will attach a story: the old couple shading themselves under the ample umbrella; the ladies, with their 'uglies', casting sly glances at all that is passing around them; the widow and her lover, . . . and above all, the lovely little girl with her naked feet in the water (said to be the artist's child) which the mother is trying to coax into the love of bathing, are perfect portraits of natural life which stir up the best emotions of the heart.[3]

This review, which passed over the more raucous, 'Cockney' elements in the painting – the musicians, showmen, donkey boys and peddlers touting for custom – shows how its author read the painting as an uplifting series of familiar stories: some touching and amusing, others, like the widow and her lover, exciting speculation or pointing a moral.[4] It also suggests how the attention of the audience could be caught and the narrative carried by clothing. Amid the flurry of colourful parasols, the elderly couple's umbrella and the man's old-fashioned breeches and gaiters signal their age and their membership of a generation more used to coach than railway travel. Shielded by the umbrella's cover, his companion does not need to attach an 'ugly' (Fig. 109)[5] to her bonnet brim to reduce the glare of the sun. 'Uglies' belonged to the present, to a generation eager to purchase the latest novelty for a trip to the seaside.

DRESS AS ART

Frith's characterisation of modern dress as ugly and unpicturesque was a view shared by many artists and both the ordinariness of everyday clothing and the specificity and luxury of high fashion were seen to be potentially alienating and distracting. Women's fashions were also criticised on aesthetic, moral, economic and hygienic grounds. Frith typically decried fashions like the

108. *Life at the Seaside (Ramsgate Sands)*, 1856. The Royal Collection. Detail of Fig. 14.

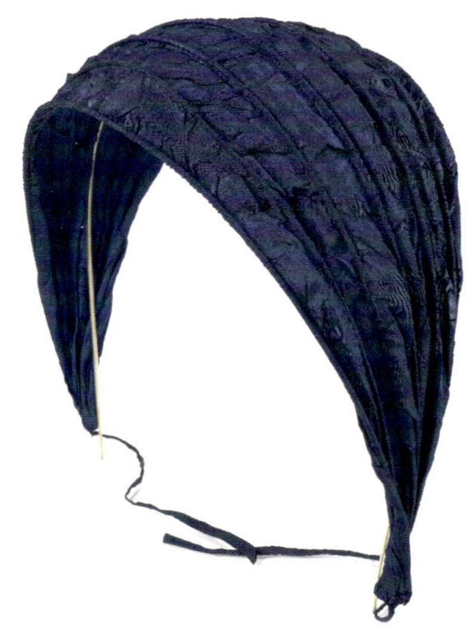

109. An ugly, *c.* 1852, silk and cane. Museum of London.

gigot sleeves of the 1830s (Fig. 110) and constrictively tight skirts of the 1870s (Fig. 111) that ignored the natural shape and proportions of the body, distorting, exaggerating or confining it. He remonstrated with women for their subservience to the dictates of fashion and blamed their dressmakers for leading them on, capitalising on the fast changing styles emanating from Paris. The bustle was the greatest travesty, 'a fashion so monstrously ugly, so gross an exaggeration of nature, indeed, so unlike any natural form, as to rob the female figure of all its grace. . . . This thing, composed . . . of steel, or wool, or "all sorts of things", must have been an attempt of the Parisian *modiste* to see how easily the servile followers of fashion could be imposed upon.'[6] Frith does not mention colour in the context of mainstream fashion but his paintings suggest that he shared the distaste of many artists and designers for the vivid colours that the new synthetic dyes had made possible.[7]

How women should dress was a debate that had preoccupied artistic circles and dress reformers since at least the middle of the century. In 1854 Mary Merrifield, a writer on art history, published *Dress as a Fine Art*, a compilation of essays that had first appeared in the *Art Journal* and the *London Magazine*. She recognised the impact of modernity on her contemporaries and the pressures to conform and consume that were encouraged by the fashion trades and the persuasive imagery of the French fashion plates published in the British media. Acknowledging the 'constant demand for novelty which exists in an improving country',[8] she recommended her readers to respect the natural form and movement of the body in the cut of their clothes and to gratify their desire for novelty from the wide range of colours[9] and constant supply of new fabrics which mechanisation and technological innovation had made possible. They should emulate the portrait painter, developing his eye for form, line and colour,[10] and apply this to selecting dress

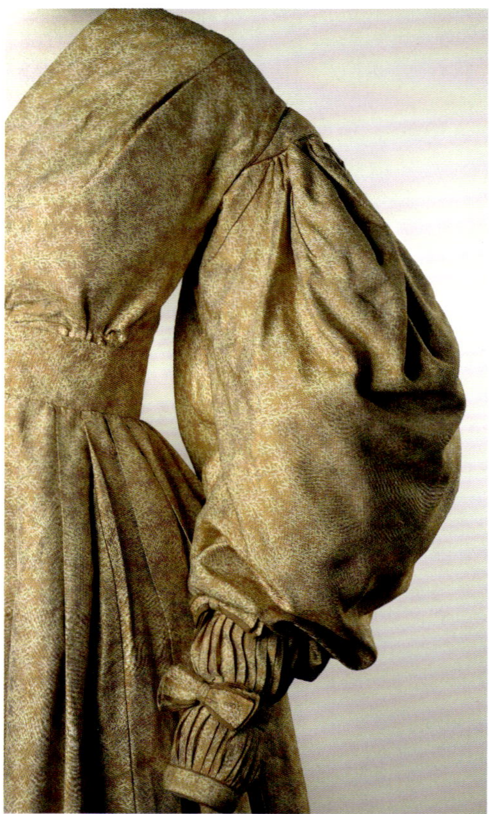

110. Silk dress with *gigot* sleeves, *c.* 1834. Museum of London.

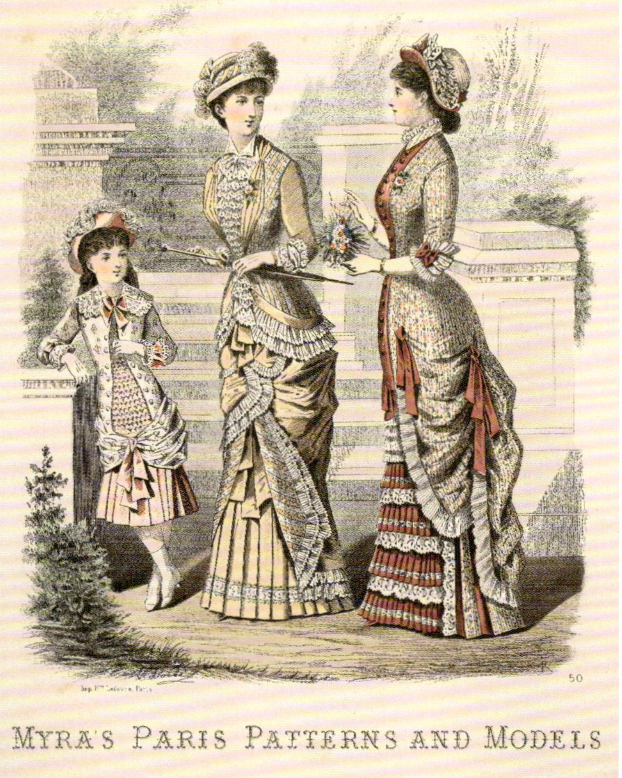

111. 'Myra's Paris Patterns and Models', from *Myra's Journal of Dress and Fashion*, 1 September 1879. Museum of London.

that accorded with their figure, complexion, age and status, enhancing their appearance and health, and saving time and money.

In the 1870s Mary Eliza Haweis, the daughter of the artist Thomas Joy and an acquaintance of the Friths, took up the baton of reform. Frith had encouraged the eighteen-year-old to submit a painting to the Royal Academy after her father's untimely death[11] and Frith's daughter Jane Ellen, or 'Cissie', attributed her decision to write to Haweis's influence.[12] Mary Eliza and her husband, the charismatic preacher Hugh Reginald Haweis, moved between aristocratic and artistic circles, socialising with artists such as Alma Tadema and Walter Crane whose wives, like Mary Eliza, were in the vanguard of the aesthetic movement. Her dress drew on historical styles,[13] which she recommended for their individuality, flowing drapery and economy, requiring less fabric and fewer trimmings, and being easier to fit and make than conventionally fashionable garments. References to period dress were a feature of high fashion throughout the nineteenth century but their interpretation accorded with the current season's silhouette, fabrics, colours and trimmings and orthodox ideals of femininity. Like Mrs Merrifield, Mrs Haweis argued that dress was 'most beautiful and most becoming when it follows the outlines of the human form'[14] and that its proportions should obey the proportions of the body. Both women were opposed to tight lacing as disfiguring and detrimental to health. Mrs Haweis repeated these admonishments in the *Art of Dress* (1879) urging those who eschewed the historical styles she preferred to follow 'the broad outlines of the prevailing mode' avoiding the 'vagaries of its details'.[15]

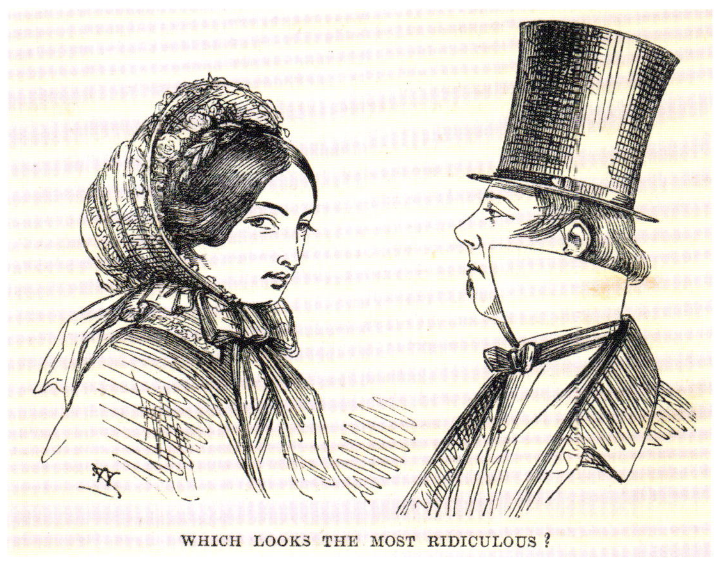

112. 'Which looks the most ridiculous?', from *Punch*, vol. XXV, September 1853, p. 145. Museum of London.

The disparaging term 'hat and trousers picture' reflects similar concerns about male dress caused not by excess but by its increasing uniformity. From the 1840s the clothing worn by the upper and respectable middle classes gradually became more sober. The chief garment for sartorial display was the waistcoat but by the 1860s colour had been largely abandoned in favour of a dark waistcoat for daywear and a white one for the evening. As Aileen Ribeiro has pointed out the sobriety of male dress was so uniform that attacks on fashion were directed almost entirely at women until the appearance of masculine aesthetic styles in the late 1870s.[16] Elizabeth Rigby, a journalist and writer on art who married the artist Sir Charles Lock Eastlake, discussed male clothing in an essay published in *The Quarterly Review* in 1847 in which, writing as a man, she contrasted the flamboyance of male dress in the past with its current plainness. Contemporary men's clothing was 'a mysterious combination of the inconvenient and unpicturesque . . . as ugly as the staunchest Puritan could have devised'.[17] Another commentator on dress, the novelist and writer Margaret Oliphant, who was well-known for her caustic attitude to the male sex, agreed that men's clothes were ugly but argued that their respectable but 'monotonous livery' was convenient and, unlike most women's costumes, allowed freedom of movement. The wealthy too enjoyed a wide range of clothes designed for every occasion and activity, all subject to the 'unwritten code of [their] kind'. 'Though these additions of modern dress are in reality luxurious . . . they are rarely extravagant in appearance, and in fact are as comfortable, as well adapted for the work (meaning play) which has called them into being, as could be devised.'[18] Neither she nor Elizabeth Rigby found anything commendable in the 'unimaginably hideous' top hat (Fig. 112).

Mrs Oliphant also cast her eye further down the social scale. While the poor working man made do with the minimum number of basic garments, shop and office workers and artisans on a regular income enjoyed more choice. For these men ready-made clothes offered a range of styles

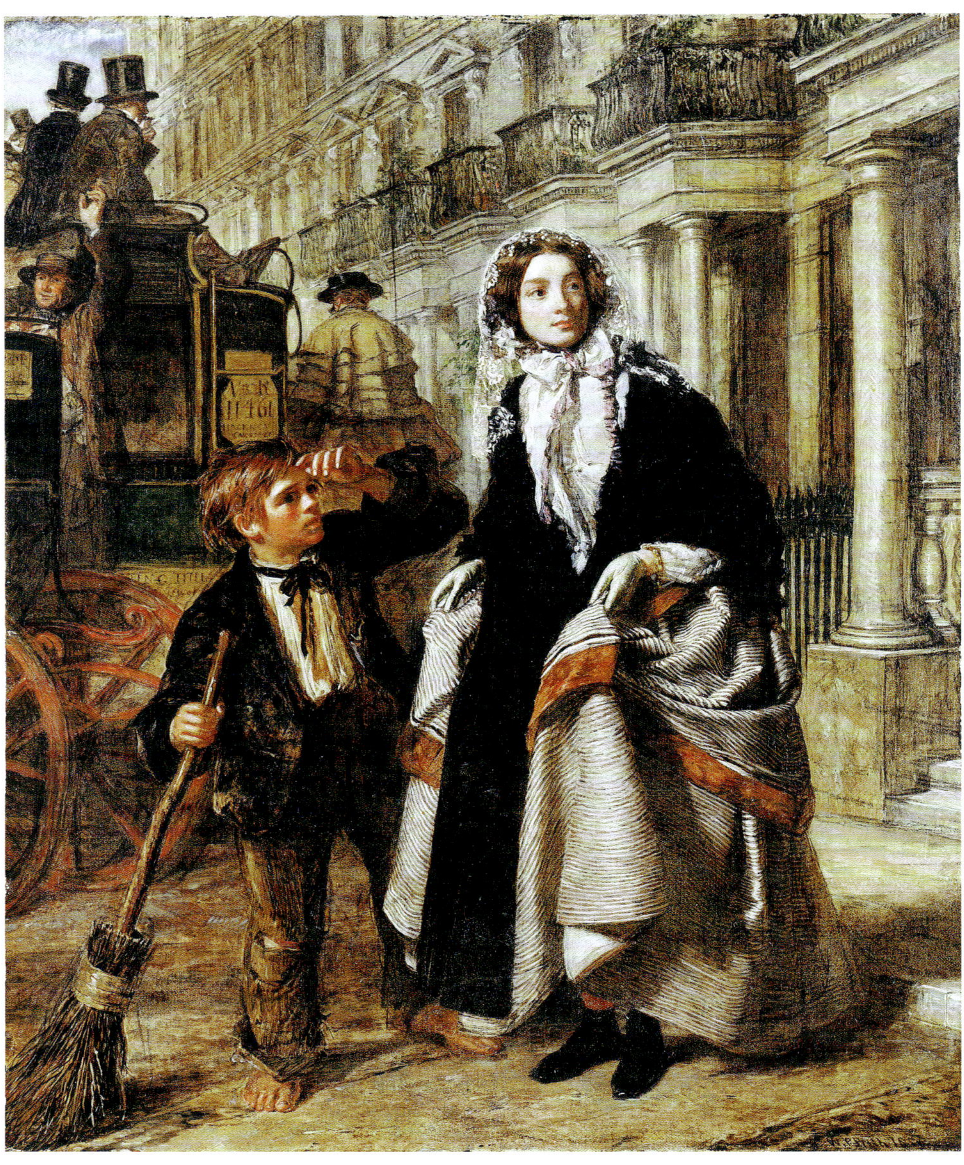

113. *The Crossing Sweeper*, 1858. Museum of London.

and an alternative to second-hand. The quantity production of ready-made clothing had been made possible by the mechanisation of the textile industry, which reduced the price and increased the variety of fabric available to clothing manufacturers, who employed sweated labour to keep costs down and boost production.[19] 'Business' wear was advertised alongside 'mechanics' clothes made in a range of durable fabrics such as fustian, jean, corduroy and moleskin. However evidence from the 1860s suggests that many London artisans wore the same outfit of black coat and waistcoat, and moleskin or cord trousers six days a week. The trousers were put on clean on Saturday evening and worn for a week.[20] Mrs Oliphant noticed this increasing uniformity, commenting a decade later that their dress was 'losing much of its distinctive character', and would soon be 'a mere reproduction in rougher material' of the dress worn by gentlemen.[21]

Occupational clothing was also disappearing in favour of standardised fashionable dress or uniforms. The novelist Anthony Trollope in *Can You Forgive Her?* (1864) wistfully compared the horseman's dress worn by innkeepers in the days of coach travel – a 'long parti-coloured waistcoat', birds-eye patterned neckerchief, breeches and top boots – to the 'undertaker's' garb and top hat they had since adopted.[22] Frith too looked back fondly on the dress worn in the coaching era. Describing a journey from Harrogate to London in 1837, he recalled the clothes of a very old post-boy, 'a figure quite strange to the present generation' who wore an old white hat, a weather-stained jacket that had once been blue, buckskin breeches 'all too wide for his shrunk shanks' and worn boots.[23] Both quotations suggest nostalgia for a pre-industrial past and an appreciation of the picturesque potential of working dress. Indeed one of Frith's earliest memories of London, the amazing number of capes on a hackney-coach driver's greatcoat,[24] found substance in paint in *The Crossing Sweeper* (Fig. 113). There the ample layers and folds of just such a coat echo the buoyant curves and horizontal stripes of the young woman's horsehair petticoat and pattern woven flounced skirt and offer a stark contrast to the bare-footed crossing sweeper's torn trousers and gaping shirt. The very poor covered their bodies as best they could from street markets and rag fairs. Their motley clothes undoubtedly appalled but inspired artists. They were a graphic reminder of the social deprivation that existed side by side with the prosperity the Industrial Revolution had brought others, but their rags, like those of Frith's crossing sweeper, whose jacket and tie impart an air of honest respectability, could be sanitised to render poverty pathetic but picturesque.

Like many artists,[25] Frith assembled a large collection of costume to dress the subjects in his genre and modern life pictures, purchased from junk shops, costumiers and, occasionally, his sitters. The latter included the 'wonderful green coat' worn by the drummer in the animal act depicted in *Life at the Seaside*, which he used in many subsequent paintings.[26] His wife Isabelle also made and arranged costumes and drapery for her husband.[27] Frith found historical costume very picturesque but it too was 'troublesome', and expensive to purchase or make. At the beginning of his career he found it difficult to find reliable information about historical dress. Visits to the Print Room at the British Museum often proved frustrating.[28] Later, when working on *Claude Duval* in 1859, he consulted F.W. Fairholt, the author of *Costume in England* (1846)[29] and used other unnamed contemporary sources. These may have included J. W. Planché's *History of British Costume* (1834), which informed Mary Merrifield's writing on dress.

Given Frith's reservations about fashion it was ironic that his first painting depicting a scene from the recent past should have triggered a brief fashion sensation, the 'Dolly Varden' polonaise (Fig. 114). Frith's painting of *Dolly Varden*, a character in Charles Dickens's novel *Barnaby Rudge*, set in the 1770s and 80s, came to public attention at the sale of Dickens's picture collection in 1870. This coincided with the Franco-Prussian War when the fashion cycle in Paris was temporarily halted and British dressmakers had to look for novelties at home to inspire the public. The polonaise, whose bodice was extended to form an overskirt, short at the front, looped up at the sides and gathered into a puff behind, resembled an eighteenth-century garment of the same name. The 'Dolly Varden', in its original form, consisted of a bodice of printed cotton or flannel worn with a plain underskirt matched to the dominant colour in the print.[30] The dress in Frith's painting was actually his grandmother's

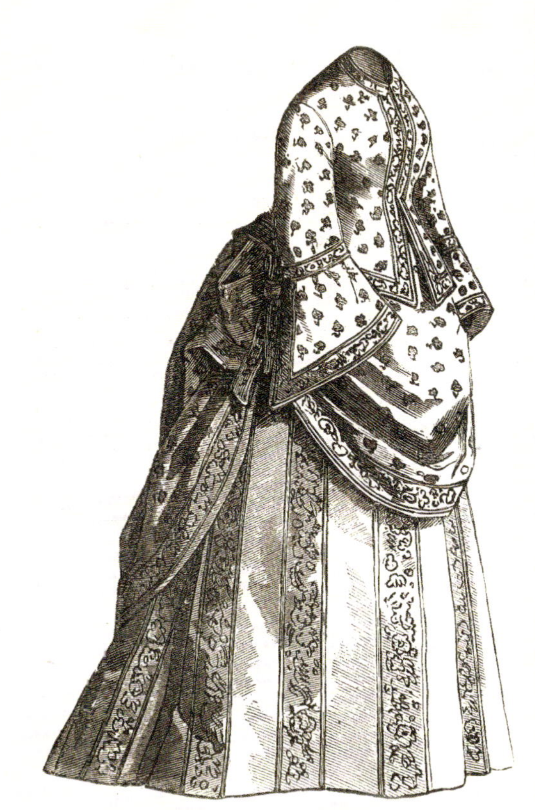

114. 'Costume of Dolly Varden Chintzes' from *The Queen*, 18 May 1872. Museum of London.

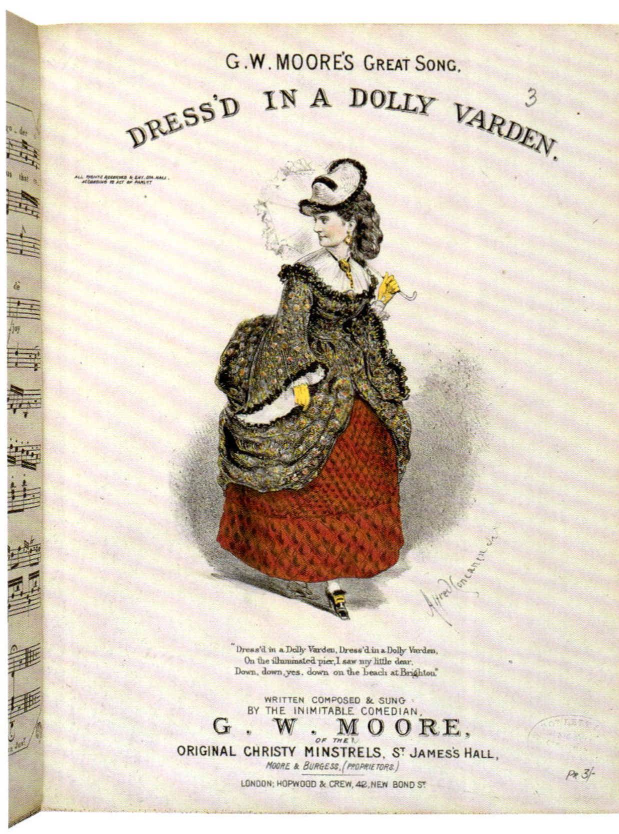

115. 'Dress'd in a Dolly Varden', song sheet cover published by Hopwood & Crew, *c.* 1871–2. The British Library.

wedding dress. His daughter Cissie, who was to wear it for a fancy dress party, described it as made

> of very thick cream-coloured striped silk, powdered with tiny rose-buds worked by hand,[31] . . . looped up *en panier* over a rose-coloured quilted silk skirt: the bodice . . . laced with cherry coloured ribands . . .; the cherry-coloured silk stockings were clocked, and the delightful little shoes had square paste buckles and cherry-coloured heels; and a dainty hat with some cherry coloured ribands . . .[32]

The Dolly Varden fad lasted into 1872 and spawned hats, caps, aprons and many versions of the polonaise costume, some of which were offered as paper dress patterns. Elizabeth Wordsworth spotted the popular author Charlotte M. Yonge in 1872 in a red and black 'Dolly Varden' with a pink skirt, 'showing a very pretty pair of feet in open-work stockings', looking 'more like an old French *Marquise* than ever'.[33]

However eccentric Charlotte M. Yonge appeared, the 'Dolly Varden' was essentially an English style. For the society fashion magazine *The Queen*, Dolly was 'quintessentially English' and a type found in 'every rank . . . with her simple beauty, her trimness, her tinge of pertness and coquetry, her briskness, and under all these her modesty, her constancy, her truth, and her purest of pure hearts, [Dolly Varden] is nothing less than a type of our national, our English maidenhood.'[34] This romantic assessment of the English girl's character and its perceived manifestation in a fictional character typifies a particular aspect of Englishness, steeped in emotions and nostalgia.[35] Popular songs (Fig. 115), on the other hand, emphasised Dolly's sex appeal:

> While promenading the other day
> I chanced to stray, in a careless way,
> I met a pretty girl, she looked so gay
> Dress'd in a Dolly Varden.
>
> I said, 'My dear, now draw it mild.
> I like your style', she gave a smile,
> I followed her fully a mile,
> Eyeing her Dolly Varden.

The denouement to this ditty, set in the seaside town of Brighton, is the heroine's saucy admission that her skirt is none other than 'Ma's bed quilt'.[36]

The fashions worn by Victorian men, women and children may have been influenced at times by the past but they also reflected the modernity of the world they lived in, from their materials and method of making to where they were purchased. Mechanisation and technological and scientific advances were the driving forces behind change. The sewing machine and band knife made quantity production possible and the discovery of synthetic aniline dyes introduced new ranges of brighter, cheaper colours. Innovation, progress and improvement were celebrated in the great international exhibitions where Britain presented herself as an imperial, industrial and commercial power. The novelty and seasonality of fashion and textiles, which were displayed under the same roof as the machines that made them in the Great Exhibition of 1851, epitomised the constant flow and ever increasing variety of goods available to the consumer – goods that could be purchased in that most modern of retail concepts, the department store. But just as the physical redevelopment of the capital reflected London's 'equivocal and piecemeal' engagement with the new,[37] so did the consumption of fashion. As we have seen there were concerns about the aesthetics of contemporary fashion, materialism and the increasing uniformity of dress, accompanied by palpable nostalgia for the past.

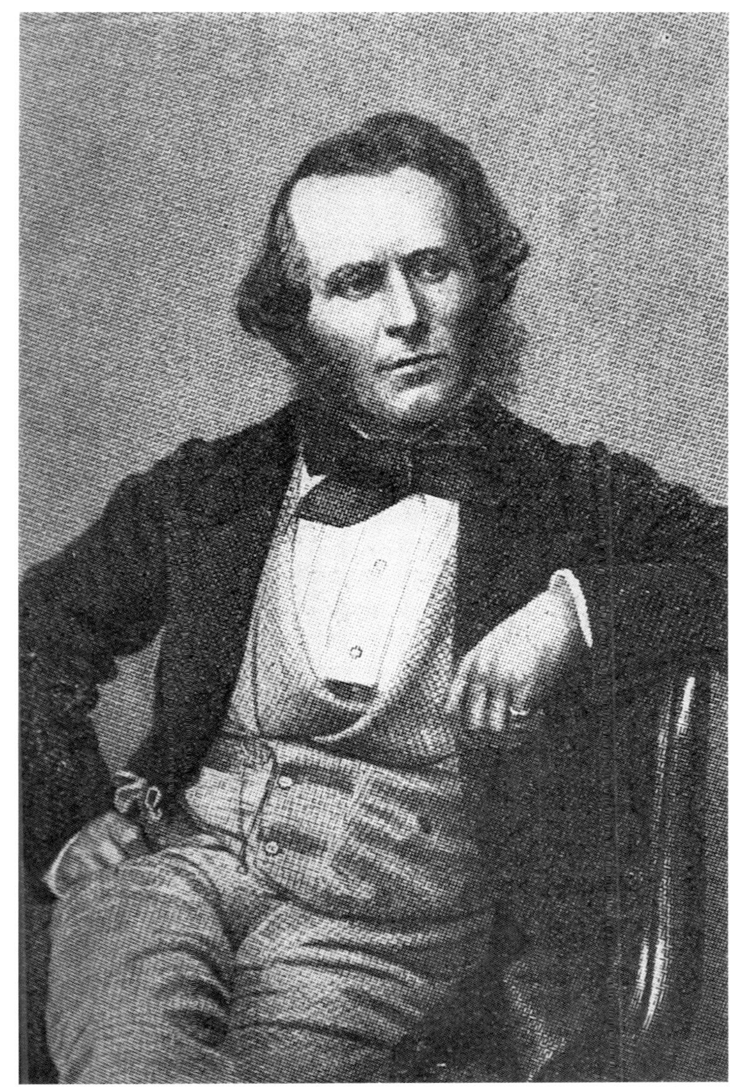

116. Photograph of William Powell Frith, from *The Graphic*, 6 November 1909. Guildhall Library, City of London.

FASHION WITHIN FRITH'S FAMILY CIRCLE

As a youth of sixteen, just arrived from Yorkshire to study at Sass's Academy in London, Frith embraced fashion. He appealed to his father and wheedled his mother to send him adult clothes. On the receipt of his first frock coat he wrote gleefully to his mother. 'I . . . wore it for the first time last Sunday. "Oh, what a dandy!" says one fellow. "What a swell!" says another. Every blackguard seemed to know I had a new coat on.' His mother sent him a mackintosh and replaced the cloak he had lost but not, it seems the handkerchief that was picked from his 'swallowtails'.[38] Large, colourful, printed handkerchiefs worn trailing from the pocket were particularly fashionable in the 1830s and 1840s and were an easy target for pickpockets. Frith's friend, the journalist and writer George Augustus Sala was another youthful victim.[39] Waistcoats too were colourful. Frith 'set his heart' on a crimson velvet one. 'Mr. Sass has one, and they are very fashionable.'[40] As an adult he continued to follow mainstream trends dressing more soberly according to current taste. The black coat, waistcoat and cravat selected for self-portraits and dark coat worn with matching waistcoat and trousers in a striped or discreetly checked lighter fabric in which he sat for photographs were the uniform of respectable men (Fig. 116).[41]

Cissie Frith's memoirs offer intriguing glimpses of the family's clothing practices. In early-married life her mother patronised Miss Jones, a local dressmaker, who received her clients in her front parlour, where fashion magazines were laid out for their inspection. 'I can . . . smell the mingled odour of warm irons, linings and "materials" that dominated the chamber, and see little Miss Jones, in a very flounced dress . . . while her six little curls, three on each side of her face, bobbed up and down, as she held forth to our mother on the different modes . . .'[42] Mrs Frith was artistic and a gifted needlewoman, who devoted much of her spare time to 'fancy' work. She knitted socks and when it was necessary to economise made the family underwear, sometimes from cloth sent by Mr Miller, the cotton magnate and owner of Horrocks, Miller & Company of Preston, who was one her husband's most important patrons.[43] The girls' governess, Miss Wright, taught her charges to sew and trimmed, renovated and altered their clothes to extend their wear. This combination of home sewing with the occasional use of professional dressmakers was standard practice for the middle classes.[44]

After it opened in 1863 the family shopped at William Whiteley's ever expanding department store in Westbourne Grove which Erika Rappaport characterised as symbolising 'the mass culture and economy' that was becoming visible throughout the West End of London between the 1860s and 1880s.[45] In his *Autobiography* Frith described how Whiteley invited him to paint his shop. An

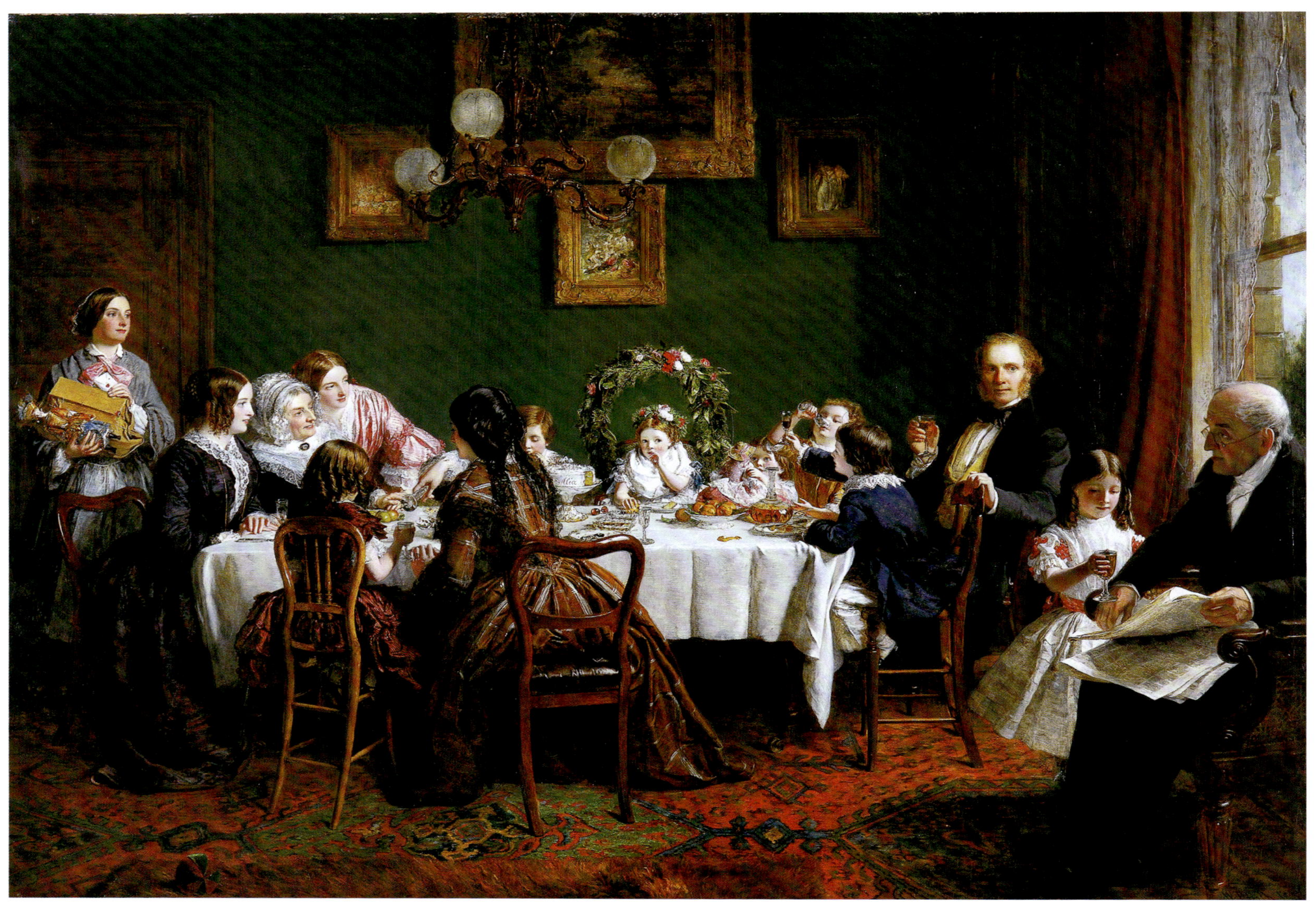

117. *Many Happy Returns of the Day*, 1856. Mercer Art Gallery, Harrogate Museums and Arts.

interior view could show the shop walkers, assistants and customers but, if Frith preferred the street aspect, Whiteley insisted that he paint the window displays along the shop's full frontage to show the diverse range of goods offered by the 'Universal Provider'.[46] Frith voiced concerns that the painting might be construed as an advertisement but he may have rejected the subject because of a hotly contested local debate about the economic and moral effect of the department store on the area. The dispute between Whiteley and his neighbours reflected a more widespread discussion about consumption and the moral dangers it posed for the female shopper, introducing her into an uncontrolled and potentially corrupting environment.[47]

Paintings of modern life demanded contemporary clothing and Frith sometimes drew on the wardrobe of his family circle. He borrowed their governess's best Sunday mantle for the woman pictured in the *Crossing Sweeper* and for *Claude Duval*.[48] One of Cissie's own dresses, or another very similar, was worn by the girl offering her grandfather a glass of sherry in *Many Happy Returns of the Day* (1856) which depicts three generations gathered together to celebrate a sixth birthday (Fig.

117).[49] The dress had great significance for Cissie as she wore it the first time she met Edwin Landseer. 'I was in a very, very stiff white frock, trimmed with a great many of Miss Wright's "cart-wheel" embroideries (Fig. 118), and a broad scarlet sash was gaily tied round my waist. The bodice had short, full-puffed sleeves, and in each puff was a rosette of very narrow scarlet velvet . . .'[50] The dress's short wide skirt supported by starched and frilled petticoats echoed the very full skirts held out by cage crinolines worn by adult women. Older women who eschewed fashion like Mrs Frith's mother modified current styles to suit their age. Cissie remembered her wearing gowns of 'unfailing black' that felt 'very horrid' and an old-fashioned cotton cap which covered her hair and denoted her status as a married woman.[51] Her daughter's refusal to wear this type of cap marked a shift in manners and attitudes. Miss Wright, who worked the cartwheel embroideries for Cissie's frock, brought her own sense of style to the family circle. Cissie remembered her as 'a slight "elegant female" with the usual curls, pinched waist, black silk apron, worked collar and cuffs, and flounced petticoats of the period, very much accentuated by the fact that she had been some years in France to learn the language, and was in consequence supposed to be not only next best to a native, but to be an authority on the latest fashions, which then, and until the Franco-Prussian war taught us we could make our own, always came or were said to come from Paris'.[52]

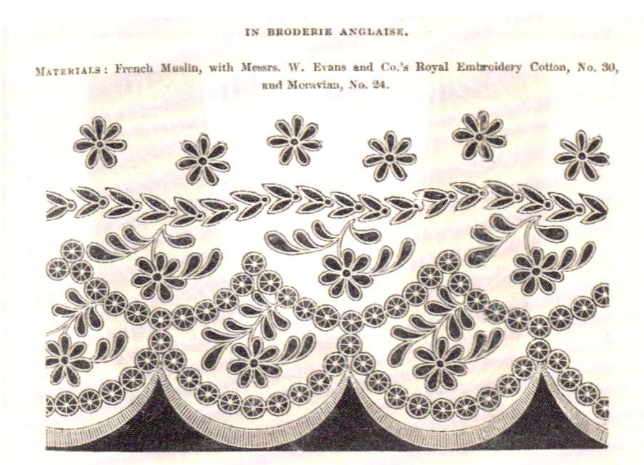

118. 'Petticoat trimming in Broderie Anglaise', *La Belle Assemblée*, May 1853. Museum of London. This pattern includes 'cartwheels' to be worked in buttonhole stitch.

The French dominance of fashion was a cause for economic concern and nationalist complaint. The British fashion media did cover London dressmakers and British-made textiles but recognising the undeniable authority of Paris they gave equal or greater prominence to the latest French modes and novelties. Setting aside conversations with friends and relatives, Mrs Frith and her daughters learned about fashion from their dressmakers and milliners, from Miss Wright, with her insider knowledge of French style, from fashion plates and from papers like the weekly *Illustrated London News*, which the family read 'from cover to cover'.[53] They were also exposed to the bohemian and aesthetic styles worn in artistic circles but anything '*outré* or "artistic"' in his daughters' clothing provoked 'the most fearful scorn' from their father.[54] This glut of information was balanced by their 'beloved' *Punch*, which regularly debunked the latest trends and exposed the dark side of the dress and tailoring trades and their ruthless exploitation of their workers.[55] The clothing worn by Frith's family represented a negotiation between these influences and other constraints such as budget, taste, morality and social need.

THE CROWD: SCENES OF MODERN LIFE

The locations Frith selected for his three great panoramas of modern life enabled him to bring together a cast of all ages from a cross-section of classes, backgrounds and occupations. Fashionable dress could be interspersed with location-specific garments – 'uglies' for the beach, dust coats and 'puggarees'[56] for the race course, cloaks made with capes for travel – and balanced with less period-specific, non-fashionable clothes – uniforms, livery, rural dress and the random outfits of the itinerant entertainers that followed the London crowd from Epsom to the south coast resorts. Clothing and accessories, particularly headwear, together with the physiognomy and deportment of the figures in the paintings, enabled the spectator to identify the social and moral status of the 'actors' and to unravel the incidents taking place within the overall drama. In some cases dress might have more than an identifying role conveying emotions such as loss and separation (mourning clothes, military uniforms) or nostalgia for a pre-industrial age (linen smocks, red cloaks).

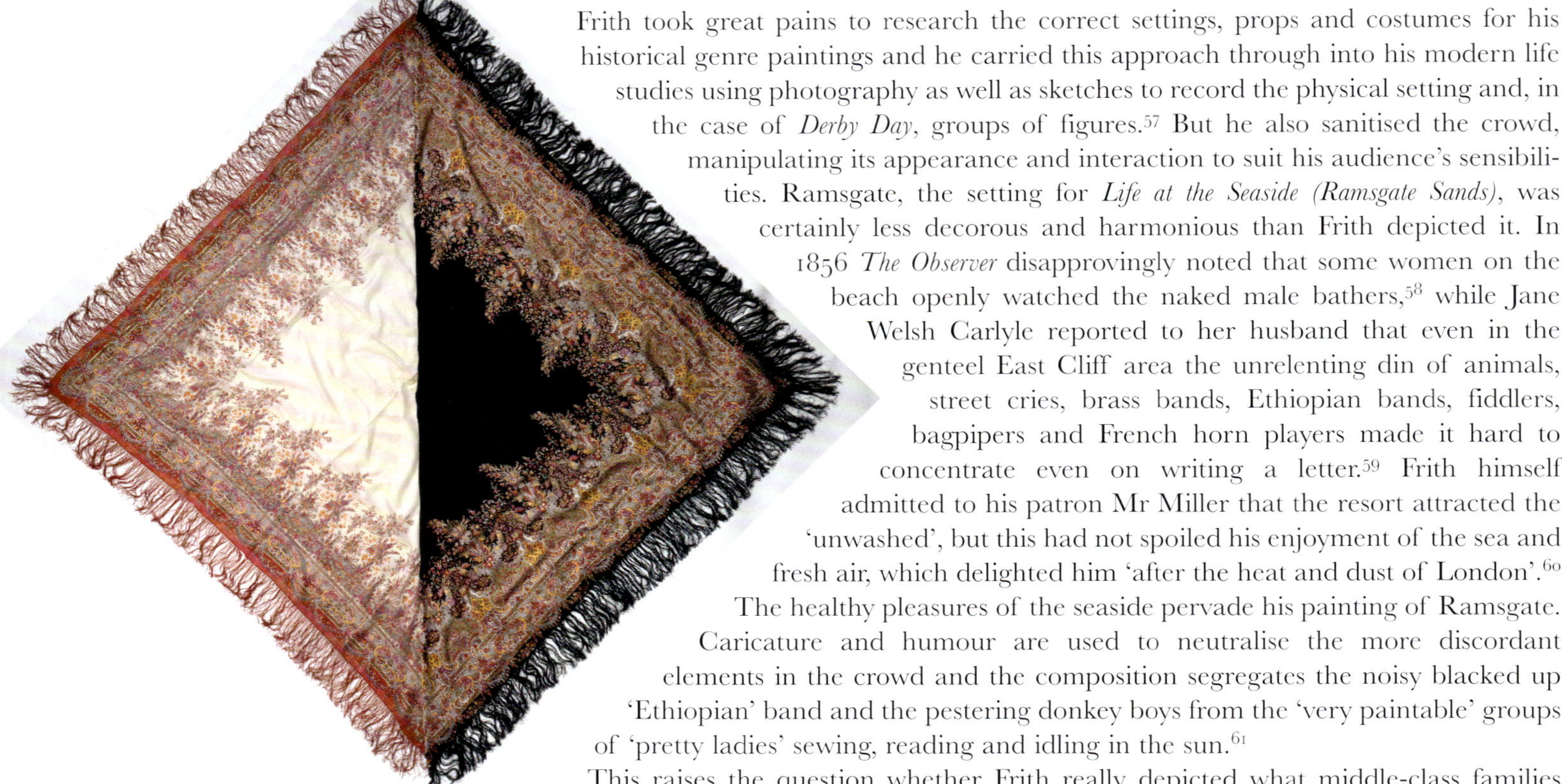

Frith took great pains to research the correct settings, props and costumes for his historical genre paintings and he carried this approach through into his modern life studies using photography as well as sketches to record the physical setting and, in the case of *Derby Day*, groups of figures.[57] But he also sanitised the crowd, manipulating its appearance and interaction to suit his audience's sensibilities. Ramsgate, the setting for *Life at the Seaside (Ramsgate Sands)*, was certainly less decorous and harmonious than Frith depicted it. In 1856 *The Observer* disapprovingly noted that some women on the beach openly watched the naked male bathers,[58] while Jane Welsh Carlyle reported to her husband that even in the genteel East Cliff area the unrelenting din of animals, street cries, brass bands, Ethiopian bands, fiddlers, bagpipers and French horn players made it hard to concentrate even on writing a letter.[59] Frith himself admitted to his patron Mr Miller that the resort attracted the 'unwashed', but this had not spoiled his enjoyment of the sea and fresh air, which delighted him 'after the heat and dust of London'.[60] The healthy pleasures of the seaside pervade his painting of Ramsgate. Caricature and humour are used to neutralise the more discordant elements in the crowd and the composition segregates the noisy blacked up 'Ethiopian' band and the pestering donkey boys from the 'very paintable' groups of 'pretty ladies' sewing, reading and idling in the sun.[61]

This raises the question whether Frith really depicted what middle-class families wore at the seaside in the mid-nineteenth century or whether his selection of dress was also contrived. The silhouettes of the women's dresses and their accessories, the parasols, bonnets, 'uglies' and shawls, are correct for the date. Although the patterns of the shawls are not depicted in detail, several appear to have similar colouring and designs to examples manufactured in Norwich and exhibited at the Great Exhibition in 1851 (Fig. 119).[62] The man reading a newspaper dressed in an informal grey lounging jacket and matching waistcoat is wearing buff slippers of the kind *Punch* mocked in 1850 as 'so slippery' that they usually ended up 'embedded in the sand'.[63] These portraits of fashionable dress would not jar with Frith's audience. They are sufficiently well-observed to carry the narrative but not so detailed that they dominate it. But did children really wear silk dresses to play at the water's edge, or did Frith introduce the fabric to catch the light and provide an effective contrast with their cotton drawers and petticoats?

119. Block printed silk shawls manufactured by Towler, Campin and Company, 1851. Norfolk Museums Service.

The Railway Station (1862) poses the same question. How appropriate are the clothes to the situation? Confessing that the clothes of the 'ordinary traveller' offered the painter little attraction, Frith solved his problem by introducing two groups that included people not intending to travel. These are the wedding party saying goodbye to the bride and groom, and the family group, modelled by Frith and his family, putting their sons on the train to return to school. The railways transformed transport but stations and trains were dirty. Mrs Walford who travelled on the night train from Scotland to stay with relatives for her first London season in 1864 remembered the soot and grime of the journey and the shabby carriage. Women wore their oldest clothes and she and her sisters covered their hair with handkerchiefs before their heads touched the cushions of their compartment. 'No one going by train thought of being neat and trim; still less of having any specially designed costume; – and the useful coat and skirt we all now wear was not in existence.'[64] Frith's travellers wear practical clothes but not perhaps their oldest. The pristine clothes 'without a stain, a patch, or a rub' worn by the working men in *The Railway Station* amused Charles

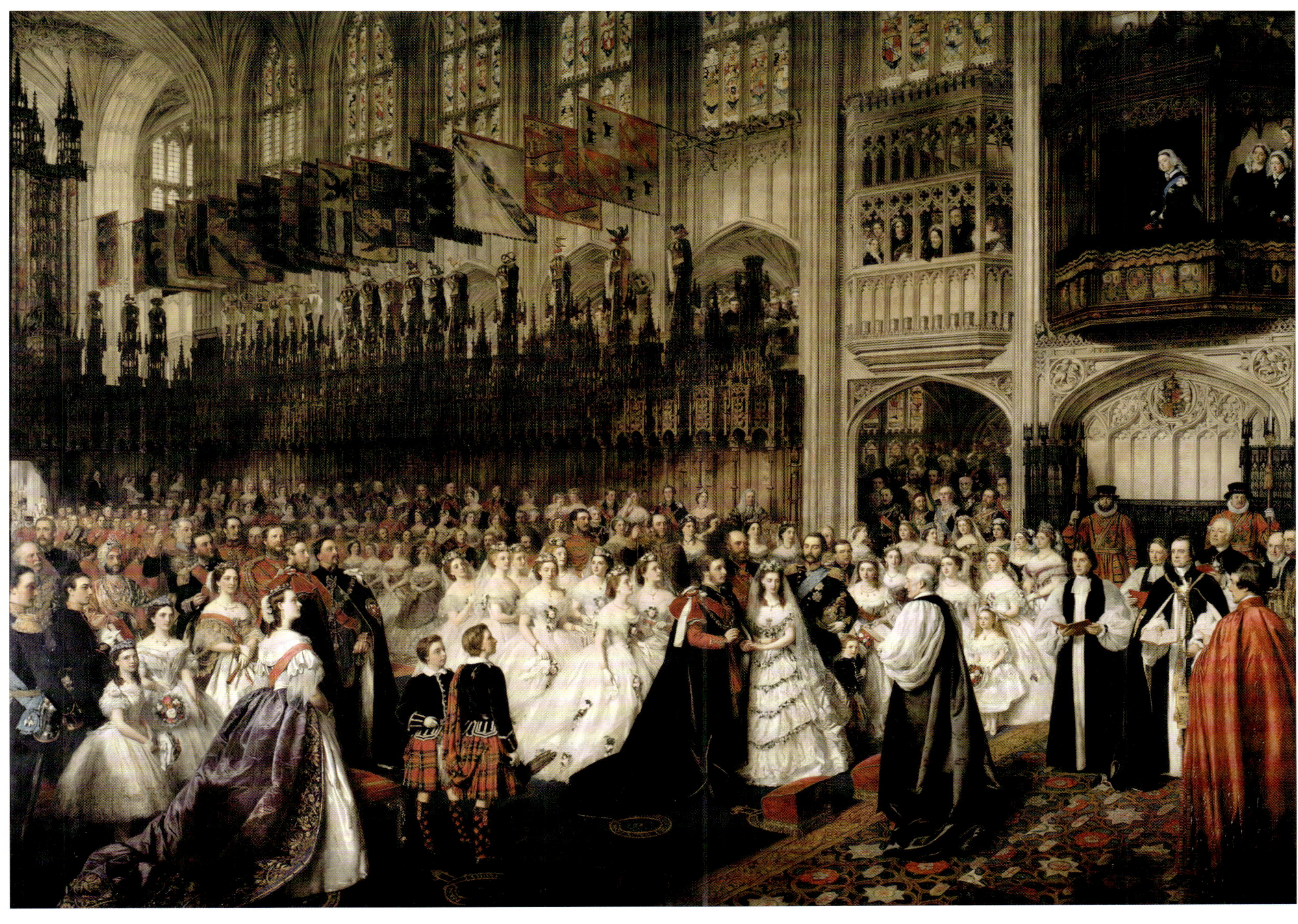

120. *The Marriage of the Prince of Wales 10 March 1863*, 1865. The Royal Collection.

Dickens. 'The pile is unworn upon the rough overcoat of the cabman, . . . The countryman's smock-frock is spick-and-span from neck to wristbands. . . . Even the cinderous stoker in the background has got a fresh fit-out of fustian, as though aware he was going to have his likeness taken . . .'[65] Frith again tempered reality knowing that his audience found the pungent, worn clothes of the common man neither uplifting nor morally improving.

Frith's expertise with large complex compositions led Queen Victoria, who had acquired *Life at the Seaside (Ramsgate Sands)*, to commission a painting of the marriage of the Prince of Wales which took place in St George's Chapel, Windsor, on 10 March 1863. Frith attended the wedding but only had time to jot down the position of the principal guests. The spectacle, which he compared to 'an illuminated page of Froissart', and the 'clang of drum and trumpet', impressed him.[66] He was deeply moved by the weeping, widowed Queen, clad in black silk and crepe,[67] who

121. Fragment of the cloth of silver used to make 'Princess Alexandra s wedding dress', woven in Spitalfields, 1862–3. Private Collection.

watched the ceremony from Catherine of Aragon's closet high above the choir. Although her guests were allowed to wear colours, the Ladies of Her Household were restricted to the half-mourning colours of grey, lilac or mauve and her daughters to combinations of 'grey or silver and gold . . . but not merely gold and white'. The bride, Princess Alexandra of Denmark, wore a dress of British manufacture made from white satin and cloth of silver woven in Spitalfields, swagged with deep flounces of Honiton lace and trimmed with festoons of orange blossom and myrtle (Figs 120 & 121). Her eight bridesmaids wore complementary dresses of white glacé silk covered with tulle.[68] Everyone agreed that the subject was difficult. The review in the *Illustrated London News* drew particular attention to the problems presented by the 'crude and ill-assorted colours' of the costumes; 'the cold masses of the silk and lawn of the bishops, the lace and tulle of the bridesmaids, the violet (sic) of the garter robes, the mauve ladies' trains, and the blue of a very obnoxious carpeting, cutting with cruel harshness against scarlet, crimson and gold uniforms'.[69] The volume of the women's dresses, whose skirts were fashionably ample, contributed to this awkward massing of colour. However, Frith's greatest problems were persuading the guests to sit for him and obtaining access to the garments, orders and jewellery worn at the wedding. His method had always been to paint costume 'from life' whether worn by his sitter, a model or lay figure but on this occasion he was forced to paint some of the guests, including most of the Danish royal family, from photographs. He claimed to find this 'most unsatisfactory'[70] but painters were wary of admitting to using photographs, feeling that it compromised their artistic integrity. Queen Victoria did not share this reservation and frequently offered photographs for reference to painters she had commissioned.[71]

WOMEN AND FASHION

From the mid-1850s Frith painted a number of pictures of attractive young women in fashionable dress enjoying the pleasures of middle-class life. *At the Opera* (1855) was admired by Prince Albert (Fig. 122).[72] Opera box studies had been a stock subject for artists and satirists since the eighteenth century. The box suggested the conceit of a theatre within a theatre and its position offered an opportunity for romantic intrigue, surveillance and gossip. It was also a favourite setting for fashion plates inviting the viewer into an inner circle of elegance. Rejecting titillation and idealisation Frith presented a young girl completely absorbed by the performance, oblivious to her fellow spectators. The colours of her clothes, a cornflower blue evening dress trimmed with geranium pink ribbons and white opera cloak, convey her youth and gentility, and Frith's delicate delineation of the cloak's quilted silk lining and the dress's fragile lace collar add to the overall impression of artlessness.

One of Frith's most delightful portraits of his family shows his eldest daughter Isabelle similarly absorbed, focussing on the subject of her sketch (Fig. 123). Painted in the mid-1860s she is depicted wearing a sheer white muslin dress whose skirt is so voluminous that it fills the lower third of the canvas. To preserve the fragile grace of the fabric women's magazines recommended supporting the skirts with starched flounced petticoats or a moderate sized steel crinoline worn with extra petticoats to create the necessary fashionable volume without compromising the softness of the material.[73] Apart from the gilt and turquoise buttons that fasten the bodice and a suggestion of a matching sash her dress is completely unadorned. The fabric is so fine that

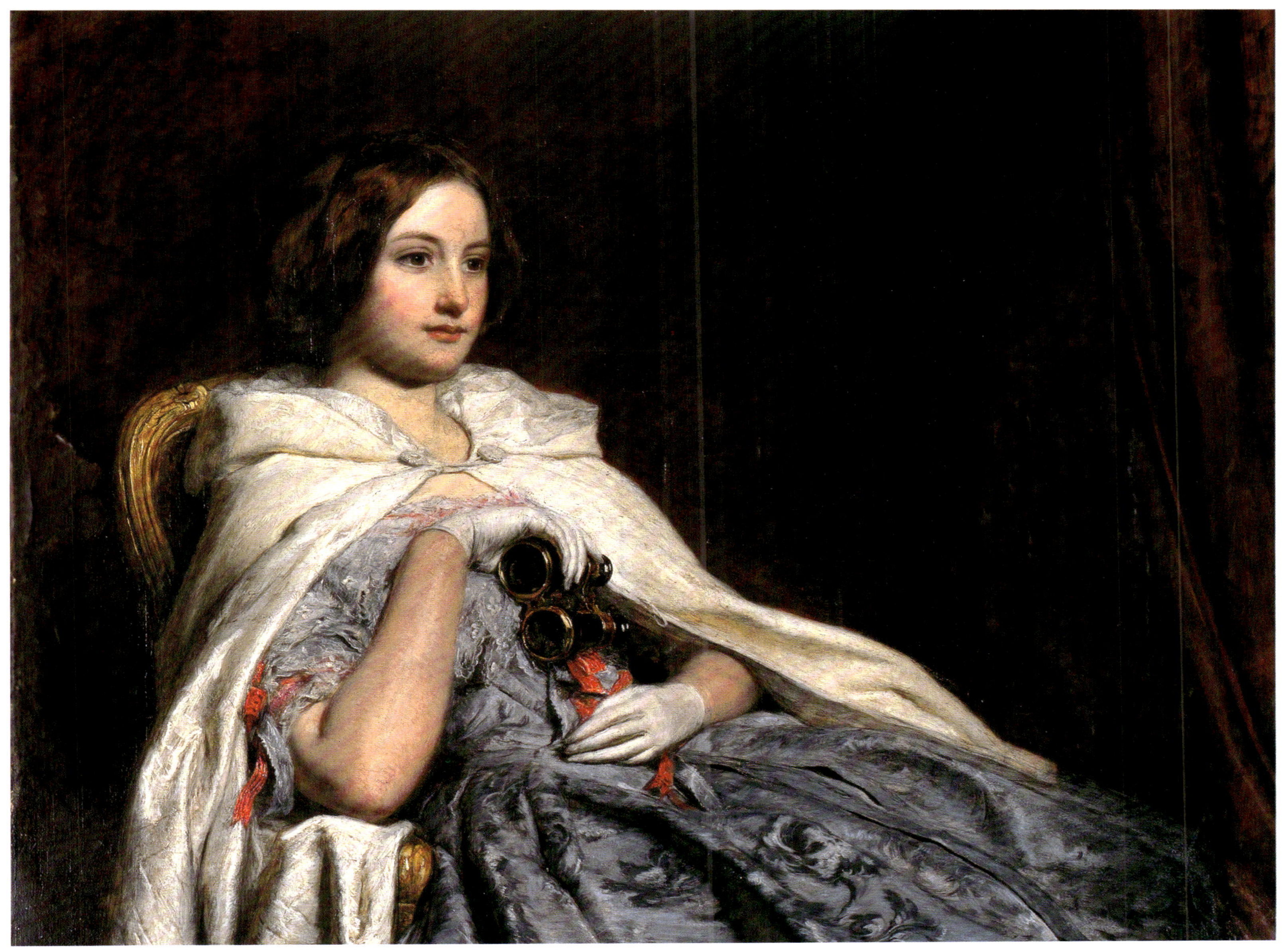

122. *At the Opera*, 1855. Harris Museum and Art Gallery, Preston, Lancashire.

Isabelle's chemise is clearly visible, its matt white surface contrasting with the pink flesh tones of her arms and upper chest. Muslin dresses were very popular for summer, and were thought to be particularly flattering and appropriate for the young. 'Nothing is so becoming to a young face as attendant clouds of muslin; there is poetry and modesty in its very appearance.'[74] Frith's daughters prized the few white dresses they possessed. Their father approved of their simplicity but London's polluted atmosphere and their 'very shallow purses' limited their purchases.[75]

Louey, Alice and Fanny Frith were the models for their father's 1873 painting *English Archers, Nineteenth Century* (Fig. 124). Following a revival of interest in archery in the late eighteenth century

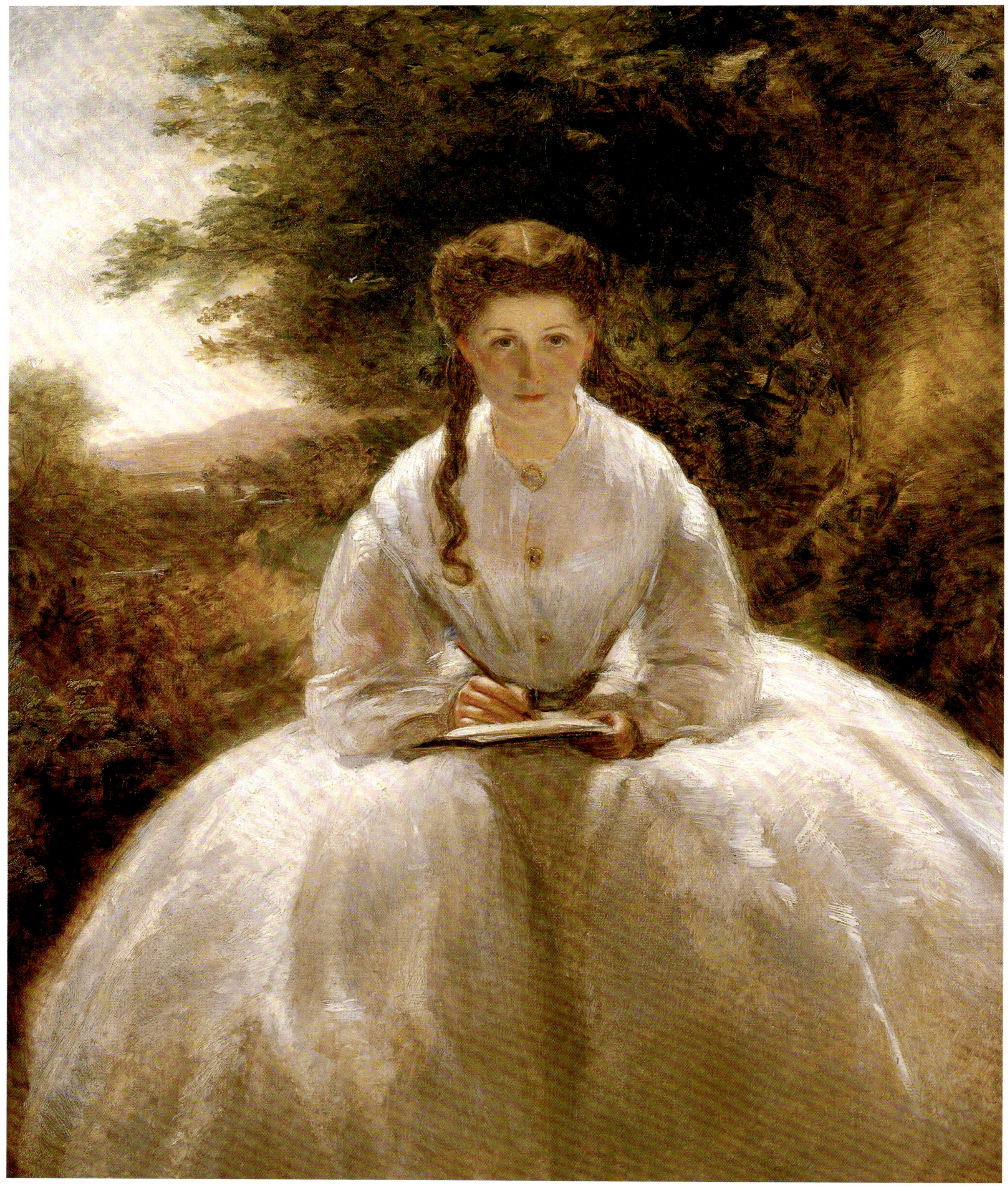

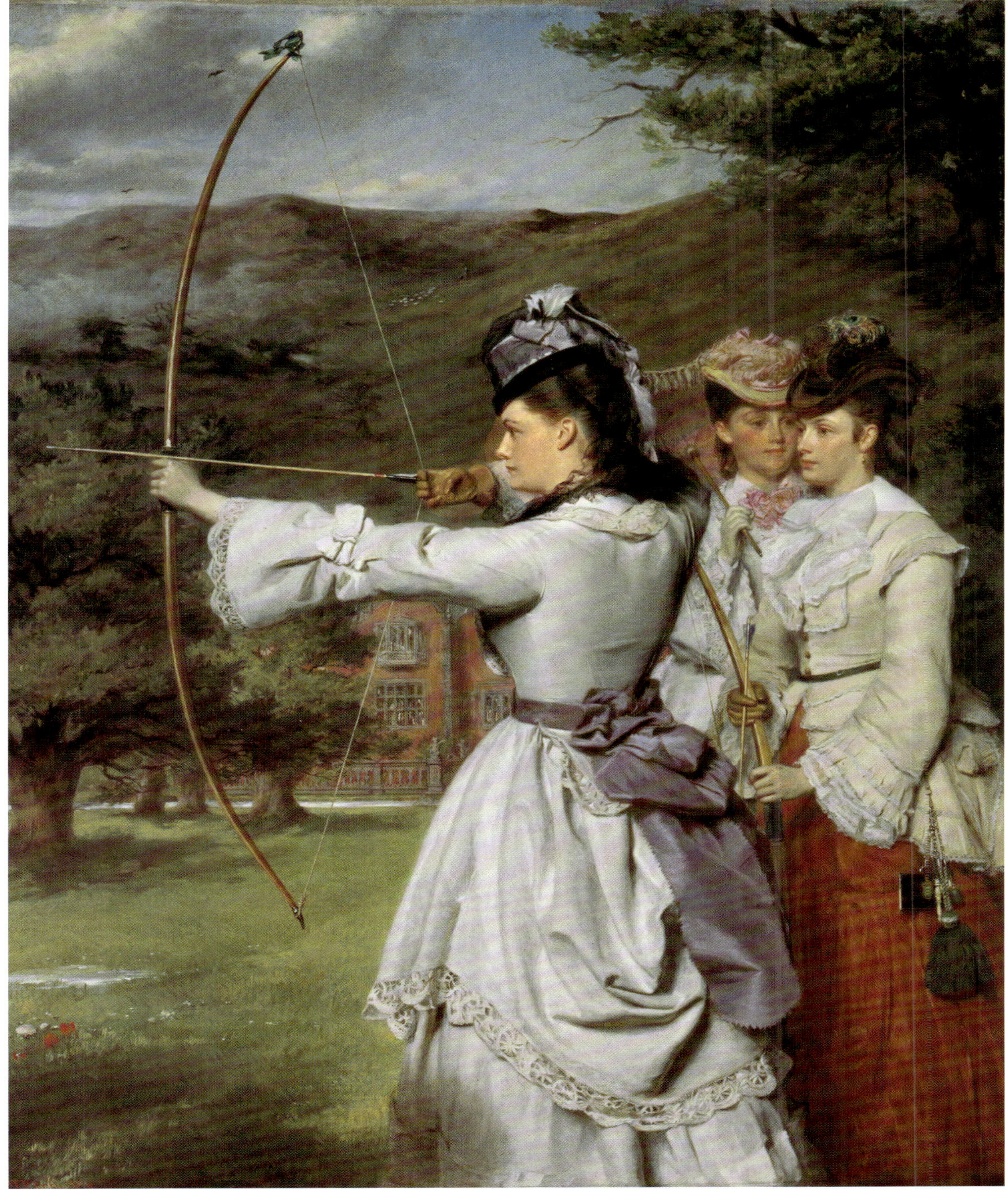

124. *English Archers, Nineteenth Century*, 1873. The Royal Albert Memorial Museum, Exeter, Devon,.
Also known as 'The Fair Toxophilites', the picture depicts Frith's daughters Alice, Louise and Fanny. Shown here in the grounds of a country house, they may have practised at the archery club in Kensington Gardens, near their Bayswater home.

a number of societies were founded which were open to both sexes. Members wore green uniforms but in the early nineteenth century some women adopted white muslin dresses worn with green sashes and these colours remained popular whether or not the wearers belonged to a society.[76] Louey's smart white cotton outfit, consisting of a jacket bodice with fashionable trumpet sleeves, a skirt and softly draped and puffed overskirt, is trimmed with Bedfordshire Maltese lace,[77] and finished with an amethyst silk sash. Simplified versions of fashionable dress were worn for

Facing page:
123. *Mrs Oppenheim*, c. 1864. Private Collection.
A portrait of Frith's eldest daughter Isabelle, who married Charles Oppenheim in 1864.

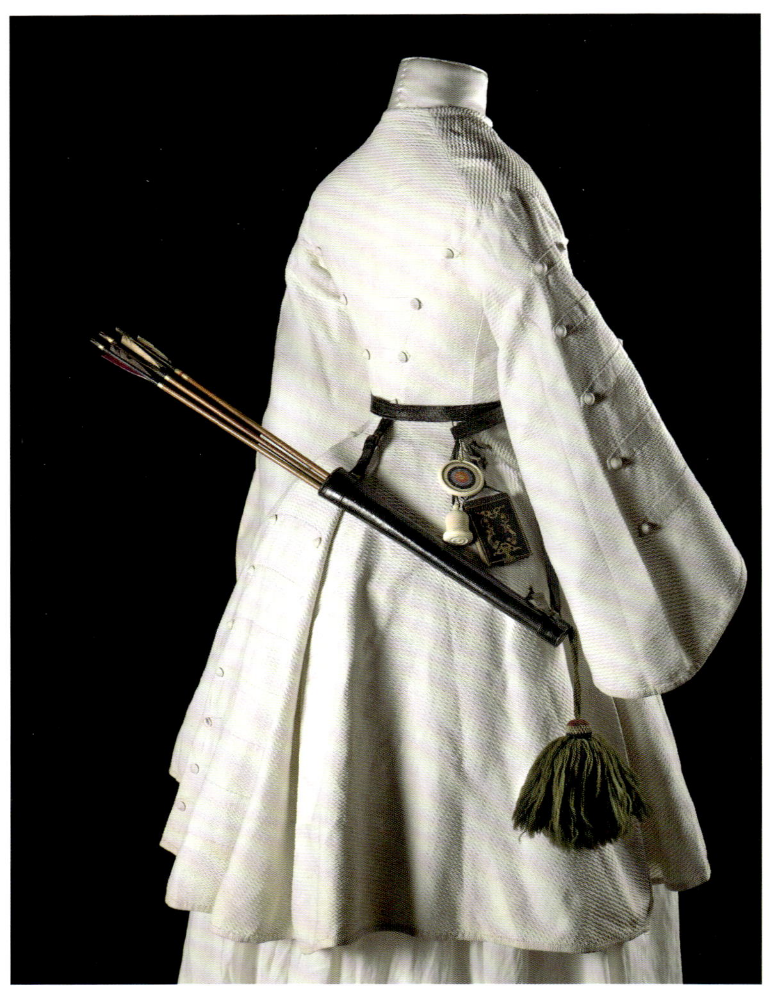

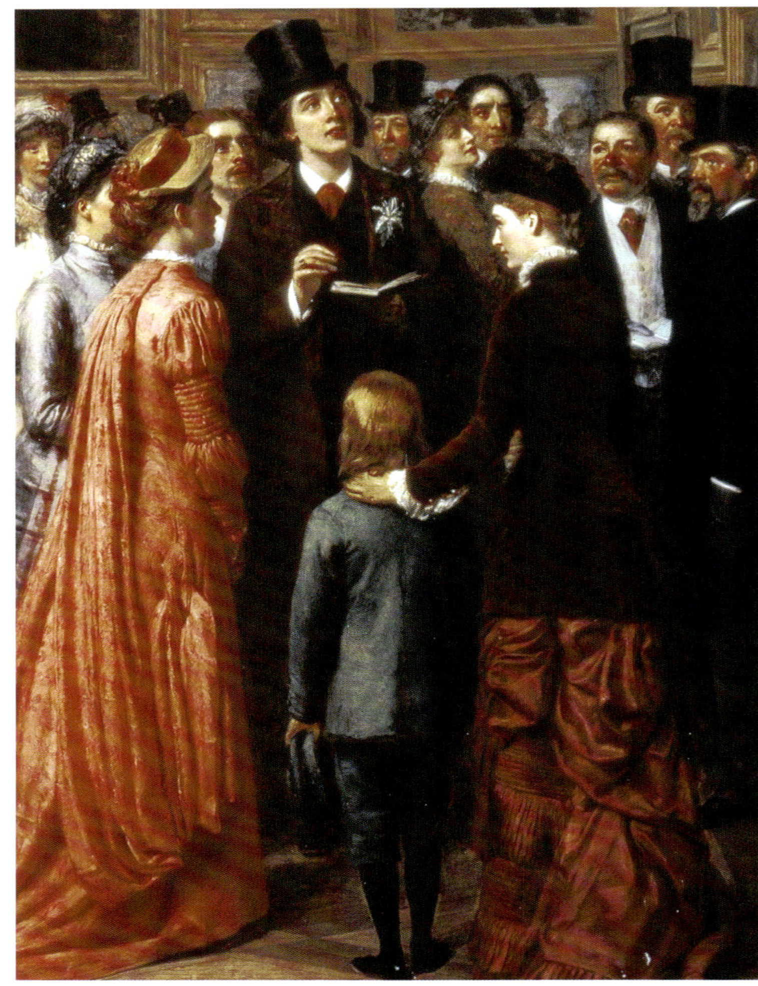

125. Left: Archery outfit worn by Mrs. Fanny Giveen: cotton marcella jacket, leather belt supporting a quiver, wool tassel, grease-pot, notebook and score card, *c.* 1854. Museum of London.

126. Right: *Private View at the Royal Academy, 1881*, 1883. Private Collection. Detail of Fig. 67, showing Oscar Wilde at the centre of a group that includes Ellen Terry on the right with her young son Edward Gordon Craig, G. A. Sala in the white waistcoat and Du Maurier with the beard at the extreme right.

summer sports but women were urged to wear bodices with some give over specially designed exercise stays that provided support while allowing freedom of movement.[78] Fanny wears an archery belt (Fig. 125) carrying a memorandum book to record the scores, a grease box and a tassel of wool used for cleaning the arrow tips. Both sisters wear archery gloves and modish feather-trimmed high-crowned hats, tipped forward over their brows.

Archery tournaments, like croquet matches, were thought to be suitable occasions for young men and women to meet and their antics were gently mocked in cartoons and short stories like 'Archery versus Love'.[79] The young narrator is initially captivated by Miss O'Brian's outfit 'which set off her complexion as a leaf will a strawberry' and by her archery belt whose 'little strappings' reminded him of 'a new rocking-horse', but her energy and determination soon exhaust him. Although Frith picked a topical subject with humorous and sentimental overtones the critics panned *English Archers*. *The Graphic* found the subject vacuous and Frith's treatment lacking in vivacity.[80] *The Times* was also dismissive and like *The Graphic* sardonically questioned the archers' skill suggesting that they were really 'scholars of that great bow-boy Cupid' and after a man.[81]

162 PUNCH, OR THE LONDON CHARIVARI. [April 14, 1877.

FLIPPANCY PUNISHED.

The Cimabue Browns, and their Friends, form one of the Nicest and most Artistic Sets in Brompton, but they hold all things Modern in Contempt, especially Modern Music. One evening Grigsby volunteers to Sing them what he calls a "Florentine Canzonet of the Fifteenth Century," but what is in reality a Maundering Improvisation of his own, in a Minor Key, with mock Italian Words of the most idiotic description, also invented by him on the spur of the moment. The Effect is Magical, tears flow freely, and an enthusiastic Encore greets the Performer. Unfortunately, the Performance being an Extempore one, he cannot repeat it, and is much Embarrassed by the Success of his Feeble Joke.

Frith's appreciation of the social and cultural significance of dress and his expertise in painting crowds came together in *A Private View at the Royal Academy 1881* (Fig. 126). The subject was prompted by his desire to record the 'aesthetic craze' and to 'hit at the folly of listening to self-elected critics in matters of taste, whether in dress or art'.[82] The private views at the Royal Academy and the Grosvenor Gallery, which opened in 1877, were highlights of the London social calendar and *The Queen* regaled its readers with descriptions of the celebrities spotted in the crush and the most striking and *outré* fashions. In 1880 it justified its attention to the appearance of the crowd in an article on the history of the Royal Academy accompanied by a reproduction of P. A. Martini's engraving of Johann Heinrich Ramberg's 1787 drawing *The Exhibition of the Royal Academy*. The company and their costume offered an insight into the 'manners of the time' and, the magazine asserted, revealed the improving influence of neo-classical artists such as Sir Joshua Reynolds and Angelica Kauffmann on contemporary fashion.[83] Standing slightly apart from the mêlée of dogs, children and gossips the Prince of Wales gazes up listening intently as Reynolds, whose *Discourses* asserted the importance of reason and philosophy to aesthetic judgement, describes the paintings to him. In Frith's view of the scene, Lord Leighton, the current President of the Academy, is absorbed in conversation and it is Oscar Wilde, Frith's self-elected critic and 'well known apostle of the beautiful' who expounds his aesthetic theories to a group of devotees. Wilde's unusually long hair which touches his collar, velvet waistcoat and above all the lily in his buttonhole distinguish him from the other men in the gallery. His genius for self-publicity and studied cultivation of his image made him the butt of satirists but Frith's portrayal is more measured. Although some men nearby look askance his depiction lends credence to the artist Louise Jopling's sympathetic appreciation of his intellectual playfulness and her delight in the 'extravagant, enthusiastic way' in which his conversation mingled sense and nonsense.[84]

Aesthetically dressed women were in the minority at Royal Academy private views, but Frith carefully included a range of approaches to the style from more extrovert historically inspired costumes to the simpler smock dresses originally favoured by women within Pre-Raphaelite circles such as Janey Morris, whose dress reflected their rejection of the materialism and artifice of high fashion. The effect of the aesthetic movement on art, dress, interior decoration and speech was wittily parodied by George Du Maurier in *Punch* in a series of cartoons featuring the Cimabue Browns who lived in 'passionate Brompton'. 'Flippancy Punished' (Fig. 127) which appeared on 14 April 1877 highlights the eclectic and escapist nature of the style which put a premium on originality, individuality, and age, believing that the clothing of the past was inherently more beautiful than modern dress.[85] Old lace, antique fans and archaeological and historical jewels and accessories like chatelaines were all prized. 'Forswear[ing] fashion plates as guides'[86] aesthetic dressers looked for inspiration in old and modern paintings, particularly those by the Pre-Raphaelite artists, in books about period costume and in the historically inspired theatrical costumes of role models like Ellen Terry,[87] who wore aesthetic styles on and off stage.

Both Du Maurier and Terry appear in Frith's painting close to the groups of aesthetes (the key suggesting that Terry is the woman whose head and upper body only are seen between Wilde and Irving). The tawny colouring and soft texture of Terry's dress might be interpreted as aesthetic

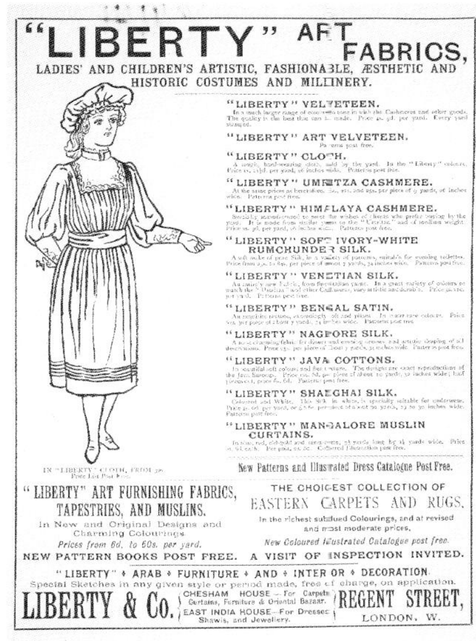

127. Top: George Du Maurier (1834–96), *Flippancy Punished*, from *Punch*, vol. LXXII, 14 April 1877. Museum of London.

128. Bottom: Advertisement for Liberty Art Fabrics from *Album of Fancy Costumes*, ed. Marie Schild, *c.* 1885. Museum of London.

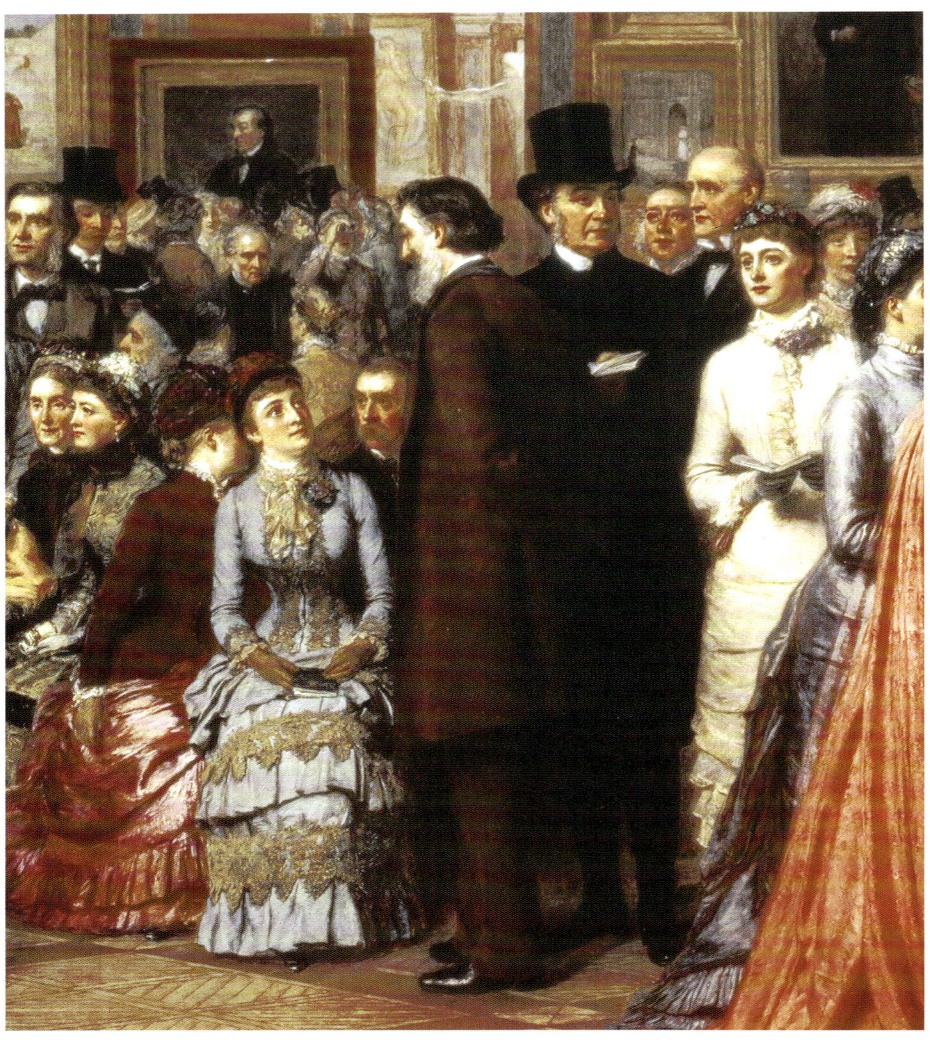

129. *Private View at the Royal Academy, 1881*, 1883. Private Collection. Detail of Fig. 67, showing Sir Frederic Leighton in his brown suit, the Archbishop of York and Lily Langtry

but it is difficult to assess the dress's cut and construction. Although many surviving aesthetic dresses from the 1880s and 1890s have boned bodices, some who affected the style wore no or bone-free corsets in favour of a natural waist.[88] They also rejected other foundation garments dictated by high fashion, such as the bustle, preferring loose-fitting, draped styles shaped to the body with smocking and gathering. These styles were ideally suited to softer, more clinging fabrics like muslin, cotton and the lightweight undressed Indian and Japanese silks sold by shops like Liberty's, which opened in 1875, the School of Art Needlework and Lewis & Allenby.[89] Synthetic dyes were rejected in favour of subdued, natural shades, such as pale blue, yellow, gold, green, terracotta and 'mouse', brightened with flashes of colour selected according to the colour theories expounded by reformers like Mrs Haweis.[90] Decoration was largely restricted to historically inspired sleeve treatments and embroidery worked by the wearer. As *The Queen* reported, and Frith's painting suggests, aesthetic dressing encompassed a range of styles from the 'few figures [who] boldly carried out the creed to its utmost limits of eccentricity' to those who combined 'a zeal for originality . . . yet kept within certain discreet bounds of loyalty to the prevailing fashions'.[91]

Given Frith's criticisms of high fashion, particularly its tendency to distort the body and restrict its movements, and its dominance by France, it is perhaps surprising that he did not support a home-grown movement that had its roots in artistic circles and shared his reservations. While granting that some costumes were 'pretty enough' he criticised others for their 'ugliness of form', 'oddity of colour' and 'eccentricity'. The style favoured *gigot* sleeves, which Frith disliked. Loose-fitting clothes, like the Watteau-style dress worn by the woman next to Wilde, were associated with sensuality and loose morals, while the Renaissance-inspired green dress with its sunflower corsage reeked of exhibitionism and was akin to fancy dress. The 'sad' colours too did not suit every complexion. Frith, who was essentially conservative, found the undiscriminating acceptance of fashion and anti-fashion and their extremes problematic whether it emanated from Paris or a London artist's studio. Perhaps too, after the death of his wife Isabelle, who had helped him with the costume in his paintings, he lost patience with it. Why else would he depict Lillie Langtry, a professional beauty and icon of style, in a dress that had previously clothed one of the bridesmaids in *For Better, For Worse* (1881, Fig. 58). The clothes of Ellen Terry are also borrowed from this painting.[92] This careless approach to a topic at the core of his subject suggests exasperation or lassitude.[93]

Although much of the topical interest of *A Private View* lies in its depiction of aesthetic dress the painting also enabled Frith to bring together the celebrities of the day with many of the friends and acquaintances remembered in his *Autobiography*. *The Queen* damned the painting for its inept portraiture and protested on behalf of Lord Leighton whose 'figure in the hideous brown suit in which it has pleased the artist to represent him . . . is surely about as unlike the special character of the original's handsome and active form as possible'.[94] (Fig. 129) Other assessments of Leighton's character disagreed, drawing attention to his unconventionality and supporting Frith's observation. Leighton might stand 'for English respectability', and seek 'the homage of the great' but according to J. McLure Hamilton he was 'an artist in everything': his hair was long and his hats, coats and shoes were all peculiar to him.[95] Frith understood the importance of clothing to self-image and indulged his friends' foibles honouring Sala's request to be painted in *A Private View* in his habitual white waistcoat, which, the writer claimed, had kept him within the bounds of respectability for twenty-five years.[96] Even though Frith might have preferred his daughters to wear white or black to private views – 'black because it was unobtrusive, and white because it would not interfere with the colour on the walls'[97] – clothes were one of the primary tools of his trade, which he relished for their ability to express character, taste and morality, to encapsulate memories and emotions, and for their social, cultural and economic resonance.

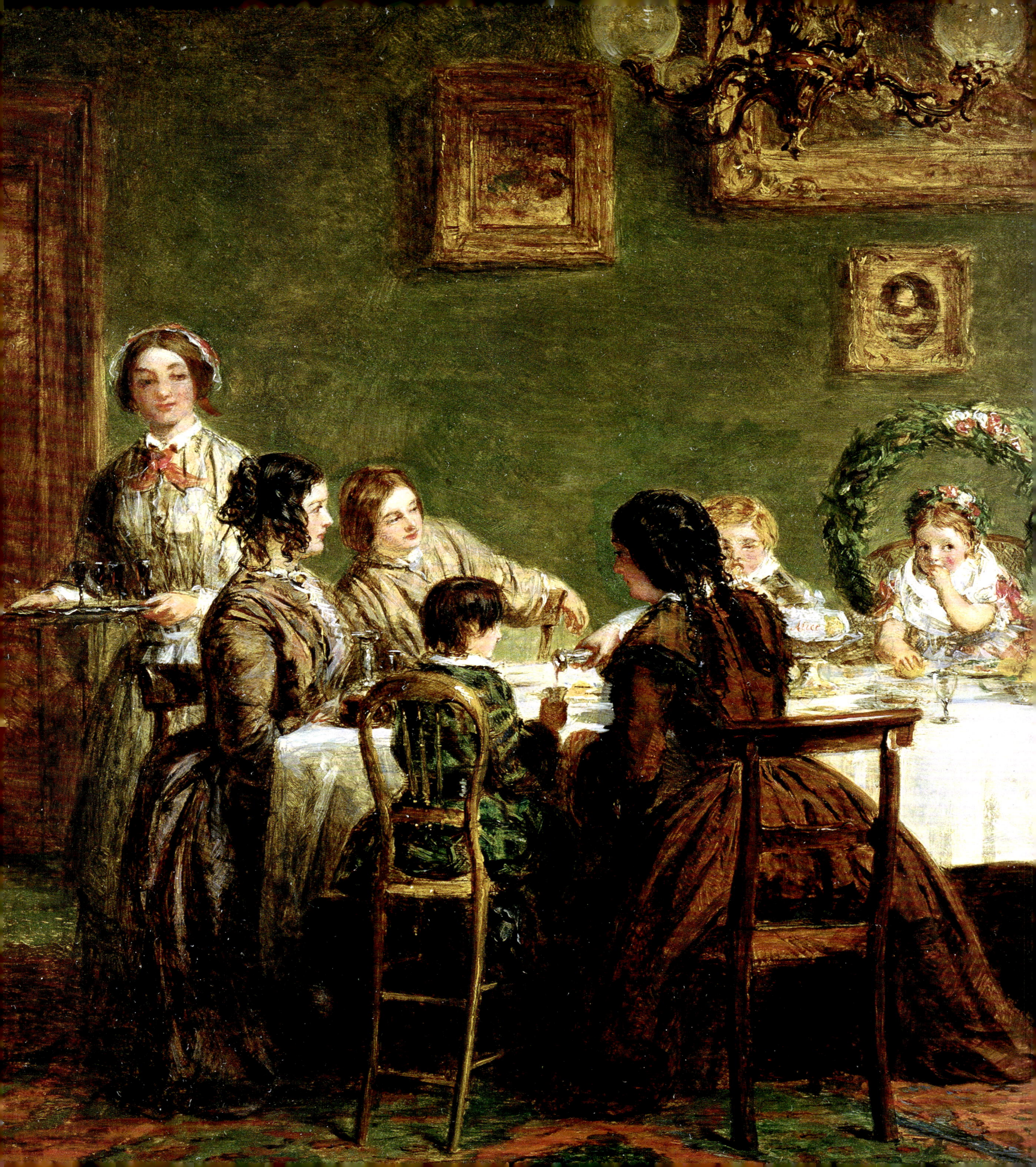
Alice

Chapter 8

Frith's Women: William Powell Frith and the Female Model

JANE SELLARS

William Powell Frith painted women in many guises. He began with Shakespeare's heroines, with scenes from Dickens, Goldsmith, Molière and Sterne, and historical genre subjects depicting an imagined English rural life. He cast women in the roles of devout maidens, jilted lovers and adoring mothers in his many female figure paintings. In common with most other artists of his day, he painted female portraits. In his grandest and most celebrated panoramas of Victorian life – *Life at the Seaside (Ramsgate Sands)* (1854; Fig. 14), *Derby Day*, (1856–8; Fig. 61), and *The Railway Station* (1860–2; Fig. 63) – a multitude of women smiled, swooned and suffered at every level of society. Victorian artists in general, with their allegiance to the ideal of 'Truth to Nature' and their conformity to the popular taste for literary, historical and genre subjects, relied heavily on the services of the artist's model. Few more so than Frith.

> I am filled with astonishment, not unmixed with envy, when I hear from one of my most distinguished colleagues that his pictures . . . are painted without models, either for human beings or accessories.
>
> I should scarcely be believed if I were to sum up the outlay for dresses, models etc, necessary for me to incur . . . Fuseli used to say that 'nature put him out', and Maclise seldom, if ever, used models. Let the student take note by the example of these men of the fatal effects of 'painting without nature'.[1]

Although much has been written about the nineteenth-century female artists' models who became the lover, wife or muse of a famous artist, notably Lizzie Siddall, Jane Morris and other Pre-Raphaelite 'stunners', little documentary material exists from which to construct a reliable account of the everyday working lives of female models. Perhaps the main reason for this dearth of information is that female models were regarded pretty much as prostitutes. There was general public belief that all artists' models were used for sexual purposes as well as sittings. The artist William Mulready, who was chastised by Ruskin for his paintings of the female nude, offered practical advice to the aspiring female model:

> An intelligent woman who at the commencement of this dangerous profession, is well prepared for . . . danger, will have much fewer cases of trouble, than poor innocent creatures who with distracted minds are flung unprepared among its smiling faces, flattering manners, its painting and gilding.[2]

The best account of the history of the Victorian studio model is to be found in *The Artist's Model*

Facing page:
130. *Study for 'Many Happy Returns of the Day'*, 1854. York Museums Trust (York Art Gallery). Detail.

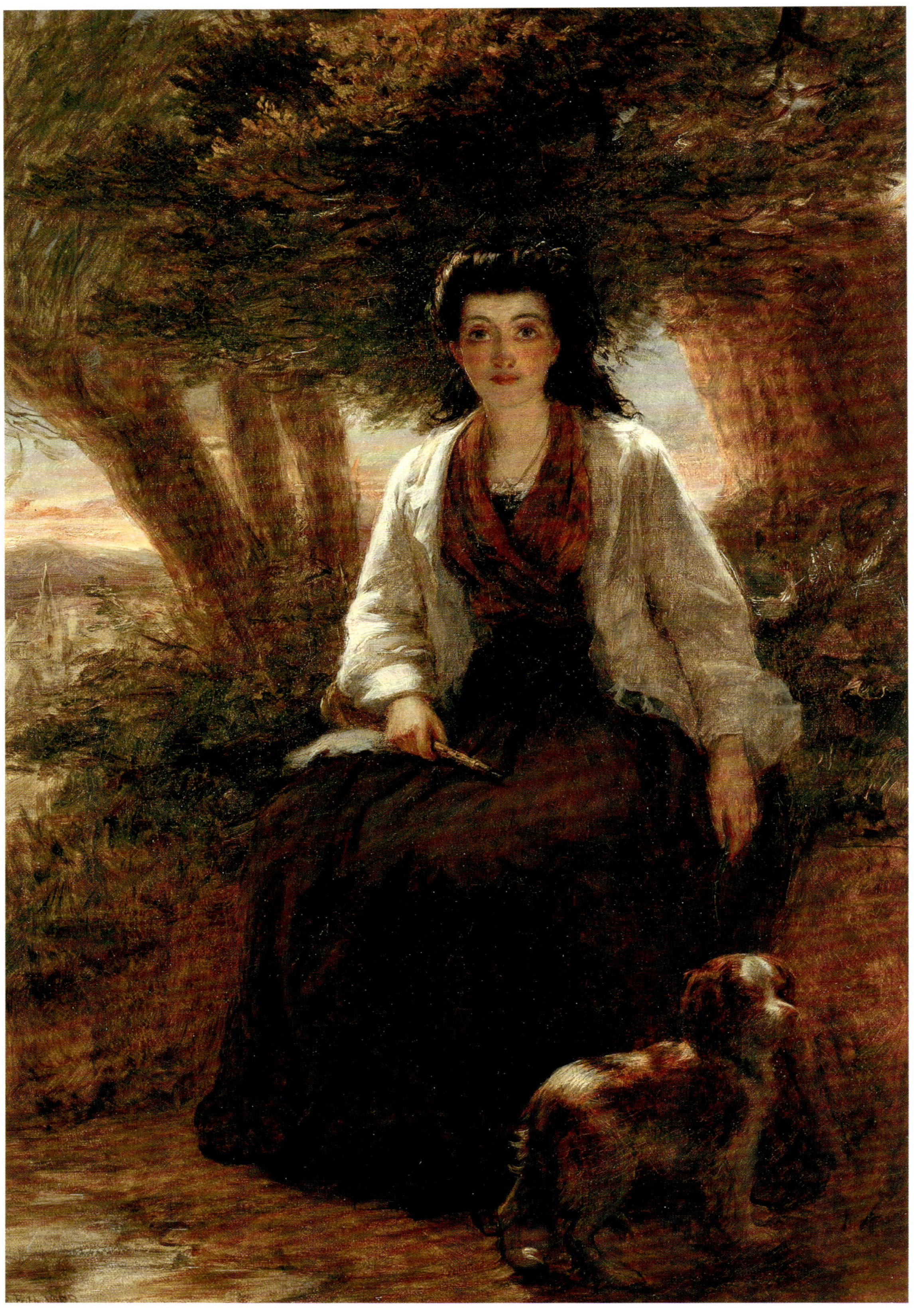

131. *Sterne's Maria, from 'A Sentimental Journey'*. Private Collection.

from Etty to Spencer by Martin Postle and William Vaughan (1999). The authors trace the progression of what was regarded as a lowly, rather dubious occupation into a profession. Frith, of course, played a major role in the development of the popularity of modern life genre painting, which led to a demand for more and more models and narrowed the gap between the social situation of the model and the role she was required to play for the artist. The flower-sellers and the shop girls came in from the streets to play themselves in the studio. As Postle and Vaughan point out, behind the mythology of the privileged existence of the artist and model in the site of the studio there existed the reality of a financial transaction; the reality of social and sexual inequality; and the reality that studio models were not only young, female and nubile, but old, infirm, orphaned or plagued by debt and disease.[3]

We can find names in artists' studio records and other scattered information, but it is in fact Frith himself to whom we turn as a major source of consistent and detailed information about the female model's working life. In *My Autobiography and Reminiscences* and *Further Reminiscences*, (1887–8), Frith makes numerous references to the female models who worked for him at his studio. We learn who his models were and how he engaged them; their personal histories; their professional strengths and weaknesses, and how Frith regarded both male and female models in general. Throughout his writings, the artist makes us keenly aware of the great importance of models to his work:

> Amongst the ignorant . . . the idea commonly prevails that pictures are evolved out of the painter's inner consciousness, or, in other words, are created out of nothing. The fact that nature is constantly referred to, that for the most trifling detail the artist never trusts to his memory, that he not only uses models for the human beings which may fill his compositions, but that he seeks far and wide for the smallest object to be represented, will be a revelation to most people.[4]

At the same time, there could be said to be a subtext to Frith's reflections on female models. In many references to them, especially in his accounts of the personal histories of the women who worked for him, he is at pains to underline the respectable nature of his model. He overcompensates with these stories of his models' indisputable virtue in a bid to convince his readers that whatever went on in other artists' studios, it did not happen in his own. For example, there is his recollection of a girl who modelled for his representation of Laurence Sterne's 'Poor Maria' (Fig. 131):

> The model for 'Maria' was a pretty, gentle creature, who had a history. She sat to me many times for many pictures; and it was her sad expression as much as her beauty that suggested 'Maria' to me, and induced me to try the subject. I drew from her – reluctantly on her side – something of her history. Her superiority to an ordinary model was apparent in many ways; her manner and address were ladylike, and her grammar never caused a shudder.[5]

It transpires that the model had been a Sunday School teacher who had been duped into marrying a rogue who beat and then abandoned her, thus it was her poor circumstances that had forced her into becoming an artist's model. Frith's only quibble with her was that she disappeared without notice, leaving him with her head unfinished.

Frith's apparent fascination with the subject of artists' models in his writing is something that he also explores in his self-portraits, the earliest of which occurs in his 1853 Royal Academy Diploma picture, *The Sleeping Model*, or 'The Sleepy Model' as he calls it in his autobiography (Fig. 132). Frith did not only use professional models. He was in the habit of looking out for suitable

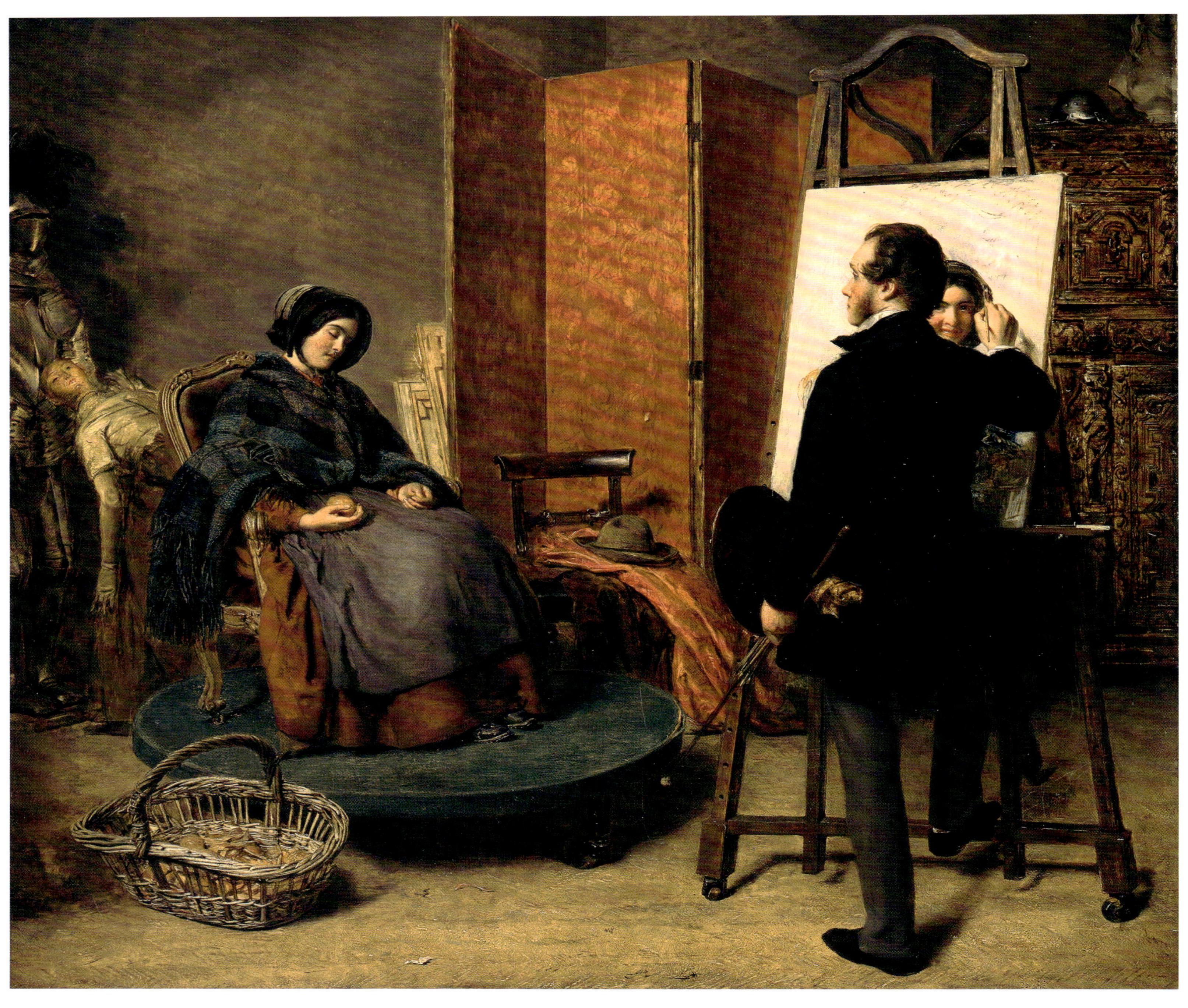

132. *The Sleeping Model*, 1853. Royal Academy of Arts, London.

subjects as he walked the streets of London. This girl was an orange seller, in whom Frith identified 'a rare type of rustic beauty'. Eventually he persuaded her to sit for him.

> I determined to paint a laughing face from her . . . I could not find anything to talk to her about that would amuse her, and she could not talk to me . . . After many attempts to rouse an expression that would help make a laughing face, I found the worst of hindrances that can afflict a painter come upon me – my model fell fast asleep.[6]

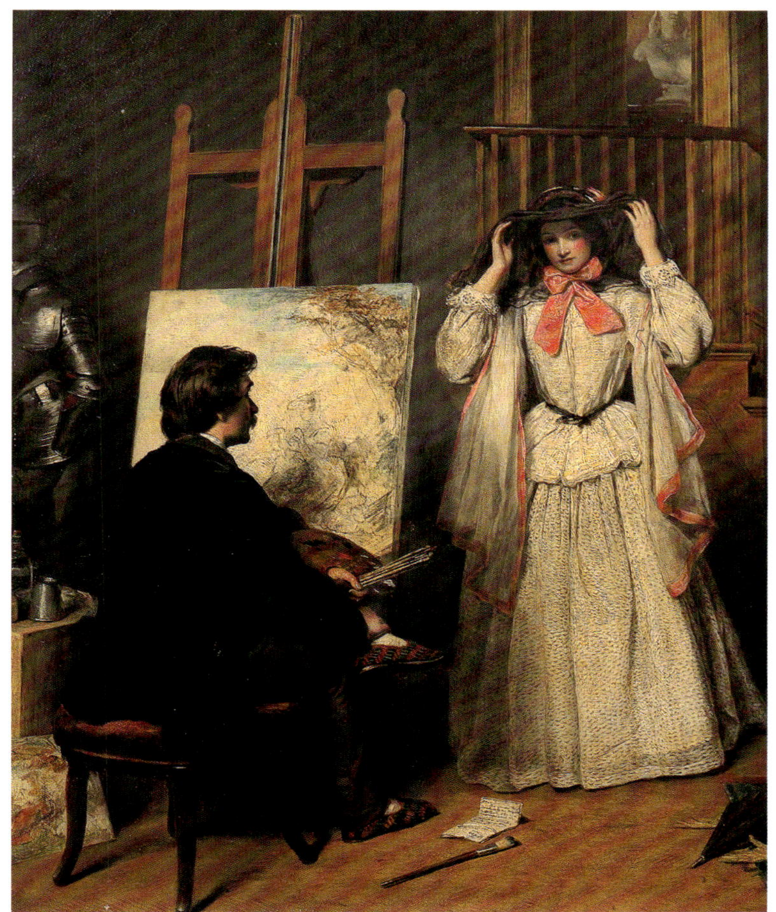

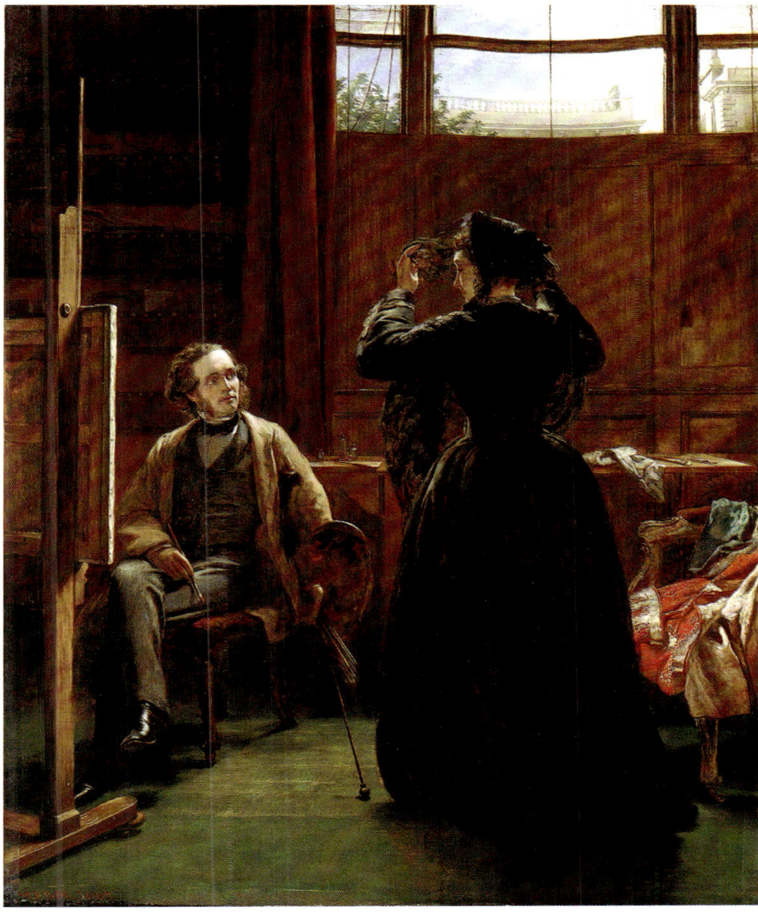

133. Left: *The Artist's Model*, 1860. Derby Museum and Art Gallery.

134. Right: *The Artist in his Studio*, 1867. National Portrait Gallery, London.

Frith does not try to glamorise either himself or the artist's studio in this painting. The picture takes in the clutter of a workplace, with its folding screen, a lay figure slumped in the corner and a stack of canvases against the wall. He avoids the suggestion of sexual overtones in the relationship between artist and model. This model, her face and hands the only naked flesh on view, dozes on the dais, unintimidated by the presence of the artist. She is a tired, working woman, unable to resist the warmth and peace of the studio as a place to take a well-earned rest. In contrast, Frith's later treatments of the subject make more pointed reference to the nature of the model's profession and her relationship with the artist. The 1856 version of the artist and his model in the studio (Fig. 133) has the artist seated at his easel with the model standing before him, lifting the veil from her hat with upraised arms in a revealing gesture. The sketch of a woman in a similar pose is just discernable on the canvas in front of the artist. The artist's self portrait of 1867 (Fig. 134) is more subtle in its delineation of the artist/model relationship. This time we look into the space of the studio over the shoulder of the newly arrived model. Her arms, too, are raised as she lifts her veil so that he might look at her face. Whereas in his Diploma picture the artist is at the mercy of the somnolent model, here he takes control. Frith was by this date both wealthy and famous, having already painted the three major modern life subjects that made his name.

As well as keeping a lookout for suitable models on the London streets, Frith also employed women whom he encountered in the course of his social life, such as Isabella Eyre. Isabella's granddaughter inherited a replica of the painting for which her grandmother had modelled and presented it in 1994 to the Mercer Art Gallery, Harrogate (Fig. 135), because of Frith's early association with the town. In letters to the Mercer, the donor tells how this came about.

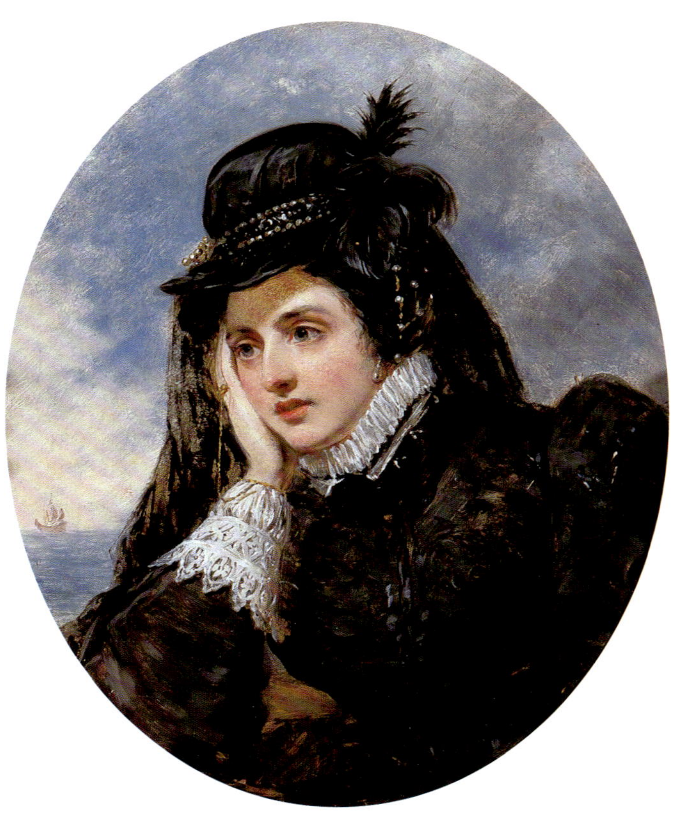

135. *Study for 'L' Adieu de Marie Stuart'*, *c.*1893. The Mercer Art Gallery, Harrogate Museums and Arts.

> This portrait of my grandmother, Miss Eyre, was painted by W. P. Frith RA who met her in a London ballroom. He was struck by her beauty and asked her to sit for him as 'Mary Queen of Scots' for his large picture *L'Adieu.* In recognition of the fact that she did so he presented her with this lovely portrait. The picture was exhibited in the Royal Academy in 1890 and there is a picture of it in the Illustrated London News. The portrait was given to Miss Eyre in recognition of her acting as the model for that picture. My mother was told that she was chaperoned by her mother and her aunt at each sitting.[7]

It is interesting to note, in the letters, how the family's history of the painting carefully distances itself from the idea that Miss Eyre could have been regarded as a paid artist's model. For every story he tells about a pretty and punctual young woman, there is one about the misdemeanours of a male model. For example, Brunskill, a guardsman, turns up for work at the Royal Academy Life Class both late and drunk. He attempts his pose, that of a sailor pushing a boat from the shore with a heavy oar, but is defeated by it and exits from the studio, for the last time, with a succinct speech. 'I can't do it. I ain't fit to do it. This 'ere thing what I hold ain't right. Nothing's right; so I wish you gentlemen good-night. There now.'[8] Drink, in Frith's view, was the greatest impediment an artist's model could possess. One particularly fruitful source of models for him had at one time been the workhouse, but the supply of elderly characters, much to his inconvenience, came to a halt for the same reason.

> We are shut out from the workhouses; and the reason given us is the impossibility of the 'inmates', whether male or female, being able to pass the public-house on their homeward route, without leaving there much of their sitting-money in exchange for drink.[9]

Only occasionally in Frith's autobiography, as Martin Postle has pointed out, does he reveal a distaste for the ordinary working class model.[10] In the final volume of his *Reminiscences*, Frith relates how people calling themselves models often arrived at his studio door to offer their services, regardless of the fact that they had neither beauty nor character.[11] He records one such incident in telling detail:

> A knock at the studio door, and enter a woman, extremely plain, not to say ugly, with a face artificially whitened and deeply marked by small-pox; age about fifty . . . 'You use models, I believe? I want to sit. Can you employ me? . . . You should do Scriptures subjects, that's what you should do. Them's what I've sat for – Holy Families, and that . . . Lots of Virgin Marys has been done from me.[12]

However, in general, Frith appears to have had more respect for his female models than his male subjects.

> My experience of the ladies who honour us by sitting is extensive. As a rule, they are all that could be desired – patient, kindly, long suffering, and well-behaved . . . indeed, instances of

misbehaviour amongst the females are very rare indeed, and they usually consist of unpunctuality, which is a deadly sin.[13]

One such sinner was Miss Jenny Trip (the principal aesthete on the left of the *Private View at the Roayl Academy* 1881), daughter of a railway stoker on the Chatham and Dover line, who was incapable of arriving less than two hours late. Little wonder that Frith made such frequent use of members of his own family, friends and, sometimes, servants as models.[14] One of Frith's female servants was the subject of one of his best known pictures, *Sherry, Sir?* (Fig. 20) popularised by an engraving.

> A little study, done from a good-looking girl who was in my service as housemaid, had a great success as an engraving. I painted the girl not only in her habit as she lived, but in her habits also, for she was carrying a tray with a bottle of wine on it.[15]

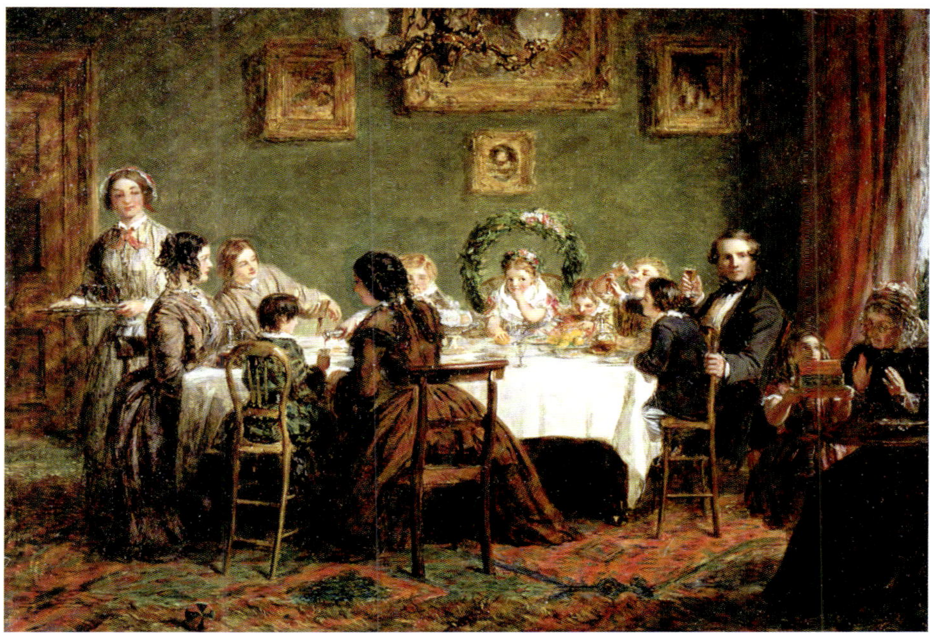

136. *Study for 'Many Happy Returns of the Day'*, 1854. York Museums Trust (York Art Gallery) purchased with the aid of grants and donations from the National Art Collections Fund, the Victoria and Albert Museum through the Museums and Galleries Commission, the Friends of York Art Gallery, the R. M. Burton Charitable Trust and Anthony Boynton-Wood, Esq., 1991.

The title of the engraving, invented by its owner, the publisher Jacob Bell, was an embarrassment to Frith, but he grudgingly acknowledged that it was a marketing success. Servants generally appear anonymously in Victorian paintings, with portraits of individuals being a rare exception. As Giles Waterfield has pointed out, in his depictions of servants, Frith, as ever, applies 'a bland quality to the social issues which other artists addressed with sighs'.[16]

In 1854, Frith began work on his painting *Many Happy Returns of the Day*, or the 'Birthday Party' as he refers to it (Fig. 117).

> The scene is laid in a dining room, where a family is assembled to do honour to a small person who may have attained the mature age of six, and is at the moment an object of attention to the whole party; for the ceremony of health drinking is taking place. The heroine sits in a high chair, which has been decorated for the occasion with a wreath of flowers, and is somewhat bewildered by her uproarious brothers and sisters, whose wishes for many happy returns of the day are screamed by half a dozen shrill voices. The parent pair preside, of course, assisted by friends; whilst the grandfather and grandmother look sympathetically on.[17]

This painting is a quintessential portrayal of Victorian middle-class family life. The fact that Frith includes a self-portrait as the paterfamilias, and uses his own wife, Isabelle, daughter Alice, the birthday girl, and his young sons as models would suggest that it is to some extent an equation to his own position in life. As Deborah Cherry has pointed out, 'Whereas paid working-class models were often perceived as impure, immoral and unrespectable, a middle-class sitter, especially a friend or family member, was considered to guarantee the purity and respectability of the image and to provide a suitable target for a respectable woman's gaze.'[18] In the painting, Frith's bewildered birthday girl is the point in the composition that separates the feminine from the masculine sphere in a reflection of Victorian society. To the left of the canvas, the women lean together, looking beyond the little child to the group of men and boys, who toast the occasion with glasses of wine. Interestingly, in Frith's preparatory oil sketch (Fig. 136) the action of the composition is dominated by the women rather than the men. The grandfather, prominent in the foreground, is supplanted by the grandmother, who is offered a sweetmeat by a little girl. The male and female figures around the table are intermingled rather than segregated; the maid brings in wine rather than presents, and the toast to the birthday girl includes all the members of the family.

This visual delineation of Victorian values becomes all the more significant when one considers the actual condition of the artist's marriage. Frith married Isabelle in 1845 when he was twenty-six, and between 1846 and 1860 they had seven sons and five daughters (of whom not all survived). But for most of his married life Frith had a mistress, Mary Alford. There is some speculation that Mary Alford could originally have worked as a model for Frith herself. It was extremely common for artists to cohabit with or marry their models, often for quite pragmatic reasons. Models were a significant expense for the artist and it often made economical sense to enter into a more intimate partnership. For example, Ford Madox Brown's second wife, Emma Hill, was his model, whom he made pregnant and later married. Frith had seven children with Mary Alford; according to the census, the first of these, Mary Powell, was born in 1856, the very year *Many Happy Returns of the Day* was exhibited at the Royal Academy. It is impossible to know, but possible to conjecture, that in creating this image Frith was publicly reinforcing his commitment to family life, when in reality this was not the case. Frith worked hard in his career as an artist and he took great pride in his achievements and the admission to the upper echelons of society that his success had bought him. A consummate self-publicist, he was quite capable of producing a picture with a propaganda slant to it. Frith was, however, not alone in living in such hypocritical style. Charles Dickens, Frith's friend, whose portrait and fictional characters he painted, led a high profile life, with marriage to Georgina in the foreground and his secret mistress, the actress Ellen Ternan, in the background.[19] Dickens found his double life stressful, whereas Frith, with greater *sang froid*, kept his two households just ten minutes walk apart in Paddington.

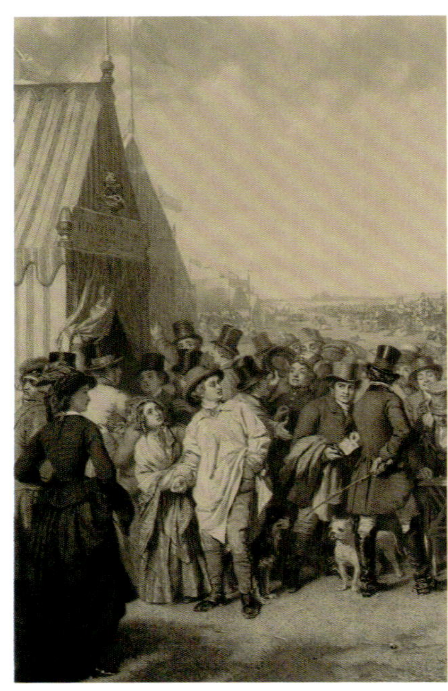

137. *The Derby Day*, 1858. Museum of London. Detail of engraving showing Miss Gilbert.

Frith was inclined to develop strong dislikes of his own paintings. It is perhaps worth noting that he was never fond of his *Birthday Party* picture, describing it as 'one of the worst pictures I ever painted'. When it was hung at the Royal Academy, it was 'in a well-known and dreaded dark part of the large room, and being a low-toned picture, the consequences were dreadful. I can never forget the shock of the first sight of it.'[20] Ruskin noted 'the advancing Pre Raphaelitism in the wreath of leaves around the child's head', an accusation that filled Frith with horror.[21] He loathed the Pre-Raphaelites, who in his opinion painted pictures where 'Ugliness and angularity took the place of beauty and grace . . . unimportant details were made important, to the utter destruction of breadth; and atmosphere was ignored altogether.'[22] Another of his own works that he took against in later life was the well-known *The Fair Toxophilites*, 1872 (Fig. 124), for which his own daughters, Alice, Fanny and Louisa, were the models.

> My desire to discover materials for my work in modern life never leaves me, and will continue its influence as long as my own life lasts; . . . though I have occasionally been betrayed by my love into themes somewhat trifling and commonplace . . . In obedience to this impulse I began a small work suggested by some lady-archers, whose feats had amused me at the seaside . . . The subject was trifling, and totally devoid of character interest; but the girls are true to nature, and the dresses will be a record of the female habiliments of the time.[23]

Facing page:
138. *Annie Gambart*, *c.* 1851. The Mercer Art Gallery, Harrogate Museums and Arts.

Portraiture provided Frith with a constant source of income throughout his life. His paintings of young women often display a tender response to his subject. Outstanding amongst these is his portrait of Annie Gambart (Fig. 138), painted about 1851. This is no mere costume piece, nor is it

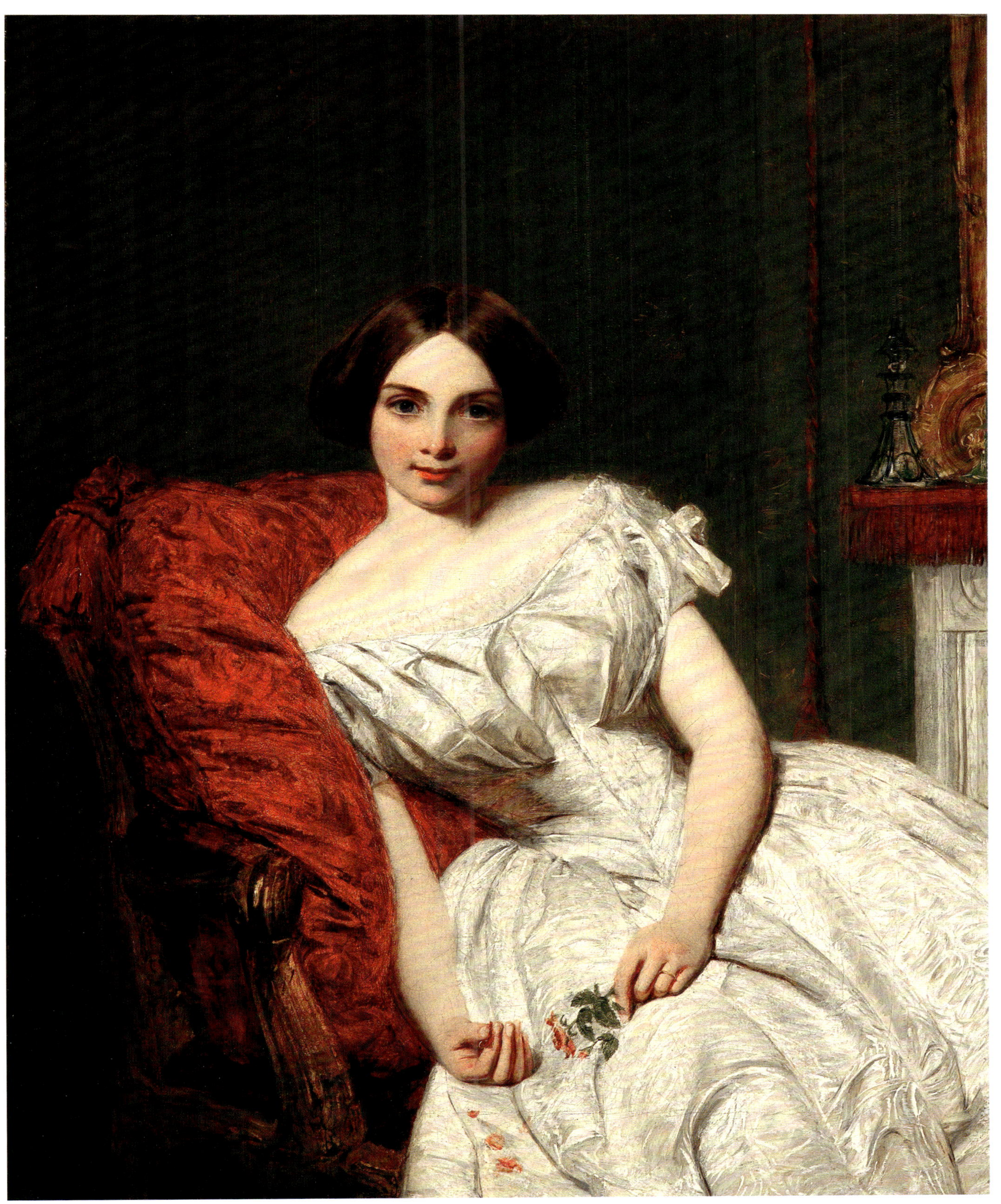

devoid of character interest. It is a picture with an intriguing subtext, one that is related to the sitter's personal history. It was painted in the year that the sixteen-year-old Annie married Ernest Gambart, the greatest of all Victorian art dealers and publishers. Annie is pictured in a white satin evening gown, enveloped by a plush red chair. As she gazes at the viewer, she plucks the petals from the rose in her hand, the falling petals symbolizing the loss of her virginity.

Annie Gambart née Baines (1835–1870), was the third wife of Ernest Gambart (1814–1902). The Gambarts were happily married and famous for their lavish parties, held at their home 'Rosenstead', near Regent's Park. Annie was a charming hostess, always expensively dressed, who reportedly behaved with the irrepressible waywardness of a spoilt child. On the evening of Derby Day in May 1866, a devastating gas explosion occurred as the Gambarts prepared their home for a fancy-dress ball, destroying part of the house and sending paintings flying into neighbouring gardens where they were impaled on the branches of trees. Annie was in such a state of anxiety that Ernest despatched her to friends nearby. The following year, Annie and Ernest Gambart separated. He allegedly kept various little girls in different lodgings around London. Although they never legally divorced, Annie moved to Bayswater, where she remained until her untimely death at the age of thirty-five. The cause of her death was diagnosed as liver disease, the same as for Gambart's second wife, Mary Matilda, who had died in 1848. This portrait of Annie is known to have hung at Gambart's home 'Les Palmiers' in Nice until the end of his days in 1902.

Frith's panoramic masterpieces, *Life at the Seaside (Ramsgate Sands), Derby Day*, and *The Railway Station* provided him with the greatest challenges of his career in many ways, not least the task of finding huge numbers of models. *Ramsgate Sands*, for example, took up the greater part of 1853, with many delays because of the difficulty of locating suitable models.[24] For the painting *Derby Day*, he acknowledges a particular source of help in finding them.

> The owner [of Derby Day], Mr Bell, was very useful to me in procuring models. Few people have a more extensive acquaintance, especially amongst the female sex, than that possessed by Jacob Bell; and what seemed singular, was the remarkable prettiness that distinguished all these pleasant friends . . . I owe every female figure in the 'Derby Day', except two or three, to the foraging of my employer.[25]

Frith, while acknowledging the professionalism of artists' models, tried whenever possible to employ working people in their natural roles. Sometimes this worked well, as in *The Railway Station*, where he used two detectives well-known at the time, Messrs Haydon and Brett, to represent the police officers arresting a criminal on the eve of his escape.[26] On other occasions the difficulties of using amateur models overcame the bid for authenticity. Frith found acrobats, father and young son, in a Drury Lane theatre, to model the central scene of the hungry little boy eyeing the race-goers' picnic. Unfortunately, the boy could not be dissuaded from somersaulting around the studio, with disastrous consequences.

> I soon saw that it would be impossible to use my acrobats in painting the whole of their figures, so by increased payment I acquired their dresses, which were donned by those 'to the manner born' . . . I laid my children and my friends largely under contribution, as well as professional models.[27]

Frith often used actresses as models in his work. Mrs Rousby, for example, sat for the character of Amy Robsart in a scene from Sir Walter Scott's *Kenilworth*, a 'vision of beauty that burst upon us when she entered the drawing-room at Pembridge Villas'.[28] For *Derby Day*, he employed two actresses, Miss Gilbert (Fig. 137) and 'Miss H.', with varying degrees of success.

> In the left-hand corner of the picture stands a lady in a riding-habit. To those who remember

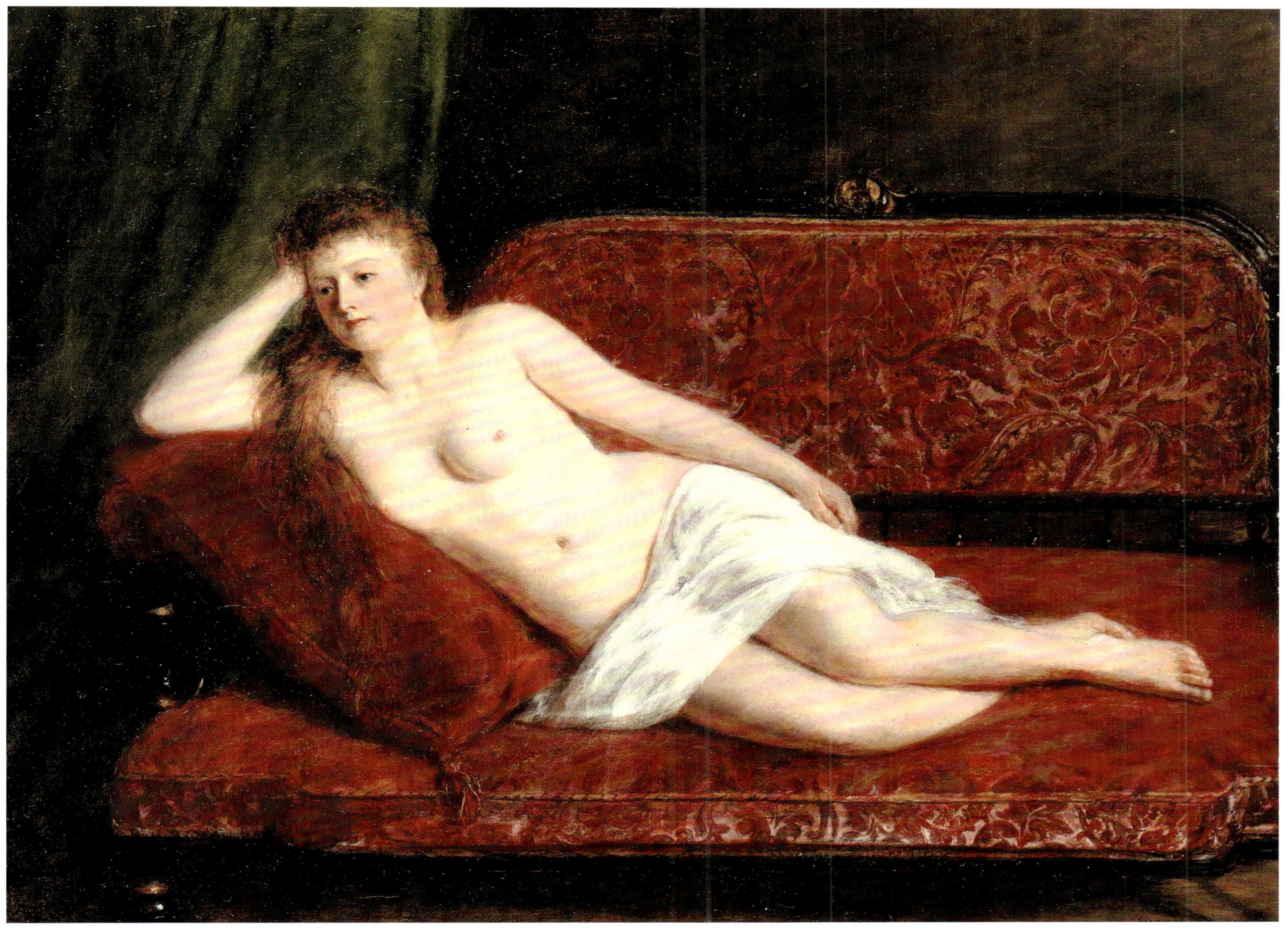

139. *After the Bath*, 1897. Private Collection.

the beautiful Miss Gilbert, my rendering of that witty, charming creature will not be satisfactory. The face was perforce in shadow, and in profile, thus handicapping me terribly . . .[29]

Miss H., one of Jacob Bell's recommendations, was an even less successful choice. Frith struggled and failed to capture her charm and beauty, and resorted to rubbing out the figure and replacing her with one of his own daughters, an act that brought down on him the full dramatic wrath of both Miss H. and Miss Gilbert.[30] This is one of many stories that Frith tells against himself in which he is his own harshest critic.

One of Frith's earliest surviving drawings is a study of the Venus de Milo (Fig. 5). For most of his working life, he claimed that he drew every figure naked in his compositions before he clothed them.[31] However, it was not until the last part of his career that he turned to paintings of the

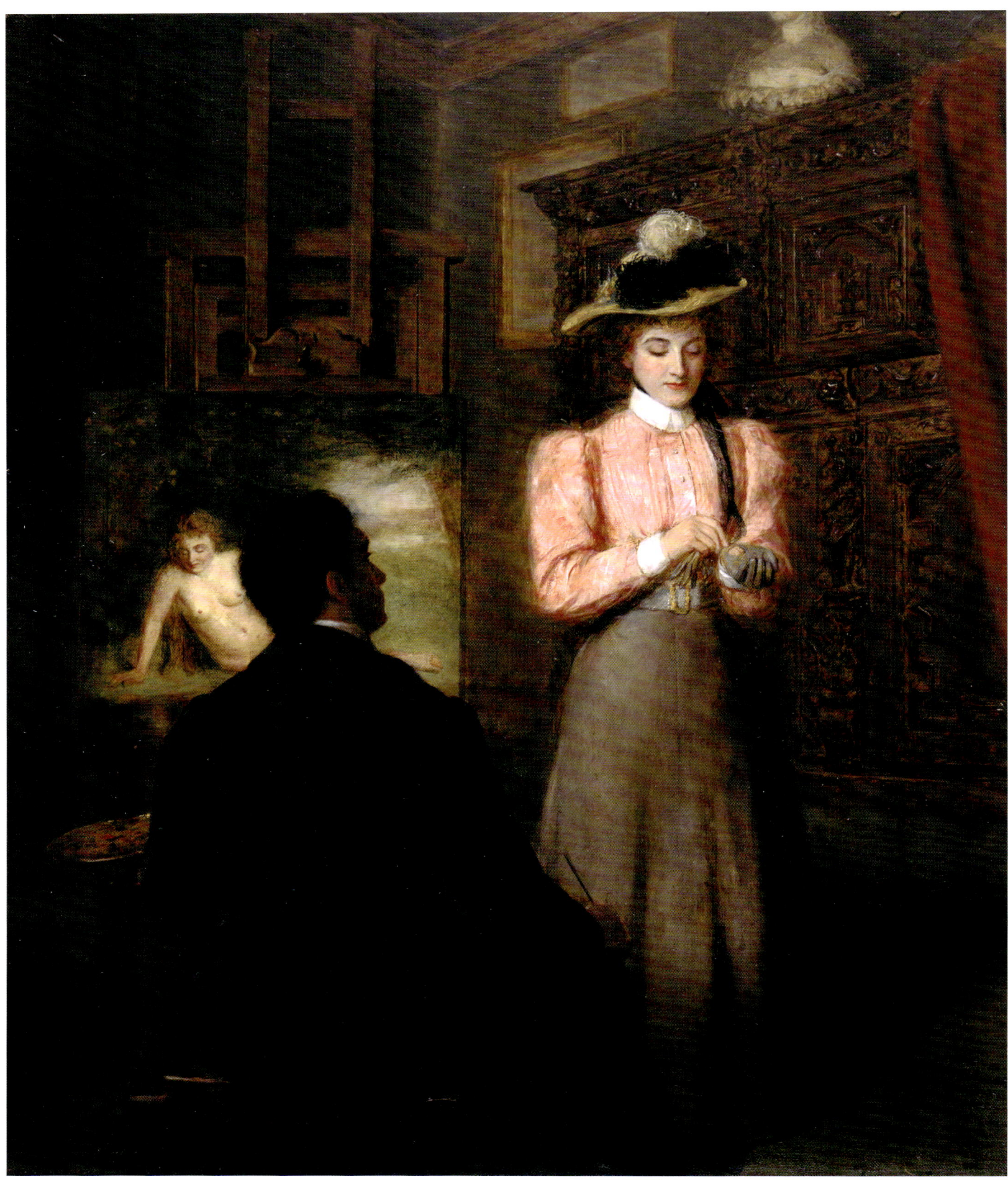

female nude *per se*, such as *After the Bath* (1897; Fig. 139). He also returned to the subject of the artist and model in the studio, only with more explicit sexual overtones. In *The New Model* (1898; Fig. 140), the newly-arrived young woman unbuttons her gloves. On the easel is the unfinished study of a nude for which she is a model. Frith discoursed at some length on the subject of the female nude, condemning the moralists who tried to prevent the study of the female nude.

> If the well-meaning objectors knew half as much as I do of the subject, they would hesitate before they charge a small section of the community with immorality, which exists only in the imagination of accusers. I declare I have known numbers of perfectly respectable women who have sat constantly and habitually for the nude, and if even it were constantly otherwise, we painters could not do without them.[32]

One particular anecdote in his autobiography underlines Frith's defence of the 'perfectly respectable woman'. He describes attending a life class at the Royal Academy, taking a position from where he could see the model's profile, and was surprised to see 'tears slowly falling down the model's cheek'. Later, the same girl turns up as a (clothed) model in his own studio. He asks her why she modelled for the life class if it had caused her so much distress.

> 'I did it', said she, 'to prevent my father going to prison. He owed three pounds ten, and if he couldn't have paid it by that Saturday night, he was to be arrested. The Academy paid me three guineas for the week, and saved him. I never sat in that way before, and I never will again.'[33]

Frith was not unusual for his day in taking on a mistress and family as well as a marriage, but his personal situation does give added resonance to his published views on women in the art world. Socially, he was a parvenu. He could be as critical of the snobbish upper-class women whom he had to manage for the production of his major portrait of the marriage of the Prince of Wales as he was of the uneducated women who inhabited his studio.

> One – the aged wife of an ambassador – was so shocked by my portrait of her that she implored me to rub it out . . . she sent me a drawing done from her when she was a lovely girl of eighteen, with an urgent request that I would correct my libel of her immediately. I declined; and the figure remains a by no means unflattered copy of a very plain old lady.[34]

He made his models enter his studio by an outside staircase so as not to have them in the house, and he went out to dine rather than lunch with them in the studio. But at the same time he was dependent on creating viable working relationships with his female models, and he clearly did develop some understanding of the trials and tribulations of women's lives. Despite his occasional patronising comments, he had considerable respect for working women. It is revealing, for example, to explore Frith's views on women as artists, in particular on their ability in the life class.

> I cannot recall the precise date of the admission of lady students to the Royal Academy, but a very few years ago they were inadmissible; now they are almost equal in number to the male students, from whom they constantly carry off prizes. Whether the means and methods of shared study, shared equally (except in one important particular) with their rougher rivals, will in course of time qualify them to become old mistresses to future ages, time can only prove. My position as visitor, or teacher, in the higher schools has brought me into contact with numbers of lady students whose admirable studies from life have often surprised and delighted me; and in the Antique School I have seen drawings by mere girls that could not be surpassed.[35]

Facing page:
140. *The New Model*, 1898. The Beaverbrook Art Gallery, Fredericton, NB.

Women, therefore, featured significantly in Frith's life, both in his family life and in his career as a celebrated Victorian artist. The female model was essential to his art, and in his *My Autobiography and Reminiscences* he provides us with a glimpse of the lives of Victorian artists' models, which, although not entirely without the prejudices of his age, adds another dimension to his art.

Chapter 9

'Very efficient as a painter'[1] The painting practice of William Powell Frith

SALLY WOODCOCK

> I know very well that I never was, nor under any circumstances could have become, a great artist; but I am a very successful one . . .[2]

Frith's unembarrassed commercialism, his pride in the prices he commanded and the crowds he attracted, the high speed and duplication of his artistic output and his apparently unquestioning confidence in his own powers attracted comment, both affectionate and malicious, from his contemporaries. Shirley Brooks's well-known doggerel 'I ups and paints, hears no complaints, and sells before I'm dry'[3] sums up his combination of energetic self-assurance, speed and commercial acumen, not always considered so endearing: 'It is amusing – or saddening as one's mood may take it, to mark your serene satisfaction in having reached your own ideal.'[4]

Frith's ostensible complacency appears to extend to his painting practice, and his three volumes of autobiography suggest that technique was the least of his worries. In some ways this is probably true – he had a thorough early training, spending four years practising drawing, successively at Sass's art school and as a probationer at the Royal Academy Schools, before returning to Sass to start painting.[5] His belief in the value of this system half a century on, is demonstrated in his article in the *Magazine of Art* of 1888, where he advises young artists to serve a similarly long apprenticeship, drawing before learning to paint 'as the great masters did'.[6] The impression given is that once he had found a system that worked, he stuck to it.

In terms of the condition and stability of his paintings, posterity appears to have endorsed his judgement, and in 1922 A. P. Laurie, Professor of Chemistry to the Royal Academy of Arts, singled out pictures by Frith as examples of paintings from the first half of the nineteenth century, that had 'stood best the test of time'.[7] These sentiments were echoed by Frith in old age, on seeing his painting *Life at the Seaside (Ramsgate Sands)* at the Guildhall in 1897: 'I have not seen it for many years, & I was pleased to find it without the slightest change of any kind – in fact exactly as it left me five & forty years ago.'[8]

However, this apparently flawless combination of sound training, dependable technique, willing and wealthy purchasers and the longevity of both the artist and his paintings conveys an over-simplified impression of Frith's artistic life, although containing elements of truth. Frith, like almost all artists, had moments of insecurity and confusion, doubted his own judgement and changed his mind. While it is clear that he could be ostentatious and somewhat disingenuous, particularly where he saw financial advantage, examination of some of his surviving papers reveals a more interesting picture of the artist at work than being merely a 'painter of popular pictures'.[9]

WORKING METHODS: PRELIMINARY STAGES

Contemporaries ascribed Frith's success in great part to his fortuitous choice of subject – popular, populous paintings that were well-received by both royalty and commoner.[10] Although some of his critics decried the vulgarity and 'sham realism' of his output,[11] Frith recognised his own limitations, declaring that he neither understood nor could paint spiritual subjects.[12] Early on he was anxious to demonstrate a versatility that his later career failed fully to establish, proposing to a patron a humorous scene for the forthcoming Royal Academy exhibition in 1848, which, 'if I can carry it out as well as the others it will do my reputation much good by shewing a command over variety of subject'.[13] However, once he had found a genre that offered both critical success and lucrative returns, he was largely content to repeat the formula, even offering a reward of £200 for suggestions of a suitable subject to follow up the success of *Derby Day*.[14]

Once he had hit upon his subject, early stages of composition developed along conventional lines. He describes the progress of *Life at the Seaside (Ramsgate Sands)* in his biography, making the first pencil drawings on site in 1851, beginning the oil sketch at the end of September, completing it in mid-November and then starting the full-size painting on 9 April 1852.[15] He records that the first touch of paint did not go on until 7 May, so it is assumed that the intervening month was spent preparing the canvas and mapping out the composition. His account with the artist's colourman Charles Roberson & Co. records that by the end of 1851 he must have decided upon the dimensions of the painting, ordering '2 Primed Cloths on stretcher 5ft . 2ft 6 4 in allwd extra cloth' on 15 December 1851 at a cost of one guinea, putting the sale price of 1,000 guineas somewhat in perspective. Usually Roberson's accounts recorded double primings by the abbreviation 'dble' and therefore this suggests a loose-lined canvas with an additional four inches of cloth to facilitate re-stretching or alterations in dimensions at a later date.[16]

While continuing to work on *Ramsgate Sands* until early April 1854, Frith completed other, smaller paintings, including his diploma piece for the Royal Academy, in order to maintain his income and fulfil commissions. His Roberson account in the period from April 1852 to April 1854 records the purchase of four panels, five canvases of given dimensions, at least seven listed simply as 'canvases', one stretcher (subsequently stretched by Roberson, presumably with Frith's own canvas) and two millboards. While perhaps not all of these would have led to completed paintings in this period, he may also have worked on supports already in the studio. Whichever is the case, the volume of purchases indicates the maintenance of a steady output in the two years during which he was at work on his large painting.

The schedule for *Derby Day*, completed four years later, shows that Frith could work still faster, completing a painting with almost double the surface area of *Ramsgate Sands* in fifteen months between January 1857 and March 1858. The 'rough drawing' was completed between 21 and 24 May 1856, then several weeks were spent on two oil sketches, sufficient to persuade the picture dealer Ernest Gambart to pay £1,500 for engraving rights, equalling the price of the painting. On 20 January 1857 Frith used charcoal to sketch the figures onto the canvas bought only three days earlier from Roberson's, his account for 17 January 1857 reading 'Double canvas extra primed 7ft 4 × 3ft 4 edges 55/-'.[17] He records that he completed the painting after 'fifteen months' incessant labour', and it is notable that his account shows no additional supports of any kind being purchased in this period.[18]

It is possible that by this time he had engaged studio assistance, contributing to his increased speed, or the income from *Ramsgate Sands* and other sales may have given him the luxury of virtually uninterrupted work on *Derby Day*.[19] Whether or not he was working alone,[20] during the 1850s Roberson carried out a variety of activities at Frith's studio, usually concerned with preparing supports for the artist. These included re-stretching canvases, stretching his canvas on their stretchers, inserting sketches in panels, reducing and enlarging canvases, removing varnish, cleaning and restoring portraits and lining paintings. It was only in the last years of his life when Frith had retired from the Royal Academy and virtually ceased to submit work that Roberson's services were no longer required, or possibly no longer affordable.

WORKING METHODS: MATERIALS

In studying Frith's painting practice, it is tempting to dismiss him as merely a conservative product of the nineteenth-century art academy: unadventurous in his choice of materials and repetitious in application. In comparison to his more experimental or unconventional contemporaries, several of whom have attracted scholarly attention,[21] it seems difficult to justify studying the technique of an artist who appears so ordinary. However, in some ways Frith provides a benchmark of normality against which to judge the immoderation of nineteenth-century materiality. Perhaps his significance is in being an exemplar of normal practice for the period, similar to countless nineteenth-century artists now forgotten by posterity, who used unadventurous materials to produce uninteresting pictures that have resolutely refused to deteriorate in noteworthy ways.

Technical issues receive little attention in Frith's writings and are rarely alluded to by his critics and observers. This is not surprising, as his paintings generally exhibited uncontroversial surface characteristics and remained in good condition throughout his life. He neither experimented with surfaces like Watts, nor adopted the vibrant 'eye-jarring' colours of the Pre-Raphaelites and their circle. There was no swift deterioration, as with Turner, and, unlike Ford Madox Brown, he had sufficient funds with which to buy good-quality materials. After an initial period of minor experimentation with paint media, he appears to have settled on a painting technique that never failed him. This left him in an ideal position to concentrate on the finished product, rather than struggling with the means by which it was to be achieved.

Information on Frith's materials is largely found in his account with his colourman, Roberson, which lasted from 1850 until his death in 1909. By 1850 he had been elected ARA for five years and had already exhibited some well-received paintings, but it is unclear who supplied his materials prior to his dealings with Roberson. Frith himself appears unsure about this towards the end of his life, writing to Roberson in 1900: 'I am anxious to know for how long I have dealt with you & used your medium – if you can tell me when I received my first tube of your medium you will oblige me. There is a picture of mine at the Guildhall exhibition which was exhibited at the RA. in 1848 – I think I was a customer of yours then?'[22]

It is possible that Frith bought his materials over the counter, and therefore unrecorded, before opening an account with the company, or bought from a variety of sources before settling on a single colourman.[23] He may have chosen Roberson both for their reputation for quality and because they were used or recommended by fellow-artists. Frith and four of his closest friends all opened accounts in the first three months of 1850: Richard Ansdell's account began on 2 January, Frith opened his account eight days later, followed by Augustus Egg on 15th of the month; by March John Calcott Horsley was also an account-holder. Seven members of the Clique were also Roberson customers, opening their accounts at irregular intervals between 1836 and 1879.

Frith may also have chosen Roberson to solve his dilemma over painting media. This is one area in which he expressed technical uncertainty and seemed to experiment with a limited range of materials. In 1848–50 his patron and later friend, Thomas Miller, discussed the issue of a suitable painting vehicle with a number of artists, including Alfred Elmore, Robert Huskisson and Frith. The discussion principally concerned copal, about which the artists expressed misgivings, Elmore writing that he was like Frith 'in my fear of the copal'[24] and Huskisson referring to advice similarly given by Frith that 'copal would certainly crack if used over the weaker drier' for finishing a picture.[25] Miller supplied Frith with a sample of copal from a Mr Bolton, which the artist tried for the first time in September 1849 and by which he expressed himself 'charmed'.[26] The following year he asked Miller to clarify what appears to be a test of copal's quality suggested by Mr Bolton: 'I should be pleased to know what the suddenly plunging copal into cold water is to prove & how the cold water is to affect the good copal & how the bad – will you kindly ask this?'[27] He also asked for a bottle of Bolton's washed linseed oil, although seemed to be favouring the copal: 'I am more & more pleased with the copal, & if I can only get something to thin it with safety I shall feel settled for life – as to vehicle.'[28]

Frith's uncertainty continued once he had received the oil, which Augustus Egg immediately commandeered, in March 1850 and by June was again sending Bolton questions via Miller:

> I do want Mr Bolton's opinion on this simple matter – namely whether fat drying oil – twenty five years in bottle is safe as a vehicle – will it dry hard – & will it change colour? Is it true that it turns yellow? Is fat linseed oil better? Such as what he kindly sent me through you. As far as I can tell this is the usual drying oil – pale I think & it works more delightfully than any vehicle I ever used. I feel ashamed of bothering you and Mr Bolton with this, but I know you would do anything to enlighten me on the puzzling question of vehicles. Why is fat oil in the most perfect state for use?[29]

Frith's Roberson account shows that he largely resolved these questions by adopting Roberson's Medium[30] as his main vehicle, buying it regularly for all but the last two years of his account lasting fifty- nine years. In a letter to Roberson, later used by the firm for publicity purposes, he confirmed his use of the medium for *Derby Day* and its satisfactory results: 'it is just fifty years since I painted the Derby Day with your colours and medium, and . . . in so long a time there is no change whatsoever in the materials used.'[31]

In addition to Roberson's oil paints prepared in linseed oil, which Frith bought throughout his working life, there are isolated purchases of other materials, likely to have been used as painting media. These include regular purchases of linseed oil and also periods using poppy oil, first purchased in 1876, largely in the 1870s and 90s. The 'fat oil' mentioned in his letter to Miller, is abandoned after 1851, as is copal, apart from a few isolated purchases, and although he tries 'McGuelp' [megilp] in 1856–7, it did not supplant its close relative, Roberson's Medium. Thus it appears that Frith used other media in small quantities for limited periods, but his account clearly shows a sustained reliance on Roberson's Medium throughout the second half of the century. In endorsing this product he seems to have found the medium on which he could truly 'settle for life'.

CANVASES

The majority of Frith's paintings are on a canvas support and as he increased in affluence, the quality of the canvases he ordered increased accordingly. At the start of the 1850s he bought single primed and possibly unprimed canvas, sometimes having it stretched by Roberson. It is likely that some of these canvases were attached to strainers, as the early accounts refer to 'frames' rather than 'stretchers' and in a letter to Miller written in 1854 Frith explained that he had to re-stretch a painting as he had been unwise enough to use a strainer, rather than a stretcher, and it had lost tension.[32]

It is notable that the larger canvases that Frith employed were often double, or loose-lined, presumably as a protective measure. For example on 23 April 1863 he ordered 'Canvas on best stretcher 10ft .7f 2 [i.e. 10ft x 7ft 2ins] to fold at 5ft prepared cloth strained at back of above.'[33] The cost of the stretched canvas was £5 10s, with an additional £2 10s for the back protection, which therefore comprised over a quarter of the total cost, perhaps explaining why this preventive measure was not more widely applied.

By 1856 he had started to order extra primed canvases as well as best quality stretchers, reflecting his first period of financial success, although they are not consistently used and Frith seemed to vary between different qualities of support, sometimes appearing to have old canvas re-stretched for use. It is possible that he ordered cheaper materials for those paintings he termed 'pot-boilers' or for copies, and spent more money on his larger works. There certainly seems to be a hierarchy in terms of Frith's working practice between the larger and smaller paintings. When writing to Miller about a less important picture in 1848, he reassured him that 'by having gas laid on in my painting room & working at night I have managed to get this last subject forward without neglecting the large picture.'[34] The primacy of working in natural light was emphasised in a later letter in which he apologised for the delay in visiting Egg to see his picture on account of being so busy with his own work that he 'could not spare daylight' and Egg refused to show the painting by candlelight.[35] He also wrote to Miller in reference to working when the daylight resembled 'diluted yolks of eggs', and while working on site at Knowle in 1848 he said that the 'thick weather' made him afraid to work on the heads, instead spending his time on the drapes and background, again showing that the most important work was executed when the light was good.[36]

Even before embarking on his series of very large paintings of the 1850s and 60s, he realised that the size of his compositions was important, explaining in 1847 that he felt compelled to paint at least one large work a year, 'for the sake of upholding and advancing my reputation & in doing this I neglect all my commissions'.[37] At this point Frith said he had twenty-three commissions, all comparatively small works, but felt confident that they could be completed without too much effort. Large paintings presented difficulties in execution and transportation, especially when the painting had to travel to the sitters, as in the case of Frith's *Marriage of the Prince of Wales* (1865).[38] The canvas measured 10ft × 7ft 2ins (3 × 2.2 m) and was attached to a folding stretcher. However, to transport the canvas to Windsor for numerous sittings over a seven-week period, Roberson evidently decided to roll the painting and pack it in a 'strong packing case lined with stout brown paper.' The whole operation, including van hire and manpower cost £11 15s, more than the price of the stretched canvas in the first place, supporting Frith's assertion that royal commissions were both time-consuming and expensive.[39]

The remainder of Frith's purchases in terms of supports are a small number of panels and millboards. He also had his sketches stretched up or mounted on, or inserted into, panels, presumably to preserve them during their use as aids to the final composition, or for posterity. It is clear that Frith's sketches were preserved and even displayed, as in 1885 he writes to 'My dearest B' saying that there is to be an article in the *Pall Mall Gazette* and that he has promised them 'the first idea' for *Derby Day*, 'the little gem which hangs in your small room.'[40]

A list of the paint used by Frith is preserved in an undated notebook in the Roberson Archive.[41] Apart from 'Special Grey Oker', the list contains nothing unusual: 'Permanent Flake White, Genuine Naples Yellow, Yellow Ochre, Special Grey Oker, Medium, French Ultramarine, Indian Red, Light Red, Madder Carmine, Vermilion, Cobalt, Raw Umber, Vandyke Brown, Ultramarine Grey, Ivory Black, Ultramarine Ash, Raw Sienna, Burnt Sienna.' Frith continued to buy his Naples yellow in bladders until 1906, even though all his other paints were supplied in collapsible tubes, presumably because of the fear that the lead antimonite would react with the metallic tube.

His account reveals that he started to buy natural ultramarine in various grades from 1859 – it is specifically named by grade or as 'genuine', and differentiated from the other colours he bought. This is clearly supplied as tube oil paint, and there is little evidence that Frith bought dry pigments and made up his own paint.[42] As with other aspects of his account, the quality of his purchases follows his fortunes, with ultramarine being replaced by the cheapest grade of ultramarine ashes from the 1870s onwards.

The only development in his palette can be seen in the directions he gave his colourman for the preparation of his paint. In 1861 he first asked for 'extra ground' flake white as a special order.[43] Subsequently, from the 1860s to 90s his account included orders for his colours to be extra or double ground, presumably allowing him to achieve transparent glazes and fine detail in his busy pictures. In the 1870s, like several of his contemporaries, he also began to ask for his colours to be supplied 'extra stiff'. This continued in tandem with the orders for extra ground colours into the 1890s. In particular, flake white was singled out for this special order. Artists were aware of the potentially yellowing effect of the medium and it seems likely that by reducing the proportion of oil to pigment, Frith hoped to maintain the brightness of his whites.

VARNISH

There is very little indication of Frith's choice of varnish for his paintings. There are isolated references in his account to varnish brushes and one purchase of a pint of mastic in 1865, but otherwise he says little on the subject.[44] A letter written to Miller in 1854 suggests that there was barely enough time for the paint, let alone varnish, to dry before the painting had to leave the studio, and perhaps gives a new meaning to Shirley Brooks' charge of Frith 'selling before he was dry': 'Today I worked over the sky of the "Lady Hawking" getting it clearer and better I hope. I also glazed and strengthened the figure a little, which does it no harm. As soon as it is dry enough which will be in a day or two I will have it packed and forwarded.'[45]

Several times Frith talks of the benefit of putting a picture away for anything from a week to a month and returning to work on it with a fresh eye. However, he was usually in too much of a hurry to achieve this. An exception was *An Old Woman Accused of Witchcraft* (1848), which he planned to put away for a week or fortnight at the start of 1848: 'I should always do this if I had time & this year by beginning so much earlier than usual I have been able to avail myself of it.'[46]

There are isolated references to Roberson removing varnish from pictures for Frith, but it is unclear whether these are paintings in his own collection (he is known to have owned paintings by other artists, buying two works by Hogarth in 1861)[47] or paintings on which he was working. It is possible that Frith was returning to older works or having a temporary varnish removed, so these references should alert conservators to the fact that paintings may have been treated at an early stage in their development or cleaned before they were completed. Frith had Roberson carry out restoration procedures fairly infrequently, but there are isolated account entries for 'transferring panel picture to canvas', 'Lining and adding to pic stopping & priming', etc.; therefore this aspect of his practice should be borne in mind when assessing the originality or otherwise of additions and alterations.

There is one specific discussion of varnish in a letter to C. W. Carey, the curator of the Royal Holloway College Picture Gallery, owners of *The Railway Station*. After a discussion of the benefits of glazing, of which Frith approved although his own painting was obviously too large for this protection, he agreed to Royal Holloway doing whatever they felt to be necessary for the preservation of his picture. He suggested that the painting be washed with water or very lightly varnished with Roberson's Medium, 'but the latter process not to be resorted to unless the picture requires it from having sunk much in the darker parts.'[48] He also suggested that Carey did whatever he felt needful for the protection of the back, as the original canvas had neither loose lining nor back protection, unlike *Ramsgate Sands*, *Derby Day* and *The Marriage of the Prince of Wales*.[49] It therefore seems likely that any original varnish remaining on a painting by Frith will be mastic, but there may also be local applications of Roberson's Medium as an intermediary layer or on top of the final varnish.

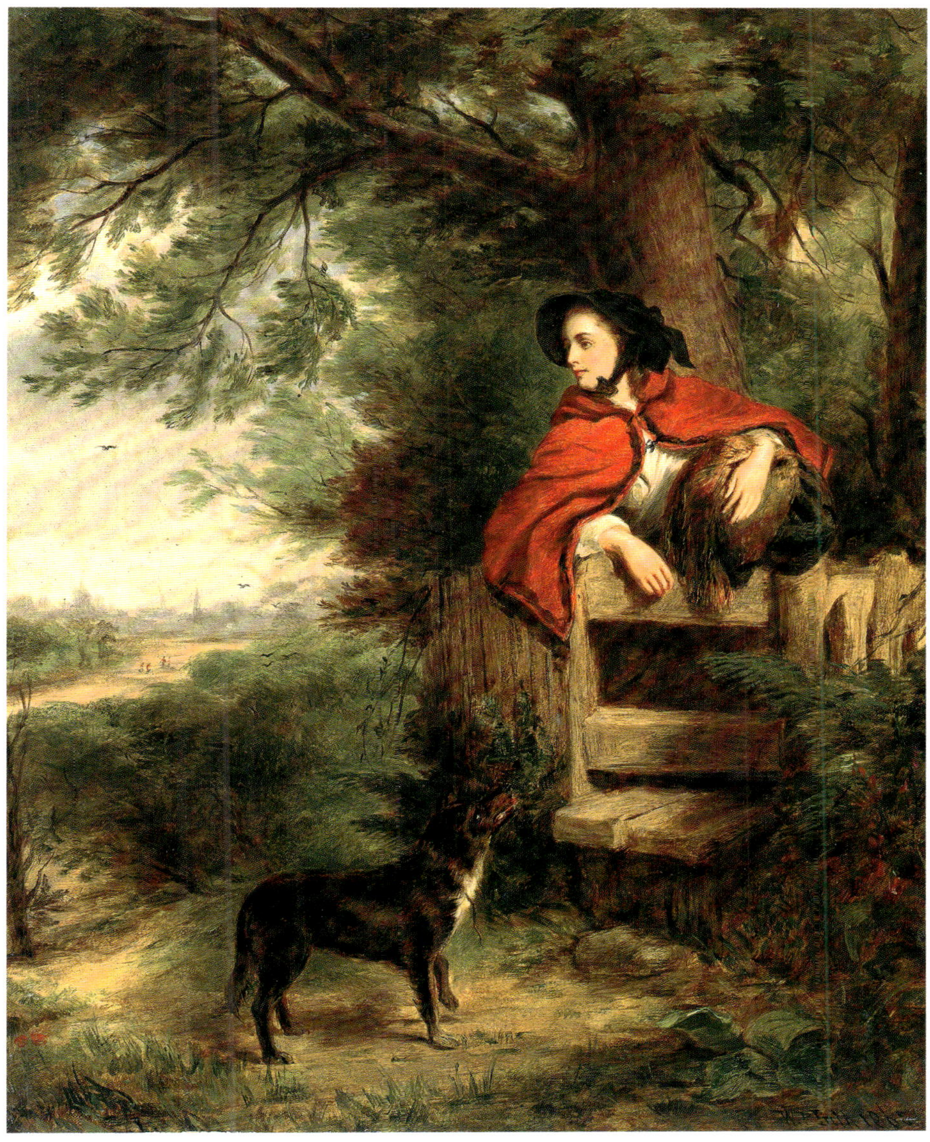

141. *A Dream of the Future*, 1865. The Mercer Art Gallery, Harrogate Museums and Arts.
This is a replica of an original composition of 1856 (Bolton Art Gallery) in which the dog was painted by Ansdell and the landscape by Creswick.

COLLABORATION AND ADVICE

Frith sought both advice and assistance from other artists. In turn his advice was sought by his friends, often concerning prices, probably because it was evident that Frith was a shrewd negotiator of his own sales.[50] In this respect, much has been made of his early ambition to be an auctioneer.

Frith collaborated on a number of paintings with his contemporaries, and Creswick, Egg and Ansdell are known to have worked with him (Fig. 141).[51] One unusual assignment was from Thomas Miller, who asked Frith and Egg to paint a new pub sign for the Hornby Arms, bought as part of his estate at Singleton, Lancashire, and eventually renamed the Miller Arms.[52] Frith refers to it as 'The Pilgrim', and the sign showed a weary traveller arriving on one side and emerging refreshed on the other.[53] Frith described the scene as 'still in embryo' on 8 October 1854, as he was still waiting for a suitable panel from his colourman who had advised well-seasoned wood to withstand wind and weather.[54] Roberson prepared a panel 43 × 33 inches to Frith's order, charging it to Egg's account[55] and Egg painted the 'before' side of the sign first to ensure uniformity, as Frith observed to Miller 'it should never do to have two different looking pilgrims'.[56] Despite being intended for external display, Frith records that the sign ended up being hung inside in the bar, where it was more likely to retain its 'carnations'.

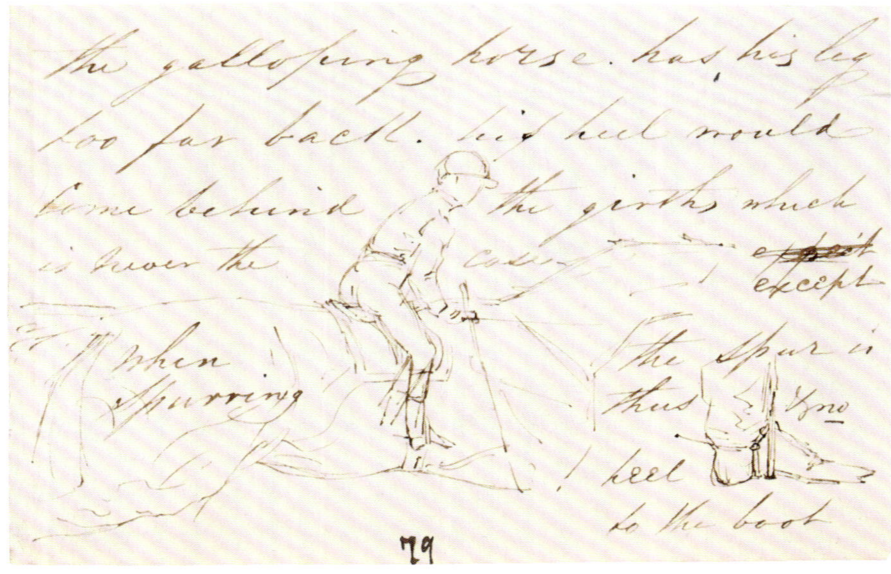

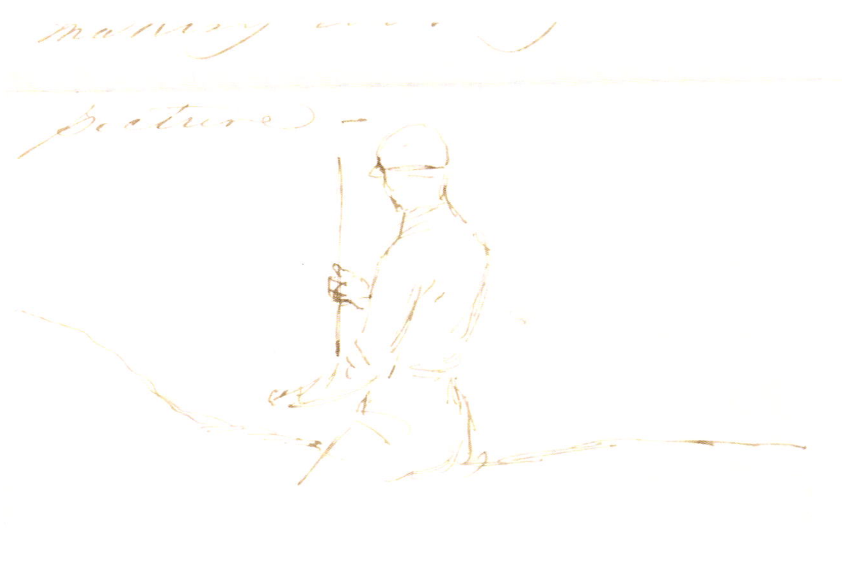

Top: 142. John Frederick Herring (1795–1865). Drawing showing the position of a jockey's leg. Victoria and Albert Museum.

Bottom: 143. John Frederick Herring. Drawing showing how a jockey holds the reins. Victoria and Albert Museum.

Although later in his career Frith implies that painting animals took less skill than painting people, commenting 'after acquiring a certain power of painting the human being, animals ought not to be very difficult',[57] much of his early collaborations involve getting other artists to paint the animals in his paintings. In 1848 when working on *An Old Woman Accused of Witchcraft,* Ansdell painted in the dogs, Frith commenting that 'the bloodhound is one of the finest things he has done.'[58] The witch's cat was also painted by Ansdell: 'I got Ansdell to paint on the black cat, holding it up for him myself & I assure you I was pretty well scratched.'[59]

The following year, while painting a small picture of a lady hawking, Frith was teaching Frederick Taylor, the watercolourist, to paint in oils in return for him painting the horse, which Frith acknowledged to be entirely Taylor's work.[60] He was still collaborating with Ansdell, even after his great success with *Ramsgate Sands,* painting *The Milkmaid* for Miller in 1855 and commenting – 'the animals are certainly his best work'.[61] It is interesting to note that the animals appear to be all that Ansdell was allowed to contribute, Frith relating to Miller: 'What do you think of my knocking Ansdells background, in the milkmaid, – all out – yesterday – what is more – what will he think? However it is done – all his neatly painted ugly cottage &c is gone to immortal smash – lights put where there were darks and vice versa & I risk I am as certain of going to Heaven as I am of the picture being the better for it.'[62]

Frith's most important collaboration was with J. F. Herring, a celebrated sporting painter over twenty years his senior, on *Derby Day* (Fig. 61), although this was not always acknowledged in later years. Frith seems a little sensitive on the subject of the horses in the painting, noting in his autobiography that it was the primacy of the human interest in the painting that kept the horses and riders in the background and not 'from the fact of my not being able to paint them properly'.[63] This opinion does not appear to have been held by Herring, who writes friendly, but slightly exasperated letters in 1857–8 concerning Frith's lack of understanding of harnesses, jockeys and racing. In January 1858 Frith had sent some sketches to Herring, at the latter's suggestion. Herring corrects some of Frith's mistakes, accompanied by his own sketches (Figs 142 and 143):

> . . . the man who is on the galloping horse has his leg too far back his heel would come behind the girths which is never the case except when the spur is spurring.
>
> The rein is tied in a knot & held thus . . . the jockey invariably holds the rein through the 3rd & little fingers.[64]

As the painting was too large to bring to Meopham Park, Herring's home in Tonbridge, in December 1857 he invited the Friths to visit him, offering to bring a horse into his painting room if it were needed.[65] By February 1858 relations seem a little less cordial, and in response to evident criticism of the painting Herring wrote a long letter in his own defence:

> The But's I fancy lay with the R.A. and not with me – I can see that I am a more matter of fact man than you – 'Why' – because you told me to make the chestnut horse as bright as I possibly could – & you did not tell me that the brown horse was the nearest therefore not knowing the latter to be the case, & that horses even on a Race Course pass on the off side – invariably – or there would be some awful collisions – I fell into the error you complain of the brown horse*
>
> How I do wish you would take a Holiday & get down here by an early train (You might get up for once in a Day) and I would paint all day for you & then you could have what you want. I am sure 'twould be the very best way.
>
> *If the brown horse is to be the largest or nearest object rely on it he should be going (to be correct) the contrary way, in which case you might save painting his the jockeys face by making him looking into the picture.[66]

The pains Herring took to help the younger artist, volunteering unsolicited to give advice when he first heard that Frith was painting a racing subject, makes Frith's later disregard for his contribution seem all the more ungrateful. This was not always the case, however, and in at least one instance he was at pains to correct a misattribution. In a letter to *The Times* in 1850 he points out that the figures in Ansdell's *The Halt*, attributed to Frith and praised by the paper for their design and execution, were in fact by Ansdell: 'All this belongs to Mr. Ansdell, for he designed and executed the whole. My share of the work was confined to the faces only, of the figures, which I painted upon without in any way altering the original design.'[67]

His collaboration did not only extend to artists, but also to his patrons, with letters from both Ansdell and Frith to Miller, asking him to send them a milk pail for their painting of a milkmaid. Jacob Bell, known to have supplied Frith with many of the models for *Derby Day*, was also asked to help with difficulties Frith had over painting the tent to the left of the composition.[68] If he had got the basic shape right, Frith thought of having a scale model made by a carpenter and covering it with canvas to help with the composition: 'I am at my wits end how to manage as the first booth is an important feature.'[69] He later sent a sketch to Bell, who had evidently offered to help: 'I don't know if you can make the above intelligible to the Tent Maker – as far as I can recollect the gambling booths were ordinary striped tents with a sort of ornamented sign over the door on which was inscribed the different games played within. If the tent maker could be induced to come here I feel sure I could explain the matter so that he would easily make me a small model & so save me no end of time & trouble.'[70] (Fig. 144) Never one to waste an opportunity, as a postscript Frith also mentions being 'awfully in want of a pretty round hat' for one of his female figures.

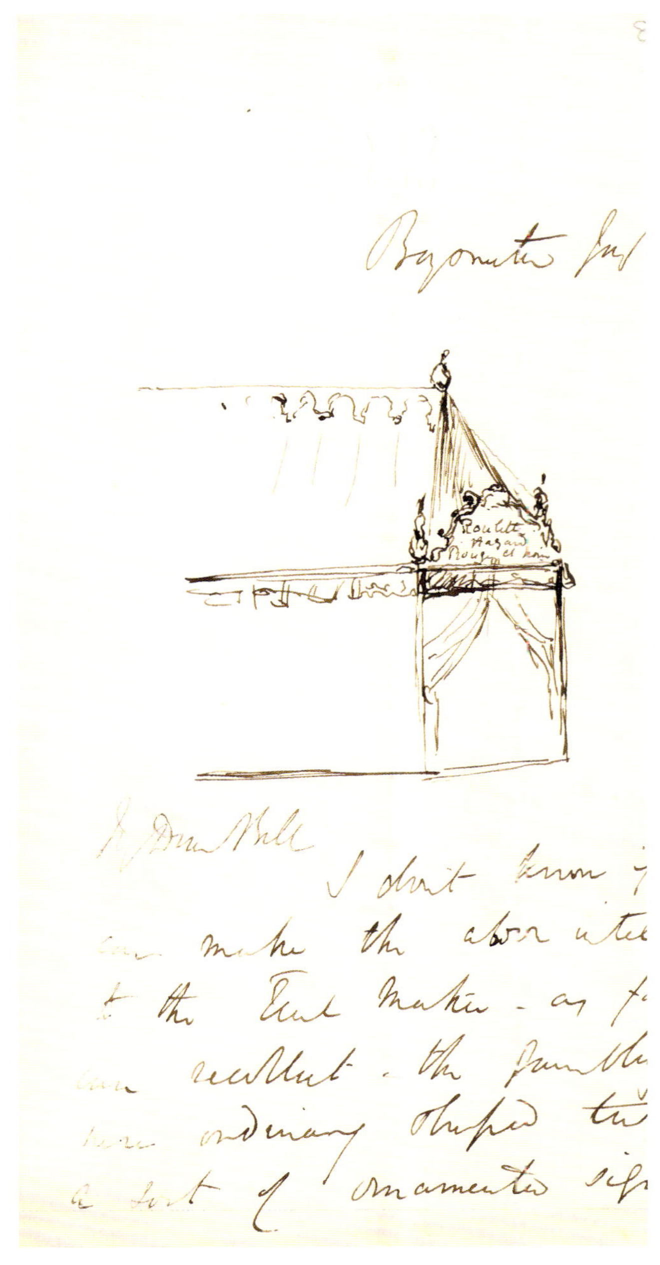
My dear Bell
I don't know
make the above
to the Tent maker – as
recollect – the gambl
ordinary striped
a sort of ornamented

144. Sketch of a gambling booth in a letter to Jacob Bell, 11 January 1858. Tate, London.

Frith's profitability and business acumen in his transactions with patrons and dealers have been more harshly criticised than that of some of his equally successful colleagues, perhaps because of the prominence Frith gave these matters in his memoirs. After his death, sales lists single out Frith by mentioning the decline in the value of his pictures, for example when *Claude Duval* (1860) was sold for 620 guineas in 1910, *The Times* drew attention to the fact that it had been bought from Frith by Louis Victor Flatow for £1,700.[71] A similar falling off in value could have been highlighted for many other artists in the sale, but perhaps Frith's candour about prices made it easier for the journalist to comment. Looking at Frith's account with Roberson, it is interesting to note that in 59 years of buying his materials, probably almost exclusively from the firm, he spent a total of less than £800, two thirds of the price of *Before Dinner in Boswell's Lodgings* (1868), which Frith sold to Agnew's for £1,200 in 1867.[72] The maximum he spent in any one year was £55 in 1864, but his usual expenditure was around £10 a year for canvas, paint, varnish, equipment and a range of services from Roberson.

Frith was a businessman, acutely aware of the value of copyright, both to himself and to publishers of engravings. He was prepared to make multiple copies of his paintings, both at the time of their inception and years later in old age, but after a number of early disputes with the owners of the originals, he was careful either to sell all rights with the painting or expressly arrange for works to be copied with permission at the time of a commission. He refers to 'the vice of copying' in his autobiography, but seemed unable to resist capitalising on his success in the form of copies. In addition to his well-known use of photography to aid his original compositions, he also used largescale photographs of his paintings when making copies, such as the small version of *Ramsgate Sands* for Thomas Miller: 'I have a large photograph – two feet long – which is as good as the picture to me.'[73] In making his copies, Frith does not appear to have intended to produce an exact replica, telling Miller that his version of *Ramsgate Sands* would have 'one or two small and unimportant points which will perhaps give an interest and an additional originality to the small work.'[74]

Frith was in favour of tighter legal controls to protect artists' rights, signing a resolution drawn up by the Copyright Committee of the Royal Society of Arts, active in the late 1850s, hoping to change the copyright laws to offer artists and the public greater protection. This resolution wanted to protect copyright for thirty years after an artist's life for works signed or made by the artist's own hand or by his or her assistants, giving similar protection for imitative works, such as engravings and photography. One intention of this was to protect the public against the fraudulent sale of copies as originals and the passing off of fraudulently re-touched engravings as first proofs or as works of the original engraver.[75] The lack of what are now termed intellectual property rights had relevance later in Frith's life when his painting *The New Frock* (Lady Lever Art Gallery, 1889) was used by Lever Brothers as an advertisement for Sunlight soap without Frith's permission. Having sold the copyright to Lever, Frith had no recourse to law and could only write, complainingly, to *The Pall Mall Gazette*, Lever shrewdly countering that if advertising had been mentioned at the time of sale, the price would have increased. Recalling this incident a few years later, Frith wrote of 'a system degrading enough when the painter of a picture consents to his work being prostituted, & infamous in my opinion when his picture is seized & vulgarised without his knowledge.'[76] As the son of a former servant, now in the class that employed such staff, Frith was sensitive to accusations of vulgarity. One of his early paintings of a female servant had attracted criticism when the engraving carried the title, not given by Frith, of *Sherry, Sir?*, something he tried, but was unable to alter. By the time he was painting the many royal and aristocratic sitters for *The Marriage of the Prince of Wales*, he had formulated a strategy to deal with condescension, confusing the daughter of the Duke of Buccleuch, 'a little plain Scotch girl who thinks herself made of different stuff from me & evidently considers me a sort of superior cabinet maker', by treating her with such familiarity that she didn't know whether he was a 'Duke in disguise'.[77]

CONCLUSION

Frith was aware of being in the right place at the right time, capturing the public's imagination and capitalising on collectors' enthusiasm for modern pictures at mid-century. He did not seek novel effects, and his painting practice reflects that consistency and conventionality. Even his detractors recognised that he was the product of a particular period's tendencies and taste, which had perhaps diverted him from better work: 'To hold you responsible for being the man of your hour, is not fair, and now that the hour is happily past, we may honestly regret that the real energy you displayed, albeit in ways artistically vicious, did not chance on a more worthy period.'[78] His glory days were short-lived and he fell out of fashion and out of sympathy for the age in which he lived fairly abruptly, in 1888 identifying two of the more lasting influences on British nineteenth-century painting, Impressionism and Pre-Raphaelitism, as transient 'crazes in art' with no lasting value.[79] Although his pride in the production of his younger days lingered, he was aware of having outlived his popularity, commenting in 1890 'How pleased old Leslie must be to be dead & independant [*sic*] of the present taste for pictures',[80] perhaps referring to the father of his friend George Dunlop Leslie, Charles Robert Leslie, who had died in 1859.

The importance of Frith's works in recording mid-nineteenth-century life and their stable condition as a result of his thorough, unadventurous technique and painstaking approach to finish have enabled his paintings to outlive the twentieth-century eclipse of Victorian art and return to the limelight almost a century after his death. This is something that Frith, always an artist with an eye to posterity, would have enjoyed, perhaps inducing the serenity he felt when finally completing one of his paintings and achieving 'the quiet, pleasing state of mind one gets into, when ones troubles are once more conquered.'[81]

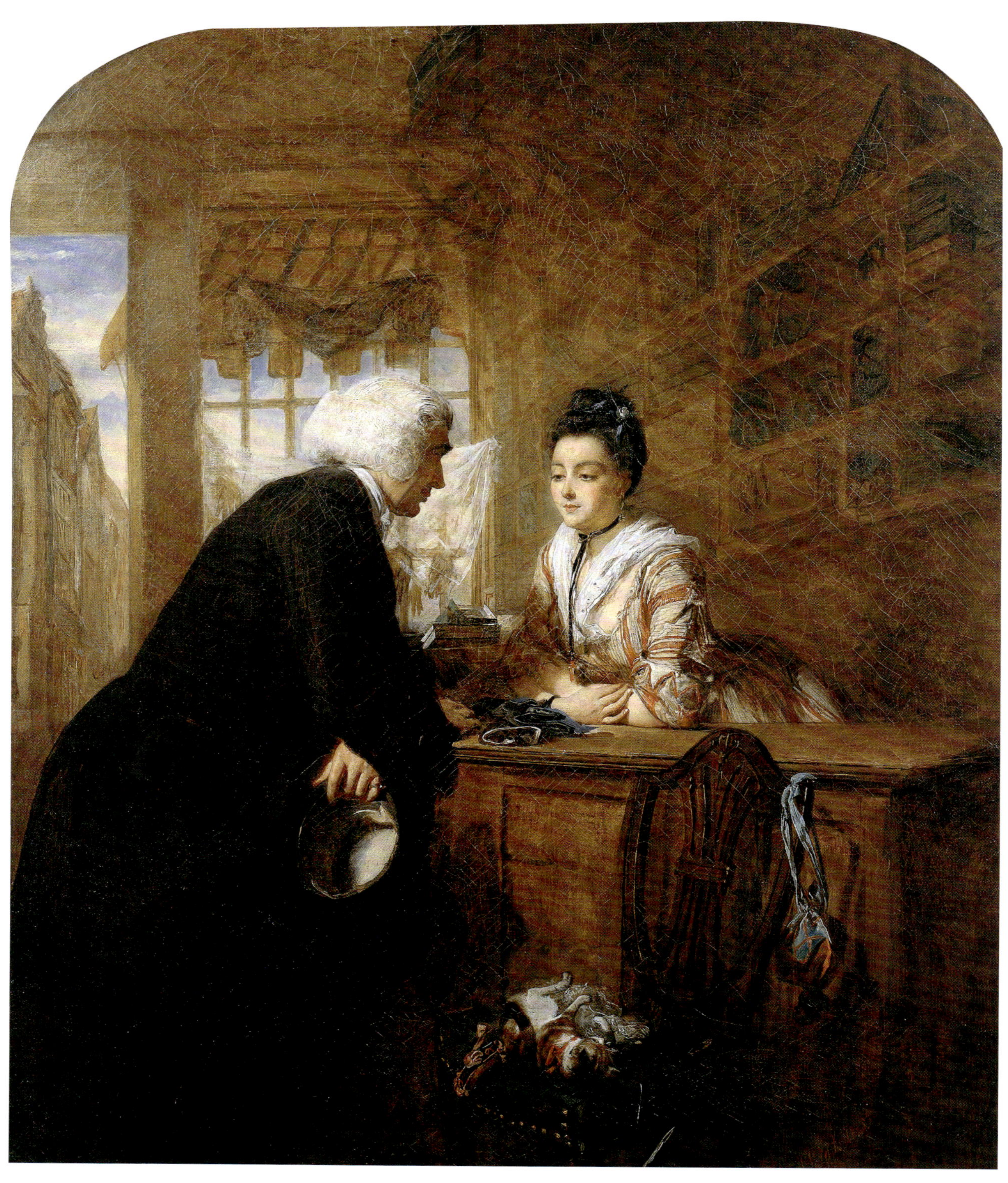

Chapter 10

Frith's frames and the business of frame-making

VICTORIA DORAN

The way in which the nineteenth century frame-making trade was organised can present challenges in identifying the origins of frames. Furthermore, artists often leave little indication of their taste in framing or their choice of frame-maker.

Fortunately, William Powell Frith does reveal the name of at least one of his frame-makers. Writing to his patron Thomas Miller on 9 October 1848 about the return of the case in which *An Old Woman Accused of Witchcraft* had been delivered, he named his frame-maker as 'Mr Haynes 16 Windmill St Haymarket London'.[1] The following August, discussing Miller's purchase of a picture by Frederick Taylor, Frith told him he was sending it to Haynes, the framing cost to be included in the bill for another picture (by Egg).[2] He had already had to explain to Miller – who seems to have been unaware of the custom – that: 'the frames are never included in the sum named but always paid for by the purchaser separately ... I merely mention the rule as no doubt you are not aware of it.'[3] It may have been Haynes who supplied the frame – almost certainly original to the painting and quite different to Frith's frames of a decade later – for the picture of the glove shop episode from *A Sentimental Journey* which Frith painted in 1845 for another early patron, John Gibbons (Fig. 146). This is an occasion when a frame from the 1840s can be dated precisely despite the absence of documentation and it provides a valuable reference point for future research.

In the 1850s there is evidence to link Frith and Miller to another frame-maker. J. & W. Vokins may have been slightly unusual in that they were also leading picture dealers (another notable example was Thomas Agnew & Sons).[4] William Vokins (1815–95) appears to have been better known on the dealing side of the partnership than John, and it may be that the latter had more responsibility for the frame-making side of the business; certainly they operated from two premises by the mid-1850s, and one is thought to have been a shop. Clearly Miller was using the dealing side of the firm to acquire paintings in 1855, as both a receipt and an invoice for paintings by John Lewis indicate; the invoice records 'purchased by T Miller thru' J & W Vokins, Gilders, Decorators & Dealers in Works of Art – 14 & 16 Gt Portland Street'.[5]

J. & W. Vokins's feigned oval ink stamp or stencil (bearing the same address) appears on the back of the neoclassical frame to Frith's sketch for *Sancho Panza Tells a Tale to the Duke and Duchess* (Victoria & Albert Museum, Jones Bequest). The painting was commissioned by the merchant banker Frederick Huth and exhibited at the Royal Academy in 1850 (this sketch is signed and dated the same year). Vokins is recorded at the Great Portland Street address close enough to 1850 to allow speculation that the frame is original to the painting. The frame to Frith's *Charles Dickens in his Study* (Victoria & Albert Museum, Forster Bequest) has an identical pattern to the scotia (or scoop of the frame) and the sight edge ornament, although the dimensions of the frame and pattern are larger than the previous example. This portrait was commissioned by Dickens's friend

Facing page:
145. Scene from *A Sentimental Journey*, 1845. Private Collection.
This was the second of Frith's pictures from Laurence Sterne's *A Sentimental Journey* (the first is in the Victoria and Albert Museum). Representing the episode when the hero flirts with a 'grisette' in a Paris glove shop, it was commissioned by Birmingham industrialist John Gibbons. He went on to commission further paintings by Frith, carefully specifying in his letters to him the detail and the level of 'finish' he required. The taste of prosperous middle-class patrons like Gibbons encouraged Frith and his circle to favour historical and literary scenes such as this, painted in a colourful, polished manner.

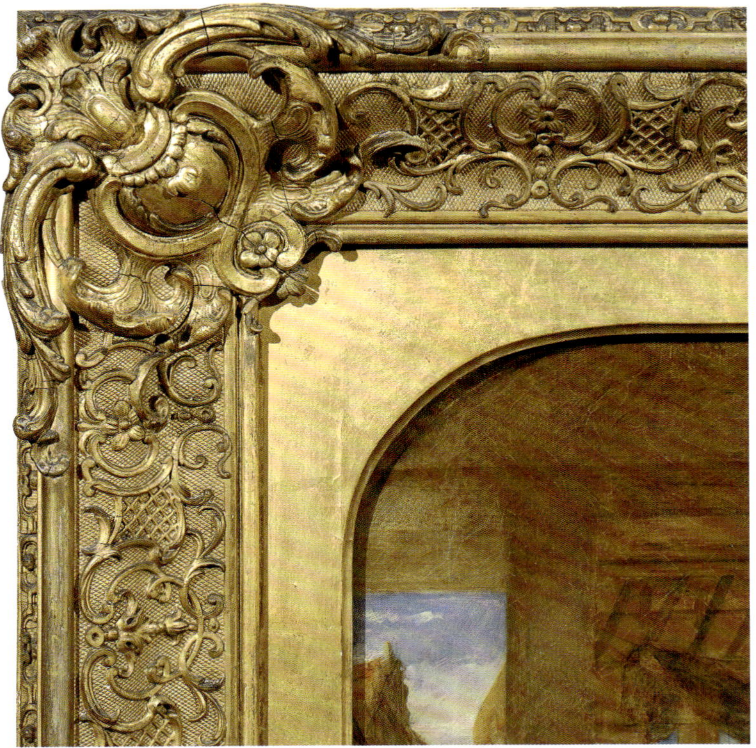

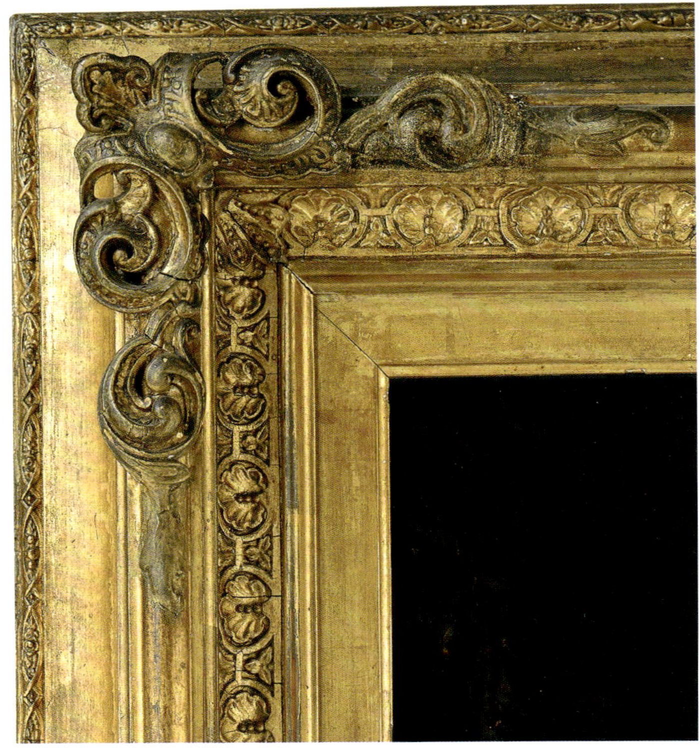

Left: 146. Detail of the frame to *Scene from a Sentimental Journey*. Private Collection.

Right: 147. Detail of the frame to Frith's portrait of Mary Braddon. National Portrait Gallery, London.

and biographer John Forster (1812–76) and exhibited at the Royal Academy in 1859. In this case it is not known if the frame is by Vokins but considering the unique nature of composition moulds and patterns as well as the similarities of these frames, it is possible that they are by the same frame-maker and that therefore Vokins supplied virtually the same frame pattern to two patrons. However, the frames of one of these patrons, John Jones (1800–82; discussed below), are so specific in style and pattern as to suggest that the appearance of one within the collection of another patron might be the result of a mistake. Possibly the frames were swapped by accident at some point after the paintings arrived at the museum, for example during conservation work to painting or frame.[6]

Within the Jones Bequest there are other Vokins frames for pictures by Frith that are similar in style to those above but with quite a different pattern. As they also appear around works by other artists in the bequest they probably reflect the taste of the collector John Jones and were chosen by him to complement his collection of eighteenth-century French furniture. Examples with identical patterns are the frames to Frith's *Measuring Heights* (Fig. 149) and *Scene from A Sentimental Journey* (V&A version), in the Louis Seize revival style with a guilloche pattern in the scotia, ribbon and stick along the top edge and beading to the back edge.[7]

Jones probably acquired *Scene from a Sentimental Journey* in or around 1871 when it was sold at Christie's, and Vokins would have made the frame in his particular style after that date. It is unlikely that Jones would have reframed his entire collection at the same time, but rather that he exchanged existing frames for his own style as he acquired pictures over time. Although his frames are characterised by the same distinctive guilloche pattern in the scotia, the slight variation in the other design elements also suggests they may have been made over a period of time. Works by other artists within the Jones bequest which have frames where entire or main scotia decoration is identical to the examples above include Frederick Goodall's *The Irish Piper*; Thomas Webster's *The Lesson* and *Beating for Recruits* and Clarkson Stanfield's *On the Dogger Bank*, all of which are by Vokins.[8]

Another pattern worthy of attention appears on the frame to Frith's oil sketch for *The Derby Day* (Fig. 148). It bears the printed label of the prominent London frame-makers, James Bourlet and Sons Ltd at 17–18 Nassau Street, Mortimer Street.[9] The style is consistent with the late 1850s to mid-1860s, after which time it would have been somewhat old fashioned. The distinctive applied composition ornament in an arabesque knotwork and bell flower pattern pressed into the scotia, takes its inspiration from the patterns in Owen Jones's *Grammar of Ornament* published in 1856, which popularised designs from the Alhambra. An identical main pattern (and sight edge) is found in the frame to *Interior with two women examining cloth* by the French painter Théophile Emmanuel Duverger (Victoria & Albert Museum, Dixon Bequest). There are a few differences such as the orientation of the main pattern which is laid over a cushion profile (instead of a scotia) and the addition of corner elements. However, the similarities are so strong as to again suggest both frames are from the same maker, and that the patterns were chosen by (or for) the owner of both pictures, Joshua Dixon (1811–85).[10]

At other times Frith himself chose the frames for pictures commissioned by his patrons. In 1864, the novelist Mary Braddon wrote telling him to order whatever frame for her portrait he thought best, as she wanted the picture to be entirely to his taste (Fig. 147).[11] However, the style of

Left: 148. Detail of the frame to the oil sketch for *Derby Day*. Victoria and Albert Museum

Right: 149. Detail of the frame to *Measuring Heights*. Victoria and Albert Museum.

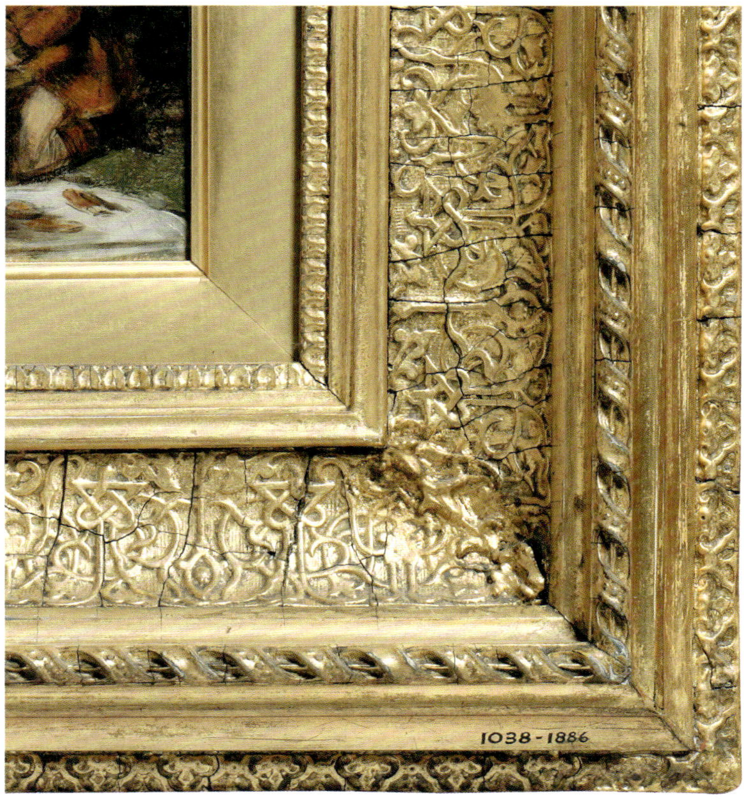

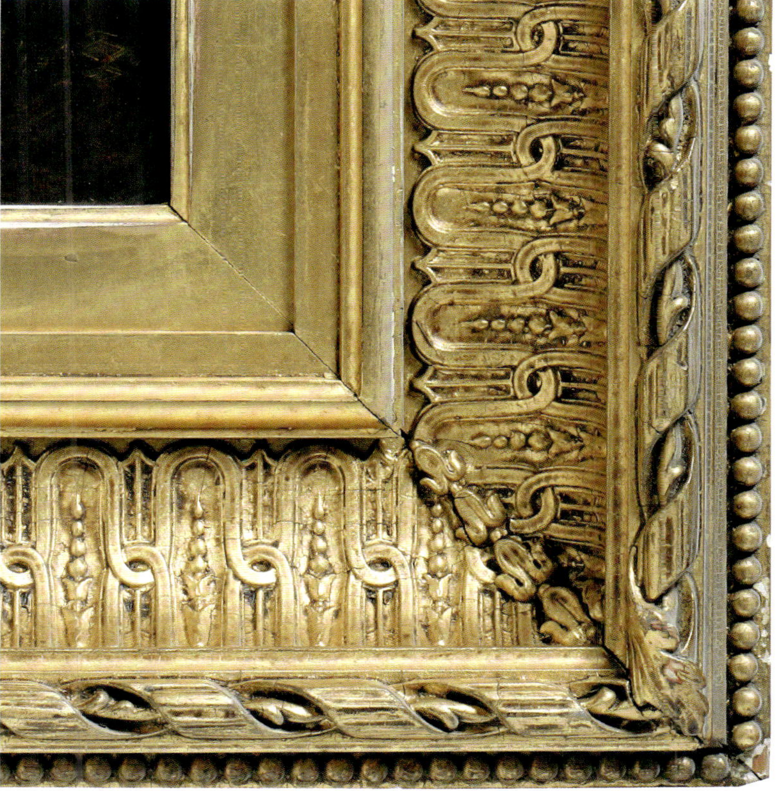

the portrait's current frame is unremarkable, and not particularly characteristic of the 1860s, so further evidence is needed to confirm whether it is original to the portrait and thus the frame mentioned by the sitter.[12]

When Haynes, Vokins and Bourlet were making frames for Frith's paintings in the second half of the nineteenth century, little in the way the trade operated had changed since the beginning of the century. Crucially, the objects themselves still reflected the trade structure and its traditional manual techniques, although the number of stages involved in producing a frame had been reduced by this time for all but the most exceptional projects. 'Composition' (or 'compo') ornament was produced by specialist manufacturers from raw linseed oil, rosin, scotch glue and whiting or whitening, perhaps with the addition of other minor ingredients. The moulds were carved (in reverse) by skilled craftsmen into a block of close-grained hardwood, usually box, to produce a durable mould into which the composition was pressed. As each design was hand carved no two are exactly alike, and the compo pressings formed from these moulds, provided they survive in good condition, reflect all the unique detail of their moulds. Produced in lengths of about one foot (the usual size of a mould) the resulting ornament could be sold to framemakers (or other manufacturers) 'soft from the press' and kept flexible by being covered with damp cloths.[13] It could then be glued onto a long length of what was often a softwood moulding to make up a frame.

Frame-making firms describing themselves as 'carvers and gilders' might be involved neither in carving nor composition production but would buy in compo ornament from different manufacturers, apply it to the basic frame and gild it, or they would buy the frame complete with ornament and ready to gild. Frames could thus be made up of a variety of elements from different sources and it was the distinctive combination of these elements that assigned a particular frame or object to an individual maker.[14] However, large London firms like Jackson's and Charles Nosotti (whose 'artists will execute for you any design you choose – a medallion of your own features if you wish it') were involved in every stage of production from carving the moulds to retailing the finished objects.[15] And Bourlet, associated with at least one of Frith's frames, also continued to provide a bespoke service for the more expensive and specialised end of the market.

A distinctive pattern such as the main guilloche for the Jones Collection frames is almost certainly the product of a unique mould produced by one firm, perhaps specifically for Jones. But different sizes would usually have been produced for frames of varying profile. It is not known whether J. & W. Vokins commissioned moulds from elsewhere, perhaps Jackson's, or produced them in-house like Charles Nosotti. However investigation reveals that both and indeed further levels of subcontracting were possible and therefore these 'Frith' frames exhibit a degree of complexity that is very particular to each of those firms. The precise nature of that complexity may be better understood with further research.

Notes

CHAPTER 1

THE PRIVATE LIFE OF WILLIAM POWELL FRITH

My thanks to Stephen Kirkman for sharing his family history research and for helping clarify some details. I am also indebted to the following: Dawn Baly, the current owner of Fitz Manor; Philippa Bassett, Archivist, Birmingham University; Marijke Booth, Archives Assistant, Christie's Archives Department; Rita Boswell, archivist, Harrow School; Ms M. J. Boustead, Senior Archivist, North Yorkshire County Record Office; Hazel Cook, Local Studies Collection, Royal Borough of Kensington and Chelsea; Mark Frost, Dover Museum; Alison Hawley, Shropshire Archives; Malcolm Holmes and Richard Knight, Camden Local Studies and Archives Centre; Anne Lyles, Tate; Mark Newman, Territory Archaeologist, North, The National Trust; Mark Pomeroy, Royal Academy Library; Sarah Pymer, York City Archives; Somerset Studies Library; Caroline Stockdale, York Reference Library; Neila Warner, Berkshire Record Office; Sally Woodcock. Extracts from The Roberson Archive are published by permission of the Syndics of the Fitzwilliam Museum, Cambridge.

1. *Boswell* fetched £4,567 10s at the sale in April 1875 of Sam Mendel's Manley Hall collection (Frith had originally received £1,200 for it). The pictures which had the distinction of a rail were: *Derby Day* (1859), *The Marriage of the Prince of Wales* (1865), *Charles II's Last Sunday* (1867), *The Salon d'Or, Homberg* (1871), *The Road to Ruin* (1878), and *The Private View at the Royal Academy* (1883).
2. Record of Frith's baptism, 10 January 1819, North Yorkshire County Record Office. It has often been stated incorrectly that Thomas was the butler at Studley, a far less significant position.
3. Jane Powell and Thomas Frith married at Hornby by Bedale on 26 May 1814. Her great-grandfather Robert Wood had bought Fitz Manor in 1697. His daughter Jane Wood married a clergyman, the Rev. William Powell, but their son William was 'a Shropshire squire who spent a tolerable fortune in extravagance and self-indulgence' (*My Autobiography and Reminiscences* and *Further Reminiscences*, 3 vols. (London: Richard Bentley and Son, 1887–8), 3. 30) and died in 1824. His property was auctioned on 22 May 1825 (Shropshire Archives 103/1/3/55), his widow Mary Davies (Frith's grandmother) dying in January 1840 'in the last house that remained of the Powell property' (see SA 322/2/306/1). SA 322/2/306/31 lists a number of Powell family births, marriages and deaths. Jane Powell's sisters Kate and Maria married well, to Charles Ade, gentleman, of Handcomb Hall, Sussex, and Francis Scaife, hotelier, respectively, but another married a carpenter. Her brothers William and Robert Wood were respectively a gentleman farmer and a chemist in Shrewsbury.
4. Properties in Harrogate and Wardour Street, London, are mentioned in the Will of Thomas Frith, Gentleman of Harrogate, 1832 and Codicil of January 1836, proved 1 April 1837.
5. Pigot's *Yorkshire Directory* 1829 lists three gentlemen's (and two ladies') boarding schools at Thorp Arch, but it is unknown which Frith attended.
6. Sass's was then the only independent art school in London. It was taken over by F. S. Carey *c.* 1840.
7. *My Autobiography*, 3. 45–6.
8. *Ibid.* 32–75.
9. *My Autobiography*, 2. 100. With the 4s 9d he earned for one portrait of an old man in a red nightcap he bought a 'beautiful-looking, shiny, tall hat', but it did not survive the first shower. Years later Frith saw the portrait at the house of his friend Tommy Brooks – Brooks thought it was by Sir Thomas Lawrence (Walter Frith, 'A Talk With My Father', *Cornhill Magazine*, vol. 20, January–June 1906, 598).
10. *Ibid.*, 600.
11. *My Autobiography*, 3. 178: 'My painting-room and Dadd's were next door to each other in Charlotte Street, Fitzroy Square. It is not possible for two persons to be more intimate than we were. We saw each other every day . . . in my many pictorial difficulties a tap at my wall would bring my friend with ready suggestions to my relief.' The context of this paragraph – in Frith's account of Dadd's employment by Sir Thomas Phillips – suggests the date would have been around 1842.
12. *My Autobiography*, 1. 152: 'Shakespeare inspired me with terror as well as admiration . . . I have never meddled with Shakespeare without regretting my temerity, for though I have painted several pictures from different plays, I cannot recall one that will add to my reputation'.
13. *My Autobiography*, 3. 201–2. In addition to the *Sentimental Journey*, Gibbons commissioned or purchased: *The Village Pastor* (1845), *Scene from the Bourgeois Gentilhomme* (1846), *A Stage Coach Adventure* (from Smollett's *Roderick Random*, 1848), and *Sancho Panza* (referred to in a letter to Miller, 11 November 1849, Royal Academy Library).
14. Dadd addressed Frith as 'Powell', 'Billy' or 'my dear little flower' (*My Autobiography*, 3. 189–91); letters from Egg to Frith's wife (in National Art Library MSL/1922/186) are the only ones in the album to 'Dear Isabel' [sic] rather than 'Dear Mrs Frith'.
15. *My Autobiography*, 3. 179–80; J. E. Panton, *Leaves from a Life* (London: E. Nash, 1908), 6 (Cissie mistakenly thought Dadd accompanied Frith and Egg to France, and that it was Egg whom he attacked in a diligence); *Edmund Yates, His Recollections and Experiences* 2 vols (London: Richard Bentley, 1884), 2. 104.
16. Soliciting a donation in 1852, Frith told Miller he had formerly been a director of the Artists' Benevolent Fund (letter to Miller 21 March 1852); and he continued to be associated with it until at least 1892. *The Times* also shows him attending dinners of the Yorkshire Society, founded in 1812 to

educate and maintain the sons of respectable Yorkshire parents reduced by misfortune, as well as of Middlesex Hospital and the Actors' Benevolent Fund. Among instances of private charity, in 1868–9 Frith helped Dickens to raise funds for the widow of the illustrator George Cattermole.

17. National Art Library, MSL/1922/186/2: letter from Dickens dated 15 November 1842.
18. Panton, *Leaves from a Life*, 141–5.
19. J. E. Panton, *More Leaves from a Life* (London: E. Nash, 1911), 155–6. Like Frith, Isabelle was born at Studley.
20. George Baker (1793–1867). See *Baines's Yorkshire Directory*, 1823 and William White's *Gazetteer of the East and North Ridings of Yorkshire*, 1838 and 1840.
21. *My Autobiography*, 1. 153–4 and 2. 141.
22. The 1845 Post Office Directory lists Frith at No. 75, but in 1846 and 1847 he is shown at No. 31, the address from which his RA exhibits were sent.
23. 'I work from six o'clock in the morning to half-past seven at night, so I think you can't say I am idle' (*My Autobiography*, 3. 43); 'if some of my young friends could see my diaries for the last five-and-forty years, they would see a record of incessant work – no day, literally, without a line – that I do believe would surprise them. My work has never been interrupted, I am thankful to say by illness, and I never allowed it to be interrupted by anything else' (*My Autobiography*, 1. 187).
24. *Cornhill Magazine*, vol. XXIII, July–Dec. 1907, 803. Frith said he found the gipsy outside their Park Village West house, although they had not yet moved in. He may also have been mistaken about which workhouse the old model came from.
25. *My Autobiography*, 2. 199–200.
26. Letter to Miller, 19 September 1847 (Royal Academy Library).
27. Park Village West, 'a colony of enchantingly sophisticated cottages . . . the epitome of the picturesque' (Ann Saunders, *Regent's Park – a Study of the Development of the Area from 1086 to the Present Day* (Newton Abbot: David and Charles, 1969)), was designed by John Nash and completed by James Pennethorne. Frith's brother Charles, now a barrister, was already living at No. 14 with his wife and two children.
28. Letter to Thomas Miller, 5 March 1848 (Royal Academy Library).
29. Letter to Miller, 16 November 1848 (Royal Academy Library): 'We are just about moving into a larger house next door to the painting room on the other side – number 12 . . . By the 28th, the time you mention for your visit, I hope to be comfortably settled in the new house.'
30. Panton, *Leaves from a Life*, 2 and 4.
31. The household shown in the 1851 Census. Geneology sources name the baby born in 1851 as Thomas, but remarks in letters to Miller of 16 November 1851 and 31 October 1852 (Royal Academy Library) suggest that it was Charles who was born in October this year.
32. Panton, *Leaves from a Life*, 2.
33. Panton, *Leaves from a Life*, 4; Joe Wall nursed the dealer L. V. Flatow in his last illness (*My Autobiography*, 2. 239) and later worked for Cissie's friend Basil Hodges (Panton, *More Leaves from a Life*, 191).
34. *Ibid.*, 23.
35. Letter to Miller, 2 July 1848 (Royal Academy Library).
36. Roy Strong has shown that Frith used Joseph Nash's *The Mansions of England in the Olden Times* (1839–49) as his source. Frith alluded to visiting the British Museum Print Room in search of authentic costume (*My Autobiography* 1. 186), but actually used F. W. Fairholt's *Costume in England* (1846): Roy Strong, *And When Did You Last See Your Father?* (London: Thames and Hudson, 1978), 90–2.
37. *The Times*, 23 May 1851.
38. Panton, *Leaves from a Life*, 289, 293–4.
39. Panton, *More Leaves from a Life*, 181.
40. *My Autobiography*, 1. 243–5.
41. Panton, *Leaves from a Life*, 7.
42. Letter to Miller, 16 November 1851 (Royal Academy Library).
43. Pembridge Villas fell within twenty-eight acres of land owned by James Weller Ladbroke who brought a private bill before Parliament in 1844 and signed an agreement with William Henry Jenkins to develop it. The largest builder on the estate was James Hall, who became Frith's neighbour at No. 12; both that house and No. 10 were erected by a coal merchant, C. Hedges of Pimlico, nominated by Hall in 1848 (*Survey of London*, vol. 37, and Middlesex Land Registers, London Metropolitan Archives).
44. William Mulready lived in nearby Linden Gardens from 1828 to his death in 1863, and fellow-Yorkshireman Thomas Creswick lived from 1838 in the same road at No. 42.
45. *The Times*, 12 December 1853 (sale was 14 December).
46. Panton, *Leaves from a Life*, 129; *My Autobiography*, 2. 271.
47. Panton, *Leaves from a Life*, 27–8. The road did not appear in the Post Office Directory until 1853, when No. 10 also appeared for the first time in the Kensington ratebook. The house probably had not been occupied beforehand and had been left in this condition by its speculative builder.
48. *Ibid.* Letter to Miller, 3 October 1852 (Royal Academy Library); Ladbroke had placed constraints on additions to property on his estate, but if Frith made any planning applications they seem not to have survived.
49. 'It has been my habit to insist upon enforced idleness, as regards the actual practice of my profession for at least a month or six weeks of every year' (*My Autobiography*, 2. 152).
50. Letter to Miller, 8 August 1852 (Royal Academy Library); *My Autobiography* 1. 246. Later he would successfully make use of a photograph by Robert Howlett of the grandstand for *Derby Day*, and of photographs by Samuel Fry and drawings by the architect William Scott Morton of Paddington Station for the background of *The Railway Station*. He commissioned photographs of students' rooms at Cambridge for the first painting in his series *The Road to Ruin*, and of the casino at Homburg for *The Salon d'Or*.
51. Letter to Miller, 2 October 1852 (Royal Academy Library): '"never trust bricks & mortar" how often is one told that by experienced people & among the latter I now class myself & so say I unto you if it had not been for those confounded materials I should not be at Ramsgate at the present moment.'
52. Letter to Miller, 31 October 1852 (Royal Academy Library).
53. Letter to Miller, 2 January 1853 (Royal Academy Library).
54. *My Autobiography*, 1. 252.
55. Letter to Miller, 3 Feb 1853 (Royal Academy Library).
56. e.g. subjects from *The Bride of Lammermoor* and *Kenilworth* painted for Lloyds to engrave as illustrations in a new edition of Scott's *Waverley* novels and for a private patron, Mr Bassett (letter to Miller, 28 March 1852, Royal Academy Library); he gives a slightly different account of these pictures in *My Autobiography* 1. 224–5. 'My father hated pot-boilers with a deadly hatred, all the same they were necessary evils' (Panton, *More Leaves from a Life*, 26).
57. *My Autobiography*, 1. 218.
58. Panton, *Leaves from a Life*, 10, 13, 35.
59. Letter to Miller, 8 August 1852 (Royal Academy Library).
60. The gross estimated rental value was £140 and the ratable value was £125. In 1854 rates were 11d in the £1 and Frith paid £5 14s 7d: in 1855 the rate soared to 1s 4d in the £1, and Frith paid £8 6s 8d.
61. Letters to Miller, 22 February 1852 and 10 February 1853 (Royal Academy Library).
62. Letter to Miller, 27 March 1853 (Royal Academy Library); The children who are known to have survived were Isabelle (b.1846), Jane Ellen

(1847–1923), William (1849–76), May Louise (b.1850), Charles George (b.?1851/2–1923), Alice (b.1853), Mary Fanny (b.1855), Walter (1857–1941), and Philip (b. 1860). Nine children are shown in the sketch 'The Great Western has finished his work nobly' (Fig. 24). However, Cissie wrote: 'As . . . the whole of our ten grew to man's estate, I suppose we must have been among the fittest who are supposed to survive all ills' (Panton, *More Leaves from a Life*, 5). Presumably therefore either Thomas (*c.*1851–64?) or Alfred Elmore (1858 – before 1871?) (both listed in the Frith genealogies http://www.genforum.genealogy.com/frith and http://www.stephen.kirkman.btinternet.co.uk but not in any census) in fact survived.

63. Panton, *Leaves from a Life*, 69–70.
64. Charles William Shirley Brooks (1816–74), journalist and dramatist; his wife was Isabelle's 'stand-by and champion'. (Panton, *Leaves from a Life*, 159).
65. Panton, *Leaves from a Life*, 28–29. The dining room was not redecorated until about 1870, when it was made 'artistic and beautiful' after Isabelle's taste; Letter to Miller 3 November 1852 (Royal Academy Library).
66. Frith owned seventeen cloud studies by Constable, bought in one lot at C.R. Leslie's sale, 25 April 1860, see G. Reynolds, *The Early Paintings and Drawings of John Constable* (New Haven and London: Yale University Press, 1996). He told Miller he had bought Hogarth's *Before and After* for 25 pounds in a letter of 30 June 1862 (Royal Academy Library). None of these was among the twenty-six pictures he sold at Christies on 14 June 1884 (which included works by Ansdell, Egg, Creswick, Landseer and other modern British and Continental painters, and by, or attributed to, Turner and Aert van der Neer). He intended to leave a portrait of James Northcote by George Henry Harlow to the Royal Academy (see Walter Frith, 'Small Talk with my Father', *Cornhill Magazine*, vol. XXIII, July–Dec 1907, 809) but appears to have changed his mind.
67. Panton, *Leaves from a Life*, 236; Panton, *More Leaves from a Life*, 184.
68. Panton, *Leaves from a Life*, 30. Frith, though 'very particular' about his wine was 'the most abstemious of men' and claimed to have been drunk only once, after a Corporation dinner during his summer holiday at Weymouth in 1857 (Panton, *Leaves from a Life*, 101; Frith, 'Small Talk with my Father', 802).
69. *My Autobiography*, 1. 262 and 2. 251, 253.
70. *Ibid.* 1. 262. One cause may have been the birth and death of a new baby in 1854 (Kirkman).
71. No. 47 in the sale of Baron Albert Grant's pictures, Christie's 14 November 1863.
72. Panton, *Leaves from a Life*, 55, 58; letter to J. C. Horsley, 26 April 1867 from the Mount Ephraim Hotel, Tunbridge Wells: 'my wife is so completely upset that I thought it well to give her a complete change of scene . . . We buried our dear little child today so you may suppose it has been a trying day.' (Bodleian Library Ms Eng 2223 fols. 78–9).
73. Panton, *Leaves from a Life*, 56.
74. *The Graphic*, 1908, 74; *My Autobiography*, 1. 270.
75. Library of Congress, Manuscripts Division, Pennell-Whistler collection.
76. Their marriage certificate names Mary's father as William Alford and his occupation as 'gentleman'. Could Mary have been connected to Frith on his mother's side? Alfords occurred in Shropshire, and in 1882 a William Powell Alford was stipendiary curate in the Shropshire parish of Dawley Magna (Shropshire Archives, P89.E/1/5). The Powell name was said to have been added to the Alfords on the female side in the 17th century (W. H. K. Wright, *West-Country Poets, their Lives and Works* (1896), 4–6).
77. 'For one knows that temptation comes from the woman and not from the man first.'; 'there never was a beautiful woman yet who could not twist him round her little finger'; '. . . the curious fascination he had for the female sex, as they had for him, lasted until well over his ninetieth birthday' (Panton, *More Leaves from a Life*, 205, 215, 265).
78. Letter to J. C. Horsley, 6 November 1855 (Bodleian Library, Ms Eng 2221, fols. 213–15).
79. Panton, *Leaves from a Life*, 23.
80. Census returns give Mary Powell Alford's birth as 1856, the first year Pierce is listed in the London Post Office Directory. (Civil registration was introduced in England and Wales in 1837 but was not compulsory until 1875; none of the Alford children's births appear to have been registered.)
81. Mary Powell (1856), Agnes Catherine (1859), William Powell (1862), Ronald (1865), Reginald (1867), Guy (1868) and Bertram Septimus (1870).
82. Isabelle died on 28 January 1880. Frith married Mary Alford on 30 January 1881.
83. 'But Papa always preferred to walk any day; he had his reasons unfortunately'; (Panton, *Leaves from a Life*, 73); '. . . my father hums to himself, looks at the picture this way and that, lights a monstrous cigar and gets ready for the unfailing walk that takes him away from us – alas! – from the time his day's work is done until he returns to dress for dinner' (Panton, *More Leaves from a Life*, 7).
84. The censuses of 1861, 1871 and 1881 show Mary and Sophia at the same address, with Mary listed as head of the household. While the ratebooks (Westminster Archives) also record her as the occupier of 12 Oxford Terrace, only Sophia's name appears in the Post Office directories from 1859 onwards – presumably Mary's whereabouts had to be kept secret from Isabelle. Conceivably Mary and Sophia were related: Alford is predominantly a West Country surname but is also prevalent in Berkshire, while it is at Hampton that they both first appear in the story.
85. 'What do you think of three thousand pounds! . . . Surely I should have been foolish to have refused such an offer. . .'. (Letter to Miller 10 Febuary 1857, Royal Academy Library); *My Autobiography*, 1. 273.
86. *The Times*, 1 May 1858.
87. Bell's letters of 3, 4, and 5 May, and reports of PC Briginshaw and Henry Eyre, are in the National Art Library album of letters MSL/1922/186.
88. Frith found the subject in Macaulay's *History of England* (1855). A copy of his contract with L. V. Flatow, dated 3 January 1859, is in MSL/1922/186/9; *My Autobiography*, 1. 307.
89. *The Times*, Monday, 25 March 1861, 1; *My Autobiography*, 1. 334; *Illustrated Review*, 5 June 1873; Advertisements in *The Times*, January 1863 – December 1864.
90. Willie was not strong enough to be sent to public school (Panton, *Leaves from a Life*, 83) but Charles attended Harrow School between September 1866 and summer 1868 and Walter from September 1871 to summer 1875. *My Autobiography*, 1. 3: 'It is a great satisfaction to me to feel that I have been able to give my own children such educations as have enabled them to take positions, and to do work, utterly denied to me.'
91. Panton, *Leaves from a Life*, 59, 61.
92. *Ibid.*, 13; Panton, *More Leaves from a Life*, 273; 1881 Census. Nonetheless Cissie later employed Miss Wright at £70 a year to instruct her own children, and she was still working as a governess when she died at the age of 75.
93. Panton, *Leaves from a Life*, 67, 83.
94. *Ibid.*, 84; *My Autobiography*, 3. 58; 1871 census. Egg painted her as one of the little girls building a house of cards in *Past and Present* and she appeared in Henry O'Neil's *Eastward Ho!* and in *The Landing of Princess Alexandra at Gravesend*; he also painted portraits of Fanny (1870) and Louise and Alice (1873). Cissie was also painted by John Phillip and Alfred Elmore, and she recalled George du Maurier drawing her in 1868 for *Punch*.
95. Panton, *Leaves from a Life*, 32.
96. The commission was later cancelled in favour of one for *King Charles II's*

Last Sunday, and the subject exists only as sketches. Frith regretted the lost opportunity.

97. *Art Journal*, 1863, 58. It withdrew an earlier claim that Frith had demanded a 'preposterous sum' for the picture in addition to the privileges of engraving and exhibiting it.
98. Henry Vizetelly, *Glances Back Through Seventy Years* (1893), vol. 2, 77.
99. Panton, *Leaves from a Life*, 31–2.
100. *My Autobiography*, 1. 366.
101. Panton, *Leaves from a Life*, 34.
102. Ibid., 26, 33, 37: 'I should much like to know if royal personages ever really realise what ordinary people really think of them'; letter to Miller, 22 February 1852.
103. Ibid., 'our dinner-parties were usually on a Sunday because actors could come then, and many others; notably John Parry, Sala and Shirley Brooks, and men who were busy at the newspaper offices until late on Saturday night, and always treated Sunday as a day off.'
104. Ibid., 10, 102, 214–19.
105. Ibid., 264.
106. Ibid., 259.
107. *My Autobiography*, 1. 374, 384: 'With [the great actors] who have appeared within the last thirty years I have been on more or less intimate terms . . . I think I may boast that I have an acquaintance more or less intimate with most of the best actors of the present day.'
108. *Claude Duval* and *The Railway Station* were also represented on stage as tableaux vivants, 'with a result in each case woefully disappointing to me'. (*My Autobiography*, 3. 416).
109. Panton, *Leaves from a Life*, 253–4.
110. Ibid., 260; *My Autobiography*, 2. 21.
111. *My Autobiography*, 1. 376–82.
112. Frith claimed to be a 'tolerable horseman' but that his horses were too spirited (*My Autobiography*, 3. 261–7); according to Cissie he left them in their livery stable for days or weeks so they were highly excitable when brought out. The Wild West Show was part of the 1887 American Exhibition, and included cowboys, Indians, Mexican vaqueros, lasso throwers, bucking broncos and a herd of buffalos. Annie Oakley was one of the performers.
113. *My Autobiography*, 2. 41–2.
114. Ibid., 328. 'If one thing enraged Papa more than anything else it was to receive a summons to serve on a jury, or else to appear as a witness in the many trials caused by the photographic piracies of his pictures, by the Belt case, the Whistler–Ruskin case and one or two other causes celèbres of his time.' Frith preferred to pay a fine rather than serve on a jury.
115. Ibid., 339–40; Frith was noted for his good health and robust constitution. He later claimed that he had only been ill once, with measles when he was four: 'I don't count double pneumonia, three or four years ago; that might have happened to anybody' (Walter Frith, 'A Talk with my Father', *Cornhill Magazine*, vol. 20, January–June 1906); *The Graphic*, 1908, 74.
116. *My Autobiography*, 2. 25. *The Relapse*, or *Virtue in Danger* by John Vanbrugh, played at the Gaiety Theatre in 1870. Frith's sequence of ten drawings is now in the Government Art Collection.
117. 'Representative Men at Home: Mr W. P. Frith at Sydenham', *Cassell's Saturday Journal*, 1890.
118. Panton, *More Leaves from a Life*, 14. When Cissie's friend Basil Hodges took up art against his parents' wishes, Frith told his father how glad he would have been if one of his own sons had done as Basil had. His eldest son Willie was a writer, Charles became a partner in J. H. Agnew & Co, Commission Agents in Manchester and Walter Frith was a barrister and author. Cissie was a novelist, journalist and writer on domestic economy and interior design. Louise became an antique dealer at 18 Fulham Road and, with Fanny, later an interior decorator (Post Office Directories 1892–1933, 1901 census).
119. Frith's account with Roberson's records materials ordered by Agnes and William: Canvas sent to 'Miss Alford', 24 September 1880 (HKI MS 248–1993, p. 17): paint and medium sent to 'Miss Alford', 23 and 26 June 1881 (HKI MS 250–1993, p. 13); goods ordered by 'Mr W Alford' in 1891 entered at end of Frith's account in 1894 (HKJI MS 250–1993 p. 219); goods 'had by Mr Alford' on 18/3/98 and 24/4/98, entered in Frith's 1899 account (HKI MS 313–1993 p. 14). In 1887 Frith was in the audience at the Royal Academy to see William receive a £10 prize for his architectural drawings. William and Guy appeared in the 1891 census as artists, and in 1901 Guy was listed as a sculptor.
120. Frith claimed the immediate inspiration for the picture was a wedding he witnessed in Cleveland Square, not far from Oxford Terrace (*My Autobiography*, 2. 208–12).
121. Frith genealogies (see note 62).
122. Panton, *Leaves from a Life*, 169.
123. Ibid., 127–8.
124. Local Studies Collection, Kensington and Chelsea Central Library.
125. Panton, *Leaves from a Life*, 128. A planning application dated April 1875 for the double height (basement and ground floor) bay windows is in the Local Studies Collection, Kensington and Chelsea Central Library. Applications for the other works do not seem to have survived.
126. Announcement of the sale of 7 Pembridge Villas in *The Times*, April 28 1888; application to lay a drain with plan 1872, Local Studies Collection, Kensington and Chelsea Central Library.
127. *My Autobiography*, 2. 141.
128. *The Times*, 24 and 28 April 1877.
129. Agnew had bought *Boswell* for £1,200 directly from Frith in 1868 before its exhibition at the RA, selling it to Sam Mendel at the private view.
130. George Redford, *Art Sales* (1888), 1. 253–57, and 316–18; *The Times*, 24 and 28 April 1877 and 16 May 1882.
131. Panton, *Leaves from a Life*, 120–1, Panton, *More Leaves from a Life*, 204.
132. Ibid., 215; *My Autobiography*, 1. 317: 'So great was the demand for modern art a quarter of a century ago, that copies of successful pictures – and sometimes of unsuccessful ones – were in great demand. I found myself included amongst the popular men to such a degree, that scarcely one of my more important works escaped what Scheffer called being 'bred from'. Large and small replicas – to give them a fine name – were made; but in no instance without the consent of the owners of the original pictures . . . I think the only popular painter who kept himself free from the vice of copying was Edwin Landseer.'
133. Frith told Miller he was teaching Frederick Taylor to paint in oil. Letter, 6 June 1849 (Royal Academy Library).
134. Frith believed 'the French system of the large atelier presided over by one or two distinguished artists . . . by which the student is directed by one man and always on the same principles' was better than the Royal Academy system where the teachers (Academicians and Associates) changed monthly, 'each inculcating his favourite method . . . the effect being, in my opinion, confusion and bewilderment to the student.' (*My Autobiography*, 3. 334).
135. 'W. P. Frith at Sydenham', *Cassell's Saturday Journal*.
136. 'Lucky dog, in a rainy day you can go to the Crystal Palace Gardens and look at the Mastodon & Ichiosaurus (can't spell it) in the middle of the fountains, whilst here I see only mist.' (letter from Millais, 15 November 1895, National Art Library album MSL/1922/186).
137. The names of some of Frith's students are known through the Roberson Archive: Miss L. A. Lord was listed in 1889 as 'pupil of W P Frith', Innes

Watson's address was care of Frith in 1890 and a Mrs Wood was listed in 1891.

138. Walter Frith, *A Talk With My Father,* Cornhill Magazine, 1907; Panton, *More Leaves from a Life,* 189.
139. 1901 Census; Frith's will (4 August 1908).
140. *Morning Post,* 3 November 1909; *Paddington, Kensington and Bayswater Chronicle,* 6 November 1909.
141. Inscriptions on the backs of pictures show that Frith was giving his children paintings from at least 1866, when he gave *My First Attempt at Nature* to Walter; he gave a replica of his mother's portrait to Louisa in 1896, the family collection includes another copy of 1902, and he gave his daughter Isabelle his self-portrait in 1908.
142. The sale included finished and unfinished oil paintings, proof and other engravings, a small library of books, antique silver plate, a Louis XV bracket clock and Louis XV armchairs, oak cabinets and oak dining room furniture, ebonised drawing room furniture upholstered in velvet (Phillips, Son and Neale, sale notice, *The Times,* 3 December) and portraits of Frith by Augustus Egg and Douglas Cowper (*The Times,* 8 December 1909). The Furniture and Fine Art Depository's advertisements for unspecified furniture and paintings of Frith's among other collections of 'genuine superior second-hand furniture' appeared in *The Times* until 20 May 1911.

CHAPTER 2

DICKENS AND FRITH

1. For an informative brief account of who was in and who was out, see Philip Collins, 'The Dickens Circle', in Paul Schlicke, ed., *Oxford Reader's Companion to Dickens* (Oxford: Oxford University Press, 1999), 176–9.
2. William Powell Frith, *My Autobiography and Reminiscences* and *Further Reminiscences*, 3 vols. (London: Richard Bentley and Son, 1887–8), 1. 101–6, 307–17.
3. *The Letters of Charles Dickens*, ed. Madeline House, Graham Storey, and Kathleen Tillotson, 12 vols. (Oxford: Clarendon Press, 1965–2002), 9. 71. Letter of 31 May 1859 to Mrs Richard Watson.
4. *My Autobiography*, 3. 232.
5. Richard Lettis, 'Dickens and Art', *Dickens Studies Annual*, 14, 1985, 93–146.
6. Letter of 11–12 November 1855, in *Letters*, 7. 742–4.
7. Leonee Ormond, 'Dickens and Painting: Contemporary Art', *Dickensian*, 80, 1984, 3–25, 3–6.
8. *Letters*, 7. 743.
9. 'Old Lamps for New Ones', first published in *Household Words*, 15 June 1850; *Dickens' Journalism*, ed. Michael Slater (London: J.M. Dent, 1994–2000), 2. 242–8.
10. 'Old Lamps', 245.
11. Ibid., 244, 247–8.
12. *My Autobiography*, 1. 101–2, 104.
13. Thomas J. Rice, 'The Politics of *Barnaby Rudge*', in Robert Giddings, ed., *The Changing World of Charles Dickens* (London: Vision Press, 1983), 51–74.
14. *Barnaby Rudge*, ed. Clive Hurst (Oxford: Oxford University Press, 2003), 161.
15. Michael Slater, *Dickens and Women* (London: J.M. Dent, 1983), 248.
16. 'Notes on the Present State of Engraving' (1872), in *Works*, ed. E.T. Cook and Alexander Wedderburn, 39 vols. (London: Longmans, Green, 1907), 22. 467.
17. *The Seven Lamps of Architecture*, in *Works*, 8. 148–9, 226.
18. Ibid., 8. 226.
19. *On Liberty and Other Essays*, ed. John Gray (Oxford: Oxford University Press, 1991), 81.
20. W. M. Thackeray, *Vanity Fair: A Novel without a Hero*, ed. John Sutherland (Oxford: Oxford University Press, 1983), 502.
21. Review of John Leech, *The Rising Generation: A Series of Twelve Drawings on Stone*, in *The Examiner*, 30 December 1848; *Dickens's Journalism*, 2. 142–7, 144.
22. *My Autobiography*, 1. 311–13.
23. My account of her last laugh draws heavily on Vanda Foster, 'The Dolly Varden', *Dickensian*, 73, 1977, 19–24.
24. *Queen*, 16 July 1870; quoted by Foster, 'The Dolly Varden', 19.
25. 'The Dolly Varden', 20–1.
26. *Englishwoman's Domestic Magazine*, June 1871; quoted by Foster, 'The Dolly Varden', 21–2.

CHAPTER 3

FRITH AND THE INFLUENCE OF HOGARTH

1. William Powell Frith, *John Leech His Life and Work*, 2 vols (London: Richard Bentley and Son, 1891), 2. 96.
2. John Ruskin, 'Introduction', in Ernest Chesneau, *The English School of Painting*, 3rd edn (London: Cassell & Co, 1887), xiii.
3. *The Times* 21 May 1863, 13.
4. Chesneau, note 2 above, 5–6.
5. William Powell Frith, *My Autobiography and Reminiscences* and *Further Reminiscences*, 3 vols (London: Bentley & Son, 1887–8), 3. 316.
6. William Makepeace Thackeray *Hogarth* in *The English Humourists of the Eighteenth Century: The Four Georges: etc.* (London: MacMillan and Co., 1904), 131–2.
7. op cit, 133.
8. *My Autobiography*, 3. 315.
9. Thackeray, *English Humourists*, 136.
10. *Art Journal*, 1864, 64.
11. *The Times* 19 April 1862, 5, review of *The Railway Station.*
12. *The Times* 17 May 1860, 11 (about G. E. Hicks, *General Post Office at One Minute to Six*)
13. Hogarth also notes on his plate for his print *Characters and Caricaturas*: 'For a further Explanation of the Difference Betwixt Character & Caricatura see ye Preface to Jos Andrews.' In the preface to his novel, Henry Fielding praises Hogarth's ability 'to consist in the exactest Copy of Nature; insomuch that a judicious Eye instantly rejects any thing *outré* . . . Whereas in the *Caricatura* we allow all Licence. Its aim is to exhibit Monsters, not Men; and all Distortions and Exaggerations whatever are within its proper Province.'
14. Hazlitt quoted in Thackeray, *English Humourists*, 132.
15. *The Times*, 17 May 1860, 11.
16. *The Times*, 18 May 1857, 9.
17. *The Times*, 8 April 1858, 12.
18. *The Times*, 8 February 1858, 11, review of Hicks's paintings, *A Winter Morning in St. James's Park* (no. 281) and *A Summer Afternoon in Hyde Park* (no. 449) at the British Institution.
19. Frith, *Leech*, 2. 97.
20. Ibid., 2. 101.
21. Ibid., 2. 5.
22. Hogarth's 'Gate of Calais'
    To the editor of *The Times.*
    Sir, I have just seen Hogarth's 'Gate of Calais,' at Messrs. Agnew's offices. The dirt has been removed from it by skilful hands, and the picture is as perfect when it left the painter's easel. I implore the authorities at the National Gallery not to let slip the opportunity – rare in the extreme – of

acquiring one of Hogarth's finest works, when they can have it for the price for which it was knocked down at Christie's, Messrs. Agnew being willing to forgo any profit.
I am, Sir, your obedient servant,
W. P. FRITH, RA.
7, Pembridge-villas, W., July 15
The Times, 16 July 1874, 5.
23. Walpole quoted in 1851 Royal Academy catalogue and Algernon Graves, *The Royal Academy of Arts: a complete dictionary of contributors and their work, 1769–1904*, London 1904.
24. Paul Jonathon Barlow, *'The Backside of Nature', The Clique, Hogarthianism and the Problem of Style in Victorian Painting*, PhD Thesis, University of Sussex, 1989, 149.
25. *My Autobiography*, 1. 206.
26. *Art Journal* 1851, 156.
27. *My Autobiography*, 1. 336.
28. The scheme of 'Twice Round the Clock' was suggested by a little eighteenth-century book, by an anonymous writer, called *One Half the World Knows Not How the Other Half Lives*, which gives an account of the humours and sorrows of Metropolitan existence from midnight on Saturday until midnight on Sunday early in the reign of George III. The book, which had been given to him by Charles Dickens, is praised by Sala for its evocation of scenes worthy of Hogarth: G. A. Sala, *The Life and Adventures of George Augustus Sala Written by himself* (London 1896).
29. *My Autobiography*, 1. 337.
30. Copy of contract from the Jeremy Maas archive.
31. Ibid.
32. *My Autobiography*, 1. 337.
33. Ibid., 2. 121.
34. *The Times*, 2 May 1879, 3.
35. *The Builder*, 11 May 1878, 474.
36. Arthur Fish, 'The Painter as Preacher and Chat about Mr W. P. Frith, R. A.', *The Quiver*, June 1898, p.722.
37. *My Autobiography*, 2. 122.
38. Fish, 'The Painter as Preacher', 722.
39. *My Autobiography*, 2. 124.
40. Ibid., 130.
41. 'Mr Green stood for me for many figures in the "Road to Ruin", and I parted from him with real regret', Ibid. 126.
42. 'Representative Men at Home – Mr W. P. Frith at Sydenham', *Cassell's Saturday Journal*, 7 June 1890, 874.
43. Fish, 'The Painter as Preacher', 719.
44. Unpublished letter, private collection, dated 1889.
45. Ibid.
46. *My Autobiography*, 2. 130.
47. *Illustrated London News*, 4 May 1878, 410.
48. *Punch*, 18 May 1878, 225.
49. *Athenaeum*, 11 May 1878, 610.
50. *My Autobiography*, 141.
51. In subject and treatment it owes much to the influence of Anthony Trollope's *The Way We Live Now* (1875).
52. Caroline Arscott's enlightening article on the series explores the depiction of Victorian prison scenes and outlines the importance of the works: 'the fascinating thing about Frith's series *The Race for Wealth* is that it takes the form of a progressive narrative, and yet it starts with the bubble and then ends with the circle of the prison yard. The financial bubble is caused by speculative investment where the accumulation of value far outstrips the present worth of the holding. In this particular speculation, money is entirely divorced from production, since the mine's potential is illusory. The bubble consists of the stretching of exchange value around the absence of use value. If we can connect the exercise circle with the punitive regime of the prison we find once again that exchange has ousted use, insofar as the prisoners' labour at the treadmill of the crank to no purpose.' Caroline Arscott, 'Convicted Labour: masking and interchangeability in Victorian prison scenes', *Oxford Art Journal*, 23 February 2000, 125–6.
53. *Fun*, 23 June 1880, 250.
54. *My Autobiography*, 2. 144.
55. Fish, 'The Painter as Preacher', 723.
56. *My Autobiography*, 2. 144.
57. *The Times*, 1 July 1878, 6.
58. *Morning Post*, quoted in *Times*, 22 April 1880, 5.
59. *The Times*, advertisement, Thursday, 21 October 1880.
60. *Morning Post*, 23 April 1880; See also *Art Journal* 1880, 207.
61. *Athenaeum*, 20 March 1880, No. 2734, 383.
62. *The Times*, 22 April 1880.
63. *The Builder*, 1 May 1880, 534.
64. Ibid.
65. 'The fashionable things to do are to rush to the Prince of Wales Theatre and see Miss Genevieve Ward perform in the new and very popular piece, "Forget Me Not", and in the morning to see the new great sensation picture by Frith, "The Race for Wealth".' Quoted in *The Times*, 22 April 1880, 5.
66. *Academy* 3 April 1880, 258.

CHAPTER 4

FRITH AND HIS FOLLOWERS

1. William Powell Frith, *My Autobiography and Reminescences*, 2 vols. (London: Richard Bentley and Son, 1887) 1. 246.
2. *Art Union*, August 1840, 127.
3. *My Autobiography*, 1. 37.
4. Henry Mayhew, *London Character: Illustrations of the Humour, Pathos and Peculiarities of London Life* (London: Chatto and Windus, 1874), 10.
5. Henry Mayhew and John Binny, *The Criminal Prisons of London* (London: Griffin, Bohn & Co., 1862), 28.
6. *Illustrated London News (ILN)*, 23 May 1863, 566.
7. *My Autobiography*, 1. 272.
8. *My Autobiography*, 2. 233.
9. *My Autobiography*, 1. 269.
10. *ILN*, 23 May 1863, 567.
11. [Hablot K. Browne] Phiz, *The Derby Carnival* (London: H. Vickers, 1869), 10–11.
12. *Athenaeum*, 1 May 1858, 565.
13. *My Autobiography*, 1. 271–2.
14. *Athenaeum*, 1 May 1858, 565.
15. *My Autobiography* 1. 288.
16. W.R. Sickert, ed. Osbert Sitwell, *A Free House!*, (London: Macmillan, 1947), 202.
17. Tom Taylor, *The Railway Station* (London: Haymarket Gallery, exh. cat., 1862), 5.
18. *Art Journal*, March 1862, 95.
19. D. Lieven, 'Through the GWR Museum, no. 2: Frith's "Railway station"', *Great Western Railway Magazine*, March 1930, n. 110.
20. For the complex financial details relating to the picture and the subsequent print, see Jeannie Chapel, *Victorian Taste: The Complete Catalogue of Paintings at the Royal Holloway Collection* (London: Zwemmer, 1984), 87–91.

21. Ibid., 90.
22. *Observer*, 20 April 1862, 6.
23. *Daily News*, 18 April 1862, 2.
24. *My Autobiography*, I. 280, quoting Jacob Bell who assisted in finding models for *Derby Day*.
25. Taylor, *The Railway* Station, 7.
26. 'On the Decay of Fine Manners', *Cornhill Magazine*, XXXVII, March 1878, 333.
27. *The Era*, 11 May 1862, 6.
28. See Mary Cowling, *Victorian Figurative Painting: Domestic Life and the Contemporary Social Scene* (London: Andreas Papadakis, 2000), 154–5.
29. Jeremy Maas, *Gambart* (London: Barrie and Jenkins, 1975), 158.
30. *The Times*, 30 April 1881, 10.
31. *The Forbes Collection of Victorian Pictures and Works of Art*, vol. 1, Christie's, London, 19 February 2003, 99.
32. *The Times*, 5 May 1888, 14.
33. *Athenaeum*, 26 May 1888, 668.
34. Oscar Wilde, 'The Critic as Artist', *Intentions Dialogues*, 1927 (1891), 95. 100; 'The Rout of the R. A., *Court and Society Review* (27 April 1887), 390.
35. W. P. Frith, 'Crazes in Art: "Pre-Raphaelitism" and "Impressionism"', *Magazine of Art*, vol. 2, 1888, 190–1.
36. W. P. Frith, 'Realism versus Sloppiness', *Magazine of Art*, vol. 3, 1889, 7.
37. Dante Gabriel Rossetti, *His Family Letters, with a Memoir by William Michael Rossetti*, (London: Ellis & Elvey, 1895), 229.
38. Rosamond Allwood, *George Elgar Hicks* (Geffrye Museum, exh. cat., 1983), 26.
39. Charles Dickens, 'Valentine's Day at the Post Office', *Household Words*, 30 March 1850, 6. For M'Connell and Charles Manby Smith, see Allwood, *Hicks*, 26.
40. George Elgar Hicks, *A Guide to Figure Drawing* (London: G. Rowney, 1853), 38.
41. *ILN*, 22 May 1858, 521.
42. *Athenaeum*, 30 April 1859, 587.
43. Ernst Chesneau, *The English School of Painting* (London: Cassell & Co., 1885) 273–5.
44. See Cowling, *Victorian Figurative Painting*, 155–7.
45. Roger Fry, *Reflections on British Painting* (London: Faber, 1934), 109.
46. Charles Lamb, 'On the Genius and Character of Hogarth', *The Works of Hogarth* (London: Bell and Daldy, 1873), vol. 1, 7.
47. Frederick Wedmore, 'Genre in the Summer Exhibitions', *Fortnightly Review*, June 1883, XXXIII, ns., 865.
48. John Ruskin, *Pre-Raphaelitism* (1853), *Works*, ed. E. T. Cook and A. Wedderburn, 39 vols. (London: G. Allen, 1903–12), 7. 151.
49. W. M. Rossetti, 'London Exhibitions of 1861', *Fraser's Magazine*, LXIV, November 1861, 588.
50. W. M. Rossetti, *Fine Art, Chiefly Contemporary* [1867] (New York: AMS Press, 1970), 265.
51. W. P. Frith, *Further Reminiscences*, (London: Richard Bentley and Son, 1888), 9.
52. *The Graphic*, 18 January 1908, 7.

CHAPTER 5

CLASSIFICATION AND THE CROWD

I would like to thank Griselda Pollock for supervision of my thesis on modern-life painting at the University of Leeds, and for many discussions on the representation of the city. This essay incorporates material that was presented at a symposium 'En Masse: the Crowd and its Subjects' at the Whitechapel Art Gallery in February 2005. I would like to thank the organisers of that day and speakers and participants at that symposium, in particular Steve Edwards and Gail Day for thought-provoking discussion on issues of classification and the crowd.

1. For this kind of modern-life painting see E. D. H. Johnson, *Paintings of the Social Scene from Hogarth to Sickert* (London: Weidenfeld and Nicolson, 1989); *George Elgar Hicks: Painter of Victorian Life* (London: Geffrye Museum, exh, cat., 1983); M. C. Cowling, *The Artist as Anthropologist; The Representation of Type and Character In Victorian Art* (Cambridge: Cambridge University Press, 1989); M. C. Cowling, *Victorian Figurative Painting: Domestic Life and the Contemporary Social Scene* (London: Andreas Papadakis, 2000); C. Arscott, 'Modern-Life Subjects in British Painting 1840–60', PhD thesis, Department of Fine Art, University of Leeds, 1987; C. Arscott, '*Ramsgate Sands*, Modern Life and the Shoring-Up of Narrative', in B. Allen, ed., *Towards A Modern Art World*, (New Haven and London: Paul Mellon Centre and Yale Center for British Art, Yale University Press, 1995), 157–68; T. Barringer, *Men At Work: Art and Labour In Victorian Britain* (New Haven and London: Paul Mellon Centre/Yale University Press, 2005).
2. See Jeannie Chapel, *Victorian Taste: The Complete Catalogue of Paintings at the Royal Holloway College* (London: Zwemmer, 1982), 87–92. The catalogue entry in this publication is an excellent source of information on Frith's painting and the commercial transactions surrounding it.
3. See Caroline Arscott and Griselda Pollock, 'The Partial View: the Visual Representation of the Early Nineteenth-century City', in J. Wolff and J. Seed, eds., *The Culture of Capital: Art, Power and the Nineteenth-Century Middle Class* (Manchester University Press, 1988).
4. Mary Cowling (citing D. Lieven) points out that the closing in of third-class carriages was a result of the Cheap Trains Act of 1844, and the incorporation of third-class carriages into the fast trains that left during peak hours from Paddington only commenced in about 1860. The mingling of the full range of classes as they assembled for one train was therefore highly novel. Cowling, *Victorian Figurative Painting*, 126.
5. Tom Taylor gives a version of this observation when he refers to the newspaper reading man's obliviousness to the events unfolding, due to his absorption in the paper, and his surprise when he looks up, perhaps from reading about the fraud committed by the man, to find that the muffled passenger did not get on the train after all. The correlation between the picture's incidents and newspaper items is also suggested by him with reference to the juxtaposition between the cover of *Punch* and the grief of the aged mother weeping on the shoulder of her ne'er-do-well son who has just signed up for the army. T. Taylor, *The Railway Station, Painted By W. P. Frith, Esq., R.A., Described by Tom Taylor, Esq., M.A.* (London, Haymarket Gallery, exh. cat., 1862), 22, 9 and 14.
6. W. P. Frith, *Further Reminiscences*, 1888, 354.
7. For an account of this character, his physiognomic appearance and the link made by reviewers to his criminal propensities, see Cowling, *The Artist as Anthropologist*, and Cowling, *Victorian Figurative Painting*. Cowling points out that the actual face of a notorious murderer Thurtell served as a reference point for one reviewer in the case of Frith's earlier painting *Derby Day* (1858). She suggests that Frith drew on the features of Thurtell for this particular figure in *The Railway Station*. The consensus in published reviews as to this figure's villainous disposition could be attributed to viewers' familiarity with physiognomic signs and readiness to interpret them, or to recognition of Thurtell's features. One possibility for the great prominence afforded to this small figure in the critical responses to the picture, not considered by Cowling, is that reviewers followed each other's lead or drew on Tom Taylor's account in the catalogue printed for the exhibition.

8. T. Taylor, *The Railway Station*, 22. The catalogue cost 6d unbound and 1s bound.
9. Elias Canetti, *Crowds and Power* (1960), trans. Carol Stewart (London: Victor Gollancz, 1962).
10. Caroline Arscott, 'Representations of the Victorian City', in M. Daunton, ed., *Cambridge Urban History of Britain: Volume Three (1840–1950)* (Cambridge: Cambridge University Press, 2000), 811–32.
11. Gustave Doré and Blanchard Jerrold, *London: a Pilgrimage* (1872). On Doré see I. B. Nadel, 'Gustave Doré: English art and London life', in I. B. Nadel and F. S. Schwarzbach, *Victorian Artists and the City* (New York: Pergamon, 1980); G. Pollock, 'Vicarious excitements: *London: a Pilgrimage*, by Gustave Doré and Blanchard Jerrold, 1872', *New Formations*, no.4, spring 1988. T. Annan, *Photographs of Old Closes and Streets of Glasgow, taken 1868–77* (Glasgow, City Improvement Trust, 1878/79), T. Annan, *Old Closes and Streets, a series of photogravures, 1868–1899* (Glasgow, James Maclehose, 1900). On Annan, see A. V. Mozley, 'Introduction', to T. Annan, *Photographs of the Old Closes etc.* (New York: Dover, 1977), and S. Stevenson, *Thomas Annan 1829–1887* (Edinburgh: National Galleries of Scotland, 1990). For Grimshaw, see A. Robertson, *Atkinson Grimshaw* (Oxford: Phaidon, 1988). For Fildes, see *Hard Times: Social Realism in Victorian Art*, (Manchester, Manchester City Art Gallery, exh. cat., 1987–88), and C. Arscott, 'Luke Fildes: from Graphic to Academic', in Colin Trodd and Rafael Cardoso Denis, eds., *Art and the Academy in the Nineteenth Century* (Manchester: Manchester University Press, 2000), 102–16. For O'Connor, see M. Galinou and J. Hayes, *London In Paint: Oil Paintings in the Collection of the Museum of London* (Museum of London, 1996).
12. Leigh Hunt, 'The Conductor', in Kenny Meadows, *Heads of the People, or Portraits of the English*, drawn by Kenny Meadows and engraved by Orrin Smith, 2 vols. (London: Robert Tyas, 1840), I. 193.
13. Leigh Hunt, 'The Conductor', I. 193–200.
14. Ibid., 195.
15. Ibid.
16. Ibid., 200.
17. Ibid.
18. Henry Mayhew, *London Characters: Illustrations of the Humour, Pathos and Peculiarities of London Life* (1870, new edition 1881), 2.
19. Ibid., 20.
20. Ibid., 21.
21. Ibid., 38.
22. Ibid., 39.
23. Ibid., 41.
24. Ibid., 40.
25. This is something I have argued in an article on Frith's *The Race For Wealth* (C. Arscott, 'Convict Labour: Masking and Interchangeability in Victorian Prison Scenes', *Oxford Art Journal*, vol. 23, no. 2, 2000, 119–42). My argument is that a vision of pure exchange value colours Frith's presentation of the criminal in the prison, undoing the viewer's ability to make classificatory judgements.
26. The more insistent the naturalistic emphasis of the depiction the greater the dependence on that assumption becomes, and the greater the strain on genre as a workable mode. Therefore one of the drivers for the shift in modes that I am describing in this essay is the intensification of naturalism in British art in the period from the mid-1850s.
27. Frith, *My Autobiography*, 1887, I. 331.
28. Wilkie Collins was part of Frith's circle, along with Dickens. Frith claimed that he had known Collins all his life and recounts playing bagatelle with him at Dickens's house at Christmas 1858, Frith, *My Autobiography*, 1887, I. 314.
29. T. Taylor, *The Railway Station*, 7.
30. 'The Police of London', *Quarterly Review*, Vol. 129, no. 257, 1870, 98–100.
31. Ibid., 99.
32. T. Taylor, *The Railway Station*, 7.

CHAPTER 6

THE *LONDON SOCIETY* MAGAZINE

1. See Lindsay Errington, *Tribute to Wilkie* (National Gallery of Scotland, exh. cat. 1985), 53–69.
2. For the growth of illustration in magazines see Michael Wolff and Celina Fox, 'Pictures in Magazines', in H. J. Dyos and Michael Wolff, eds., *The Victorian City, Images and Realities*, vol. 2, section 24, 1973, 559–82 and Celina Fox, 'The Development of Social Reportage in English Periodical Illustration during the 1840s and early 1850s', *Past and Present*, 74, February 1977, 90–111.
3. See Mary Cowling, *The Artist as Anthropologist* (Cambridge: Cambridge University Press, 1989), 138–42 for an examination of the aristocratic types portrayed by Millais in the novel, *Orley Farm*.
4. *The Young George Du Maurier, a Selection of his Letters*, 1860–7 ed. Daphne Du Maurier (London: Peter Davies, 1951), 93.
5. British Library Add MS46665, f171, 295. Hogg wrote to advertisers that the print run of the 1868 Christmas Number would be between 45,000 and 55,000 copies.
6. *The Times*, 3 February 1862.
7. *London Society*, July 1862, 26. O'Neil's exhibit was *Mary Stuart's Farewell to France*.
8. Gleeson White, *English Illustration: The Sixties*, (1897) and Forrest Reid, *Illustrators of the Eighteen Sixties*, (1928).
9. White, *English Illustration*, 55.
10. Laurence Housman in *Arthur Boyd Houghton* (1896) referred to how 'Houghton and the rest – made a closer alliance with life, with the facts and passions of every day existence, and threw themselves with personal enthusiasm into an idyllic rendering of the Victorian age of crinolines, breaking away from the somewhat cramped and cloistral point of view which had marked the earlier days of the movement', 17.
11. *London Society*, February 1862, 9.
12. Ibid., 4.
13. *Illustrated London News*, May 1862, 516.
14. See Lynda Nead's *Victorian Babylon – People Streets and Images in Nineteenth-Century London* (New Haven and London: Yale University Press, 2000), for a reading of the blind person in the visual presentation of the urban space, 59–62
15. *The Young George Du Maurier*, 86.
16. *London Society*, 1862, 219.
17. *London Society*, 1862, 222.
18. Charles Altamont Doyle is best known as Arthur Conan Doyle's father. He worked as a civil servant in Edinburgh but also supplemented his income as an illustrator, sharing many of the skills of his brother Richard (Dickie) Doyle. His family may have known the Hoggs before their move to London. He illustrated an edition of Bunyan's *Pilgrim's Progress* for them in 1860. Sadly, later in his life, he suffered from alcoholism and epilepsy, spending the last seventeen years of his life in nursing homes and asylums.
19. Reid, *Illustrators of the Eighteen Sixties*, 168.
20. *London Society*, August 1862, 97.
21. *London Society*, August 1862, 98.
22. George Somes Layard *The Life and Letters of Charles Samuel Keene* (1892), 64.

23. *London Society*, July 1863, 35.
24. Cowling, *The Artist as Anthropologist*, 352.
25. Quoted in *The Young George Du Maurier*, 303.

CHAPTER 7

FRITH AND FASHION

The author would particularly like to thank Aileen Ribeiro for her pertinent advice and for sharing her expertise. She also offers sincere thanks to Charlotte Gere; Helen Hoyte; Harry Matthews; Shirley Nicholson; Barbara Underwood; Mike Ashington, Mark Bills, Sally Brooks, Oriole Cullen and Alex Werner at the Museum of London; Vivien Knight, Guildhall Art Gallery; Lucy Johnston and Jenny Lister, Victoria & Albert Museum; Daniel Robbins and Reena Suleman, Leighton House Museum; Siobhan Barratt and Paul Meredith, National Trust, Smallhythe, Kent; Beatrice Behlen, Kensington Palace, State Apartments and Royal Ceremonial Dress Collection; Sharon Boak, Museum of Costume, Bath; Miles Lambert, Gallery of English Costume, Manchester; Heinz Archive, National Portrait Gallery, London; Royal Academy Archive, London; The London Library; and the photographic department and picture library at the Museum of London.

1. William Powell Frith, *My Autobiography and Reminiscences* and *Further Reminiscences*, 3 vols. (London: Richard Bentley and Son, 1887–8), 1. 243. 'Costume painting' was a commonly used term in the mid-nineteenth century for historical genre paintings depicting scenes from history and literature in which the characters were presented in period costume. 'Modern life' paintings depicted contemporary subjects with the characters dressed accordingly.
2. Ibid., 185. Paintings of scenes of contemporary life were sometimes referred to as 'hat and trousers' pictures. Trousers, which were originally worn only by working men, and top hats became fashionable in the early nineteenth century, transforming the appearance of men. See also p.113.
3. *The New Monthly Belle Assemblée* (June 1854), 331.
4. For the middle-class taste for anecdotal narrative paintings and the preference for the 'familiar, the sentimental, and the pathetic' see Dianne Sachko Macleod, 'Art Collecting and Victorian Middle Class Taste', *Art History*, vol.10, no.3, 1987, 332–8.
5. An ugly, which was worn on the front of the bonnet like an extra brim and secured under the chin with ties, was made of half-hoops of cane covered in silk. When it was not in use it the hoops folded flat on to each other.
6. *My Autobiography*, 3. 314–15.
7. William Henry Perkins discovered mauveine, an aniline dye based on benzene oil extracted from coal tar and combined with acid to form colour in 1856. This was quickly followed by magenta, violet, blue and green synthetic dyes.
8. Mrs Mary Merrifield, *Dress as a Fine Art* (London, 1854), 90.
9. This quotation predates the introduction of synthetic dyes, which were criticised in artistic circles for their harshness and vulgarity.
10. Merrifield, *Dress as a Fine Art*, 98.
11. Bea Howe, *Arbiter of Elegance* (London: Harvill Press, 1967), 62.
12. J. E. Panton, *Leaves from a Life* (London: E. Nash, 1908), 137.
13. Howe, *Arbiter of Elegance*, 114 (a 'plain white silk [dress] with Charles II sleeves' worn with 'big' amber beads for a dinner Haweis hosted at home), 120 ('I dress in the Watteau style – cheap which pays' for a house party given by the Cowper Temples at Broadlands in Hampshire). Mrs Haweis also dressed her children in historically inspired aesthetic dress.
14. Mrs Hugh Reginald Haweis, *The Art of Beauty* (London: Chatto and Windus, 1878), 17.
15. Mrs Hugh Reginald Haweis, *The Art of Dress* (London: Chatto and Windus, 1879), 54.
16. Aileen Ribeiro, *Dress and Morality* (London: B. T. Batsford, 1986), 125. An exception to this were the colourful, exaggerated styles worn at this period by 'Gents' who formed a distinct sub-cultural group drawn from the middle and working classes who aped the lifestyle of the upper classes.
17. Lady Elizabeth Eastlake, *Art of Dress* (London: John Murray, 1854), 65–6.
18. Mrs Margaret Oliphant, *Dress* (London: MacMillan and Co., 1878), 40–1
19. Christopher Breward, Edwina Ehrman and Caroline Evans, *The London Look: fashion from street to catwalk* (New Haven and London: Yale University Press, 2004), 31–4.
20. Anne Buck, 'Clothes in Fact and Fiction', *Costume*, vol.17, 1983 93, quoting Thomas Wright, *Some Habits of the Working Classes, by a Journeyman Engineer* (1867).
21. Oliphant, *Dress*, 43–4.
22. Buck, 'Clothes in Fact and Fiction', 93.
23. *My Autobiography*, 1. 72–3.
24. Ibid., 21.
25. The Museum of London has collections of clothes assembled by the historical genre painters John Seymour Lucas (1849–1923), Edwin Austin Abbey (1852–1911) and Frank Moss Bennett (1874–1952).
26. *My Autobiography*, 1. 250.
27. Panton, *Leaves from a Life*, 9.
28. *My Autobiography*, 1. 186.
29. Ibid., 305.
30. Anne Buck, *Victorian Costume and Costume Accessories* (London: Herbert Jenkins, 1961), 51–2.
31. Although Cissie Frith believed the rosebuds to have been embroidered the silk was probably brocaded.
32. Panton, *Leaves from a Life*, 115.
33. My thanks to Charlotte Gere for this information quoted in Georgina Battiscomb's biography of Charlotte M. Yonge.
34. *The Queen* (16 December 1871), 384.
35. Aileen Ribeiro, 'On Englishness in Dress'. In Christopher Breward, Becky Conekin and Caroline Cox, eds, *The Englishness of English Dress* (Oxford and New York: Berg, 2002), 17.
36. G. W. Moore, 'Dress'd in a Dolly Varden', n.d. (British Library song sheet cover).
37. Lynda Nead, *Victorian Babylon* (New Haven and London: Yale University Press, 2000), 6.
38. *My Autobiography*, 3. 41, 61, 53.
39. George Augustus Sala, *The Life and Adventures of George Augustus Sala*, 2 vols. (London: Cassell and Co., 1895), 1. 264–5.
40. *My Autobiography*, 3. 72.
41. See for instance a photograph of 1857 by Maull & Polyblank showing Frith wearing a dark coat with light-coloured checked waistcoat and trousers (illustrated in National Portrait Gallery, *Victorian Art World*, London, 1984) and a photograph by F. Joubert where he wears a dark coat with chalk-striped dark waistcoat and trousers (NPG 25263).
42. Panton, *Leaves from a Life*, 1–2.
43. Frith to T. Miller (10 July 1851), RAA 397/236/42/2.
44. Jane Welsh Carlyle and Mrs Haweis followed this practice. Carlyle made her own clothes and occasionally patronised Madame Elise, one of London's most fashionable dressmakers. Haweis had her clothes made at home by her children's nurse and by a 'small dressmaker who knows my figure and fits me, always, to a T' (Howe, *Arbiter of Elegance*, 134).

45. Erika Diane Rappaport, *Shopping for Pleasure: women in the making of London's West End* (Princeton and Oxford: Princeton University Press, 2000), 18.
46. *My Autobiography*, 2. 38–40.
47. Rappaport, *Shopping for Pleasure*, 29–33.
48. Panton, *Leaves from a Life*, 104.
49. The review of 'Many Happy Returns of the Day' in *The Times* noted that the family dynamics introduced a 'poetical element' into a 'humdrum subject'. 'Children are the salvation of such a scene – children and aged people – . . .' *The Times* (12 May 1856), 12.
50. Panton, *Leaves from a Life*, 93.
51. Ibid., 10.
52. Ibid., 62–3.
53. Ibid., 68.
54. Ibid., 172.
55. For examples of the cartoons and verses published in *Punch* drawing attention the working conditions of Victorian needlewomen see: Christina Walkley, *The Ghost in the Looking Glass: The Victorian Seamstress* (London: Peter Owen, 1981), passim.
56. A puggaree, derived from the Indian word for a turban, denoted the veil worn around the crown of the top hat (or sun helmet) to protect the wearer from dust and flies.
57. Jeremy Maas, *Victorian Painters* (London: Barne and Rockliff, 1969), 194–5.
58. Quoted in Ribeiro, *Dress and Morality*, 134.
59. Jane Welsh Carlyle to Thomas Carlyle (6 & 7 August 1861). Jane Welsh Carlyle, *Letters and Memorials of Jane Welsh Carlyle*, ed. James Anthony Fronde, 3 vols, (London: Longman, Green and Co., 1883), 3. 81–4.
60. Frith to T. Miller, (8 August 1852), RAA 397/236/42/14.
61. *My Autobiography*, 1. 243.
62. My thanks to Helen Hoyte for this information. The black shawl with the deep, coloured patterned border worn by the elderly woman seated at the water's edge on the left of the painting and the greenish shawl worn by the woman carrying the child behind the elderly couple beneath the umbrella could both have been made in Norwich. The cream-coloured shawl with crimson in the border pattern worn by the woman behind the mother encouraging her child to paddle is similar in colour and style of design to a shawl made by Towler & Campin in 1851 in the collection of Carrow House, Norwich.
63. *Punch* (August 1850), vol. 19, p. 77, 'Gentlemen's Fashions for the Sea-side'.
64. L. B. Walford, *Memories of Victorian London* (London: Edward Arnold, 1912), 1–2.
65. Quoted in *The Illustrated Review* (5 June 1873), 594, 'William Powell Frith, R.A.'
66. Frith to T. Miller (12 April 1863), RAA 397/236/46/9/1–2.
67. Queen Victoria was in mourning for her husband Prince Albert who had died on 14 December 1861. A rigid etiquette, based on the relationship of the mourner to the deceased, dictated the degree and length of mourning, which was divided into stages in which the mourner moved from wearing matt black fabrics to black with a sheen and then lighter, 'half-mourning colours'. Although the officially proscribed period of mourning ended in 1863 the Queen continued to wear black to express her acute personal loss.
68. Kay Staniland, *In Royal Fashion: the clothes of Princess Charlotte of Wales and Queen Victoria. 1796–1901* (London: Museum of London, 1997), 159.
69. *Illustrated London News* (6 May 1865), 439.
70. *My Autobiography*, 1. 344.
71. Maas, *Victorian Painters*, 195.
72. *My Autobiography*, 1. 264.
73. C. Willet Cunnington, *English Women's Clothing in the Nineteenth Century* (London: Faber and Faber, 1937), 210.
74. *The Englishwoman's Domestic Magazine*. Quoted in Aileen Ribeiro, *Whistler, Women and Fashion* (New Haven and London: Yale University Press, 2003), 45.
75. Panton, *Leaves from a Life*, 210, 212, 172, 113.
76. Anne Buck, 'Dress for Archery, 1790–1825', *Documenta Textilia: Festschrift für Sigrid Müller-Christrensen*, ed. M. Flury-Lemberg and K. Stolleis, *Deutscher Kunstverlag*, 1981, 393–404.
77. My thanks to Barbara Underwood for this information. Bedfordshire Maltese lace being closely made of heavy cotton or linen would be appropriate for the firm fabric from which Louey's outfit is made and would also be less likely to snag than other laces. It was very cheap and not very well made because of the speed at which the lacemaker had to work to earn a pittance.
78. Quoted in Phillis Cunnington and Alex Mansfield, *English Costume for Sports and Outdoor Recreation* (London: Adams and Charles Black, 1969), 177–8.
79. *London Society* (October 1866), 357.
80. *The Graphic* (7 June 1873), 539.
81. *The Times* (3 May 1873), 12.
82. *My Autobiography*, 2. 256.
83. *The Queen* (8 May 1880), 412.
84. Louise Jopling, *Twenty Years of My Life 1867–1887* (London: John Lane The Bodley Head Ltd., 1925), 78–82.
85. Leoneé Ormond, 'Female Costume in the Aesthetic Movement of the 1870s and 1880s', *Costume*, vols. 1 and 2, 1970, 47–8.
86. *The Queen* (8 May 1880), 420.
87. Zuzanna Shonfield, 'Miss Marshall and the Cimabue Browns', *Costume*, vol.13, 1979, 69, 71. Terry's stage outfits, several of which were designed by the architect E. W. Godwin, who was appointed Director of Liberty's Costume Department in 1884, were reported in *The Queen*. See for instance an article on her costumes for 'The Cup': *The Queen* (15 January 1881), 69, and Valerie Cumming, 'Ellen Terry: an Aesthetic Actress and her Costumes', *Costume*, vol.21, 1987, 68.
88. Shonfield, 'Miss Marshall and the Cimabue Browns', 69. Sophia Wilson, ed., *Simply Stunning: The Pre-Raphaelite Art of Dressing* (Cheltenham Art Gallery and Museum, 1996), 26.
89. *The Queen* (27 March 1880), 275; *The Queen* (27 April 1872), 286.
90. Haweis, *The Art of Dress*, 108–17.
91. *The Queen* (7 May 1881), 466.
92. Lionel Lambourne, *Victorian Painting*, has identified this figure as Ellen Terry and the boy as her son Edward Gordon Craig, but the picture's key does not seem to support this.
93. Lillie Langtry probably refused to sit for Frith but her image was widely circulated in photographic form and the press reported her appearance in detail. See for instance *The Queen* (8 May 1880), 420.
94. *The Queen* (12 May 1883), 434.
95. J. McLure Hamilton, *Men I have Painted* (London: Fisher Unwin, 1921), 111. My thanks to Daniel Robbins for drawing my attention to this quotation.
96. *My Autobiography*, 3. 259.
97. Panton, *Leaves from a Life*, 172.

CHAPTER 8

FRITH'S WOMEN

1. William Powell Frith, *My Autobiography and Reminiscences* and *Further Reminiscences*, 3 vols. (London: Richard Bentley and Son, 1887–8), 2. 295.
2. Susan Casteras, *The Substance or the Shadow: Images of Victorian Womanhood* (New Haven: Yale Center for British Art, 1982).

3. Martin Postle and William Vaughan, *The Artist's Model from Etty to Spencer* (London: Merrell Holberton, 1999), 55.
4. *My Autobiography*, 2. 56.
5. Ibid., 58–9.
6. Ibid., 248–9.
7. Archives of the Mercer Art Gallery, Harrogate.
8. *My Autobiography*, 1. 57.
9. Ibid., 263.
10. Postle and Vaughan, *The Artist's Model.*
11. *My Autobiography*, 3. 385.
12. Ibid., 383.
13. Ibid., 2. 130.
14. Ibid., 2. 249.
15. Ibid., 1. 218.
16. *Below Stairs: 400 Years of Servants' Portraits* (London: National Portrait Gallery, 2003).
17. *My Autobiography*, 1. 262–3.
18. Deborah Cherry, *Painting Women: Victorian Women Artists* (London: Routledge, 1993), 126–7.
19. See Claire Tomalin, *The Invisible Woman: The Story of Nelly Ternan and Charles Dickens* (London: Viking, 1990).
20. *My Autobiography*, 1. 268–9.
21. John Ruskin, *Academy Notes*, 1856.
22. W. P. Frith, 'Crazes in Art, Pre Raphaelitism and Impressionism,' *The Magazine of Art*, 1888, vol. 11, 190. Although Frith disliked Pre-Raphaelite painting, personally he was a close friend of both Millais and Holman Hunt.
23. *My Autobiography*, 2. 34–5.
24. Ibid., 1. 249.
25. Ibid., 1. 278–80.
26. Ibid., 2. 330.
27. Ibid., 1. 274.
28. Ibid., 2. 21.
29. Ibid., 1. 278–80.
30. Ibid., 1. 280–2.
31. Ibid., 1. 59.
32. Ibid., 1. 59–60.
33. Ibid., 1. 58–9.
34. Ibid., 1. 356.
35. Ibid., 2. 323–4.

CHAPTER 9

THE PAINTING PRACTICE OF WILLIAM POWELL FRITH

The author is most grateful to the staff of numerous archives and libraries with holdings of material on Frith, including the British Library, National Art Library, Cambridge University Library and Tate Archives and also to Anne Young at the John Rylands University Library, Manchester, for making accessible material I did not manage to consult. Thanks also go to Vivien Knight, Guildhall Art Gallery, London; Régine Page, Hamilton Kerr Institute, Cambridge; Mark Pomeroy, Royal Academy Archive, London; Jane Ruddell, Royal Holloway Archives, Egham; and Colin Harris, Bodleian Library, Oxford. Material from the Roberson Archive is published by kind permission of the Syndics of the Fitzwilliam Museum.

1. This was the highest accolade in Frith's testimonial for the lithographer John Alfred Vintner, 23 August 1887, and might also have been said of Frith himself (Tate Archive 7922/2/6).
2. William Powell Frith, *My Autobiography and Reminiscences* and *Further Reminiscences*, 3 vols. (London: Richard Bentley and Son, 1887–8), 1. 7.
3. Recorded in Mrs J. E. Panton, *Leaves from a Life* (London: Eveleigh Nash, 1908), 171. The amiable and teasing friendship between Brooks, editor of *Punch*, and Frith is described in Frith's autobiography and corroborated in the letters and notes from Brooks to the artist preserved in the National Art Library, MSL/1922/186.
4. Anon, *Letters to Living Artists* (London: Elkin Mathews, 1891), 134. The author is Joseph William Gleeson White, first editor of *The Studio* (1893–4) and an admirer of Whistler. Frith's appearance as a witness for Ruskin, albeit as an apparently unwilling participant, at the famous trial of 1878 may, in part, explain White's extreme antipathy to the artist.
5. *My Autobiography*, 35–50.
6. William Powell Frith, 'Crazes in Art, Pre-Raphaelitism and Impressionism', *The Magazine of Art*, vol. 11, 1888, 187 and 191.
7. A. P. Laurie, 'The Late Mr Holman Hunt's Experiments on the Permanency of Artists' Oil Colours', *Royal Society of Arts Journal*, LXX (5 May 1922), 432. Ironically, the other group of painters singled out for this commendation by Laurie were the Pre-Raphaelites, whom Frith felt to be a short-lived craze in his *Magazine of Art* article of 1888.
8. Letter from Frith to Roberson, 7 April 1897 (Hamilton Kerr Institute, Roberson Archive, hereafter HKI, MS 645–1993).
9. 'A Painter of Popular Pictures', newspaper cutting, 3 November 1909 (Bodleian Library MS Autograph b. 9 1333).
10. In 1858 Jacob Bell, the owner of *Derby Day* reported visiting the Royal Academy at 4 p.m. and finding 'the people smelling the picture like bloodhounds'. (National Art Library MSL/1922/186/205).
11. Anon, *Letters to Living Artists*, 135.
12. Frith to Thomas Miller, 31 October 1852 (Royal Academy Library, 236/43/1).
13. Frith to Miller, 5 March 1848 (Royal Academy Library, 236/33/8).
14. Paula Gillett, *The Victorian Painter's World* (Rutgers University Press, 1990), 99.
15. *My Autobiography*, 1 243–5.
16. HKI MS 245–1993, p. 16; *Derby Day* similarly had an original Roberson loose lining (Tate Gallery Conservation Department Folders: Roberson p.615).
17. HKI MS 245–1993, p. 28. The reference to 'edges' is likely to indicate additional canvas at the tacking margins, as for *Ramsgate Sands.*
18. *My Autobiography*, 1. 272–84
19. It is known that the caricaturist 'Spy', Leslie Ward (1851–1922), was Frith's apprentice at a later date and a Miss L. A. Lord is recorded as 'pupil of Mr Frith' in her Roberson account. In 1890 Innes Watson's address is given as 'c/o WP Frith' as is a Mrs Wood in 1891. However, these entries may indicate nothing more than a period of collaboration, a convenient postal address or a temporary visit to Frith, as in 1850 Edward Lear's account with Roberson has its first address as 'at Mr Frith's'; therefore, presumably Lear was working or staying with Frith at that time, having been pupils together at Sass's Art School.
20. He is known to have had some help with the background and assistance from John Frederick Herring, senior, although he did not always acknowledge it.
21. See, for example, Joyce Townsend on Blake and Turner, Melissa Katz on Holman Hunt, Stephen Hackney, Jacqueline Ridge & Joyce Townsend on the Pre-Raphaelites, Libby Sheldon on the Pre-Raphaelite circle,

Jacqueline Ridge & Joyce Townsend on Watts, Carol Willoughby on Watts, Stephen Hackney on Whistler.

22. Frith to Roberson, 15 April 1900 (HKI MS 646–1993). The picture in the Guildhall's Loan Collection of Pictures by Living British Painters, 1900, was *An Old Woman Accused of Witchcraft* (no. 36).
23. It is possible that Frith had accounts with other colourmen as well, but it is more usual to find artists dealing with a single firm, where they held an account.
24. Alfred Elmore to Thomas Miller, 14 September 1850 (Royal Academy Library, 346/34/14). For a discussion of the use of copal by Frith's contemporaries, the Pre-Raphaelites, see Joyce Townsend, Jacqueline Ridge and Stephen Hackney, *Pre-Raphaelite Painting Techniques* (London: Tate Publishing, 2004), 47–8.
25. Robert Huskisson to Thomas Miller, n.d. (Royal Academy Library, 236/13/20).
26. Frith to Miller, 25 September 1849 (Royal Academy Library, 236/40/4).
27. Frith to Miller, 25 February 1850 (Royal Academy Library, 236/41/2).
28. Ibid.
29. Frith to Miller, 2 June 1850 (Royal Academy Library, 236/41/8).
30. A gelled painting medium comprising 'Genuine Mastic Varnish, Fine Body Copal, Turners light drying Oil' according to Charles Roberson's own recipe written in 1868 (HKI MS 891–1993).
31. Frith to Roberson, 7 July 1897 (HKI MS 597–1993).
32. Frith to Miller, 8 October 1854 (Royal Academy Library, 236/45/1).
33. HKI MS 246–1993, p. 14. This is the canvas for *The Marriage of the Prince of Wales* (1865).
34. Frith to Miller, 5 March 1848 (Royal Academy Library, 236/38/8).
35. Frith to Miller, 27 January 1850 (Royal Academy Library, 236/38/15).
36. Frith to Miller 3 February 1853 (Royal Academy Library, 236/43/7 and 8 January 1848 RA 236/38/5).
37. Frith to Miller, 9 October 1847 (Royal Academy Library, 236/38/3).
38. The reference by a prospective buyer to one of Frith's paintings in its early stages 'with all the scaffolding around it' indicates that he had to work from scaffolding for some of his larger works, William Grapel to Frith, 20 January 1859 (National Art Library MSL/1922/186/193).
39. 2 November 1863, 'Roller for picture 20/- Strong packing case lined with stout brown paper &c £9.15.0 iron and brass plates & screws & fixing do in frame 13/6 Van hire & men's time removing picture to Windsor 7/6' (HKI MS 246–1993, p. 15). Roberson's account entries confirm the accuracy of Jeremy Maas's book on the painting, where it is noted that Frith and his ten-foot canvas would arrive at Windsor on Monday 2 November 1863, exactly the day on which Roberson were engaged to deliver it. J. Maas, *The Prince of Wales's Wedding. The Story of a Picture* (London: Cameron & Tayleur, 1977), 66. The picture's return is not noted in the account.
40. 'B' is not identified, but if one of his children, it could be Bertram Septimus Alford, born in 1870, Frith to B, 26 May 1885 (National Art Library, MSL/1980/99).
41. HKI MS 795–1993, f. 27v.
42. His purchase of dry pigments is almost exclusively confined to vermilion, bought in 1878, 1890, 1892 and 1903 (HKI MS. 248–1993, pp. 16–17; HKI MS 250–1993, p. 15 & p. 219, HKI MS 313–1993, p. 15).
43. HKI MS 246–1993, p. 14.
44. HKI MS 246–1993, p. 16. His isolated purchases of copal in 1850–2, 1858, 1863, 1870, 1889 and 1896 may have been used either as additions to his paint or for varnish.
45. Frith to Miller, 5 October 1854 (Royal Academy Library, 236/44/15).
46. Frith to Miller, 30 January 1848 (Royal Academy Library, 236/38/6).
47. Frith to Miller, 2 June 1861 (Royal Academy Library, 236/46/3).
48. Frith to W.C. Carey, 9 October 1887 (Archives, Royal Holloway, University of London, AR 500/217/2).
49. HKI MS 246–1993, p. 13.
50. In 1860 he advised J. C. Horsley on how much to ask for a painting (Bodleian Library, Ms Eng 2222 fols. 125–6) and in 1867 Wilkie Collins consulted Frith on the value of 'certain small pictures & sketches by my father' (National Art Library, MSL/1922/186/37) as well as Frith frequently advising Thomas Miller as to price, value and condition of prospective purchases.
51. J. C. Horsley may also have done so, as a telegram dated 10 November 1855 was sent by him to his wife, saying 'I am working for Firth [*sic*] and cannot come down till late as soon as I can' (Bodleian Library, Ms Eng 2221 fol. 220).
52. It appears to have been known as the Miller Arms from at least 1869 (*Preston Guardian*, 2 October 1869, p. 7) and may have been renamed after Thomas Miller's death in 1865. The Hornby family were the previous owners of the Singleton Park estate, bought by Miller in 1852.
53. Frith to Miller, 25 September 1853 (Royal Academy Library, 236/44/6).
54. Frith to Miller, 8 October 1854 (Royal Academy Library, 236/45/1).
55. HKI MS 245–1993, p. 27.
56. Frith to Miller, 17 September 1854 (Royal Academy Library, 236/44/11).
57. Neville Wallis, ed., *A Victorian Canvas, The Memoirs of W.P. Frith, R.A.* (London: Geoffrey Bles, 1957), 155.
58. Frith to Miller, 13 February 1848 (Royal Academy Library, 236/38/7).
59. Ibid.
60. Frith to Miller, 3 June 1849 (Royal Academy Library, 236/39/13 and 21 August 1849, 236/40/3).
61. Frith to Miller, 18 January 1855 (Royal Academy Library, 236/45/10).
62. Frith to Miller, 3 October 1854 (Royal Academy Library, 236/44/14).
63. Wallis, *A Victorian Canvas*, 91.
64. J. F. Herring to Frith, (National Art Library, MSL/1922/186/79). Herring has dated the letter 23 January 1857, in error for 1858.
65. J. F. Herring to Frith, 17 December 1857 (National Art Library, MSL/1922/186/78).
66. J. F. Herring to Frith, 6 February 1858 (National Art Library, MSL/1922/186/77).
67. Frith to the editor of *The Times*, 28 December 1850, 5. The cynical reader might attribute the correction to a desire not to have Ansdell's inferior work attributed to Frith, the rising artist.
68. Bell was not only an important patron of Frith's, but had also, briefly, attended Sass's art school with him: Walter Frith, 'A Talk with my Father', *Cornhill Magazine* ns vol. 20, May 1906, 605. Note that the tent was not included in the sketch for the painting now in the Victoria and Albert Museum (no. 1038–1886).
69. Frith to Jacob Bell, 1 January 1858 (Tate Archive TGA 8524/32).
70. Frith to Bell, 11 January 1858 (Tate Archive, TGA 8524/33).
71. *The Times*, 28 May 1910, 12. This is, however, not the true figure, as the contract from Flatou exists in Frith's papers at the National Art Library. In it, the price for the painting is £850, plus £300 for copyright. Two smaller paintings were also bought at the same time, costing £250 each, making a total of £1,650. Flatou is often also spelt Flatow, but in the contract with Frith, the former spelling is used.
72. *My Autobiography*, 1. 389. This painting was sold for £4,567 10s at Christie's in 1875, at the time the largest price paid for the work of a living artist.
73. Frith to Miller, 22 October 1854 (Royal Academy Library, 236/45/5).
74. Ibid.
75. Royal Society of Arts, Minutes of Committees 1856–7, Committee on Copyright on Fine Art, 31 December 1857, 196.

76. Frith to Frederick George Kitton, 10 July 1892 (National Art Library, MSL/1979/5116/79).
77. Frith to Miller, 5 July 1863 (Royal Academy Library, 236/46/11).
78. Anon, *Letters to Living Artists*, 140.
79. *My Autobiography*, 3. 187–91. Despite his antipathy to the Pre-Raphaelites in later life, it is interesting to read his initial impressions: 'I hear wonders of Hunt the P. R. B. painters new picture . . . Philip says he never saw *light* painted till now', Frith to Thomas Miller, 2 January 1853 (Royal Academy Library, 236/43/5); Millais '. . . is a "genius" & will throw everything into the shade – confound him – & I for one am as pleased at being thrown into the shade as you could expect a man of my temper to be . . . It is somewhat remarkable that the work of a man who has no sympathy for the old masters should forcibly remind you of some of them – there are qualities in these works that are not surpassed by the Venetians', Frith to Miller, 9 April 1856 (RA 236/45/14). By 1860 he has changed his opinion, excepting Millais: 'As to the other P.R.B. I hear nothing – the whole thing seems dying out & we shall require a good deal of brown paper to get rid of the unpleasant odour & think no more about them', Frith to Miller, 19 February 1860 (RA 236/46/1).
80. Frith to Bosanquet, 7 June 1890 (Bodleian Library MS Autograph d.41 29–30).
81. Frith to Miller, 30 January 1858 (Royal Academy Library, 236/38/6).

CHAPTER 10

FRITH'S FRAMES AND THE BUSINESS OF FRAME-MAKING

1. William Powell Frith, letter to Thomas Miller, Royal Academy Library. The framer was Henry Haynes. I am grateful to Sally Woodcock for drawing this information to my attention.
2. William Powell Frith, letter to Thomas Miller, 21 August 1849, Royal Academy Library.
3. William Powell Frith, letter to Thomas Miller, 5 April 1848, Royal Academy Library. Miller may not have been accustomed to dealing with frame-makers, either directly or indirectly through the artist, but the accounts of the frame-makers John Smith show that dealing directly with the frame-maker had been quite common among even such illustrious clients as the Prince Regent, the Earl of Yarmouth and Lord Byron.
4. In 1949 the Reverend G. H. Porter told the Victoria and Albert Museum that he had a number of De Wint's oil paintings and a sketchbook which had been given to his grandfather John Vokins (the dealer friend of De Wint) by the artist's widow.
5. Thomas Miller papers, Royal Academy Library, 19 May 1855
6. J. & W. Vokins, 5 John Street, Oxford Street to Thomas Miller Esq., 19 May 1855, 236/6/1/a-c and 23/6/6/7/a Royal Academy Library.
7. Further research is required to determine if this frame pattern is found around many other paintings in the Forster bequest.
8. Jacob Simon *The Art of the Picture Frame*, London, National Portrait Gallery, 1996, pp. 117, 202.
9. While Jones used Vokins as a framer, evidence suggests that he generally preferred to acquire his works through other dealers (perhaps simply because he had had no previous business with the firm before he sought to re-frame his collection). However Vokins the dealer did buy other examples of Frith's work, perhaps strengthening the probability that the firm worked directly with Frith, even perhaps as his principal frame-makers.
10. Trade directories do not show the firm at this address before the mid-1860s, but the information may have been out of date
11. An identical main pattern (again laid over a cushion profile) appears on the frame to *Men of Science Living in 1807–8* (1858) by Sir John Gilbert, Frederick John Skill and Elizabeth Walker (National Portrait Gallery). This points to Bourlet as the maker, although no good reason can be found for Bourlet to use 'Dixon's pattern or mould' for other customers (even though essentially the firm could use them for any frame they chose). There is thus a question as to whether this frame was connected with the Dixon bequest at one time.
12. William Powell Frith, letter from Mary Braddon, National Art Library, MSL/1922/186.
13. Furthermore, the applied corners are more prominent and defined and less fussy than many examples from the 1860, making them more typical of the 1880s or later. But moulds were used for many years within an ever increasing mélange of pattern and style, making the task of positively attributing a date to a frame of the second half of the nineteenth century ever more difficult.
14. Thomas Martin, *The Circle of the Mechanical Arts*, 1813, pp. 211–13.
15. Henry Mayhew, ed., *The Trades and Manufacturies of Great Britain*, vol. 1, London, Strand Printing & Publishing, 1865, pp. 203–5.

INDEX

Page numbers in italics indicate illustrations

PICTURE CREDITS

Gift of The Second Beaverbrook Foundation. The Beaverbrook Art Gallery, Fredericton, NB, Canada, fig. 140
© Bonhams, London, UK/The Bridgeman Art Library, figs 20, 21
Private Collection, © Bonhams, London, UK/The Bridgeman Art Library, fig 22
The British Library, fig. 115
Private Collection/© Christie s Images Ltd. 1994, fig. 40
© Copyright of Christie's Images Ltd. 1996, figs 8, 33
© Copyright of Christie s Images Ltd. 2003, figs 18, 19, 65, 139
Private Collection © Christopher Wood Gallery, London UK / The Bridgeman Art Library, figs 10, 131
City of London, London Metropolitan Archives, figs 12, 28
Cornhill Magazine (1861–2), figs 88, 89
Derby Museum and Art Gallery, fig. 133
Dover Museum, figs 3, 6
European Art Gallery, Dallas, Texas, USA, fig. 9
Guildhall Library, City of London, figs 17, 27, 34–38, 59, 60, 62, 76, 81–85, 116
© Harris Museum and Art Gallery, Preston, Lancashire, UK/The Bridgeman Art Library, fig. 122
Ironbridge Gorge Museum Trust, Elton Collection, fig. 79
London Society (February 1862–July 1863), figs 87, 90–107
© Manchester Art Gallery, fig. 23
The Mercer Art Gallery, Harrogate Museums and Arts, figs 5, 117, 135, 138, 141
Museum of London, figs 4, 26, 42, 45–57, 68, 69, 71–75, 78, 109–112, 114, 118, 125, 127, 128, 137
Museum of London, purchased with the assistance of the National Art Collections Fund, and the Resource/V&A Purchase Grant Fund, fig. 113
Peter Nahum at The Leicester Galleries, London, www.leicestergalleries.com, figs 58, 66
National Portrait Gallery, London, half title page, frontispiece, fig. 134, 147
Norfolk Museums Service, fig. 119
Private collection of author, fig. 70
Private Collection, © Copyright Pope Family Trust/The Bridgeman Art Library, figs 67, 126, 129
© Royal Academy of Arts, London, fig. 132
Royal Albert Memorial Museum, Exeter, Devon, UK/The Bridgeman Art Library, fig. 124
Royal Borough of Kensington & Chelsea Family and Children's Services, Local Studies, fig. 15
The Royal Collection © 2006, Her Majesty Queen Elizabeth II, figs 14, 108, 120
Royal Holloway, University of London, figs 63, 77
Roy Miles Fine Paintings/The Bridgeman Art Library, fig. 25
By courtesy of Sotheby's Picture Library, London, figs 13, 16
© Tate, London 2004, figs 61, 144
© Copyright the Trustees of The British Museum, fig. 7
© V & A Images/ Victoria and Albert Museum, figs 24, 142, 143
© V & A Images/ Victoria and Albert Museum, Dixon Bequest, fig. 148
© V & A Images/ Victoria and Albert Museum, Forster Bequest, figs 30, 31, 32
© V & A Images/ Victoria and Albert Museum, Jones Bequest, fig. 149
York Museums Trust (York Art Gallery) purchased with the aid of grants and donations from the National Art Collections Fund, the Victoria and Albert Museum through the Museums and Galleries Commission, the Friends of York Art Gallery, the R.M. Burton Charitable Trust and Anthony Boynton-Wood, Esq., 1991, figs 130, 136